BY JOSEPH WOOD KRUTCH

Comedy and Conscience After the Restoration
Our Changing Morals (with others)
Edgar Allan Poe: A Study in Genius
The Modern Temper
Five Masters
Living Philosophies (with others)
Experience and Art
Was Europe a Success?
America Now (with others)
The American Drama Since 1918
Samuel Johnson
Henry David Thoreau
The Twelve Seasons
The Desert Year
The Best of Two Worlds
Modernism in Modern Drama
The Measure of Man
The Voice of the Desert
The Great Chain of Life
Grand Canyon: Today and All Its Yesterdays
Human Nature and the Human Condition

EDITED BY JOSEPH WOOD KRUTCH

The Plays of William Congreve
Nine Plays by Eugene O'Neill
Marcel Proust's Remembrance of Things Past
Representative American Dramas
The Selected Letters of Thomas Gray
Great American Nature Writing
The Gardener's World

Edited by

JOSEPH WOOD KRUTCH

The Gardener's World

G. P. Putnam's Sons  New York

DESIGNED BY MARSHALL LEE

To Ruth Stout

ACKNOWLEDGMENTS

The author wishes to thank the following authors and publishers for permission to include copyright material in this volume:

The American Folklore Society, publisher of *The Journal of American Folklore,* for the selection from *Taos Tales* by Elsie Clews Parsons; Dodd, Mead and Company for the selections from *North with the Spring* by Edwin Way Teale, Copyright © 1951 by Edwin Way Teale, and *Sex and the Nature of Things* by N. J. Berrill, Copyright 1953 by N. J. Berrill; Farrar, Straus and Cudahy, Inc. for the selection from *Sido* by Colette; Harper & Brothers for the selection from *The World of Night* by Louis J. and Margery J. Milne, Copyright 1948, 1953, 1956 by Louis J. Milne and Margery J. Milne; Harvard University Press, Cambridge, Massachusetts, for the selection from *Abbé David's Diary,* translated and edited by Helen M. Fox, Copyright 1949 by The President and Fellows of Harvard College; Houghton Mifflin Company for the selections from *A Thousand-Mile Walk to the Gulf* by John Muir, *Truly Rural* by Richardson Wright, and *Insect Invaders* by Anthony Standen; The Huntington Library, San Marino, California, for the selections from *The Wisdom of God Manifested in the Works of the Creation* by John Ray, London, 1709, HM 229540, *The Theory and Practice of Gardening* by Antoine Joseph Dezallier d' Argenville (Alexandre Le Blond), London, 1728, HM 152011, and *The Curious and Practical Gardener* by John Cowell, London, 1730, HM 130326–9; The Macmillan Company and Mrs. David Fairchild for the selection from *Exploring for Plants* by David Fairchild, Copyright 1930 by the Macmillan Company; Beverly Nichols for the selection from *Down the Garden Path* by Beverly Nichols; G. P. Putnam's Sons, Inc. for the selections from *An Almanac for Moderns* by Donald Culross Peattie, Copyright 1935 by Donald Culross Peattie, *Flowering Earth* by Donald Culross Peattie, Copyright 1939 by Donald Culross Peattie, and *The Arctic Year* by Peter Freuchen and Finn Salomonsen, © 1958 by G. P. Putnam's Sons; William Sloane Associates, Inc. for the selection from *The Voice of the Desert* by Joseph Wood Krutch, © 1955 by Joseph Wood Krutch; Smithsonian Institution, publishers of the *Annual Report of the Bureau of American Ethnology,* for the selection from *Science Fiction, Legends and Myths;* University of New Mexico Press for the selection from *Gold on the Desert* by Olga Wright Smith, Copyright 1956 by the University of New Mexico Press; University of Pittsburgh Press for the selection from *Penn's Woods West* by Edwin L. Peterson; The Viking Press, Inc. for the selections from *Cream Hill* by Lewis Gannett and Ruth Gannett, Copyright 1949 by Lewis Gannett and Ruth Gannett.

Some of them will saye, seynge that I graunte that I have gathered this booke of so manye writers, that I offer unto you an heape of other mennis laboures. . . . To whom I aunswere, that if the honye that the bees gather out of so manye floure of herbes, shrubbes, and trees, that are growing in other mennis medowes, feldes and closes: maye justelye be called the bees' honye . . . so maye I call it that I have learned and gathered of manye good autoures . . . my booke.

WILLIAM TURNER
[*A New Herbal* (1551)]

Contents

Section Two

HERBALISTS AND
EARLY GARDEN BOOKS

Section Three

FASHIONS IN GARDENS

Section Four

THE LINNAEAN AGE

Section Five

EXPLORING FOR PLANTS

Section Six

ROMANTICISM AND THE LANDSCAPE GARDEN

Section Eleven

MECHANISMS AND MYSTERIES

Illustrations

Greek Herbal of Dioscorides, written in the 1st Century A.D., illustrated by a Byzantine artist, C. 512 A.D.

following page 92

MANDRAKES, NARCISSUS AND THE TREE OF KNOWLEDGE, from *Ortus Sanitatus*, 1491. [*Courtesy of the New York Botanical Garden Library.*]

EARTHLY PARADISE, title page of *Paradisi In Sole* by John Parkinson, 1629. [*Courtesy of the New York Botanical Garden Library.*]

following page 124

BOCCACCIO'S GARDEN, from an early edition of *The Decameron* by Boccaccio. [*Courtesy of the New York Public Library Prints Division.*]

PEARS ON AN ESPALIER. [*Courtesy of the New York Botanical Garden Library.*]

THE PEAR ("*Pyra*") and THE APPLE ("*Malus*"), from *Commentarii* by Mattioli, 1565. [*Courtesy of the New York Botanical Garden Library.*]

THE GARDENER'S ATTIRE, *Habit du Jardinier* by N. de l'Armessin, Paris. [*Courtesy of the New York Public Library Prints Division.*]

THE GARDEN IN SUMMER, from *Hortus Floridus* by Crispin van de Pass, 1615. [*Courtesy of the New York Botanical Garden Library.*]

following page 156

THE BROAD-LEAVED TULIP, from *Hortus Floridus* by Crispen van de Pass, 1615. [*Courtesy of the New York Botanical Garden Library.*]

PARTERRE DE BRODERIE, etching by Perelle, mid-17th Century. [*Courtesy of the Metropolitan Museum of Art, Rogers Fund, 1920.*]

BOWLING GREENS AND HALLS, from *The Theory and Practice of Gardening* by Dezallier d'Argenville (Alexandre Le Blond). [*Courtesy of the New York Botanical Garden Library.*]

CHINESE FLOWERS, from Chieh tzu yüan hua chuan ("Mustard seed garden manual of painting"), 1679–1701. [*Courtesy of the New York Public Library Manuscript Division.*]

following page 172

FLOWER ARRANGEMENT, 18th Century Japanese print by Itchinsai Utagawa. [*Courtesy of the Metropolitan Museum of Art, Bequest of Mrs. H. O. Havemeyer, 1929, the H. O. Havemeyer collection.*]

CLEMATIS, from *Hortus Floridus* by Crispin van de Pass, 1615. [*Courtesy of the New York Botanical Garden Library.*]

CROWN IMPERIAL, from *Hortus Floridus* by Crispen van de Pass, 1615. [*Courtesy of the New York Botanical Garden Library.*]

PEONIES AND IRIS, Japanese print by Kubo Shunman (1757–1820). [*Courtesy of the Metropolitan Museum of Art, Bequest of Mrs. H. O. Havemeyer, 1929, the H. O. Havemeyer collection.*]

following page 220

A CHINESE TREE, from Chieh tzu yuän hua chuan ("Mustard seed garden manual of painting"), 1679–1701. [*Courtesy of the New York Public Library Manuscript Division.*]

CHINESE GRASSES, from Chieh tzu yuän hua chuan ("Mustard seed garden manual of painting"), 1679–1701. [*Courtesy of the New York Public Library Manuscript Division.*]

following page 252

PAPAYA RAMOSA, from *Journal des Observations Physiques* by Louis Feuillée, Paris, 1725. [*Courtesy of the New York Botanical Garden Library.*]

THE MOUNTAIN LILY, from *Hortus Floridus* by Crispin van de Pass, 1615. [*Courtesy of the New York Botanical Garden Library.*]

following page 300

THE WORLD OF BIRDS

PASSION FLOWER. [*Courtesy of the New York Botanical Garden Library.*]

DRAGON TREE, from *Rariorum . . . per Hispanias*, 1576. [*Courtesy of the New York Botanical Garden Library.*]

FANTASTIC FLOWERS, pen and ink by Scottie Wilson. [*Collection Museum of Modern Art.*]

DREAM OF PLANTS, "Le Reveil des Plantes" by Barbant.

following page 348

PLANT SPRAYS, etchings by Manzù from *Le Georgiche di Virgilio*, Italian version by Giulio Caprin, published by Hoepli, Milan. [*Collection Museum of Modern Art.*]

THE WORLD OF INSECTS

GIANT PLANT LOUSE, by Paul Klee. [*Collection Museum of Modern Art.*]

QUEEN ANNE'S LACE, etching by Anthony Gross. [*Collection Museum of Modern Art.*]

following page 380

TWO PERUVIAN PLANTS— *Inga Siliquis Longissimus* and *Opuntia Herbariorum*—from *Journal des Observations Physiques* by Louis Feuillée, Paris, 1725. [*Courtesy of the New York Botanical Garden Library.*]

WHEAT, etching by Manzù from *Le Georgiche di Virgilio*, Italian version by Giulio Caprin, published by Hoepli, Milan. [*Collection Museum of Modern Art.*]

THE REAPER, pen and ink by Manuel Martinez Pintao, 1935. [*Collection Museum of Modern Art.*]

following page 412

FRUIT, etching by Manzù from *Le Georgiche di Virgilio*, Italian version by Giulio Caprin, published by Hoepli, Milan. [*Collection Museum of Modern Art.*]

PEACH TREE, from Fuchs, *De historia stirpium*, 1542. [*Courtesy of the New York Botanical Garden Library.*]

APPLE TREE, pen and ink by Bernard Chaet, 1955. [*Courtesy of the artist. Photograph courtesy Museum of Modern Art.*]

following page 460

THE GARDENER'S WORLD

THE TOAD AND THE GRASSHOPPER, aquatints by Pablo Picasso, 1942. [*Collection Museum of Modern Art.*]

POLLEN, Fritzsche, 1837. [St. Petersburg. Mem 1 (Acad. des Sciences)] [*Courtesy of the Widener Library.*]

General Introduction

A CYNICAL friend once taunted me by the remark that the first horticulturist was, after all, the first murderer also. But this, as all subsequent history proves, was surely a mere coincidence. The garden is a symbol of peace and gardeners have usually been inoffensive men.

Their pleasure is not to bring death, but to help things live; and even when they grow for food only, their hands are not stained with blood. As the old writers never tired of pointing out, man's first and only state of innocence was passed in a garden from which he was expelled when his innocence was lost. Perhaps those who now make gardens are trying, whether they know it or not, to find Paradise again. And some have fancied they had found it:

> What wondrous life is this I lead!
> Ripe apples drop about my head;
> The luscious clusters of the vine
> Upon my mouth do crush their wine;
> The nectarine and curious peach
> Into my hands themselves do reach;
> Stumbling on melons, as I pass,
> Insnar'd with flowers, I fall on grass.
>
> .   .   .   .   .
>
> Such was that happy garden-state,
> While man there walk'd without a mate:
> After a place so pure, and sweet,
> What other help could yet be meet!

To the merely hardheaded and resolutely prosaic, Eden may be a myth and Andrew Marvell's Paradise Found a romantic delusion. But the more scientific one becomes, the more indisputable is the fact that man's culture—his very life indeed—are bound up with the world's greenery. The anthropologist tells us that no other step which man took on the road from brutishness to civilization was so important as the discovery he made, no more than a few thousand years ago, that food plants could be cultivated instead of merely gathered where they happened to grow. This step, so recent that many primitive people still living today have not yet learned it, made him a stay-at-home instead of a wanderer and brought with it so many other changes that Paleolithic man became Neolithic instead.

Moreover, as the biochemist will add, even the most primitive subhuman as well as the whole of animal creation has been, from the beginning, utterly dependent upon the green of chlorophyll which alone has the power of transforming the mere mineral elements present in the earth's crust into food capable of nourishing any form of animal life. Even when the earliest men were mere hunters and flesh eaters their only food derived ultimately from the plants eaten by the animals which they ate in turn. In that very real sense "all flesh is grass." Red and green are the two colors of life but the green came first.

Man might conceivably survive if every other species of animal disappeared from the face of the earth. But not unless millions of plants continued to furnish him food and to return to his atmosphere the oxygen he breathes into it in the form of carbon dioxide. Could we watch our earth from some space platform not too far away we might be disturbed to see how, year by year, the indispensable green areas shrink as populations grow and cities spread.

Anthropologists can date pretty closely the epoch when European man first domesticated and cared for the plants he could use as food. But no one knows when he first grew something for the sheer pleasure of growing it and first contemplated a flower with delight. Likely enough it was not actually he but his wife; for is it not still the tradition in many farming communities that only women tend the ornamental plants? Yet it is not certain that gardening for use and gardening for delight and beauty are as unrelated as they may at first sight seem. The aesthetic often begins as a sort of sudden flowering of the utilitarian, and what was once a necessary labor becomes an activity pleasurable because it is a ritual performance of the utilitarian. When the botanist Sir Joseph Banks visited New Zealand with Captain Cook in 1769 he found that the Maoris, though still Stone-Age cannibals, grew about their dwellings the red "glory pea" (Clianthus) now familiar to American gardeners in northern greenhouses and southern gardens.

Why should the gardener for pleasure raise tulips and roses when he might be usefully employed raising turnips? Is it (as the sour sociologists of the Veblen school would say) mere "conspicuous expenditure" and therefore a demonstration that one belongs to a privileged class not compelled to be useful? No doubt, alas, some gardens have been created for precisely that reason. But not all and not most. Nor is it only because a thing of beauty is a joy forever, though that too is an important truth. It is also because those whose business neither is nor need be the production of food can both produce beauty and at the same time participate symbolically in one of the most fundamental of human activities—helping green things to grow, and to flower as well.

Relatively few of the selections which follow in this book have to do with farming as such, though poetic farmers like Virgil and Thoreau are present. Most of the other ways in which men have dealt with plant life and most of the kinds of interest they have exhibited in it are represented by one group of writers or another. The arrangement is by topics and themes rather than chronological and the reader who follows through from beginning to end will be struck by two things: on the one hand, the persistence through time of certain themes and, on the other, changing emphases so that, for example, both gardening and botany at one time mean, first of all, medicine; at another, the classification of plants into families and genera; at still another, the search in far places for new species to be brought into cultivation at home.

Even purely aesthetic gardening goes through phases as numerous and represents as many different fundamental concepts of beauty as do painting and poetry. Thus an elegant Roman villa boasted topiary hedges trimmed into fantastic shapes; the Renaissance loved pots and tubs disposed about a walled patio; the Elizabethan a knot garden with more gravel walks than greenery; seventeenth- and eighteenth-century France the parterre primly set with enormous numbers of tulips, lilies, narcissi or what not. And so it goes. Indeed it was not before the nineteenth century that "garden" came to suggest, first of all, the "perennial border" set off by a lawn.

When man is surrounded on all sides by wild nature and when his cities, towns and houses are but islands of artificiality and order painfully wrested from nature, then he wants his garden to be as artificial (or perhaps one should say as artful) as possible, and by its artificiality to call attention to the fact that it is indeed man-made. When populations grow, cities spread, and nature not modified by man becomes rarer and rarer, then he is likely, on the other hand, to be oppressed by too much regularity, to find geometrical arrangements stiff, and to seek for some compromise under which nature is to some extent tamed but not entirely subdued.

The eighteenth-century country estate found one such compromise in landscaping which relegated flowers to a very inconspicuous role and aimed at making lawn and spinney as well as isolated tree or shrub appear, if not precisely natural, at least like a natural scene as somewhat rearranged by a romantic painter. The twentieth-century gardener who cannot usually operate on so large a scale tries for another compromise: not the gravel walk and parterre of the Bourbons but the "border" which is neither too orderly nor too rampant.

The present collection is intended first of all to provide interesting, self-explanatory reading, not to be a source book systematically documenting the history of gardening. Nevertheless the selections presented do give at least revealing glimpses into that history. Similiarly, though it does not document the history of botany as a science, much of the writing included does reveal some of the changing approaches and aims of those who studied, as well as merely loved, plants.

King Solomon, as the older botanists frequently reminded their readers, wrote a book about plants, including the Cedars of Lebanon. And the more enthusiastic of the herbalists assumed that this unfortunately lost book contained all and more about the use of herbs in medicine than had ever been discovered since. But however that may be, the earliest surviving botanical work is Aristotle's *History of Plants,* which contains a good deal of what we should call scientific knowledge and speculation mixed with a good deal of a priori reasoning which leads him to very dubious conclusions. His pupil Theophrastus wrote a treatise in which he described some five hundred species used in the treatment of disease, but his interest is already more limited than Aristotle's in scope because the intellectual horizon was already beginning to narrow and almost two thousand years were to pass before anyone would again take as broad a view as Aristotle had.

The *Natural History* of Pliny the Elder, compiled during the first century A.D., is a vast hodgepodge in which sound if secondhand information about plants and the methods of cultivation is uncritically mixed with absurd superstitions. But the great source of knowledge for all the Middle Ages was the herbal of the Greek physician Dioscorides who is believed to have written in the same century as Pliny but to whom botany was largely a matter of the "virtues" real and supposed of various plants.

Such for more than a thousand years it remained, and one may perhaps say that out of the writings of the medieval herbalists who did attempt to describe plants (often by copying Dioscorides and his other copyists rather than from genuine observation) botany was reborn much as chemistry was born out of alchemy. By the sixteenth century herbals based upon more direct observation and taking a somewhat broader view of the subject were appearing, as were also such practical, how-to-do-it garden books as (to take English examples) John Parkinson's *Paradisi in Sole* (1629) and Philip Miller's *Gardener's Dictionary* (1731).

Nevertheless the developments which at last reanimated botany as a science were typified by two: (1) Linnaeus's creation of a system of classification which for the first time made it possible to be sure that one could identify to others the plant one happened to be talking about; and (2) the discovery of the sexuality of plants which stimulated interest in the whole subject of physiology, or the study of plants as living organisms analogous to the animal.

Classification is often regarded as an arid subject and classifiers as dry men. Sometimes it is and sometimes they are. But Linnaeus wasn't. He had the sense of wonder and the enthusiasm for natural beauty which we associate with romanticism. To him nature was already what Goethe was to call it: "the living garment of God"; and when he came to sum up his life he could name as its chief blessing the fact that it had been his privilege to examine a greater number of God's works than any man who had ever lived before him. Donald Culross Peattie's account of Linnaeus's accomplishment and spirit, included in this volume, says so much that it is hardly necessary to say more here—except perhaps to add that though he was not the first to reveal what the eighteenth century liked to call "the loves of the plants" he did a good deal to win general acceptance of the fact that they do indeed reproduce by a process closely analogous to that of all the higher animals, and he based his system of classification upon the characteristics of those sex organs which are called flowers.

Since the dawn of history horticulturists as well as botanists had been on the verge of making the discovery which was to be of such enormous importance practically as well as theoretically. The Babylonians were well aware of the fact that the date palm (which happens to be one of those plants which bear their male and female flowers on different trees) would not mature fruit without the assistance of the males, and they hung clusters of these male flowers upon the female trees. Both Theophrastus and Pliny were aware of this fact and at least dimly of its implications. But Aristotle had denied on a priori grounds that plants had sex and his authority was usually followed. John Ray, in the late seventeenth century, suspected the contrary but it was the German botanist Rudolph Camerarius who, at about the same time, first demonstrated the existence of sex in plants through experiments with the mulberry—another tree which, like the date palm, bears the male and female organs on different plants instead, as is the case with most, either within the same flower or within separate flowers borne upon the same plants.

As late as the mid-eighteenth century there were still doubters like the Regius Professor of Botany at Cambridge who could write that "there is great reason to contend not only that all plants are not produced in a manner analogous to animal generation but that none are so produced." But he was already well behind the times.

A few years later James Logan, Governor of Pennsylvania, showed that a patch of Indian corn would not bear if the male "tassels" were removed; and not long thereafter the first successful attempts at artificial hybridization were made. Meanwhile the romantic possibilities of the notion that plants knew "love" were not missed. With characteristic enthusiasm and quaintness Linnaeus wrote:

> The petals of the flower contribute nothing to generation but serve only as bridal beds, gloriously arranged by the great Creator, who has adorned them with such noble bed-curtains and perfumed them with so many sweet perfumes that the bridegroom may celebrate his nuptials with all the greater solemnity. When the bed is thus prepared, it is time for the bridegroom to embrace his beloved bride and surrender his gifts to her. One can see the male organs open and emit the genital powder which falls up the tube and fertilizes the ovary.

In his long and enormously popular poem Erasmus Darwin, grandfather of Charles Darwin, went far beyond Linnaeus and attributed to the amorous plants most of the phenomena associated with eighteenth-century gallantry:

> With honey'd lips enamoured woodbines meet,
> Clasp with fond arms, and mix their kisses sweet.

Before the end of the eighteenth century came the discovery of the somewhat disillusioning fact that colored petals and sweet perfumes existed to attract insects rather than to provide "noble bed-curtains" for a bride and groom.

Ultimately, of course, knowledge of the secret sex life of plants led to the science of plant heredity and thus to the development of new or improved species for which even the gardener least interested in science is grateful. Grafting had been commonly practiced in ancient times and hybridization had taken place by accident but the true secret of the latter process was so completely unsuspected that even accidental hybrids were assumed to be the result of grafts—as is so pleasantly illustrated by the curious dialogue between Perdita and Polixenes in *The Winter's Tale:*

> PERDITA: . . . The fairest flowers o' the season
> Are our carnations, and streak'd gillyvors,
> Which some call nature's bastards: of that kind
> Our rustic garden's barren, and I care not
> To get slips of them.
>
> .   .   .   .   .
>
> POLIXENES: . . . You see, sweet maid, we marry
> A gentler scion to the wildest stock,
> And make conceive a bark of baser kind
> By bud of nobler race: this is an art
> Which does mend nature, change it rather, but
> The art itself is nature.
>
> .   .   .   .   .
>
> PERDITA: I'll not put
> The dibble in earth to set one slip of them.

Perdita was unconvinced by the argument that "nature is made better by no mean/ But nature makes that mean," and she would hardly have been mollified to learn that the fanciest Elizabethan carnations were the product of actual crossbreeding. Modern gardens would lack much of their glory if every gardener were so scrupulous.

Exploration and the plant hunting it made possible has contributed even more than hybridization to make modern gardens more varied than either an ancient or a Renaissance gardener would have dreamed possible. Plant hunting was stimulated both by Columbus's discovery that new worlds were to be found and by the fact that the new science of classification made it possible to arrange in relation to the previously known kinds the myriads of new species brought back from far-distant lands.

If the earliest gardeners for pleasure were undoubtedly like the Maoris who deliberately cutivated wild native plants, the truth now is that a pretty large proportion of the most striking flowers in a modern garden are both exotic and also the products of deliberate modification in one way or another. Comparatively few, in other words, now grow wild anywhere on earth. Some are "sports" which appeared spontaneously and were eagerly isolated; many more are the product of deliberate hybridization—which art has grown more and more complicated and in recent years has depended increasingly upon such esoteric processes as the doubling of chromosomes to increase the size of both the plant and its flower.

Nevertheless all flowers must have begun originally as wild flowers, often brought from afar to be grown by gardeners in regions where nature had never placed them. And in recent years travelers in remote places have brought back new species which proved important not so much in their natural form but because they contained new features with which the hybridizers could experiment as, to take a single example, the Chinese Clematis brought back by Robert Fortune in the mid-nineteenth century became one of the parents of the crimson, violet-blue and purple clematises of the garden. Even though some of what we call "old-fashioned" flowers are really old-fashioned, others are actually rather new—like the Bleeding Heart which was another of Fortune's introductions from China.

The great age of plant exploration did not begin until the discovery of the new world revealed to men's imagination the undreamed-of variety of the natural world, but plant hunting is, nevertheless, as old as history. More than three thousand years ago Queen Hatshepsut of Egypt sent a company of gardeners to what is now British Somaliland for new species, and a century and a half later another Egyptian queen received from an army which had invaded Assyria many new plants, including a pomegranate and a new water lily. In the Middle Ages monastery gardens sometimes grew exotics. The Crusaders seem to have brought back some from the Holy Land including the red peony and the red *Lychnis chalcedonica*. The first European to so much as see a tulip was the Austrian ambassador to the court of the Sultan who, in 1554, gathered some bulbs near Constantinople and brought them back to flower in Vienna. And the common lilac got somehow from the same region to England in the time of Queen Elizabeth.

Perhaps the first Englishman to visit a foreign land for the sole purpose of finding new flowers was John Tradescant who sailed for America in 1637, brought back the Virginia Creeper and the Cardinal Flower (*Lobelia cardinalis*), and was assured a dim sort of immortality when John Parkinson christened the little blue Spider Flower, Tradescantia. By the time Captain Cook made his voyages to the South Seas it was already a matter of course that a botanist should accompany him—Sir Joseph Banks, the real creator of Kew Gardens, on the first voyage, and Georg Forster on the second. Forster we shall meet in the main body of this book, and also some of the innumerable plant explorers—Waterton, Fortune, Belt, Wallace, the Abbé David, Douglas, and Fairchild. Perhaps all that need be said of them now is that their adventures were by no means as mild as hunting flowers might suggest. They met not only the hardships of travel in primitive countries but not seldom the ferocity of men as well.

Though knowledge has grown, fashions have changed, and gardens have been enormously enriched by exotic species and new forms; though even what might be called the various ostensible motives for gardening have been differently stressed at different times; yet it will nevertheless be evident to the reader of the selections which follow that certain of the *themes* developed by those who write about plants have persistently reappeared and that not one of them is really new. One may, for example, be struck by the fact that the seventeenth and eighteenth centuries liked to dwell upon the idea that plant study is not only useful but also, in its nonutilitarian aspects, a pious occupation because it is, after all, a contemplation of God through His works. But that is not actually a new idea though the stress put upon it is. Pope Gregory the Great was already writing in the sixth century A.D.: "The wonders of creation are the footprints of the Creator. We cannot see Him as yet but we are on the way to wisdom when we admire the things He has made."

Of all the themes the most persistent is the simplest: The garden is a refuge, a place of peace, a retreat from the worries and contentions of the world. Plato taught in a grove; Horace celebrated his Sabine farm; the monk walked in the garden to meditate; the seventeenth-century statesman longed for a country retreat—and so have men of affairs in every century since. To quote Marvell again:

Bind me, ye woodbines in your 'twines,
Curl me about ye gadding vines,

And oh, so close your circles lace,
That I may never leave this place:
But, lest your fetters prove too weak,
Ere I your silken bondage break,
Do you, O brambles, chain me too,
And courteous briars nail me through.

The Golden Age of the Greeks, like the paradise of the Hebrews and the Christians, imagined a time when the earth was a garden needing no gardening and the whole of romanticism's "return to nature movement" was a dream of that same blessed time. Nor is the least confessedly romantic of present-day gardeners wholly uninfluenced by the long tradition which assures him, not merely that a garden is a refuge from the world, but that it is such in part because it re-creates a legendary Golden Age.

Many of the other persistent themes might be grouped as various answers to the inclusive question: "Why garden? Why study plants?" Because, said the herbalists, God gave us herbs to cure our diseases. Because, said those to whom botany and gardening were more than merely handmaids to medicine, it brings us peace; because it arouses pious wonder; or because, as the nineteenth century was most likely to say, disinterested curiosity, knowledge for its own sake, is good.

Beauty may be its own excuse for being, but if so that is a truth we are loath to accept and we are prone to seek at least supporting justifications whenever we are moved to pursue beauty. Nor is the modern who likes to think that he has got rid of his sense of sin much more likely to have an easy conscience. Ask him why he gardens and he is not very likely to say, "In order to contemplate the Creator as manifest in His creations"; but he is likely enough to reply, "Wonderful exercise, you know; keeps me fit; makes me work better at the office on Monday." And it is not evident that this is a sounder or, in any event, a nobler reason.

But does the gardener really need any excuse at all? Is the beautiful the good only because it supports the utilitarian, or is the utilitarian good only because it makes possible the cultivation of the beautiful?

John Ruskin once infuriated Asa Gray, the leading American botanist of his time, by the dogmatic statement that the botanists did not know what they were talking about—as, for instance, when they explained that the purpose of a flower is the production of a seed. The truth is, said Ruskin, the other way around. The purpose of a seed is the production of a flower.

In a sense, of course, both were right. Nature's "purpose" in creating a flower is the continuation of the species through the production of a seed. But man's purpose when he gathers a seed is to get, in the end, a flower; and the greatest achievement of the human being has been just that he can have such a purpose, that he can, that is to say, value something *as an end in itself*, not merely as a means by which life, human or plant, may be enabled to continue. To the gardener at least Ruskin was more right than Gray and the gardener would be wise to admit the fact. He gardens to produce gardens and flowers, not seeds, because beauty is indeed its own excuse for being.

J.W.K.

By Way of a Prologue

[The young John Muir quotes Scripture.]

A R R I V I N G at the last house, my knock at the door was answered by a bright, good-natured, good-looking little woman, who in reply to my request for a night's lodging and food, said, "Oh, I guess so. I think you can stay. Come in and I'll call my husband." "But I must first warn you," I said, "that I have nothing smaller to offer you than a five-dollar bill for my entertainment. I don't want you to think that I am trying to impose on your hospitality."

She then called her husband, a blacksmith, who was at work at his forge. He came out, hammer in hand, bare-breasted, sweaty, be-grimed, and covered with shaggy black hair. In reply to his wife's statement, that this young man wished to stop overnight, he quickly replied, "That's all right; tell him to go into the house." He was turning to go back to his shop, when his wife added, "But he says he hasn't any change to pay. He has nothing smaller than a five-dollar bill." Hesitating only a moment, he turned on his heel and said, "Tell him to go into the house. A man that comes right out like that beforehand is welcome to eat my bread."

When he came in after his hard day's work and sat down to dinner, he solemnly asked a blessing on the frugal meal, consisting solely of corn bread and bacon. Then, looking across the table at me, he said, "Young man, what are you doing down here?" I replied that I was look-ing for plants. "Plants? What kind of plants?" I said, "Oh, all kinds; grass, weeds, flowers, trees, mosses, ferns—almost everything that grows is interesting to me."

"Well, young man," he queried, "you mean to say that you are not employed by the government on some private business?" "No,"

I said, "I am not employed by any one except just myself. I love all kinds of plants, and I came down here to these Southern States to get acquainted with as many of them as possible."

"You look like a strong-minded man," he replied, "and surely you are able to do something better than wander over the country and look at weeds and blossoms. These are hard times, and real work is required of every man that is able. Picking up blossoms doesn't seem to be a man's work at all in any kind of times."

To this I replied, "You are a believer in the Bible, are you not?" "Oh, yes." "Well, you know Solomon was a strong-minded man, and he is generally believed to have been the very wisest man the world ever saw, and yet he considered it was worth while to study plants; not only to go and pick them up as I am doing, but to study them; and you know we are told that he wrote a book about plants, not only of the great Cedars of Lebanon, but of little bits of things growing in the cracks of the walls.

"Therefore, you see that Solomon differed very much more from you than from me in this matter. I'll warrant you he had many a long ramble in the mountains of Judea, and had he been a Yankee he would likely have visited every weed in the land. And again, do you not remember that Christ told his disciples to 'consider the lilies how they grow,' and compared their beauty with Solomon in all his glory? Now, whose advice am I to take, yours or Christ's? Christ says, 'Consider the lilies.' You say, 'Don't consider them. It isn't worth while for any strong-minded man.'"

This evidently satisfied him, and he acknowledged that he had never thought of blossoms in that way before. He repeated again and again that I must be a very strong-minded man, and admitted that no doubt I was fully justified in picking up blossoms. He then told me that although the war was over, walking across the Cumberland Mountains still was far from safe on account of small bands of guerrillas who were in hiding along the roads, and earnestly entreated me to turn back and not think of walking so far as the Gulf of Mexico until the country became quiet and orderly once more.

I replied that I had no fear, that I had but very little to lose, and that nobody was likely to think it worth while to rob me; that, anyhow, I always had good luck. In the morning he repeated the warning and entreated me to turn back, which never for a moment interfered with my resolution to pursue my glorious walk.

JOHN MUIR
[*A Thousand-Mile Walk to the Gulf* (1916)]

Section One

THE PLEASURES OF GARDENING

If you would be happy for a week take a wife; if you would be happy for a month kill a pig; but if you would be happy all your life, plant a garden.

CHINESE PROVERB

Such cunning, wit and wisdom is conteined in this Art of Gardning, that the wise and mighty Emperour Dioclesian, through the delight and pleasure he tooke therein after he had reigned 18 yares, left for a season the whole government & rule of the empire: & forsaking the court, went unto a mean house, having a garden adjoining thereto, where he with his proper, hands, both sowed, set & weeded the hearbs of his garden: which kind of life so pleased him, that hardlye hee was intreated to take upon him again the government of the Empire, so much did this quiet life & beauty of the Garden please him.

THOMAS HILL
The Arte of Gardening (1608)

Dolce Far Niente in Ancient Greece

[*Greek literature abounds in references to flowers though we do not always know what their names referred to. Their hyacinth, for example, "that ensanguined flower marked with woe" is certainly not ours, and no one is quite sure what it was. Of their gardens also little is known except the fact that they enjoyed them. Here is at least a hint from Theocritus.*]

SO, I and Eucritus and the fair Amyntichus, turned aside into the house of Phrasidamus, and lay down with delight in beds of sweet tamarisk and fresh cuttings from the vines, strewn on the ground. Many poplars and elm-trees were waving over our heads, and not far off the running of the sacred water from the cave of the nymphs warbled to us: in the shimmering branches the sun-burnt grasshoppers were busy with their talk, and from afar the little owl cried softly out of the tangled thorns of the blackberry; the larks were singing and the hedge-birds, and the turtle-dove moaned; the bees flew round and round the fountains, murmuring softly; the scent of late summer and of the fall of the year was everywhere; the pears fell from the trees at our feet, and apples in number rolled down at our sides, and the young plum-trees were bent to the earth with the weight of their fruit.

THEOCRITUS
[*Idyll VII,*
TRANSLATED BY WALTER PATER]

A Friar's Garden

[*Every well-ordered monastery of the Middle Ages and Renaissance had its kitchen garden and, usually, its garden of medicinal "simples" also. That even flowers were not always regarded as worldly vanities is evident from this passage in an early life of Saint Francis.*]

ST. FRANCIS used also to say to the friar who made ready the wood for the fire, that he should never cut down a whole tree; but so that always some part of a tree should remain whole for the love of Him who did work out our salvation on the wood of the cross. Also he said to the friar who made the garden, not to use it all for pot-herbs. He should leave some part to produce herbs which in their time would produce flowers for the love of Him who is called the "flower of the field" and "the lily of the valley." He used to say, even, to the brother gardener that he ought always make a fair place in some part of the garden, planting there all sweet smelling herbs which bring forth beautiful flowers, so that those who looked on them might be called to praise God.

ANONYMOUS
[*The Mirror of Perfection* (14th century)]

The First English Essayist
Considers the Garden

[*Almost inevitably the first English essayist, Lord Bacon, wrote on the pleasures of gardening and almost as inevitably (at least so it now seems) he began with: "God Almighty first planted a garden."*

Innumerable poets and essayists since (as well as, no doubt, before) have played with the idea. The first man and the first woman lived in a garden while they were blessed and expulsion from it was the first of the punishments inflicted upon them.

Rationalists of today are likely to approach the subject from the opposite direction. Men imagined Adam and Eve in a garden because so many pleasant ideas are associated with the word and the love of gardens symbolizes our nostalgia for an age of innocence. When Abraham Cowley began his letter to John Evelyn with the sentence "I never had any other desire so strong, and so like to Covetousness as that one which I have had always, that I might be master at last of a small house and large garden," he also was saying what innumerable writers since have echoed. Like many of his successors he was thinking first of all of escape from the perplexities of a wicked world; but one may escape into *as well as* from, *and it is the positive aspect—the beauty, the wonder and the mysticism of the garden—which others think of first.*]

G O D Almightie first Planted a Garden. And indeed it is the Purest of Humane pleasures. It is the Greatest Refreshment to the Spirits of Man; Without which, Buildings and Pallaces are but Grosse Handy-works: And a Man shall ever see that, when Ages grow to Civility and Elegancie, Men come to Build Stately sooner then to Garden Finely: As if Gardening were the Greater Perfection. I doe hold it, in the Royall Ordering of Gardens, there ought to be Gardens for all the Moneths in the Yeare; In which, severally, Things of Beautie may be then in Season. For December and January and the Latter Part of November, you must take such Things as are Greene all Winter: Holly; Ivy; Bayes; Juniper; Cipresse Trees; Eugh; Pine-Apple-Trees; Firre-Trees; Rose-Mary; Lavander; Periwinckle, the White, the Purple, and the Blewe; Germander; Flagges; Orenge-Trees; Limon-Trees; And Mirtles, if they be stooved; and Sweet Marioram, warme set. There followeth, for the latter Part of January and February, the Mezerion Tree, which then blossomes; Crocus Vernus, both the Yellow and the Gray; Prime-Roses; Anemones; The Early Tulippa; Hiacynthus Orientalis; Charmairis; Frettellaria. For March, There come Violets, specially the Single Blew which are the Earliest; The Yellow Daffadill; The Dazie; The Almond-Tree in Blossome; The Peach-Tree in Blossome; The Cornelian-Tree in Blossome; Sweet-Briar. In Aprill follow, The Double white Violet, The Wall-flower; The

Stock-Gilly-Flower; The Couslip; Flower-Delices, and Lilies of all Na-
tures; Rose-mary Flowers; The Tulippa; The Double Piony; the Pale
Daffadill; The French Honny-Suckle; The Cherry-Tree in Blossome;
The Dammasin, and Plum-Trees in Blossome; The White-Thorne in
Leafe; The Lelacke Tree. In May and June, come Pincks of all sorts,
Specially the Blush Pincke; Roses of all kinds, except the Muske which
comes later; Hony-Suckles; Strawberries, Buglosse; Columbine; The
French Marygold; Flos Africanus; Cherry-Tree in Fruit; Ribes; Figges
in Fruit; Raspes; Vine Flowers; Lavender in Flowers; The Sweet Sat-
yrian, with the White Flower; Herba Muscaria; Lilium Convallium; The
Apple-tree in Blossome. In July, come Gilly-Flowers of all Varieties;
Muske Roses; The Lime-Tree in blossome; Early Peares, and Plummes
in Fruit; Ginnitings; Quadlins. In August, come Plummes of all sorts
in Fruit; Peares; Apricockes; Berberies; Filberds; Muske-Melons; Monks
Hoods, of all colours. In September, come Grapes, Apples; Poppies of
all colours; Peaches; Melo-Cotones; Nectarines; Cornelians; Wardens;
Quinces. In October and the beginning of November, come Services;
Medlars; Bullises; Roses Cut or Removed to come late; Hollyokes; and
such like. These Particulars are for the Climate of London; But my meaning is Perceived, that you may have *Ver Perpetuum*, as the Place affords.

　　And because the Breath of Flowers is farre Sweeter in the Aire
(where it comes and Goes, like the Warbling of Musick) then in the
hand, therfore nothing is more fit for that delight then to know what
be the Flowers and Plants that doe best perfume the Aire. Roses Damask
and Red are fast Flowers of their Smels; So that you may walke by a
whole Row of them and finde Nothing of their Sweetnesse; Yea, though
it be in a Morning's Dew. Bayes likewise yeeld no Smell as they grow.
Rosemary little; Nor Sweet-Marioram. That which above all Others
yeelds the Sweetest Smell in the Aire is the Violet; Specially the White-
double-Violet, which comes twice a Yeare; About the middle of Aprill,
and about Bartholomew-tide. Next to that is the Muske-Rose. Then the
Strawberry-Leaves dying, which yeeld a most Excellent Cordiall Smell.
Then the Flower of the Vines; It is a little dust, like the dust of a Bent,
which growes upon the Cluster in the First comming forth. Then Sweet
Briar. Then Wall-Flowers, which are very Delightfull, to be set under
a Parler or Lower Chamber Window. Then Pincks and Gilly-Flowers,
specially the Matted Pinck and Clove Gilly-flower. Then the Flowers
of the Lime tree. Then the Hony-Suckles, so they be somewhat a farre
off. Of Beane Flowers I speake not, because they are Field Flowers. But
those which Perfume the Aire most delightfully, not passed by as the
rest, but being Troden upon and Crushed, are Three: That is Burnet,

Wilde-Time, and Water-Mints. Therefore, you are to set whole Allies of them, to have the Pleasure when you walke or tread.

For Gardens, (Speaking of those which are indeed Prince-like, as we have done of Buildings), the Contents ought not well to be under Thirty Acres of Ground, And to be divided into three Parts: A Greene in the Entrance; A Heath or Desart in the Going forth; and the Maine Garden in the midst, Besides Alleys on both Sides. And I like well that Foure Acres of Ground be assigned to the Greene; Six to the Heath, Foure and Foure to either Side; and Twelve to the Maine Garden. The Greene hath two pleasures; The one, because nothing is more Pleasant to the Eye then Greene Grasse kept finely shorne; The other, because it will give you a faire Alley in the midst, by which you may go in front upon a Stately Hedge, which is to inclose the Garden. But, because the Alley will be long, and in great Heat of the Yeare or Day, you ought not to buy the shade in the Garden by Going in the Sunne thorow the Greene, therefore you are, of either Side the Greene, to Plant a Covert Alley, upon Carpenter's Worke, about Twelve Foot in Height, by which you may goe in Shade into the Garden. As for the Making of Knots or Figures with Divers Coloured Earths, that they may lie under the Win-dowes of the House, on that Side which the Gardens stands, they be but Toyes: You may see as good Sights, many times, in Tarts. The Garden is best to be Square; Incompassed, on all the Foure Sides, with a Stately Arched Hedge. The Arches to be upon Pillars of Carpenter's Worke, of some Ten Foot high and Six Foot broad; And the Spaces between of the same Dimension with the Breadth of the Arch. Over the Arches, let there bee an Entire Hedge, of some Foure Foot High, framed also upon Carpenter's Worke; And upon the Upper Hedge, over every Arch, a little Turret, with a Belly enough to receive a Cage of Birds: And over every Space, betweene the Arches, some other little Figure, with Broad Plates of Round Coloured Glasse, gilt, for the Sunne to Play upon. But this Hedge I entend to be raised upon a Bancke, not Steepe, but gently Slope, of some Six Foot, set all with Flowers. Also I understand that this Square of the Garden should not be the whole Breadth of the Ground, but to leave, on either Side, Ground enough for diversity of Side Alleys; Unto which the Two Covert Alleys of the Greene may deliver you. But there must be no Alleys with Hedges, at either End of this great Inclosure; Not at the Hither End, for letting your Prospect upon this Faire Hedge from the Greene; Nor at the Further End, for letting your Prospect from the Hedge, through the Arches, upon the Heath.

For the Ordering of the Ground within the Great Hedge,

I leave it to Variety of Device; Advising, neverthelesse, that whatsoever forme you cast it into, first it be not too Busie or full of Worke. Wherein I, for my part, doe not like Images Cut out in Juniper or other Garden stuffe: They be for Children. Little low Hedges, Round like Welts, with some Pretty Pyramides, I like well: And in some Places, Faire Columnes upon Frames of Carpenter's Worke. I would also have the Alleys Spacious and Faire. You may have Closer Alleys upon the Side Grounds, but none in the Maine Garden. I wish also, in the very Middle, a Faire Mount, with three Ascents and Alleys, enough for foure to walke a breast; Which I would have to be Perfect Circles, without any Bulwarkes or Imbosments; And the Whole Mount to be Thirty Foot high; And some fine Banquetting House, with some Chimneys neatly cast, and without too much Glasse.

For Fountaines, they are a great Beauty and Refreshment; But Pooles marre all, and make the Garden unwholsome and full of Flies and Frogs. Fountaines I intend to be of two Natures: The One, that Sprinckleth or Spouteth Water; The Other a Faire Receipt of Water, of some Thirty or Forty Foot Square, but without Fish, or Slime, or Mud. For the first, the Ornaments of Images Gilt or of Marble, which are in use, doe well: But the maine Matter is, so to Convey the Water as it never Stay, either in the Bowles or in the Cesterne, That the Water be never by Rest Discoloured, Greene, or Red, or the like, it is to be cleansed every day by the Hand. Also some Steps up to it, and some Fine Pavement about it, doth well. As for the other Kinde of Fountaine, which we may call a Bathing Poole, it may admit much Curiosity and Beauty; wherewith we will not trouble our selves: As, that the Bottome be finely Paved, And with Images: The sides likewise; and withall Embellished with Coloured Glasse and such Things of Lustre; Encompassed also with fine Railes of Low Statuas. But the Maine Point is the same which we mentioned in the former Kinde of Fountaine; which is, that the Water be in Perpetuall Motion, Fed by a Water higher then the Poole, and Delivered into it by faire Spouts, and then discharged away under Ground by some Equalitie of Bores, that it stay little. And for fine Devices of Arching Water without Spilling, and Making it rise in severall Formes, (of Feathers, Drinking Glasses, Canopies, and the like,) they be pretty things to looke on, but Nothing to Health and Sweetnesse.

For the Heath, which was the Third Part of our Plot, I wish it to be framed, as much as may be, to a Naturall wildnesse. Trees I would have none in it; But some Thickets, made onely of Sweet-Briar and Honny-suckle, and some Wilde-Vine amongst; And the Ground set with Violets, Strawberries, and Prime-Roses. For these are Sweet, and prosper in the Shade. And these to be in the Heath, here and there, not in any Order. I like also little Heaps, in the Nature of Mole-hils, (such as are in Wilde Heaths) to be set, some with Wilde Thyme; Some with Pincks; Some with Germander, that gives a good Flower to the Eye; Some with Periwinckle; Some with Violets; Some with Straw-berries; Some with Couslips; Some with Daisies; Some with Red-Roses; Some with Lilium Convallium; Some with Sweet-Williams Red; Some with Beare's-Foot; And the like Low Flowers, being withal Sweet and Sightly: Part of which Heapes, to be with Standards of little Bushes prickt upon their Top, and Part without. The Standards to be Roses, Juniper; Holly; Beare-berries (but here and there, because of the Smell of their Blossome,) Red Currans; Goose-berries; Rose-Mary; Bayes; Sweet-Briar; and such like. But these Standards, to be kept with Cutting, that they grow not out of Course.

For the Side Grounds, you are to fill them with Varietie of Alleys, Private, to give a full Shade, Some of them, wheresoever the Sun be. You are to frame some of them likewise for Shelter, that when the Wind blows Sharpe, you may walke, as in a Gallery. And those Alleys must be likewise hedged at both Ends to keepe out the Wind; And these Closer Alleys must bee ever finely Gravelled, and no Grasse, because of Going wet. In many of these Alleys likewise, you are to set Fruit-Trees of all Sorts; As well upon the Walles as in Ranges. And this would be generally observed, that the Borders, wherin you plant your Fruit-Trees, be Faire and Large, and Low, and not Steepe; and Set with Fine Flowers, but thin and sparingly, lest they Deceive the Trees. At the End of both the Side Grounds, I would have a Mount of some Pretty Height, leaving the Wall of the Enclosure Brest high, to looke abroad into the Fields.

For the Maine Garden, I doe not Deny but there should be some Faire Alleys, ranged on both Sides with Fruit Trees; And some Pretty Tufts of Fruit Trees, And Arbours with Seats, set in some Decent Order; But these to be by no Meanes set too thicke; But to leave the Maine Garden so as it be not close, but the Aire Open and Free. For as for Shade, I would have you rest upon the Alleys of the Side Grounds, there to walke, if you be Disposed, in the Heat of the Yeare, or day; But to make Account that the Maine Garden is for the more Temperate Parts of the yeare, And in the Heat of Summer, for the Morning and the Evening, or over-cast Dayes.

For Aviaries, I like them not, except they be of that Largenesse as they may be Turffed, and have Living Plants and Bushes set in them;

That the Birds may have more Scope, and Naturall Neastling, and that no Foulenesse appeare in the Floare of the Aviary. So I have made a Platforme of a Princely Garden, Partly by Precept, Partly by Drawing, not a Modell, but some generall Lines of it; And in this I have spared for no Cost. But it is Nothing for Great Princes, that, for the most Part, taking Advice with Workmen, with no Lesse Cost set their Things together; And sometimes adde Statuas and such Things, for State and Magnificence, but nothing to the true Pleasure of a Garden.

FRANCIS BACON
[*Essays* (1598)]

Peace in a Garden

[*In his own day Abraham Cowley was far better known than his contemporary John Milton. He was, in fact, by far the most popular English poet then living. But it was only a generation later that Pope could ask, "Who now reads Cowley?"; and the answer is still "Nobody." His prose is more to the modern taste, as this open letter to his friend the diarist John Evelyn will demonstrate.*]

To J. EVELYN *Esquire*

I NEVER had any other desire so strong, and so like to Covetousness as that one which I have had always, that I might be master at last of a small house and large garden, with very moderate conveniencies joyned to them, and there dedicate the remainder of my life only to the culture of them and study of Nature,

And there (with no design beyond my wall) whole and
 intire to lye,
In no unactive Ease, and no unglorious Poverty.

Or as Virgil has said, Shorter and Better for me, that I might there *Studiis florere ignobilis otii* (though I could wish that he had rather said, *Nobilis otii*, when he spoke of his own). But several accidents of my ill fortune have disappointed me hitherto, and do still, of that felicity; for though I have made the first and hardest step to it, by abandoning all ambitions and hopes in this World, and by retiring from the noise of all business and almost company, yet I stick still in the Inn of a hired House and Garden, among Weeds and Rubbish; and without that plesantest work of Human Industry, the Improvement of something which we call (not very properly, but yet we call) Our Own. I am gone out from Sodom, but I am not yet arrived at my Little *Zoar. O let me escape thither (Is it not a Little one?) and my Soul shall live.* I do not look back yet; but I have been forced to stop, and make too many halts. You may wonder, Sir, (for this seems a little too extravagant and Pindarical for *Prose*) what I mean by all this Preface; It is to let you know, That though I have mist, like a Chymist, my great End, yet I account my affections and endeavours well rewarded by something that I have met with by the By; which is, that they have procured to me some part in their kindness and esteem; and thereby the honour of having my Name so advantagiously recommended to Posterity, by the *Epistle* you are pleased to prefix to the most useful Book that has been written in that kind, and which is to last as long as Moneths and Years.

Among many other *Arts* and *Excellencies* which you enjoy, I am glad to find this Favourite of mine the most predominant, That you choose this for your Wife, though you have hundreds of other Arts for your Concubines; Though you know them, and beget Sons upon them all (to which you are rich enough to allow great Legacies) yet the issue of this seemes to be designed by you to the main of the Estate; you have taken most pleasure in it, and bestow'd most charges upon its Education: and I doubt not to see that Book, which you are pleased to Promise to the World, and of which you have given us a Large Earnest in your Calendar, as Accomplisht, as any thing can be expected from an *Extraordinary Wit*, and no ordinary Expences, and a long Experience. I know no body that possesses more private happiness then you do in your Garden; and yet no man who makes his happiness more publick, by a free communication of the Art and Knowledge of it to others. All that I my self am able yet to do, is onely to recommend to Mankind the search of that Felicity, which you Instruct them how to Find and to Enjoy.

ABRAHAM COWLEY
[Prefatory Letter to John Evelyn's Kalendarium Hortense (1664)]

A Victorian Gardener

[*Every age has its own way of writing about plants and flowers. The seventeenth was philosophical; the twentieth most likely to be practical. The Victorians also had their characteristic tone which was likely to be didactic—often in the now-children manner. One of the most popular books,* Conversations on Botany, *was written by the two Fitton sisters for whom the familiar little terrarium plant Fittonia was named. Though it went into its ninth edition in 1840, no modern child would endure its Little Edward who obligingly asks all the right questions nor his mother who condescendingly answers them. We turn instead to a genteel essayist of the same age in whom a real charm triumphs over the didactic manner.*]

I HAVE said that there was great pleasure in watching the ways in which different plants come through the ground, and February and March are the months in which that can best be seen. The more I study flowers, the more I feel how little I know about them, and especially how very little is known of a plant by its flower only. The young shoots of a plant when it first breaks the ground are often of wonderful beauty, and are in many cases so utterly unlike the same leaves when come to maturity, that to describe a plant by its mature leaves only is to tell less than half its story. And this is only one of the wonders of young plant life. People sow seeds, and watch for the coming of the plant, but few note that every separate plant has its particular method of coming out of darkness into light, and we may be quite certain that that particular method is the only one suitable to it. Darwin noticed that some flowers break through the ground as arches, the flower being formed underneath the ground, and then coming up curled almost like a fern. He instances the parasitic *Lathrea, Helleborus niger, Epimedium,* and *Ranunculus ficaria*; I have noticed the same thing in some of the fumitories, and probably it occurs in other plants. Why these should act so differently to all other plants is a mystery. But the greatest mystery of this bursting forth of the plants is that it is done when the growth is at its tenderest age; when the shoot is tender and brittle it has power to push through everything that binds it down. Instances are on record where funguses have lifted large paving-stones, and in my own garden I have an example almost as curious. Many years ago I filled up a flower-bed, and brought a gravel path through the midst of it. By accident a bunch of white crocuses was left in the ground, and now every year there is a bunch of these white crocuses coming up through the hard gravel path, apparently quite happy in their ungenial position. When I look on that bunch of crocuses I get an excellent object-lesson in the enormous strength of even the smallest plants. The leaves and flowers of the crocus are apparently so weak that a fly settling on any of them can weigh it down; yet they can force their way through a substance as hard as concrete. From another habit of many plants I get another object-lesson, from which I learn that plant-life knows no rest. Many plants come up in the spring at a considerable distance from their position last summer. Roses will send up suckers many feet away from the parent plant; the pretty Chinese poppy, *eomecon*, will come up almost anywhere in the bed except where it was first planted, and this is more or less the case with almost all plants which in our country dialect are called "rastlers."

If we carefully study the revival of plants in the spring, we are often reminded that "great are the uses of adversity," even to a garden. An Italian professor, Signor Goiran, has recently given his opinion that earthquakes are beneficial to agriculture, "promoting a more rapid germination of seeds, a quicker rate of growth in the young plants, and a distincter greenness in all vegetation." Few gardeners would wish to have such a help in their gardens; but I feel sure that they are helped by what at first seemed almost as disastrous, for I am sure that for the abundant flowers of one year we are often largely indebted to previous very severe winters. We may have to regret the entire loss of many good plants, and no doubt only the strong ones survive; but the strong have by it gained more strength. The enforced rest which is necessary after the shock of the severe winters may make them produce few flowers the following year; but the rest was just what the plants wanted to enable them to recover all they had lost, and to gain much fresh strength; just as many an active man is brought to a severe illness by overtaxing his strength, but the enforced rest will often bring back strength that he was fast losing altogether; or just as a fruit-tree which bears beyond its strength one year takes a rest in the next year, and then fruits with

Bruegel inuet.

Martius, Aprilis, Maius, sunt tempora ueris.

H. Cock. excud. 1570.

Epigramma.

FLORA naturæ reserans receß,
Exhibet blandas violas, rosasq̃,
Quicquid et dites Arabes remittũt.
    Spargit odorum.

B.

Simon Passeus sculp. vlr.

renewed vigour the year after. And this teaches us that the true gardener is never overmuch disquieted by bad seasons, whether they are seasons of drought or of frost. The half-hearted gardener thinks that all is lost when he has lost one season; but the wise man's caution has a very wide meaning: "He that observeth the wind shall not sow, and he that regardeth the clouds shall not reap." The fair-weather gardener, who will do nothing except when wind and weather and everything else are favourable, is never a master of his craft. Gardening, above all crafts, is a matter of faith, grounded, however (if on nothing better), on his experience that somehow or other seasons go on in their right course, and bring their right results. No doubt bad seasons are a trial of his faith; it is grievous to lose the fruits of much labour by a frosty winter or a droughty summer; but after all, frost and drought are necessities for which, in all his calculations, he must leave an ample margin; but even in the extreme cases, when the margin is past, the gardener's occupation is not gone.

HENRY N. ELLACOMBE
[*A Gloucestershire Garden* (1895)]

In Praise of Dirt

[*Charles Dudley Warner, the once-famous American essayist who was also in the genteel tradition, is now almost forgotten. But he wrote much on gardens in a fashion which still retains its somewhat faint charm.*]

THE love of dirt is among the earliest of passions, as it is the latest. Mud-pies gratify one of our first and best instincts. So long as we are dirty, we are pure. Fondness for the ground comes back to a man after he has run the round of pleasure and business, eaten dirt, and sown wild-oats, drifted about the world, and taken the wind of all its moods. The love of digging in the ground (or of looking on while he pays another to dig) is as sure to come back to him, as he is sure, at last, to go under the ground, and stay there. To own a bit of ground, to scratch it with a hoe, to plant seeds, and watch their renewal of life—this is the commonest delight of the race, the most satisfactory thing a man can do. When Cicero writes of the pleasures of old age, that of agriculture is chief among them: *"Venio nunc ad voluptates agricolarum, quibus ego incredibiliter delector: quæ nee ulla impediunter senectute, et mihi ad sapientis vitam proxime videntur accedere."* (I am driven to Latin because New-York editors have exhausted the English language in the praising of spring, and especially of the month of May.)

Let us celebrate the soil. Most men toil that they may own a piece of it; they measure their success in life by their ability to buy it. It is alike the passion of the *parvenu* and the pride of the aristocrat. Broad acres are a patent of nobility; and no man but feels more of a man in the world if he have a bit of ground that he can call his own. However small it is on the surface, it is four thousand miles deep; and that is a very handsome property. And there is a great pleasure in working in the soil, apart from the ownership of it. The man who has planted a garden feels that he has done something for the good of the world. He belongs to the producers. It is a pleasure to eat of the fruit of one's toil, if it be nothing more than a head of lettuce or an ear of corn. One cultivates a lawn even with great satisfaction; for there is nothing more beautiful than grass and turf in our latitude. The tropics may have their delights; but they have not turf: and the world without turf is a dreary desert. The original garden of Eden could not have had such turf as one sees in England. The Teutonic races all love turf: they emigrate in the line of its growth.

To dig in the mellow soil—to dig moderately, for all pleasure should be taken sparingly—is a great thing. One gets strength out of the ground as often as one really touches it with a hoe. Antæus (this is a classical article) was no doubt an agriculturist; and such a prize-fighter as Hercules couldn't do anything with him till he got him to lay down his spade, and quit the soil. It is not simply beets and potatoes and corn and string-beans that one raises in his well-hoed garden: it is the average of human life. There is life in the ground; it goes into the seeds; and it also, when it is stirred up, goes into the man who stirs it. The hot sun on his back as he bends to his shovel and hoe, or contemplatively rakes the warm and fragrant loam, is better than much medicine. The buds are coming out on the bushes round about; the blossoms of the fruit-trees begin to show; the blood is running up the grape-vines in streams; you can smell the wild-flowers on the near bank; and the birds are flying and glancing and singing everywhere. To the open kitchen-door comes the busy housewife to shake a white something, and stands a moment to look, quite transfixed by the delightful sights and sounds. Hoeing in the garden on a bright, soft May day, when you are not obliged to, is nearly equal to the delight of going trouting.

Blessed be agriculture! if one does not have too much of it. All literature is fragrant with it, in a gentlemanly way. At the foot of the charming olive-covered hills of Tivoli, Horace (not he of Chappaqua) had a sunny farm: it was in sight of Hadrian's villa, who did landscape-gardening on an extensive scale, and probably did not get half as much comfort out of it as Horace did from his more simply-tilled acres. We trust that Horace did a little hoeing and farming himself, and that his verse is not all fraudulent sentiment. In order to enjoy agriculture, you do not want too much of it, and you want to be poor enough to have a little inducement to work moderately yourself. Hoe while it is spring, and enjoy the best anticipations. It is not much matter if things do not turn out well.

CHARLES DUDLEY WARNER
[*My Summer in a Garden* (1870)]

Colette Remembers Her Mother's Garden

[*In her later years "Colette," once regarded as a somewhat scandalous light novelist, became accepted in France as a classic. With equal facility she described the amorous adventures of her sophisticated Parisians and her own passionate interest in the nature she learned to love during her country childhood.*]

IN my home village there were hardly twenty houses without a garden. The worst off enjoyed a backyard, whether or not it was cultivated or roofed with a vine trellis. Each frontage hid a long back garden, joined to the others by a party wall. These back gardens gave the village its character. There we all lived in summer, and there the washing was done; in winter the wood was chopped there; and all the year round it was the place for odd jobs, while the children played under the cart-sheds and perched on the side-rails of the empty hay-wains.

The enclosures adjoining our own had no particular mystery about them, but in ours both the "upper garden" and the "lower garden" were shielded by the slope of the ground, the high and ancient walls, and screens of trees. The reverberating hill-side echoed all noises, carrying news from the little island of kitchen-gardens surrounded by houses as far as our "public park."

From our garden, to the South we could hear Milton sneezing as he dug, and talking to his white dog. Every Fourteenth of July he used to dye its head blue and its hind-quarters red. To the North there was old Mother Adolphe singing a little hymn as she tied up bunches of violets for the altar of our church, which had lost its belfry when it was struck by lightning. To the East, a sad little tinkle announced that a client had called to see the lawyer. Let no one talk to me of provincial suspiciousness. Suspiciousness indeed! Our gardens told each other everything.

How pleasant it was, that civilised life in our gardens, with its exchanges of courtesies and amenities between the kitchen-garden and the "floral," the shrubbery and the poultry-yard! What harm ever came over an espalier trained along a party-wall whose coping-stones, held together with lichen and glowing yellow stonecrop, served as a promenade for toms and she-cats? On the other side, where the houses gave on the street, cheeky children mooned about, playing marbles and tucking up their petticoats when they played in the stream; neighbours eyed each other and flung little curses, a laugh or a bit of peel in the wake of each passer-by, while the men lounged in their doorways smoking and spitting. From our own façade, iron-grey with tall, faded shutters, no sound emerged but that of my fumbling scales, the barking of a dog when the bell rang, and the song of the green canaries in their cage.

Perhaps our neighbours tried to emulate in their gardens the peace of ours, where the children never fought and where beasts and men lived their lives tranquilly together; a garden where for the space of thirty years a husband and wife dwelt with never a harsh word between them.

In those days there were bitter winters and burning summers. Since then I have known summers which, when I close my eyes, are the colour of ochre-yellow earth, cracking between stalks of corn; and beneath the giant umbels of wild parsnip, the blue or grey of the sea. But no summer, save those of my childhood, enshrines the memory of scarlet geraniums and the glowing spikes of foxgloves. No winter now is ever pure white beneath a sky charged with slate-coloured clouds foretelling a storm of thicker snowflakes yet to come, and thereafter a thaw glittering with a thousand water-drops and bright with spear-shaped buds. How that sky used to lower over the snow-laden roof of the haylofts, the weathercock, and the bare boughs of the walnut-tree, making the she-cats flatten their ears! The quiet vertical fall of the snow became oblique and, as I wandered about the garden catching its flying flakes in my mouth, a faint booming as of a distant sea arose above my hooded head. Warned by her antennae, my mother would come out on the terrace, sample the weather and call out to me:

"A gale from the West! Run and shut the skylights in the barn! And in the door of the coach-house! And the window of the back room!"

Eager cabin-boy of the family vessel, I would rush off, my sabots clattering, thrilled if, from the depths of that hissing turmoil of white and blue-black, a flash of lightning and a brief mutter of thunder, children of February and the West wind, together filled one of the abysses of the sky. I would try then to shudder and believe that the end of the world had come.

But when the din was at its height, there would be my mother, peering through a big brass-rimmed magnifying glass, lost in wonder as she counted the branched crystals of a handful of snow she had just snatched from the very jaws of the West wind as it flung itself upon our garden.

It was the reflected glow of your blazing line along the terrace, O geraniums, and yours, O foxgloves, springing up amidst the coppice, that gave my childish cheeks their rosy warmth. For Sido loved red and pink in the garden, the burning shades of roses, lychnis, hydrangeas and red-hot pokers. She even loved the winter-cherry, although she declared that its pulpy pink flowers, veined with red, reminded her of the lights of a freshly killed calf. She made a reluctant pact with the East wind. "I know how to get on with him," she would say. But she remained suspicious and, out of all the cardinal and collateral points of the compass, it was on that icy treacherous point, with its murderous pranks, that she kept her eye. But she trusted him with lily of the valley bulbs, some begonias, and mauve autumn crocuses, those dim lanterns of cold twilights.

Except for one mound with a clump of cherry-laurels overshadowed by a maiden-hair tree—whose skate-shaped leaves I used to give to my school friends to press between the pages of their atlases—the whole warm garden basked in a yellow light that shimmered into red and violet; but whether this red and violet sprang then, and still springs, from feelings of happiness or from dazzled sight, I could not tell. Those were summers when the heat quivered up from the hot yellow gravel and pierced the plaited rushes of my wide-brimmed hats, summers almost without nights. For even then I so loved the dawn that my mother granted it to me as a reward. She used to agree to wake me at half-past three and off I would go, an empty basket on each arm, towards the kitchen-gardens that sheltered in the narrow bend of the river, in search of strawberries, black-currants, and hairy gooseberries.

At half-past three everything slumbered still in a primal blue, blurred and dewy, and as I went down the sandy road the mist, grounded by its own weight, bathed first my legs, then my well-built little body, reaching at last to my mouth and ears, and finally to that most sensitive part of all, my nostrils. I went alone, for there were no dangers in that free-thinking countryside. It was on that road and at that hour that I first became aware of my own self, experienced an inexpressible state of grace, and felt one with the first breath of air that stirred, the first bird, and the sun so newly born that it still looked not quite round.

"Beauty" my mother would call me, and "Jewel-of-pure-gold"; then she would let me go, watching her creation—her masterpiece, as she said—grow smaller as I ran down the slope. I may have been pretty; my mother and the pictures of me at that period do not always agree. But what made me pretty at that moment was my mouth and the dawn, my blue eyes deepened by the greenery all round me, my fair locks that would only be brushed smooth on my return, and my pride at being awake when other children were asleep.

I came back when the bell rang for the first Mass. But not before I had eaten my fill, not before I had described a great circle in the woods, like a dog out hunting on its own, and tasted the water of the two hidden springs which I worshipped. One of them bubbled out of the ground with a crystalline spurt and a sort of sob, and then carved its own sandy bed. But it was no sooner born than it lost confidence and plunged underground again. The other spring, almost invisible, brushed over the grass like a snake, and spread itself out secretly in the middle of a meadow where the narcissus, flowering in a ring, alone bore witness to its presence. The first spring tasted of oak-leaves, the second of iron and hyacinth stalks. The mere mention of them makes me hope that their savour may fill my mouth when my time comes, and that I may carry hence with me that imagined draught.

In her garden my mother had a habit of addressing to the four cardinal points not only direct remarks and replies that sounded, when heard from our sitting-room, like brief inspired soliloquies, but the actual manifestations of her courtesy, which generally took the form of plants and flowers. But in addition to these points—to Cebe and the Rue des Vignes, to Mother Adolphe and Maître de Fourolles—there was also a zone of collateral points, more distant and less defined, whose contact with us was by means of stifled sounds and signals. My childish pride and imagination saw our house as the central point of a Mariner's Chart of gardens, winds and rays of light, no section of which lay quite beyond my mother's influence.

I could gain my liberty at any moment by means of an easy climb over a gate, a wall, or a little sloping roof, but as soon as I landed back on the gravel of our own garden, illusion and faith returned to me. For as soon as she had asked me: "Where have you come from?" and frowned the ritual frown, my mother would resume her placid, radiant garden-face, so much more beautiful than her anxious indoor-face. And merely because she held sway there and watched over it all, the walls grew higher, the enclosures which I had so easily traversed by jumping from wall to wall and branch to branch, became unknown lands, and I found myself once more among the familiar wonders.

"Is that you I hear, Cebe?" my mother would call. "Have you seen my cat?"

She pushed back her wide-brimmed hat of burnt straw until it slid down her shoulders, held by a brown taffeta ribbon round her neck, and threw her head back to confront the sky with her fearless grey glance and her face the colour of an autumn apple. Did her voice strike the bird on the weathercock, the hovering honey-buzzard, the last leaf on the walnut-tree or the dormer window which, at the first light, swallowed up the barn owls? Then—though it was certain to happen, the surprise was never failing—from a cloud on the left the voice of a prophet with a bad cold would let fall a: "No, Madame Cole . . . e . . . tte!" which seemed to be making its way with great difficulty through a curly beard and blankets of fog, and slithering over ponds vaporous with cold. Or perhaps: "Ye . . . es, Madame Cole . . . e . . . tte!" the voice of a shrill angel would sing on the right, probably perched on the spindle-shaped cirrus cloud which was sailing along to meet the young moon. "She's he . . . e . . . ard you. She's go . . . oing through the li . . . i . . . lacs."

"Thank you!" called my mother at random. "If that's you, Cebe, just give me back my stake and my planting-out line, will you? I need them to get my lettuces straight. But be careful. I'm close to the hydrangeas!" As if it were the offering of a dream, the prank of a witches' sabbath, or an act of magical levitation, the stake, wound round with ten yards of small cord, sailed through the air and came to rest at my mother's feet.

On other occasions she would offer to lesser, invisible spirits a tribute of flowers. Faithful to her ritual, she threw back her head and scanned the sky: "Who wants some of my double red violets?" she cried.

"I do, Madame Cole . . . e . . . tte!" answered the mysterious one to the East, in her plaintive, feminine voice.

"Here you are, then!" and the little bunch, tied together with a juicy jonquil leaf, flew through the air, to be gratefully received by the plaintive Orient. "How lovely they smell! To think I can't grow any as good!"

"Of course you can't," I would think, and felt inclined to add: "It's all a question of the air they breathe."

Always up at dawn and sometimes before day, my mother attached particular importance to the cardinal points of the compass, as much for the good as for the harm they might bring. It is because of her and my deep-rooted love for her that first thing every morning, and while I am still snug in bed, I always ask: "Where is the wind coming from?" only to be told in reply: "It's a lovely day," or "The Palais-Royal's full of sparrows," or "The weather's vile" or "seasonable." So nowadays I have to rely on myself for the answer, by watching which way a cloud is moving, listening for ocean rumblings in the chimney, and letting my skin enjoy the breath of the West wind, a breath as moist and vital and laden with portents as the twofold divergent snortings of some friendly monster. Or it may be that I shrink into myself with hatred before that fine-cold-dry enemy the East wind, and his cousin of the North. That was what my mother used to do, as she covered with paper cornets all the little plant creatures threatened by the russet moon. "It's going to freeze," she would say, "the cat's dancing."

Her hearing, which remained keen, kept her informed too, and she would intercept Aeolian warnings.

"Listen over Moutiers!" she used to say, lifting her forefinger where she stood near the pump, between the hydrangeas and the group of rose-bushes. That was her reception point for the information coming from the West over the lowest of the garden walls. "D'you hear? Take the garden chairs indoors, and your book and hat. It's raining over Moutiers; in two or three minutes more it'll be raining here."

I strained my ears "over Moutiers"; from the horizon came a steady sound of beads plopping into water and the flat smell of the rain-pitted pond as it sluiced up against its slimy green banks. And I would wait for a second or two, so that the gentle drops of a summer shower, falling on my cheeks and lips, might bear witness to the infallibility of her whom only one person in the world—my father—called "Sido."

Certain omens, dimmer since her death, haunt me still. One is concerned with the Zodiac, another is entirely botanical, and others again have to do with the winds, the phases of the moon, and subterranean waters. It was because those omens were only free to be effective and decisive in the wide air of our province that my mother found Paris irksome.

"I could live in Paris only if I had a beautiful garden," she would confess to me. "And even then! I can't imagine a Parisian garden where I could pick those big bearded oats I sew on a bit of cardboard for you because they make such sensitive barometers." I chide myself for having lost the very last of those rustic barometers made of oat grains whose two awns, as long as a shrimp's feelers, crucified on a card, would turn to the left or the right according to whether it was going to be fine or wet.

No one could equal Sido, either, at separating and counting the talc-like skins of onions. "One . . . two . . . three coats; three coats on the onions!" And letting her spectacles or her lorgnette fall on her lap, she would add pensively: "That means a hard winter. I must have the pump wrapped in straw. Besides, the tortoise has dug itself in already, and the squirrels round about Guillemette have stolen quantities of walnuts and cob-nuts for their stores. Squirrels always know everything."

If the newspapers foretold a thaw my mother would shrug her shoulders and laugh scornfully. "A thaw? Those Paris meteorologists can't teach me anything about that! Look at the cat's paws!" Feeling chilly, the cat had indeed folded her paws out of sight beneath her, and shut her eyes tight. "When there's only going to be a short spell of cold," went on Sido, "the cat rolls herself into a turban with her nose against the root of her tail. But when it's going to be really bitter, she tucks in the pads of her front paws and rolls them up like a muff."

All the year round she kept racks full of plants in pots standing on green-painted wooden steps. There were rare geraniums, dwarf rose-bushes, spiraeas with misty white and pink plumes, a few "succulents," hairy and squat as crabs, and murderous cacti. Two warm walls formed an angle which kept the harsh winds from her trial-ground, which consisted of some red earthenware bowls in which I could see nothing but loose, dormant earth.

"Don't touch!"

"But nothing's coming up!"

"And what do you know about it? Is it for you to decide? Read what's written on the labels stuck in the pots! These are seeds of blue lupin; that's a narcissus bulb from Holland; those are seeds of winter-cherry; that's a cutting of hibiscus—no, of course it isn't a dead twig!—and those are some seeds of sweet-peas whose flowers have ears like little hares. And that . . . and that . . ."

"Yes, and that?"

My mother pushed her hat back, nibbled the chain of her lorgnette, and put the problem frankly to me:

"I'm really very worried. I can't remember whether it was a family of crocus bulbs I planted there, or the chrysalis of an emperor moth."

"We've only got to scratch to find out."

A swift hand stopped mine. Why did no one ever model or paint or carve that hand of Sido's, tanned and wrinkled early by house-hold tasks, gardening, cold water and the sun, with its long, finely-tapering fingers and its beautiful, convex, oval nails?

"Not on your life! If it's the chrysalis, it'll die as soon as the air touches it, and if it's the crocus, the light will shrivel its little white shoot and we'll have to begin all over again. Are you taking in what I say? You won't touch it?"

"No, mother."

As she spoke her face, alight with faith and an all-embracing curiosity, was hidden by another, older face, resigned and gentle. She knew that I should not be able to resist, any more than she could, the desire to know, and that like herself I should ferret in the earth of that flowerpot until it had given up its secret. I never thought of our resemblance, but she knew I was her own daughter and that, child though I was, I was already seeking for that sense of shock, the quickened heartbeat, and the sudden stoppage of the breath—symptoms of the private ecstasy of the treasure-seeker. A treasure is not merely something hidden under the earth, or the rocks, or the sea. The vision of gold and gems is but a blurred mirage. To me the important thing is to lay bare and bring to light something that no human eye before mine has gazed upon.

She knew then that I was going to scratch on the sly in her trial-ground until I came upon the upward-climbing claw of the cotyledon, the sturdy sprout urged out of its sheath by the spring. I thwarted the blind purpose of the bilious-looking, black-brown chrysalis, and hurled it from its temporary death into a final nothingness.

"You don't understand . . . you can't understand . . . You're nothing but a little eight-year-old murderess . . . or is it ten? You just can't understand something that wants to live." That was the only punishment I got for my misdeeds; but that was hard enough for me to bear.

Sido loathed flowers to be sacrificed. Although her one idea was to give, I have seen her refuse a request for flowers to adorn a hearse or a grave. She would harden her heart, frown, and answer "No" with a vindictive look.

"But it's for poor Monsieur Enfert who died last night! Poor Madame Enfert's so pathetic, she says if she could see her husband depart covered with flowers, it would console her! And you've got such lovely moss-roses, Madame Colette."

"My moss-roses on a corpse! What an outrage!"

It was an involuntary cry, but even after she had pulled herself together she still said: "No. My roses have not been condemned to die at the same time as Monsieur Enfert."

But she gladly sacrificed a very beautiful flower to a very small child, a child not yet able to speak, like the little boy whom a neighbour to the East proudly brought in to the garden one day, to show him off to her. My mother found fault with the infant's swaddling clothes, for being too tight, untied his three-piece bonnet and his unnecessary woollen shawl, and then gazed to her heart's content on his bronze ringlets, his cheeks, and the enormous, stern black eyes of a ten months' old baby boy, really so much more beautiful than any other boy of ten months! She gave him a *cuisse-de-nymphe-emue* rose, and he accepted it with delight, put it in his mouth, and sucked it; then he kneaded it with his powerful little hands and tore off the petals, as curved and carmine as his own lips.

"Stop it, you naughty boy!" cried his young mother.

But mine, with looks and words, applauded his massacre of the rose, and in my jealousy I said nothing.

She also regularly refused to lend double geraniums, pelargoniums, lobelias, dwarf rose-bushes and spiraea for the wayside altars on Corpus Christi Day, for although she was baptized and married in church, she always held aloof from Catholic trivialities and pageantries. But she gave me permission, when I was between eleven and twelve, to attend catechism classes and to join in the hymns at the Evening Service.

On the first of May, with my comrades of the catechism class,

I laid lilac, camomile and roses before the altar of the Virgin, and returned full of pride to show my "blessed posy." My mother laughed her irreverent laugh and, looking at my bunch of flowers, which was bringing the may-bugs into the sitting-room right under the lamp, she said: "D'you suppose it wasn't already blessed before?"

COLETTE
[*Sido* (1953)]

A Gardener's Philosophy

[*Richardson Wright, for many years editor of the magazine* House and Garden, *wrote innumerable books and articles dealing with every aspect of life in the country and suburbs. But he was obviously at heart a gardener first of all, and probably no contemporary was more widely read by those who shared his interests.*]

S O M E pages back I stated that I preferred to garden *coram populo*. I cannot hold with the English theory of enclosing all gardens with walls, because, just as a man may not possess leisure to himself, or live a life to himself, so he cannot make a garden to himself.

Try to keep a garden beautiful to yourself alone and see what happens—the neighbor, hurrying by to catch his train of mornings, will stop to snatch a glint of joy from the iris purpling by your doorstep. The motorist will throw on brakes and back downhill just to see those Oriental poppies massed against the wall.

Nature is always on the side of the public. Build your wall never so high but her winds will carry the seeds of that choice variety you reserved for yourself to a dozen different dooryards and open fields, where they will blossom next season. Plant your hedgerow never so thick but a vine will stretch forth a friendly finger through it. Lock the gate never so tight but the zephyrs will waft odors of rose and hyacinth and mignonette to every passer-by.

It follows, then, that a garden is a public service and having one a public duty. It is a man's contribution to the community. It is not enough that law and order be preserved in our communities. Only the policeman with his truncheon would stand between us and chaos if law and order were all we desired. No, it is the mark of an upward-looking civilization that men make beautiful gardens, that the joy of the tulip and the flowering shrub be shared with other men. . . .

Even in the face of such poignant experiences I would not say that every man should garden. Gardening does not come naturally to every man: we should not expect it of him, any more than expecting all men to be great lovers and all women mothers of children and good cooks.

Some people make a garden because it is a fashionable thing to do. They have themselves photographed for society magazines and Sunday supplements, in their gardens (made by their hosts of gardeners), wearing smart clothes and all the jeweled panoply of Dives. I have a notion that when such pictures are taken the little birds in the tree-tops have a difficult time to prevent themselves from bursting with laughter. And yet I know that the interest of society women in gardening has a salutary effect. They are the bellwether sheep of a flock of suburban wives who, until they heard that Mrs. Chomley-Chomley works in her garden, had a vague notion that getting one's hands dirty with soil was among the things that weren't done.

Other people take gardening the way they would take a nar- cotic (the way some men take work)—to make themselves forget the bitter realities of life. This is futile because, to maintain the stimulus for oblivion they must increase the dose, and they eventually reach the point where they are not capable of increasing it.

Still others make gardens because it is part of a full life. To live happily they must invest their hours and aspirations in the activities of another world. And they draw the interest of delight and refreshment according to the measure of their investment. These are usually quaint folk, other-worldly in their manner, but capable of comprehending the idiosyncrasies of Nature as she displays them in tree and bush and passing season, across the skyline and in the infinite zenith. These, moreover, are the successful gardeners.

RICHARDSON WRIGHT
[*Truly Rural* (1922)]

Making the Earth Say Beans

[There was never a more philosophical gardener than Henry David Thoreau and there is nothing that reveals more of his philosophy than the fact that he planted his "pleasure garden" with beans.]

MEANWHILE my beans, the length of whose rows, added together, was seven miles already planted, were impatient to be hoed, for the earliest had grown considerably before the latest were in the ground; indeed they were not easily to be put off. What was the meaning of this so steady and self-respecting, this small Herculean labor, I knew not. I came to love my rows, my beans, though so many more than I wanted. They attached me to the earth, and so I got strength like Antæus. But why should I raise them? Only Heaven knows. This was my curious labor all summer—to make this portion of the earth's surface, which had yielded only cinquefoil, blackberries, johnswort, and the like, before, sweet wild fruits and pleasant flowers, produce instead this pulse. What shall I learn of beans or beans of me? I cherish them, I hoe them, early and late I have an eye to them; and this is my day's work. It is a fine broad leaf to look on. My auxiliaries are the dews and rains which water this dry soil, and what fertility is in the soil itself, which for the most part is lean and effete. My enemies are worms, cool days, and most of all woodchucks. The last have nibbled for me a quarter of an acre clean. But what right had I to oust johnswort and the rest, and break up their ancient herb garden? Soon, however, the remaining beans will be too tough for them, and go forward to meet new foes.

When I was four years old, as I well remember, I was brought from Boston to this my native town, through these very woods and this field, to the pond. It is one of the oldest scenes stamped on my memory. And now tonight my flute has waked the echoes over that very water. The pines still stand here older than I; or, if some have fallen, I have cooked my supper with their stumps, and a new growth is rising all around, preparing another aspect for new infant eyes. Almost the same johnswort springs from the same perennial root in this pasture, and even I have at length helped to clothe that fabulous landscape of my infant dreams, and one of the results of my presence and influence is seen in these bean leaves, corn blades, and potato vines. . . .

Before yet any woodchuck or squirrel had run across the road, or the sun had got above the shrub oaks, while all the dew was on, though the farmers warned me against it—I would advise you to do all your work if possible while the dew is on—I began to level the ranks of haughty weeds in my bean-field and throw dust upon their heads. Early in the morning I worked barefooted, dabbling like a plastic artist in the dewy and crumbling sand, but later in the day the sun blistered my feet. There the sun lighted me to hoe beans, pacing slowly backward and forward over that yellow gravelly upland, between the long green rows, fifteen rods, the one end terminating in a shrub oak copse where I could rest in the shade, the other in a blackberry field where the green berries deepened their tints by the time I had made another bout. Removing the weeds, putting fresh soil about the bean stems, and encouraging this weed which I had sown, making the yellow soil express its summer thought in bean leaves and blossoms rather than in wormwood and piper and millet grass, making the earth say beans instead of grass—this was my daily work. As I had little aid from horses or cattle, or hired men or boys, or improved implements of husbandry, I was much slower, and became much more intimate with my beans than usual. But labor of the hands, even when pursued to the verge of drudgery, is perhaps never the worst form of idleness. It has a constant and imperishable moral, and to the scholar it yields a classic result. A very *agricola laboriosus* was I to travellers bound westward through Lincoln and Wayland to nobody knows where; they sitting at their ease in gigs, with elbows on knees, and reins loosely hanging in festoons; I the home-staying, laborious native of the soil. But soon my homestead was out of their sight and thought. . . .

Near at hand, upon the topmost spray of a birch, sings the brown thrasher—or red mavis, as some love to call him—all the morning, glad of your society, that would find out another farmer's field if yours were not here. While you are planting the seed, he cries—"Drop it, drop it—cover it up, cover it up—pull it up, pull it up, pull it up." But this was not corn, and so it was safe from such enemies as he. You may wonder what his rigmarole, his amateur Paganini performances on one string or on twenty, have to do with your planting, and yet prefer it to leached ashes or plaster. It was a cheap sort of top dressing in which I had entire faith.

As I drew a still fresher soil about the rows with my hoe, I disturbed the ashes of unchronicled nations who in primeval years lived under these heavens, and their small implements of war and hunting were brought to the light of this modern day. They lay mingled with other natural stones, some of which bore the marks of having been burned by Indian fires, and some by the sun, and also bits of pottery and glass brought hither by the recent cultivators of the soil. When my hoe tinkled against the stones, that music echoed to the woods and the sky, and was an accompaniment to my labor which yielded an instant and immeasurable crop. It was no longer beans that I hoed, nor I that hoed beans; and I remembered with as much pity as pride, if I remembered at all, my acquaintances who had gone to the city to attend the oratorios. The nighthawk circled overhead in the sunny afternoons—for I sometimes made a day of it—like a mote in the eye, or in heaven's eye, falling from time to time with a swoop and a sound as if the heavens were rent, torn at last to very rags and tatters, and yet a seamless cope remained; small imps that fill the air and lay their eggs on the ground on bare sand or rocks on the tops of hills, where few have found them; graceful and slender like ripples caught up from the pond, as leaves are raised by the wind to float in the heavens; such kindredship is in nature. The hawk is aerial brother of the wave which he sails over and surveys, those his perfect air-inflated wings answering to the elemental unfledged pinions of the sea. Or sometimes I watched a pair of hen-hawks circling high in the sky, alternately soaring and descending, approaching and leaving one another, as if they were the embodiment of my own thoughts. Or I was attracted by the passage of wild pigeons from this wood to that, with a slight quivering winnowing sound and carrier haste; or from under a rotten stump my hoe turned up a sluggish portentous and outlandish spotted salamander, a trace of Egypt and the Nile, yet our contemporary. When I paused to lean on my hoe, these sounds and sights I heard and saw anywhere in the row, a part of the inexhaustible entertainment which the country offers.

On gala days the town fires its great guns, which echo like popguns to these woods, and some waifs of martial music occasionally penetrate thus far. To me, away there in my bean-field at the other end of the town, the big guns sounded as if a puffball had burst; and when there was a military turnout of which I was ignorant, I have sometimes had a vague sense all the day of some sort of itching and disease in the horizon, as if some eruption would break out there soon, either scarlatina or canker-rash, until at length some more favorable puff of wind, making haste over the fields and up the Wayland road, brought me information

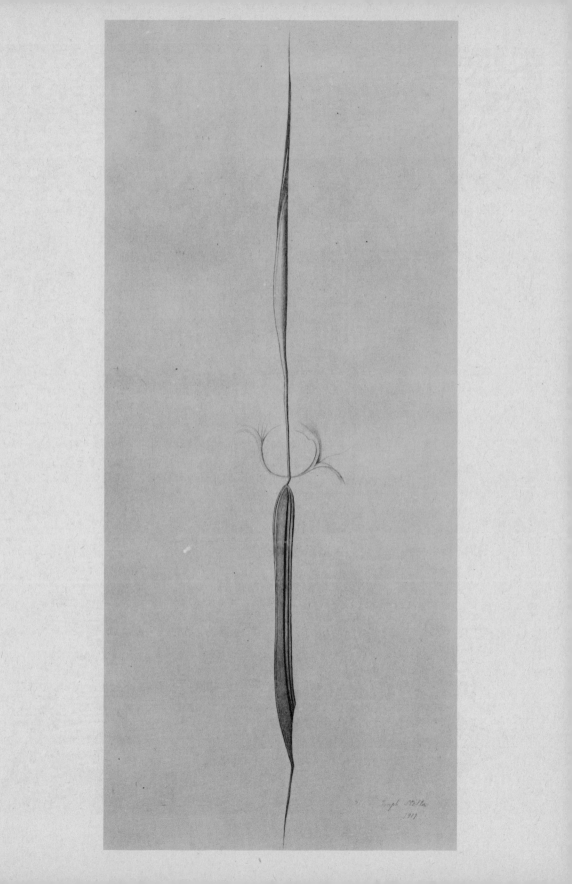

of the "trainers." It seemed by the distant hum as if somebody's bees had swarmed, and that the neighbors, according to Virgil's advice, by a faint *tintinnabulum* upon the most sonorous of their domestic utensils, were endeavoring to call them down into the hive again. And when the sound died quite away, and the hum had ceased, and the most favorable breezes told no tale, I knew that they had got the last drone of them all safely into the Middlesex hive, and that now their minds were bent on the honey with which it was smeared.

I felt proud to know that the liberties of Massachusetts and of our fatherland were in such safe keeping; and as I turned to my hoeing again I was filled with an inexpressible confidence, and pursued my labor cheerfully with a calm trust in the future. . . .

It was a singular experience that long acquaintance which I cultivated with beans, what with planting, and hoeing, and harvesting, and threshing, and picking over and selling them—the last was the hardest of all—I might add eating, for I did taste. I was determined to know beans. When they were growing, I used to hoe from five o'clock in the morning till noon, and commonly spent the rest of the day about other affairs. Consider the intimate and curious acquaintance one makes with various kinds of weeds—it will bear some iteration in the account, for there was no little iteration in the labor—disturbing their delicate organizations so ruthlessly, and making such invidious distinctions with his hoe, levelling whole ranks of one species, and sedulously cultivating another. That's Roman wormwood—that's pigweed—that's sorrel—that's piper-grass—have at him, chop him up, turn his roots upward to the sun, don't let him have a fibre in the shade, if you do he'll turn himself t'other side up and be as green as a leek in two days. A long war, not with cranes, but with weeds, those Trojans who had sun and rain and dews on their side. Daily the beans saw me come to their rescue armed with a hoe, and thin the ranks of their enemies, filling up the trenches with weedy dead. Many a lusty crest-waving Hector, that towered a whole foot above his crowding comrades, fell before my weapon and rolled in the dust.

Those summer days which some of my contemporaries devoted to the fine arts in Boston or Rome, and others to contemplation in India, and others to trade in London or New York, I thus, with the other farmers of New England, devoted to husbandry. Not that I wanted beans to eat, for I am by nature a Pythagorean, so far as beans are concerned, whether they mean porridge or voting, and exchanged them for rice; but, perchance, as some must work in fields if only for the sake of tropes and expression, to serve a parable-maker one day. It was on the whole a rare amusement, which, continued too long, might have become a dissipation. Though I gave them no manure, and did not hoe them all once, I hoed them unusually well as far as I went, and was paid for it in the end, "there being in truth," as Evelyn says, "no compost or laetation whatsoever comparable to this continual motion, repastination, and turning of the mould with the spade." "The earth," he adds elsewhere, "especially if fresh, has a certain magnetism in it, by which it attracts the salt, power, or virtue (call it either) which gives it life, and is the logic of all the labor and stir we keep about it, to sustain us; all dungings and other sordid temperings being but the vicars succedaneous to this improvement." Moreover, this being one of those "worn-out and exhausted lay fields which enjoy their sabbath," had perchance, as Sir Kenelm Digby thinks likely, attracted "vital spirits" from the air. I harvested twelve bushels of beans.

But to be more particular, for it is complained that Mr. Coleman has reported chiefly the expensive experiments of gentlemen farmers, my outgoes were—

For a hoe	$0 54	
Plowing, harrowing, and furrowing	7 50	Too much.
Beans for seed	3 12½	
Potatoes "	1 33	
Peas "	0 40	
Turnip seed	0 06	
White line for crow fence	0 02	
Horse cultivator and boy three hours	1 00	
Horse and cart to get crop	0 75	
In all	$14 72½	

My income was (*patrem familias vendacem, non emacem esse oportet*), from

Nine bushels and twelve quarts of beans sold	$16 94
Five " large potatoes	2 50
Nine " small	2 25
Grass	1 00
Stalks	0 75
In all	$23 44
Leaving a pecuniary profit, as I have elsewhere said, of	$ 8 71½

. . . Ancient poetry and mythology suggest, at least, that husbandry was once a sacred art; but it is pursued with irreverent haste and heedlessness by us, our object being to have large farms and large crops merely. We have no festival, nor procession, nor ceremony, not excepting our cattle-shows and so-called Thanksgivings, by which the farmer expresses a sense of the sacredness of his calling, or is reminded of its sacred origin. It is the premium and the feast which tempt him. He sacrifices not to Ceres and the Terrestrial Jove, but to the infernal Plutus rather. By avarice and selfishness, and a grovelling habit, from which none of us is free, of regarding the soil as property, or the means of acquiring property chiefly, the landscape is deformed, husbandry is degraded with us, and the farmer leads the meanest of lives. He knows Nature but as a robber. Cato says that the profits of agriculture are particularly pious or just (*maximeque pius quaestus*), and according to Varro the old Romans "called the same earth Mother and Ceres, and thought that they who cultivated it led a pious and useful life, and they alone were left of the race of King Saturn."

We are wont to forget that the sun looks on our cultivated fields and on the prairies and forests without distinction. They all reflect and absorb his rays alike, and the former make but a small part of the glorious picture which he beholds in his daily course. In his view the earth is all equally cultivated like a garden. Therefore we should receive the benefit of his light and heat with a corresponding trust and magnanimity. What though I value the seeds of these beans, and harvest that in the fall of the year? This broad field which I have looked at so long looks not to me as the principal cultivator, but away from me to influences more genial to it, which water and make it green. These beans have results which are not harvested by me. Do they not grow for woodchucks partly? The ear of wheat (in Latin *spica*, obsoletely *spece*, from *spe*, hope) should not be the only hope of the husbandman; its kernel or grain (*granum*, from *gerendo*, bearing) is not all that it bears. How, then, can our harvest fail? Shall I not rejoice also at the abundance of the weeds whose seeds are the granary of the birds? It matters little comparatively whether the fields fill the farmer's barns. The true husbandman will cease from anxiety, as the squirrels manifest no concern whether the woods will bear chestnuts this year or not, and finish his labor with every day, relinquishing all claim to the produce of his fields, and sacrificing in his mind not only his first but his last fruits also.

HENRY DAVID THOREAU
[*Walden* (1854)]

Wild Garden on Cream Hill

[*Most wild flowers are harder to grow than those adapted by long culti-vation to the artificial conditions of a garden. Many of even the "weeds" will flourish only where they, not where we, choose. Still, wild gardens are possible to those who will take trouble enough with them, as Lewis Gannett has proved at his Connecticut home.*]

O U R first summer on Cream Hill we thought we'd be too busy to have a flower garden. But we couldn't help ourselves. Friends with overflowing gardens of their own proudly showered us with their sur-plus iris, hollyhocks, and chrysanthemums. Whenever we admired a plant in a neighbor's beds, the instant response was a hunt for a trowel, and we would find our car loaded, whether we wanted it or not. So our flower gardens began, and they have been growing ever since.

That first year we had a superhumanly sensible dream. We wouldn't have any formal beds; we would merely naturalize a few native flowers and ferns. We wouldn't have much lawn to cut; we wouldn't have large beds to weed.

It was a good idea. I have known other people who have had it, and among them some who have clung to it for as long as two years after they bought a country place. But each spring (and sometimes in Indian summer too) a gardening instinct, sure as the sap rising in the trees, stirs within us. We look about and decide to tame another little bit of ground. After twenty-odd years of such spring-surging instincts, we have tamed far too much ground. By the end of August, discouraged by the in-pressing jungle, we resolve to restrict our tended acreage. And again in spring, and sometimes in autumn, after the first frost, when the jungle begins to wither, we violate our good resolutions.

Yet the wild-garden idea persisted. The first wild-flower bed we nursed was an extension of a somewhat fern-grown waste area on the north side of the big barn. We began moving hepatica and bloodroot and columbine into it that first spring. They made themselves at home and multiplied, and we have been moving them elsewhere ever since.

The ferns took over. There were lady ferns and hay-scented ferns in the patch before we began calling it a garden. Both are beautiful and fresh in spring, and blowsy and pestiferous weeds by midsummer. I added some handsomer wood ferns. I had spent a teen-age summer in a White Mountain boardinghouse long before, and had learned from a visiting fern specialist the names of many of the commoner ferns, and soon I had something like a "collection."

Ferns are a comfortable garden specialty. They seem a bit difficult to the tyro. They have the great and solacing advantage that there are few of them. Possibly forty species may lurk somewhere within a ten-mile radius of Cream Hill—but I doubt it. I have found fewer than thirty-five, and we usually have thirty growing in our garden. To keep limestone ferns we have to do a little work, but most of the thirty thrive all but untended, and a few actually have to be weeded out.

Most people know more ferns than they know they know. Everyone knows bracken, the coarse three-parted fern of dry pasture lands. Everyone also knows the delicate maidenhair. Everyone knows the evergreen Christmas fern, even if they miscall it Boston fern. Once you have identified the interrupted fern, its green fronds interrupted for a few pairs of brown fruiting "pinnae," you cannot fail to recognize it again. Nor can you mistake the tall handsome ostrich fern, which looks more like ostrich plumes than any fern has a right to do. (But beware of it in your garden; it will put out runners and invade everything within range, crowding out and eventually shading to death any little wild flowers you may have planted near by.) You probably also recognize at sight the boulder or hay-scented fern that is so abundant about the rocks in cow pastures, the coarse pale green fern, misnamed sensitive, which springs up in the meadows after midsummer mowings, and the spinulose wood fern, which you very likely call the florist's fern. That's eight species of fern, a good beginning.

It is easy also to identify the tall cinnamon fern, which looks like the interrupted but bears its cinnamon spores on separate stalks; the flowering fern of the swamps, which flaunts its spores at the tip, as if it were trying to be a flower; and the common evergreen wood or leather fern, whose spores crowd the margins of every subdivision of the fronds. And there is the stubby polypody, which some people call thumb fern, growing in the crevices of boulders, sometimes in great mats. If, peering under some moss-grown limestone cliff, you have ever seen the exquisite rosettes of the tiny maidenhair spleenwort, you have not forgotten its beauty, though you may not have known its name. Its cousin, the ebony spleenwort, aptly called ladder fern, which also has mahogany maidenhairlike stalks, is as easily recognizable. And once you have recognized it as a fern, you can never mistake the walking fern, another limestone addict, which bends the tips of its fronds to the mossy ground and takes root, "walking." That's seven more, and you are already halfway through our fern garden. You can take your time hunting out and identifying the rest.

We planted most of them by the barn, more than twenty years ago, and they are still there. In the spring, bloodroot and toothwort, columbine, Dutchman's breeches, and squirrel corn come up ahead of the ferns; the hepaticas which we planted there long ago succumbed to competition or were moved. The limestone ferns died out, as I should have known they would unless I remembered to give them fresh lime each year, which, of course, I didn't. The big ferns do their own weeding; they just crowd out the weeds. Once or twice a year, sometimes not even that, I pull out a few wild aster and sarsaparilla plants and some of the young maples which hopefully take root. That is all the care the fern bed requires. Of course, we do not rake the autumn leaves off it. The ferns take care of the leaves and relish the leaf mold, as their woodland neighbors do.

Eventually we built our own limestone ledges. I brought home as big weathered limestone boulders as I could carry and cleared a shaded spot for them. The boulders looked woefully small when we had them planted. I went back and got more, but they still looked small. I spaded the ground, added some mulch and a lot of powdered lime. Then we tucked maidenhair spleenwort, purple cliff brake, walking fern, and even a bit of the rare wall rue from the limestone hills north of us, into the crannies of our boulders. We watered them for a month. They liked it. Now we merely keep the goldenrod and wood asters, the sorrel and clover, from invading, and add more lime every year. And, I should confess, every few years we add new limestone ferns, for a limestone bed in a sub-acid patch of woodland is never quite the same thing as a piece of limestone cliff.

We have read of bog gardens and dreamed of a bog garden of our own. But weekend gardeners who do their own work are likely to continue merely dreaming of bog gardens. Besides, the brook that should feed our dream bog garden is usually an arroyo seco before July is out. And anyway the marsh fern, which we dubiously set in the moistest corner of the fern bed by the barn, at once made itself at home, belying its name, and soon became a spreading weed which, like the so-called sensitive fern, the bracken, the hay-scented, the lady, and the ostrich ferns, has to be yanked out to give other ferns a chance. The royal or flowering fern, another native of the swamps, seems equally at home by the barn; and we found our crested fern, another reputed swamp-lover, when scything about boulders in the dry old orchard below the house. The books sometimes make things unnecessarily hard for the amateur gardener.

There are those who conscientiously test their soil for acidity and eruditely compound their compost piles with chemicals. We have always intended to do so, but have not yet found the time for it. We lime our vegetable garden when it looks sour, lime the limestone-fern bed each spring and fall if we remember it, and annually feed a few bushels of rooted pine needles to our laurel—which never does very well, probably because we don't give it enough acid—and also feed pine needles to our pink lady's slippers, arbutus, and painted trilliums. That is about as far as we ever get, and yet we have a pretty good garden.

The art of gardening is various. Some like to twist Nature to their wills. Our theory is to adapt ourselves to Nature. We must have experimented with hundreds of plants; we continue to cultivate those which amiably demonstrate that they like our neighborhood.

"Cultivate" is perhaps hardly the word for our kind of gardening. Some twenty years ago I brought in a couple of wild red columbine plants. They multiplied and in time spread all over the place. In May they are a glorious sight. In July they are a scraggly mess, but enough have reseeded themselves so that we can afford to weed out the scraggliest. "How do you grow such beautiful columbine?" people ask us. The answer is that the columbine grows itself; it likes Cream Hill almost as well as we do ourselves.

When the CCC was excavating a parking place by the Dean's Ravine park some years ago, we noticed that the bulldozer had ripped up a whole plantation of mandrakes or May apples. We planted a few under the plum three. Within a few years we had a whole forest of mandrake umbrellas; each, in May, with a waxy blossom safe from the rain, and in June full of May apples, which small boys—no gourmets—consider good eating. But soon the mandrakes were crowding out the hepaticas, which had been one of our first transplantations, and invading the asparagus bed. We moved the hepatica; we still dig mandrake out of the asparagus bed off and on all summer.

Wild ginger is another savage invader. Why the hills about us are not all carpeted with wild ginger is as deep a mystery as that of the poison tomato. Three small plants which we set out fifteen years ago have each spread over square yards; one of them reached down through a stone wall and reappeared rods away from its base of operations. We like wild ginger. Its rusty hidden flower makes a lovely design, though you have to stoop to see it, even lower than to see the mandrake's hidden blossom; and it blooms, in its modest way, almost as early as bloodroot and arbutus. But enough is enough. For years now we have been weeding wild ginger and trying to give it away to friends who complain that nothing will grow in their dry soil.

We don't yet claim as complete success with arbutus. The wild-flower preservation societies strenuously object to digging up arbutus. But what should a conservationist do when he finds a CCC tractor in the state forest smashing down patches of this best-loved of spring flowers? We regarded it as our duty to save the arbutus. We dug up a few mats of it, carefully keeping the gritty soil in which it had been born, and set it in our wild garden. Knowing that it preferred a more acid soil than ours, we diligently bedded it in pine needles and oak leaves for a year or two. Then we forgot it. And we cut some of the trees that shaded it, to give more light to Ruth's barn studio.

The arbutus resented the neglect. It died. But we had kept it for five or six years; and it is a pleasant thing to have a patch of arbutus in your yard to remind you when to go off to the woods to smell its perfume where it grows in mass. . . . It may even be that we shall have masses of it in our own yard. For one year we found a mountain road in a neighboring town where the grader had undercut a whole bank of arbutus, so that it was falling into the ditch. With an eager sense of duty, we rescued it—quite a lot of it. We planted it with care. We acidified the soil with ammonium sulphate, with pine needles, and with oak leaves. I hope it lives. It may—if we continue to remember to do our duty by it.[1]

Bloodroot stands any kind of abuse and seems to thrive in any soil—in full sun or in shade, beneath the ferns, and even on an open ledge—and bloodroot in sunlight is one of the loveliest of spring sights. Hepatica is choosier; it does not seem to reseed itself with us, though many of our clumps have spread and are a shy joy in May. We performed another task of liberation some years ago with Dutchman's breeches. We rescued it from beside a roadside—and rescue was a truer word than we knew. When we went back for more a year later, the whole patch where it had grown in masses had been plowed. There

---

[1] It lived, though not much more than that. But in the summer of 1948 it vigorously expanded, what with God's water in June and July, irrigation in dry August and September, a little acid fertilizer, and dozens of bushels of pine needles.

wasn't a sign of Dutchman's breeches anywhere, except in our wild garden at home. There, after twenty years, it still thrives untended and multiplies.

About lady's slippers, members of the orchid tribe, I speak with diffidence. The stemless pink lady's slipper is said to be common in our woods. In my first years on Cream Hill I found plenty of it. When I wanted it for my wild garden, it seemed to have disappeared. I hunted hillside after hillside, year after year, in lady's-slipper time, which is about Memorial Day. I found the yellow lady's slipper, both the large and the small varieties, which are supposed to be rare in our town, and for years they flourished in our garden. The three plants I brought home multiplied in ten years to eighteen; then the colony began to decline. It had seven flowers in the spring of 1947, and that autumn I dug it up and separated the individual root stocks. Whether it will accept such treatment, which is certainly not that followed by Nature in the woods, I am not yet sure. In 1948 it seemed to be working.

Eventually I found a rich colony of the "common" pink lady's slipper; for some odd reason it prefers the remote south end of town to our northern hillsides. We gave it a fine rich bed of pine needles. It stood the winter well and flowered again, but in its second spring only the leaves came up, and then it disappeared. Ruth noticed that in the woods the pink lady's slipper often had its root stocks snuggled against bare rock, and accordingly she made a pine-needle bed for it on a rock ledge. I said it wouldn't work, the rock would be too hot and dry. So far—and five years have passed—it has worked. Away from the rock ledge, other pink lady's slippers which I have transplanted have also survived, though they have an odd habit of emigrating a yard or two each year. (You can trace the route of migration in long, pale, under-ground roots.) But the pink lady's slippers do not yet multiply for us; they just hold their own. I have not tried to transplant the tall Regina lady's slippers, and I won't until I get a reliable bog.

Nor can I report the faintest success at seeding fringed gentian. That late autumn beauty is notorious for its willful ways. When we first came to Cream Hill it grew in abundance by our meadow spring, the kind of wet spot a fringed gentian should prefer. Then it disappeared from the neighborhood of the meadow spring. For a few years we found it in a dry clearing that was growing up to young pine, a spot no self-respecting fringed gentian should endure. It was so abundant there that we actually committed the criminal act of picking it; it closes when picked, but will come out again in full sun. And then it began to thin out and disappear.

We next found our gentians growing on a still drier and sunnier hillside, an even more unlikely spot, and there they still flourish. I have tried to restore them by the meadow spring, but in vain. Pitcher plants, brought from Chocorua a dozen years ago, still grow there, though the meadow spring dries up in a year of bad drought, and dryness is accounted even worse for pitcher plant than for gentian. Grass of Parnassus flourishes there, and grass of Parnassus is normally the fringed gentian's closest friend. I have tried scattering ripe seed from the hillside plants. I have tried planting the seed in a sandy patch. When a farmer neighbor told me that he was going to mow a marshy field that was blue with gentian, I went, with his permission, and dug up two bushel basket-loads of gentians from his field and set them by my spring. The plant is a biennial, which accounts for part of its mystery, but I thought that if the plants went to seed normally in a spot which others of their tribe had once accepted as a happy homeland, a new colony might become established. I had no luck at all. Wild gardening, and above all gentian gardening, is a gamble.

On the other hand the tall nodding Canada or meadow lilies have responded warmly to the mildest gesture of friendship. I try to scythe an acre or two of open grassland to keep us from utter claustrophobia as the woods close in on us, and in our early years we always had one or two Canada lily plants in this patch. I scythed around them and let them scatter their own seeds. I have continued to scythe around them. Now we have scores of lilies, and we love them.

We do not have to do anything about Jack-in-the-pulpit, one of the oddest and most endearing of spring flowers, for it seeds itself and comes up throughout the fern beds and in all our wild gardens according to its own strong will. So do the dainty Solomon's seal, the foamy-flowered false Solomon's seal, the graceful miterwort, and the baneberries, which our children, for obvious reasons, used to call "doll's eyes." Both red and white baneberries flourish of themselves in our wild garden, though the books say that the one prefers acid soil and the other alkaline. With us they are at home regardless of soil, and we have a special affection for flowers which make themselves at home without demanding attention.

It doesn't pay to give too much attention to a wild flower. "More California flowers have been killed by coddling than by neglect," a California gardener once informed me. Such Western wild flowers as still grow in our garden arrived belatedly one cold December, when our Cream Hill soil was frozen. I shoveled a patch of earth clear, built a bonfire to thaw the surface, planted my "Westerns," watered them, and re-covered them with snow. Back in New York, my expert friends assured me that I had sadly misbehaved. The rootlets would absorb the water, freeze, and die. . . . They didn't. They all came up next spring, and some still thrive, reminding us each year of "Ma" Arens, who sent them to us just before she passed away in Oregon.

We used to admire the tall wild thistles—not the stingy-flowered little Canada thistle but the proud plant for which the botanical flower-christeners could think up no better name than "common thistle." We decided that actually this thistle was handsomer than most cultivated flowers, and we would accordingly give it a place of honor in our garden. We did. We mulched it and fertilized it, and our thistle plant became a magnificent giant indeed, a glorious mass of purple bloom. And the purple flowers turned to thistledown and scattered thistle seeds all over our tended areas, and ever since that summer we have been digging thistles out of the grass and painfully weeding them out of the asparagus bed, the vegetable garden, the wild gardens, the rock garden, and every other one of our most cherished plant homes.

We concluded that it was wiser to adopt a modified version of Emerson's counsel. "Hast thou . . . loved the wood-rose and left it on its stalk?" he asked sternly. We have learned to love the thistle and leave it in its faraway roadside or pasture.

LEWIS GANNETT
[*Cream Hill* (1949)]

Section Two

HERBALISTS AND EARLY GARDEN BOOKS

Anything Green that grew out of the mould
Was an excellent herb to our fathers old.

KIPLING

In such a night
Medea gather'd the enchanted herbs
That did renew old Aeson.

SHAKESPEARE
The Merchant of Venice

The First Great Herbalist

[*English garden books of the how-to-do-it sort first appeared in the six-teenth century. Their ancestors were the many medieval herbals and the two tend to merge. But they are not the same thing. In the first place, the herbals are primarily utilitarian and are concerned above all with plants supposed to have a medicinal or magic use—how to recognize them and what they were good for. In the second place, they usually embody comparatively little that is based upon actual observation, each herbalist copying his predecessors—even to the illustrations which long tended to become more and more crude. Beginning about the fifteenth century the herbals tend to improve, and finally they merge with true "garden books" which shift the interest from medicinal herb to ornamental plant and turn away from magic and tradition toward garden design and the art of horticulture.*

The most important original source of most of the herbals was that compiled (probably during the first century A.D.*) by the Greek physician Dioscorides, of whom little except his long authoritative work is known. The following selections will illustrate both a certain lack of modesty which was an enduring characteristic of the herbalists and the kind of information they dealt in.*]

W E , as I may say from our first growth, having an unceasing desire to acquire knowledge of this matter, and having travelled much (for you know that I led a soldier's life), have by your advice gathered together all that I have commented hereupon, and have committed it into five books. This compilation I dedicate to you, thus fulfilling my grateful affection for the goodwill you have towards us. It is your nature to show yourself a familiar friend to all who are led by learning, but especially to those who follow the same profession, and yet more particularly to myself. But the great affection that that most excellent man, Licinius Bassus doth bear unto thee, is no small token of the lovable goodness that is in thee, which I know, beholding when I lived with you, the goodwill worthy of emulation, that passed between you both.

But I beg that you, and all who may peruse these Commentaries, will not pay attention so much to the force of our words, as to the industry and experience that I have brought to bear in the matter. For with very accurate diligence, knowing most herbs with mine own eyes, others by Historical relation agreeable to all, and by questioning, diligently enquiring of the Inhabitants of each sort, we will endeavour both to make use of another arrangement, and also to describe the kinds and forces of every one of them. . . .

THE IRIS

Iris (Somme call it Iris Illyrica, somme Thelpida, somme Urania, somme Catharon, somme Thaumastos, the Romanes call it Radix Marica, somme Gladiolus, somme Opertritis, somme Consecratrix, the Egyptians call it Nar) is soe named from the resemblance of the rainbow in heaven, but it beares leaves like unto a little sword but greater & broader & fatter (or thicker): the flowers on the stalke, are bended in, on ouer against another, & diuers, for they are either soon white or pale or black or purple or azure. Whence for the varietie of colours it is likened to the heauenly rainebow. The rootes under are knotty, strong (or sound), of a sweet savour, which after the cutting ought to be dryed in the shade, & soe (with a linnen thread put through them) to be layd vp. But ye best is that of Illyria & Macedonia, & of these the best is that which hath a thick roote, stumped, & hard to breake, & in color of a faint-yellow, & exceeding well-scenting, & very bitter to the tast, of a sound smell, & not enclining to nastiness, & moving to sneesing in ye beating. The second is that of Lybia (or Africa) white according to the colour, bitter according to the tast, next in strength (to the former), but when they grow old they will be worm-eaten, yet then they smell the sweeter. But all of them haue a warming, extenuating facultie, fitting against coughs, & extenuating grosse humors hard to get up. They purge thick humors

& choler, being dranck in Hydromel to the quantity of seven dragms they are also causers of sleep & prouokers of tears & heale the torments of ye belly. But dranck with venegar they help such as are bitten by venomous beasts, and the splenitick and such as are troubled with convulsion fitts, & such as are chilled, & stiff with cold, & such as let fall their food. But dranck with wine, they bring out the menses, yea, & the decoction of them is fitting for women's fomentations which doe mollify & open the places, & for the Sciatica being taken by way of infusion, & for Fistulas, & all hollow sores, which it fills up with flesh. But being applyed as a Collyrium with hony, they draw out the Embryons. Being fed, & layd on by way of Cataplasme, they doe mollify the struma & the old Scirrhus, but being dryed they fill up vlcers, & cleanse them, & with hony they fill vp with flesh the bare of the bones. They are good also for the headache being layd on by way of cataplasme with acetum & Rosaceum: being dawbed on also with white Veratrum, & twice soe much hony, they cleanse off the Lentigo, & sun burning; they are mixt also with the Pessi, with ye Malagmata & with the Acopi, & in generall they are of very much use. . . .

LUPINE

Thermos that is set, (which the Latines call Lupinus, the Aegyptians Brechu) is commonly knowne. The meale, being taken as a Lohoc with hony (or dranck with vinegar) doth expell wormes, & ye Lupines themselves being macerated and eaten bitter doe performe the same, and the decoction of them doth doe the like being dranck with rue and Pepper, after which manner also it doth help the Spleneticall. It is a good fomentation of the Gangreane, & of wilde vlcers, of ye scab when it beginnes, of the Vitiligines, of spotts, & of Exanthemata, and of the running vlcers of the head. And ye same also being giuen in a Pessum with Myrrh & hony doth extract the menstrua & the Embrya. The meale doth cleanse the skinne, and ye blackness & bluenesse, and with Polenta & water it doth assuage inflammations. With Vinegar it doth assuage the paines of the Sciatica, and swellings. Being sod in vinegar, and applyed as a Cataplasme, it moues the strumae out of their place, and breakes Carbuncles round about. And Lupines, being sod with raine water till they creame, doe cleare the face, and being sod with the roote of black Chamaeleon, they cure the scabs of sheep washt with ye decoction of it luke warme; and the roote being sod with water, and so drancke, doth expell vrine. But the Lupines themselues beeing sweetened,

فاذا زاد العصير نصفه فهذا الشراب موافق لوجع الحلق والجنب والرئتين
والاسهال الرقيق والمزيه لمعدة غليظ في حلقه يصفي اللون وكثر النوم

وليسر له غائلة موافق للمثانة والكلا ع ع ع

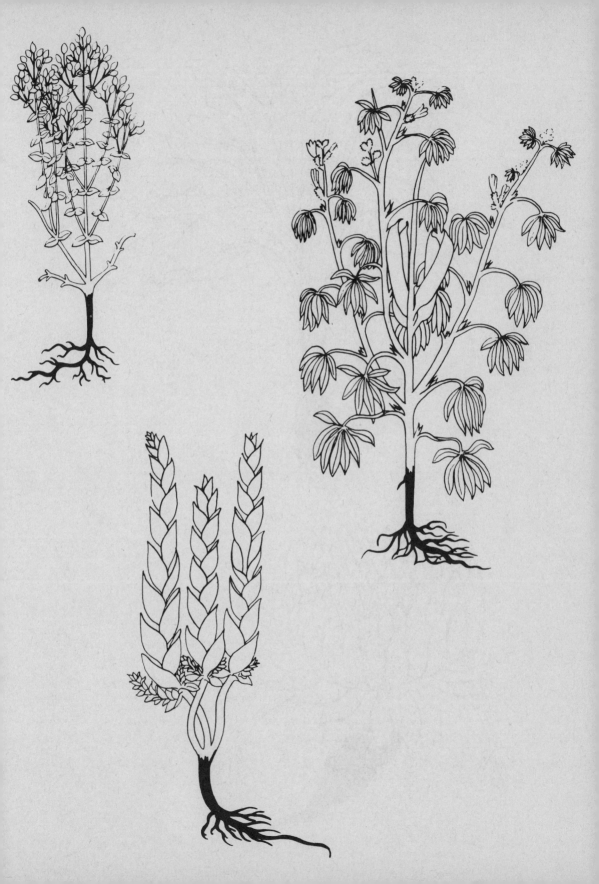

beaten small, and soe dranck with vinegar, doe assuage ye nauseousnesse of the stomach and cure the want of appetite. . . .

THE MANDRAKE

Mandagoras, which some call Antimelon, some call it Dircaea, some Circaea (some Circaeum, some Xeranthe, some Antimnion, some Bombochylon, some Minon, ye Egyptians Apemum, Pythagoras Anthropomorphon, some Aloitin, some Thridacian, some Cammaron, Zoroastres Diamonon, or Archinen, ye Magi Hermionous, some Gonogeonas, ye Romans Mala Canina, some Mala terrestria). Since that the root seems to be a maker of love medicines. There is of it one sort that is foemall, which is black, called Thridacias, having narrower & longer leaves than lettuce, of a poisonous & heavy scent to ye smell, scattered upon the ground, & amongst them ye apples like Service berries, pale, of a sweet scent, in which is ye seed as of a pear: ye roots two or three of a good bigness, wrapped within one another, black according to outward appearance, within white & of a thick bark, but it bears no stalk.

But of ye male, and white which some have called Norion, ye leaves are greater, white, broad, smooth as of the beet, but ye apples twice as big, drawing to saffron in ye colour, sweet smelling with a certain strongness which also ye shepherds eating are in a manner made asleep, but ye root is like to that before it, yet greater and whiter, & this also is without stalk. Ye bark of ye root is juiced being beaten when it is new, & set under a press. But it will behove ye beaters, after it is stirred about to lay it up in an earthen vessel, & ye apples also are juiced in like manner. But ye juice of them becomes remiss. And ye bark of the root being peeled off & done through with a thread is hanged up for store. And some do seeth the roots in wine to thirds, & straining it set it up. Using a Cyathus of it for such as cannot sleep, or are grievously pained, & upon whom being cut, or cauterized they wish to make a not-feeling pain. Ye juice being drank ye muchness of ye quantity of 2 Oboli with Melicrate, doth expel upward Phlem, and black choler, as Ellebore doth, but being too much drank it drives out ye life. And it is mixed with eye-medicines, & Anodynas, & mollifying Pessums, but being put to of itself, as much as half an Obolus, it expels ye menstrua, & ye Embryo, & being put up into ye seat for a suppository, it causeth sleep. But ye root is said also to soften Ivory when sodden together with it for six hours, & to make it ready to be formed into what fashion a man will. But ye new leaves are good both for ye inflammations of ye eyes, and those upon ulcers, being laid on with Polenta; & they dissolve also all hardness, & Apostumes, Strumas & tumors, & being rubbed on gently for 5 or 6 days, it doth deface scars without exulcerating. Ye leaves preserved in brine are laid up for ye same uses. The root being beaten small with acetum doth heal ye Erysipelata, but for ye strokes of serpents, with honey, or oil; & with water, it disperseth ye strumas, and Tumors, & assuageth ye pains of ye joints with Polenta. Ye wine of ye bark of ye root is prepared without seething but you must cast in 3 pounds into a Metreta of sweet wine, & that there be given of it 3 Cyathi to such as shall be cut, or cauterized, as is aforesaid. For they do not apprehend the pain, because they are overborn with dead sleep, but the apples being smelled to, or eaten, are soporiferous, & ye juice that is of them. But used too much they make men speechless. The seed of the apples being drank purgeth ye matrix, & given as a Pessum with brimstone that never felt ye fire it stays ye red flux. It is juiced, ye root being scarified about divers ways, & that which runs out being gathered into a concavity; but ye juice is more effectual than ye liquor. But ye roots do not bear liquor in every place: experience doth show as much. They give out also that there is another sort called Morion, growing in shady places, & about dens, having leaves like to ye white Mandrake, but less, as it were a span long, white, lying round about ye root, it being tender, & white, by a little longer than a span, ye thickness of ye great finger, which they say being drank as much as a dragm or eaten with Polenta, in Placetum, or Obsonium it doth infatuate. For a man sleeps in ye same fashion, as when he ate it, sensible of nothing for 3 or 4 hours, from ye time that it is brought him. And Physitians also, use this, when they are about to cut, or cauterize. And they say also that ye root being drank with Solanum that is called Manicum is an Antidot.

DIOSCORIDES
[*Herbal* (1st century A.D.)
TRANSLATED BY JOHN GOODYEAR]

The Herbalist Explains His Art

[*This preface to an English translation of a fifteenth-century German herbal will illustrate again that the herbalists were not modest men and that they were much given to stressing both the importance of their art and the fact that God had obligingly provided herbs to cure the diseases He permitted. The original author of this work, known as the* Herbarius zu Teutsch, *was probably a physician of Frankfort.*]

M A N Y a time and oft have I contemplated inwardly the wondrous works of the Creator of the universe: how in the beginning He formed the heavens and adorned them with goodly, shining stars, to which He gave power and might to influence everything under heaven. Also how He afterwards formed the four elements: fire, hot and dry—air, hot and moist—water, cold and moist—earth, dry and cold—and gave to each a nature of its own; and how after this the same Great Master of Nature made and formed herbs of many sorts and animals of all kinds, and last of all Man, the noblest of all created things. Thereupon I thought on the wondrous order which the Creator gave these same creatures of His, so that everything which has its being under heaven receives it from the stars, and keeps it by their help. I considered further how that in everything which arises, grows, lives or soars in the four elements named, be it metal, stone, herb or animal, the four natures of the elements, heat, cold, moistness and dryness are mingled. It is also to be noted that the four natures in question are also mixed and blended in the human body in a measure and temperament suitable to the life and nature of man. While man keeps within this measure, proportion or temperament, he is strong and healthy, but as soon as he steps or falls beyond the temperament or measure of the four natures, which happens when heat takes the upper hand and strives to stifle cold, or, on the contrary, when cold begins to suppress heat, or man becomes full of cold moisture, or

again is deprived of the due measure of moisture, he falls of necessity
into sickness, and draws nigh unto death. There are many causes of
disturbances, such as I have mentioned, in the measure of the four
elements which is essential to man's health and life. In some cases it is
the poisonous and hidden influence of the heavens acting against man's
nature, for from this arise impurity and poisoning of the air; in other
cases the food and drink are unsuitable, or suitable but not taken in the
right quantities, or at the right time. Of a truth I would as soon count
thee the leaves on the trees, or the grains of sand in the sea, as the things
which are the causes of a relapse from the temperament of the four
natures, and a beginning of man's sickness. It is for this reason that so
many thousands and thousands of perils and dangers beset man. He is
not fully sure of his health or his life for one moment. While considering
these matters, I also remembered how the Creator of Nature, Who has
placed us amid such dangers, has mercifully provided us with a remedy,
that is with all kinds of herbs, animals and other created things to which
He has given power and might to restore, produce, give and temper the
four natures mentioned above. One herb is heating, another is cooling,
each after the degree of its nature and complexion. In the same manner
many other created things on the earth and in the water preserve man's
life, through the Creator of Nature. By virtue of these herbs and created
things the sick man may recover the temperament of the four elements
and the health of his body. Since, then, man can have no greater nor
nobler treasure on earth than bodily health, I came to the conclusion
that I could not perform any more honourable, useful or holy work or
labour than to compile a book in which should be contained the virtue
and nature of many herbs and other created things, together with their
true colours and form, for the help of all the world and the common
good. Thereupon I caused this praiseworthy work to be begun by a
Master learned in physic, who, at my request, gathered into a book the
virtue and nature of many herbs out of the acknowledged masters of
physic, Galen, Avicenna, Serapio, Dioscorides, Pandectarius, Platearius
and others. But when, in the process of the work, I turned to the drawing
and depicting of the herbs, I marked that there are many precious herbs
which do not grow here in these German lands, so that I could not draw
them with their true colours and form, except from hearsay. Therefore
I left unfinished the work which I had begun, and laid aside my pen,
until such time as I had received grace and dispensation to visit the Holy
Sepulchre, and also Mount Sinai, where the body of the Blessed Virgin,
Saint Catherine, rests in peace. Then, in order that the noble work I had
begun and left incomplete should not come to nought, and also that my

journey should benefit not my soul alone, but the whole world, I took with me a painter ready of wit, and cunning and subtle of hand. And so we journeyed from Germany through Italy, Istria, and then by way of Slavonia or the Windisch land, Croatia, Albania, Dalmatia, Greece, Corfu, Morea, Candia, Rhodes and Cyprus to the Promised Land and the Holy City, Jerusalem, and thence through Arabia Minor to Mount Sinai, from Mount Sinai towards the Red Sea in the direction of Cairo, Babylonia, and also Alexandria in Egypt, whence I returned to Candia. In wandering through these kingdoms and lands, I diligently sought after the herbs there, and had them depicted and drawn, with their true colour and form. And after I had, by God's grace, returned to Germany and home, the great love which I bore this work impelled me to finish it, and now, with the help of God, it is accomplished.

[*Herbarius zu Teutsch*
(Translated 1485)]

The Doctrine of Signatures

[*One of the favorite (and most stupefying) general principles followed by the herbalists was the Doctrine of Signatures. This meant that God had indicated the use of an herb by something in its appearance—for instance that the liver-shaped leaf of the Hepatica indicated that it was a remedy for liver troubles and the tongue-shaped leaf of another herb that it was good for disorders of the mouth. Here are two pleasant statements of the doctrine.*]

BY Herbalists we mean those medicine-men of past ages—if we may use the term without danger of suggesting the medicine-men of Africa and other savage lands—who placed implicit faith in the use of herbs, and found in them virtues of amazing kinds. But the term may also be extended to include the many credulous people, even of the present day, who use flowers and herbs for various purposes without knowing anything of their medical properties, in virtue of the traditions which still cling to them with leech-like tenacity, and on account of their having been for ages past applied to these same uses. Every one knows that many of our herbs, plants, and flowers have valuable medicinal properties; with these we have here nothing to do; our present object is to look at some of the superstitious notions which have been held in the past, and are still firmly maintained in many of our country villages and hamlets, respecting the use of certain plants and herbs, owing to some peculiarity in their form, time of growth, period of coming into blossom, or other similar property.

At the very outset it will be necessary to call attention to what is popularly known as the Doctrine of Signatures. "This was a system for discovering the medicinal uses of a plant from something in its external appearance that resembled the disease it would cure, and proceeded upon the belief that God had in this indicated its especial virtues. Thus the hard, stony seeds of the Gromwell must be good for gravel, and the knotty tubers of Scrophularia for scrofulous glands; while the scaly pappus of Scabiosa showed it to be a specific in leprous diseases; the spotted leaves of Pulmonaria, that it was a sovereign remedy for tuberculous lungs; and the growth of Saxifrage in the fissures of rocks, that it would disintegrate stone in the bladder." If the more youthful reader should find this passage somewhat difficult to comprehend, we hope to make it clearer as we proceed, for it is quite possible that we may have to call up some of the plants here mentioned for closer analysis and investigation. In an old work on the "Art of Simpling" we are told that "Though Sin and Sathan have plunged mankinde into an Ocean of Infirmities, yet the mercy of God, which is over all His workes, maketh Grasse to grow upon the Mountaines, and Herbes for the use of men, and hath not only stamped upon them a distinct forme, but also given them particular Signatures, whereby a man may read, even in legible characters, the use of them." Those who live in country places, and make themselves at home with the peasants in their simple life and homely dwellings, will often have heard them say that if a child is suffering from nettle-rash some Nettle-tea should be made for it. Here we have an interesting illustration of the Doctrine of Signatures, and one which all will be able to understand. In some parts of England it is still usual to apply the blood-stone to prevent bleeding from the nose, although a key often takes its place in houses where the blood-stone is not kept. In the same way when people were suffering from jaundice, which shows itself, as its name indicates, in the *yellow* colour of the skin, they were advised to take Turmeric as a remedy. Now Turmeric is the root of a plant found in India and elsewhere, which is used for making a yellow dye. You can judge of its colour when you know that it is the Turmeric which makes the curry powder, employed so largely in the East, of such a golden hue; and it was not to be wondered at that people should suppose some affinity between jaundice, the yellow complaint, and Turmeric, the yellow herb. It was on account of the great respiratory power of the fox that his lungs were thought to be good for asthma, and from the same consideration many savage peoples will not eat the flesh of a deer lest they should become timid; while they will pay anything for the heart of a tiger, and even drink the blood and eat the flesh of a brave warrior whom they have taken in battle, in order that they may be endued with the same undaunted courage as these possessed.

THE REV. HILDERIC FRIEND
[*Flowers and Flower Lore* (1886)]

OF HORSE-TONGUE
OR DOUBLE TONGUE
(Hippoglossum Uvularia)

The little leaf-like tongue, growing upon the greater is no light argument that this plant is effectual for sores in the mouth and throat. . . . It is good also for those that have an imperfection in their speech, so as not to be natural.

WILLIAM COLES
[*Adam in Eden* (1657)]

The Authority of the Ancients

[*Like all the other sciences and arts, botany and gardening slowly emancipated themselves from the authority of the ancients who were for so long supposed to have known more than we could hope to learn. It is to*

their authority that the author of one of the early English garden books
was still appealing.]

I CALLED to remembrance the two notable sayings of the well
learned and worthy Philosopher *Xenophon* . . . that that Arte was
moste commendable, and of all men moste worthy to be allowed & accepted, which to a common wealth brought any kinde of profit and
commoditie. And because this Art of Gardning is of it self verry profitable, and bringeth moste necessarie commodities, both to Citties and
Townes, therefore in my simple judgement, it deserueth no small com-
mendation. The beginning of it is very ancient, . . . long ago found
out, first by dame Nature, & after continued and augmented by the
dilligent care and vigilant paines of the wise and skilfull Gardeners, by
whose industrie & meanes, it is now growen to such perfection, as I
thinke it therefore moste worthie to be accounted amongst other such
artes, as euery common wealth hath need of . . . forsomuch as this is
so linked and chained to the noble artes, both of Phisicke and Surgerie,
as by no meanes possible it may be separated from the other, but rather
as a dayly handmaiden, continually serueth them both.

THOMAS HILL
[*The Arte of Gardening* (1608)]

Of Roses

[*One of New England's prettiest wild flowers, Gerardia, was named in*
honor of John Gerard (1545–1612), barber-surgeon and for twenty
years manager of gardens for Queen Elizabeth's prime minister Lord
Burghley. In 1596 he published a catalogue of the plants in his own little
garden and in 1597 his large herbal. Described in the preface as "the
fruits of these mine own labours," it is said to have been cribbed in large
part from a translation of an earlier book by one Rembert Dodoens. In
any event, however, it is the earliest English example of the herbal

transforming itself into a garden encyclopedia and for twenty years it was the textbook of English gardeners. In this article on the roses of his time and country the supposed "virtues" of the plant have come to take a very subordinate place.]

THE KINDES

T H E Plant of Roses, though it be a shrub full of prickles, yet it had bin more fit and convenient to have placed it with the most glorious floures of the world, than to insert the same here among base and thorny shrubs: for the Rose doth deserve the chief and prime place among all floures whatsoever; beeing not onely esteemed for his beauty, vertues, and his fragrant and odoriferous smell; but also because it is the honor and ornament of our English Scepter, as by the conjunction appeareth, in the uniting of those two most Royall Houses of Lancaster and Yorke. Which pleasant floures deserve the chiefest place in crownes and garlands, as *Anacreon Thius* a most antient Greeke Poet affirmes in those Verses of a Rose, beginning thus:

> The Rose is the honour and beauty of floures,
> The Rose is the care and love of the Spring:
> The Rose is the pleasure of th' heavenly Pow'rs.
> The Boy of faire *Venus*, *Cythera*'s Darling,
> Doth wrap his head round with garlands of Rose,
> When to the dances of the Graces he goes.

Augerius Busbequius speaking of the estimation and honor of the Rose, reporteth, That the Turks can by no means endure to see the leaves of Roses fall to the ground, because some of them have dreamed, that the first or most antient Rose did spring out of the bloud of *Venus:* and others of the Mahumetans say that it sprang of the sweat of *Mahumet.*

But there are many kindes of Roses, differing either in the bignesse of the floures, or the plant it selfe, roughnesse or smoothnesse, or in the multitude or fewnesse of the flours, or else in colour and smell; for divers of them are high and tall, others short and low, some have five leaves, others very many.

Moreover, some be red, others white, and most of them or all sweetly smelling, especially those of the garden.

THE DESCRIPTION

1   If the Curious could so be content, one generall description might serve to distinguish the whole stock or kindred of the Roses, being things so wel knowne: notwithstanding I thinke it not amisse to say somthing of them severally, in hope to satisfie all. The white Rose hath very long stalkes of a wooddy substance, set or armed with divers sharpe prickles: the branches wherof are likewise full of prickles, whereon grow leaves consisting of five leaves for the most part, set upon a middle rib by couples, the old leaf standing at the point of the same, and every one of those small leaves somwhat snipt about the edges, somewhat rough, and of an overworne greene colour: from the bosome wherof shoot forth long foot-stalks, whereon grow very faire double flours of a white colour, and very sweet smell, having in the middle a few yellow threds or chives; which being past, there succeedeth a long fruit, greene at the first, but red when it is ripe, and stuffed with a downy choking matter, wherein is contained seed as hard as stones. The root is long, tough, and of a wooddy substance.

2   The red Rose groweth very low in respect of the former: the stalks are shorter, smoother, and browner of colour: The leaves are like, yet of a worse dusty colour: The floures grow on the tops of the branches, consisting of many leaves of a perfect red colour: the fruit is likewise red when it is ripe: the root is wooddy.

3   The common Damaske Rose in stature, prickely branches, and in other respects is like the white Rose; the especiall difference consists in the colour and smell of the flours: for these are of a pale red colour, of a more pleasant smel, and fitter for meat and medicine.

4   The *Rosa Provincialis minor* or lesser Province Rose differeth not from the former, but is altogether lesser: the floures and fruit are like: the use in physicke also agreeth with the precedent.

5   The Rose without prickles hath many young shoots comming from the root, dividing themselves into divers branches, tough, and of a wooddy substance as are all the rest of the Roses, of the height of two or three cubits, smooth and plain without any roughnesse or prickles at all: whereon grow leaves like those of the Holland Rose, of a shining deep green colour on the upper side, underneath somewhat hoary and hairy. The flours grow at the tops of the branches, consisting of an infinite number of leaves, greater than those of the Damaske Rose, more double, and of a colour between the red and damask Roses, of a most sweet smell.

The fruit is round, red when it is ripe, and stuffed with the like flocks and seeds of those of the damaske Rose. The root is great, wooddy, and far spreading.

6   The Holland or Province Rose hath divers shoots proceeding from a wooddy root ful of sharpe prickles, dividing it selfe into divers branches, wheron grow leaves consisting of five leaves set on a rough middle rib, & those snipt about the edges: the flours grow on the tops of the branches, in shape and colour like the damaske Rose, but greater and more double, insomuch that the yellow chives in the middle are hard to be seene; of a reasonable good smell, but not fully so sweet as the common damaske Rose: the fruit is like the other of his kinde.

THE PLACE

All these sorts of Roses we have in our London gardens, except that Rose without pricks, which as yet is a stranger in England. The double white Rose groweth wilde in many hedges of Lancashire in great aboundance, even as Briers do with us in these Southerly parts, especially in a place of the country called Leyland, and at Roughford not far from Latham. Moreover, in the said Leyland fields doth grow our garden Rose wilde, in the plowed fields among the corne, in such aboundance, that there may be gathered daily during the time, many bushels of roses, equal with the best garden Rose in each respect: the thing that giveth great cause of wonder, is, That in a field in the place aforesaid, called Glovers field, every yeare that the field is plowed for corne, that yeare it wil be spred over with Roses, and when it lieth ley, or not plowed, then is there but few Roses to be gathered; by the relation of a curious gentleman there dwelling, so often remembred in our history.

I have heard that the Roses which grow in such plenty in Glovers field every yere the field is plowed, are no other than Corn Rose, that is, red Poppies, however our Author was informed.

THE TIME

These floure from the end of May to the end of August, and divers times after, by reason the tops and superfluous branches are cut away in the end of their flouring: and then doe they somtimes floure even untill October and after.

THE VERTUES

The distilled water of Roses is good for the strengthning of the heart, and refreshing of the spirits, and likewise for all things that require a gentle cooling.

The same being put in junketting dishes, cakes, sauces, and many other pleasant things, giveth a fine and delectable taste.

It mitigateth the paine of the eies proceeding of a hot cause, bringeth sleep, which also the fresh roses themselves provoke through their sweet and pleasant smell.

Of like vertue also are the leaves of these preserved in Sugar, especially if they be onely bruised with the hands, and diligently rempered with Sugar, and so heat at the fire rather than boyled.

[*Gerard's Herball*, edition Th. Johnson (1636)]

The Doctrine of Signatures Rejected

[*John Ray (1628–1705), sometimes called "the father of English natural history," was both a philosopher and a true scientist in the modern sense. He was responsible for original contributions to botany and zoology and the author of the most influential book of his time on the philosophy of natural history. We shall meet him again among the early scientists but his rejection of the Doctrine of Signatures belongs here—along with his defense of one of the few superstitions which he did still countenance.*]

AS for the Signatures of Plants, or the Notes impressed upon them as *Indices* of their Virtues, tho' some lay great stress upon them, accounting them strong Arguments to prove that some Understanding Principle is the highest Original of the Works of Nature; as indeed they were, could it certainly be made appear that there were such Marks designedly set upon them; because all that I find mention'd and collected by Authors, seem to me to be rather fancied by Men, than design'd by Nature to signifie or point out any such Vertues or Qualities as they would make us believe. I have elsewhere, I think upon good Grounds, rejected them; and finding no reason as yet to alter my Opinion, I shall not further insist on them. Howbeit I will not deny but that the noxious and malignant Plants do many of them discover something of their Nature by the sad and melancholick Visage of their Leaves, Flowers and Fruit. And that I may not leave that Head wholly untouch'd, one Observation I shall add relating to the Virtues of Plants, in which I think there is something of Truth, that is, that there are, by the wise Disposition of Providence, such *Species* of Plants produc'd in every Country as are most proper and convenient for the Meat and Medicine of the Men and Animals that are bred and inhabit there. Insomuch that *Solenander* writes, that from the frequency of the Plants that spring up naturally in any Region he could easily gather what endemial Diseases the Inhabitants thereof were subject to: So in *Denmark, Friezland,* and *Holland,* where the Scurvy usually reigns, the proper Remedy thereof, *Scurvy-grass,* doth plentifully grow.

JOHN RAY
[*The Wisdom of God Manifested in the Works of the Creation* (1691)]

Mandrakes, True and False

[*Of all the "signatures" by which the purpose of an herb might be known, the completest and most sensational was written all over the mandrake root. Because this forked root sometimes bore a crude resemblance to the human body it must have inclusive virtues. And because fakers soon learned to improve on nature by manufacturing mandrake roots which were actually little puppets, the superstitions persisted and grew. The mandrake had aphrodisiacal powers among many others; it was particularly potent if collected from beneath a gallows; it shrieked when you pulled it up; and those unlucky enough to hear the shriek often went mad. The herbalist William Turner tried manfully to separate superstition from fact, but he was not prepared to give up the mandrake entirely.*]

※

T H E rootes whiche are conterfited & made like litle puppettes & mam-
mettes, which come to be sold in England in boxes, with heir, & such
forme as a man hath, are nothyng elles but folishe feined trifles, & not
naturall. For they are so trymmed of crafty theues to mocke the poore
people with all, & to rob them both of theyr wit and theyr money. I have
in my tyme at diuerse tymes taken up the rootes of Mandrag out of the
grounde, but I neuer saw any such thyng upon or in them, as are in and
upon the pedlers rootes.

WILLIAM TURNER
[*Herbal* (1568)]

How to Make a Knot Garden

[*During at least one hundred years the most often consulted English
work on horticulture was one published in 1629 by John Parkinson,
apothecary to King James I. It was a sumptuous folio and despite its
absurd punning title* Paradisi in Sole Paradisus Terrestris (*Park-in-sun's
Earthly Paradise*) *it was a solid and practical book which justified its
subtitle:*

A Garden of all sorts of pleasant flowers, which our English
ayre will permit to be noursed up: with a Kitchen garden of all manner
of herbes, rootes, and fruites, for meate or sauce used with us, and an
Orchard of all sorte of fruitbearing Trees and shrubbes fit for our Land;
together with the right orderinge, planting, and preserving of them, and
their uses and vertues.

*Parkinson was accused of having stolen a major part of his
material from the manuscript of a deceased predecessor and it seems that
he did so, but in any event here at last is a large inclusive book where the
main stress is on the pleasure garden rather than on supposedly medicinal
herbs and where full attention is given to exotics suited to the English
climate. His work was not really superseded until 1731 when Philip
Miller, chief gardener at the Chelsea Botanical Garden, published his*

Gardener's Dictionary—*the ancestor of all the modern garden books in encyclopedic form.*

    Since the taste of Parkinson's time ran to what would strike a modern as an intolerable deal of gravel walk to a pennyworth of plants, he gives directions for constructing what was called a "knot garden"— i.e., an intricately twisting but geometrical "knot" of paths surrounding beds of flowers.]

The many sorts of herbs and other things, wherewith the beds and parts of knots are bordered to set out the form of them, with their commodities and discommodities.

I T is necessary also, that I shew you the several materials, wherewith these knots and trails are set forth and bordered, which are of two sorts: The one are living herbs, and the other are dead materials; as lead, boards, bones, tyles, &c. Of herbs there are many sorts, wherewith the knots and beds in a Garden are used to be set, to shew forth the form of them, and to preserve them the longer in their form, as also to be as green and sweet herbs while they grow, to be cut to perfume the house, keeping them in such order and proportion, as may be most convenient for their several natures, and every mans pleasure and fancy: Of all which, I intend to give you the knowledge here in this place: and first, to begin with that which hath been most anciently received, which is Thrift. This is an everliving green herb, which many take to border their beds, and set their knots and trails, and therein much delight, because it will grow thick and bushy, and may be kept, being cut with a pair of Garden sheers, in some good handsom manner and proportion for a time, and besides in the Summer time send forth many short stalks of pleasant flowers, to deck up an house among other sweet herbs: Yet these inconveniences do accompany it; it will not onely in a small time overgrow the knot or trail in many places, by growing so thick and bushy, that it will put out the form of a knot in many places: but also much thereof will die with the frosts and snows in Winter, and with the drought in Summer, whereby many void places will be seen in the knot, which doth much deform it, and must therefore be yeerly refreshed: the thickness also and bushing thereof doth hide and shelter snails and other small noisom worms so plentifully, that Gilloflowers, and other fine herbs and flowers being planted therein, are much spoiled by them, and cannot be helped without much industry, and very great and daily attendance to destroy them.

Germander is another herb, in former times also much used, and yet also in many places, and because it will grow thick, and may be kept also in some form and proportion with cutting, and that the cuttings are much used as a strawing herb for houses, being pretty and sweet, is also much affected by divers: but this also will often dye and grow out of form, and besides that, the stalks will grow too great, hard and stubby, the roots do so far shoot under ground, that upon a little continuance thereof, will spread into many places within the knot, which if continually they be not pluckt up, they will spoil the whole knot it self; and therefore once in three or four years at the most, it must be taken up and new set, or else it will grow too roynish and cumbersom. Hyssope hath also been used to be set about a knot, and being sweet will serve for strewings, as Germander: But this, although the roots do not run or creep like it, yet the stalks do quickly grow great above ground, & die often after the first yeers setting, whereby the grace of the knot will be much lost. Marjerome, Savorie, and Thyme, in the like manner being sweet herbs, are used to border up beds and knots, and will be kept for a little while, with cutting, into some conformity; but all and every of them serve most commonly but for one years use, and will soon decay and perish: and therefore none of these, no more then any of the former, do I commend for a good bordering herb for this purpose. Lavander Cotton also being finely slipped and set, is of many, and those of the highest respect of late dayes accepted, both for the beauty and form of the herb, being of a whitish green mealy colour, for his scent smelling somewhat strong, and being everliving and abiding green all the Winter, will, by cutting, be kept in as even proportion as any other herb may be. This will likewise soon grow great and stubbed, notwithstanding the cutting, and besides will now and then perish in some places, especially if you do not strike or put off the snow, before the Sun lying upon it dissolve it: The rarity and novelty of this herb, being for the most part but in the Gardens of great persons, doth cause it to be of greater regard, it must therefore be renewed wholly every second or third year at the most, because of the great growing thereof. Slips of Juniper or Yew are also receved of some and planted, because they are alwaies green, and that the Juniper especially hath not that ill scent that Box hath, which I will presently commend unto you, yet both Juniper and Yew will soon grow too great & stubbed, and force you to take up your knot sooner, then if it were planted with Box. Which lastly, I chiefly and above all other herbs commend unto you, and being a small, low, or dwarf kind, is called French or Dutch Box, and serveth very well to set out any knot, or border out any beds: for besides that it is ever green, it being reasonable thick set,

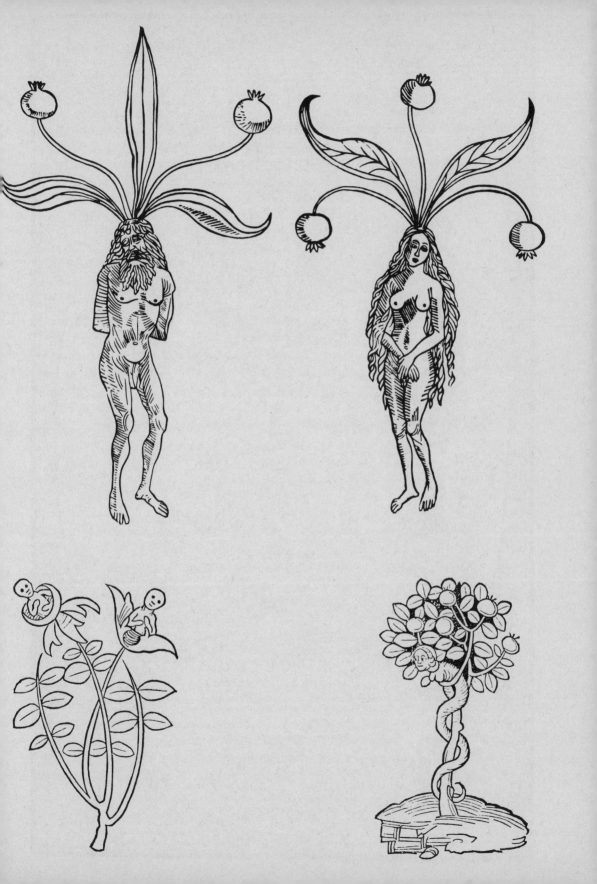

will easily be cut and formed into any fashion one will, according to the
nature thereof, which is to grow very slowly, & wil not in a long time
rise to be of any height, but shooting forth many smal branches from the
root, will grow very thick, and yet not require so great tending nor so
much perish as any of the former, and is onely received into the Gardens
of those that are curious. This (as I before said) I commend and hold to
be the best & surest herb to abide fair and green in all the bitter storms
of the sharpest Winter, and all the great heats and droughts of Summer,
and doth recompence the want of a good sweet scent with his fresh
verdure, even proportion, and long lasting continuance. Yet these inconveniences it hath, that besides the unpleasing scent which many mislike,
and yet is but small, the roots of this Box do so much spread themselves
into the ground of the knot, and do draw from thence so much nourishment, that it robbeth all the hearbs that grow near it of their sap and
substance, thereby making all the earth about it barren, or at least lesse
fertile. Wherefore to shew you the remedy of this inconvenience of
spreading, without either taking up the Box of the border, or the herbs
and flowers in the knot, is I think a secret known but unto a few, which
is this: You shal take a broad pointed iron like unto a Slise or Chesil,
which thrust down right into the ground a good depth all along the inside
of the border of Box somewhat close thereunto, you may thereby cut
away the spreading roots thereof, which draw so much moisture from
the other herbs on the inside, and by this means both preserve your herbs
and flowers in the knot, and your Box also, for that the Box will be
nourished sufficiently from the rest of the roots it shooteth on all the
other sides. And thus much for the living herbs, that serve to set or border
up any knot. Now for the dead materials, they are also, as I said before
divers: as first, Lead, which some that are curious do border their knots
withal, causing it to be cut of the breadth of four fingers, bowing the
lower edge a little outward, that it may lye under the upper crust of the
ground, and that it may stand the faster, and making the upper edge
either plain, or cut out like unto the battlements of a Church: this fashion
hath delighted some, who have accounted it stately (at the least costly)
and fit for their degree, and the rather, because it will be bowed and
bended into any round, square, angular, or other proportion as one listeth,
and is not much to be misliked, in that the Lead doth not easily break or
spoil without much injury, and keepeth up a knot for a very long time
in his due proportion: but in my opinion, the Lead is over-hot for Summer, and over-cold for Winter. Others do take Oaken inch boards, and
sawing them four or five inches broad, do hold up their knot therewith:
but in that these boards cannot be drawn compasse into any small

scantling, they must serve rather for long outright beds, or such knots as have no rounds, half rounds, or compassings in them. And besides, these boards are not long lasting, because they stand continually in the weather, especially the ends where they are fastned together will soonest rot and perish, and so the whole form will be spoiled. To prevent that fault, some others have chosen the shank bones of Sheep, which after they have been well cleansed and boyled, to take out the fat from them, are stuck into the ground the small end downwards, and the knuckle head upwards, and thus being set side to side, or end to end close together, they set out the whole knot therewith, which heads of bones although they look not white the first year, yet after they have abiden some frosts and heats will become white, and prettily grace out the ground: but this inconvenience is incident to them, that the Winter frosts will raise them out of the ground oftentimes, and if by chance the knuckle head of any do break, or be struck off with any ones foot, &c going by, from your store, that lyeth by you of the same sort, set another in the place, having first taken away the broken piece: although these will last long in form and order, yet because they are but bones many mislike them, and indeed I know but few that use them. Tyles are also used by some, which by reason they may be brought compasse into any fashion many are pleased with them, who do not take the whole Tyle at length, but half Tyles, and other broken pieces set somewhat deep into the ground, that they may stand fast, and these take up but little room, and keep up the edge of the beds and knots in a pretty comely manner, but they are often out of frame, in that many of them are broken and spoiled, both with mens feet passing by, the weather and weight of the earth beating them down and breaking them, but especially the frosts in Winter do so crack off their edges, both at the tops and sides that stand close one unto another, that they must be continually tended & repaired, with fresh and sound ones put in the place of them that are broken or decayed. And lastly (for it is the latest invention) round whitish or blewish pebble stones, of some reasonable proportion and bignesse, neither too great nor too little, have been used by some to be set, or rather in a manner but laid upon the ground to fashion out the trail or knot, or all along by the large gravelly walk sides to set out the walk, and maketh a pretty handsome shew, and because the stones will not decay with the injuries of any time or weather, and will be placed in their places again, if any should be thrust out by any accident, as also that their sight is so conspicuous upon the ground, especially if they be not hid with the store of herbs growing in the knots; is accounted both for durability, beauty of the sight, handsomnesse in the work, and ease in the working and charge, to be of all other dead mate-

rials the chiefest. And thus, Gentlemen I have shewed you all the varieties
that I know are used by any in our Countrey, that are worth the reciting
(but as for the fashion of Jaw-bones, used by some in the Low-Countries,
and other places beyond the Seas, being too grosse and base, I make no
mention of them) among which every one may take what pleaseth him
best, or may most fitly be had, or may best agree with the ground or
knot. Moreover, all these herbs that serve for borderings, do serve as
well to be set upon the ground of a levelled knot; that is, where the allies
and foot-paths are of the same level with the knot, as they may serve also
for the raised knot, that is, where the beds of the knot are raised higher
than the allies: but both Lead, Boards, Bones, and Tyles, are onely for the
raised ground, be it knot or beds. The pebble stones again are onely for
the levelled ground, because they are so shallow, that as I said before,
they rather lie upon the earth then are thrust any way into it. All this
that I have here set down, you must understand is proper for the knots
alone of a Garden. But for to border the whole square or knot about, to
serve as a hedge thereunto, every one taketh what liketh him best; as
either Privet alone, or sweet Bryer, and white Thorn enterlaced together,
and Roses of one, or two, or more sorts placed here and there amongst
them. Some also take Lavander, Rosemary, Sage, Southernwood, Lavander Cotton, or some such other thing. Some again plant Cornel trees,
and plash them, or keep them low, to form them into an hedge. And
some again take a low prickly shrub, that abideth always green, . . .
called in Latine *Pyracantha*, which in time will make an ever green hedge
or border, and when it beareth fruit, which are red berries like unto
Hawthorn berries, make a glorious shew among the green leaves in the
Winter time, when no other shrubs have fruit or leaves.

JOHN PARKINSON
[*Paradisi in Sole Paradisus Terrestris* (1629)]

Gardening as Pleasure, Profit and Physick

[*A later English Herbalist, William Coles, was backward enough both
to defend tradition against new knowledge and to appeal often to the
"signatures" plainly written upon useful plants. Writing as he did during*

the Puritan regime, he was also uneasily aware that he did not dare describe his own delight in gardening without stressing utility also.]

T H A T there is no place more pleasant than a garden, may appear from God himselfe, who after he had made Man, planted the Garden of Eden, and put him therein, that he might contemplate the many wonderful Ornaments wherewith Omnipotency had bedecked his Mother Earth. It was not so much for Adam's recreation, who at that time was not acquainted with wearinesse, as it was for his Instruction, but to us it will serve for both. There is not a Plant which growes but carries along with it the legible Characters of a Deity.

As for recreation if a man be wearied with over-much study (for study is a wearinesse to the Flesh as Solomon by experience can tell you) there is no better place in the world to recreate himselfe than a Garden, there being no sence but may be delighted therein. If his sight be obfuscated and dull, as it may easily be, with continually poring, there is no better way to relieve it, than to view the pleasant greennesse of Herbes, which is the way that Painters use, when they have almost spent their sight by their most earnest contemplation of brighter objects: neither doe they only feed the Eyes, but comfort the wearied Braine with fragrant smells which yield a certaine kinde of nourishment.

The Eares also (which are called the Daughters of Musick, because they delight therein) have their recreation by the pleasant noise of the warbling notes, which the chaunting birds accent forth from amongst the murmuring Leaves. As for the Taste, they serve it so exceedingly, that whether it be affected with sweet, sower or bitter things, they even prostitute themselves. And for the feeling likewise, they entertain it with as great variety as can be imagined, there being some Plants as soft as silke, and some as prickly as an Hedgehogge; so that there is no outward sense which can want satisfaction in this Cornucopia. And if the outward senses be so delighted, the inward will be so too, it being as it were, the School of Memory and Fancy. Hereupon it was that the antient Poets did so much extoll the Gardens of Alcinous and the Hesperides. The grove of Mars was not unknowne to Juvenal, neither were there any Poets, which had not recesses into those sacred places. The first instituter of them at Athens was Epicurus, in which he had a School, where he taught, one that knew as much what belonged to pleasure as any Man. Seneca the Philosopher was likewise a great admirer of them, and is said to have expended vast summes of Money this way.

A house though otherwise beautifull, yet if it hath no Garden belonging to it, is more like a Prison than a House.

The pleasure of a Garden being thus demonstrated, I shall conclude with the profit thereof. First for household occasions, for there is not a day passeth over our heads, but we have need of one thing or other that groweth within their circumference. We cannot make so much as a little good Pottage without Herbes, which give an admirable relish and make them wholesome for our Bodies. In a Garden there be Turnips and Carrots which serve for sauce, and if meat be wanting for that too. Neither doth it afford us Aliment only, but Physick, (no Herbes being without their Physicall use, as I have said before, especially if it be well furnished with Simples). But besides this inestimable profit, there is another not much inferior to it, and that is the wholesome exercise a man may use in it. Dr. Pinck, late Warden of New College in Oxon, whereof I was once a Member (whose memory I very much honour) was a very learned Man, and well versed in Physick, and truly he would rise very betimes in the morning, even in his later dayes, when he was almost fourscore yeares old, and going into his Garden he would take a Mattock or Spade, digging there an houre or two, which he found very advantageous to his health. A Man worthy to be imitated, not only in this, but also in many other things, especially in his charitable Provisions for bringing up of poore Children. And if Gentlemen which have little else to doe, would be ruled by me, I would advise them to spend their spare time in their Gardens; either in digging, setting, weeding, or the like, than which there is no better way in the world to preserve health. If a man want an Appetite to his Victuals, the smell of the Earth new turned up, by digging with a Spade will procure it, and if he be inclined to a Consumption it will recover him. Gentlewomen, if the ground be not too wet, may doe themselves much good by kneeling upon a Cushion and weeding. And thus both sexes might divert themselves from Idlenesse, and evill Company, which often times prove the ruine of many ingenious people. But perhaps they may thinke it a disparagement to the condition they are in; truly none at all, if it were but put in practice: For we see that those fashions which sometimes seem ridiculous, if once taken up by the Gentry cease to be so. And if you shall require another Precedent besides that before mentioned, I shall present unto you that of the wise and mighty Emperor Dioclesian, who after he had reigned eighteen yeares, left for a season the whole Government of the Empire, and forsaking the Court, betook himself to a meane House, with Garden adjoining, wherein with his owne hands he both sowed, set, and weeded the Herbes of his Garden; which kinde of life so pleased him, that he was hardly intreated to resume the Government of the Empire. By this time I hope you will thinke it no dishonour to follow the steps of our Grandsire Adam, who is commonly pictured with a Spade in his hand, to march through the Quarters of your Garden with the like Instrument, and there to rectifie all the disorders thereof, and procure, as much as in you lyes, the recovery of the languishing Art of Simpling, which did it but appeare in lively colours, I am almost persuaded, it would so affect you, that you would be much taken unto it. There is no better way to understand the benefit of it, than by being acquainted with Herballs, and Herbarists, and by putting this Gentile and ingenious Exercise in practice, that so this part of Knowledge, as well as others, may receive that esteem and advancement that is due to it, to the banishment of Barbarisme and Ignorance, which begin againe to prevaile against it. So that this Art, with the rest, being improved may bring forth much Glory to God, much Honour to the Nation, much Pleasure and Profit to those that delight in it, and much Comfort to those which have need of Physick. To which end, the Right Honourable Earle of Danby, erected the Physicke Garden in Oxford a place worth the seeing.

WILLIAM COLES
[*The Art of Simpling* (1656)]

The First Garden Calendar

[*John Evelyn, the diarist, was all his life much interested in both gardening and forestry. He claims (justifiably it seems) to have been the first to hit upon the still-so-popular scheme of giving, month by month, a list of the gardener's routine tasks and of the plants likely to flower then.*]

A GARD'NERS work is never at an end; it begins with the year, and continues to the next: He prepares the ground, and then he sows it; after that he plants, and then he gathers the fruits; but in all the intermedial spaces he is careful to dress it. . . .

Here we endeavour to present our Gard'ners with a compleat cycle of what is requisite to be done throughout every month of the year. . . .

We are yet far from imposing . . . those nice and hypercritical punctillos which some astrologers, and such as pursue their rules, seem to oblige our Gard'ners to; as if, forsooth, all were lost, and our pains to no purpose, unless the sowing and the planting, the cutting and the pruning, were performed in such and such an exact minute of the moon.

JANUARY
To be done in the Parterre and Flower Garden.

Set up your traps for vermine, especially in your nurseries of kernels and stones, and amongst your bulbous roots. . . . About the middle of this month, plant now your anemony roots, and ranunculus's, which you will be secure of without covering, or further trouble.

Preserve from too great and continuing rains (if they happen), snow, and frost, your choicest anemonies and ranunculus's sow'd in September or October for earlier flowers: also your carnations, and such seeds as are in peril of being wash'd out, or over-chilled and frozen; covering them under shelter, and striking off the snow where it lies too weighty; for it certainly rots and bursts your early-set anemonies and ranunculus's, &c. unless planted now in the hot-beds; for now is the season, and they will flower even in London. Towards the end, earth-up with fresh and light mould the roots of those auricula's which the frost may have uncover'd; filling up the chinks about the sides of the pots where your choicest are set, but they need not be hous'd: it is a hardy plant.

Flowers in prime, or yet lasting.

Winter aconite, some anemonies, winter cyclamen, black hellebor, brumal hyacinth, oriental jacinth, levantine, narcissus, hepatica, primroses, . . . præcoce tulips, &c. especially if raised in the hot-bed.

JOHN EVELYN
[*Kalendarium Hortense* (1664)]

The Herbalist Lingers On

[*A few plants are still important to medicine—quinine, digitalis, and pilocarpine. A few more linger as pleasant anachronisms—senna, rhubarb, and mint. Most have been discarded as worthless or replaced by more potent synthetic compounds. But the herbalist is not quite extinct. Following the spring northward from one end of the United States to the other, Edwin Way Teale found one who was even a part of organized commerce.*]

"MRS. TOY MILLER. Kite Hollow. Of Happy Valley. On the road to Blowing Rock."

I wrote it down in a spiral-ring pocket notebook.

We were in a huge rambling wooden building at Lenoir, North Carolina. Around us rose the smell of drying plants and roots and barks. The building was the headquarters of the Greer Drug Company, one of the country's largest dealers in medicinal herbs. Mountainfolk in hundreds of lonely spots were out in the spring weather gathering herbs, grubbing out roots, making a wild harvest to sell to the Greer Company. One of the most active of the Blue Ridge plant hunters is Mrs. Toy Miller. She ranges through Kite Hollow, along a mountain stream north of Happy Valley, and over the ridges beyond. I noted the directions for reaching her; for we hoped to go along on a hunt for mountain herbs.

The Greer Company, we found in looking over a price list, is in the market for such odd items as elder flowers, catnip leaves, balm of Gilead buds, skunk cabbage roots, wild strawberry vines, mistletoe twigs, horse nettle berries, haircap moss, shonny haw bark, and maypop pops. In the United States there are more than 250 species of roots, herbs, and barks of value in the manufacture of drugs. A bulletin put out by the U. S. Department of Agriculture, *American Medicinal Plants of Commercial Importance*, is a Who's Who of these salable herbs. It is also a dictionary of curious botanical folk names. The harvest of an American plant hunter may include badman's-oatmeal, truelove, tread-softly, simpler's joy, lords-and-ladies, shoofly, nature's mistake, or mad-dog skullcap. He may bring home Aaron's-rod, Noah's ark, Jacob's-ladder, or Devil's bones. Or he may return with juglans, kinnikinnic, hackmatack, missey-moosey, daffydowndilly, hurr-burr or robin-runs-away.

In the cavernous loft of the building at Lenoir we walked among piles of white pine and wild cherry bark, mounds of mullein leaves and blackberry roots, and rows of burlap bags filled with fragrant sassafras bark—the first product of the New World shipped back to Europe by the Pilgrims. Wooden barrels held Adam and Eve roots. Star grass roots, like small onions, were drying near adjoining mounds of yellow jessamine bark and pokeweed roots. And extending across a wide carpet of cloth lay bushels of balsam poplar, or balm of Gilead, buds. More buds were coming in every day. This was spring, the harvest-time of the budpickers. A waxy substance extracted from these buds is used in salves. For the dried buds, the Greer Company pays 60 cents a pound. Other prices range from 3 cents a pound for birch bark and 4 cents for sumac berries to $1 a pound for star grass roots and $5 a pound for golden seal roots.

The highest price of all is paid for ginseng, from $8 to $10 a pound for the dried roots. Although there is no evidence that ginseng possesses any therapeutic or pharmacological properties, it has been in constant demand in China for centuries. The superstition that it has magic ability to restore virility to the aged has resulted in as much as $700 a pound being paid for especially fine roots in Manchuria. Most American ginseng grows far back in the mountains. The roots are at their best, shrinking least and bringing the highest prices, during a few weeks in autumn. André Michaux records that, in 1793, ginseng was the only product of Kentucky that could be transported profitably overland to Philadelphia.

Mailtime at the Greer Company brings a varied assortment of letters, penciled in unregimented spelling on odd scraps of paper by mountain plant hunters. The morning we were there, a note was deciphered suggesting that the writer should get twice the regular price for his roots because they were dug at a place "where the most dangerous snakes in the world live."

Not all the wild products handled at the Lenoir warehouse go into making drugs. Leaves of deer's-tongue are in demand for flavoring smoking tobacco. Another wild herb is necessary in the manufacture of silver polish. Sassafras bark goes into making perfumes as well as medicines. A recent development has been the collection of pollens for the treatment of allergies. One year, in less than a month, the Greer Company shipped $40,000 worth of ragweed pollen to northern pharmaceutical laboratories. In a kind of nightmare chamber for hayfever sufferers, we saw row on row of glass vials and jars filled with brightly colored dust—pollen from more than a hundred different plants.

Some of the first pollen handled by the Greer Company came from Kite Hollow. The red dirt road that leads into this side valley eluded us that day and it was afternoon before we came to the beginning of the hollow. A mile or so away we had asked directions for finding Toy Miller's house.

"Anybody down there can tell you," we were assured. "They're all kinfolk in the hollow."

The house we were hunting, gray from long weathering, clung to the foot of a steep descent. A dozen rows of peas and a small patch of catnip for the cat occupied a cleared space in the weeds at the back of the house. Chickens, dogs, cats, and children swarmed over the porch and unfenced yard. The herbwoman came to the door—thin, tired looking, her left cheek and lower lip bulging with snuff used "for the toothache." She was, she said, going up the creek that afternoon—the balm of Gilead buds were right for picking—and we were welcome to come along.

While she was getting a basket, Nellie passed around some Beechnut gum to the children. The oldest, a girl of about eight, chewed her stick solemnly for a few minutes. Then, before all the flavor was gone, she stuck it, for future enjoyment, under the arm of a cane-bottomed chair on the porch. A moment later she thought better of it. She returned, unstuck the wad, and attached it high on the frame of the front door, well out of reach of the smaller children.

We started down the hollow. The herbwoman was alert, pleasant, friendly. She had been born near Blowing Rock and was, she said, "a mountain girl from the beginning." She had a kind of natural dignity and her mountain dialect was interspersed with words of an older and better diction. She had been collecting wild plants, roots and barks for fifteen years. Once, when lumbering operations felled a stand of white pines near Kite Hollow, she and her husband skinned the bark from the logs and, in seven hours, earned $41. Another time, in two days, they earned $61—piling up more than 800 pounds of bark at 7½ cents a pound. Those were long-remembered bonanza days.

Where a decaying rail fence staggered along under a load of honeysuckle vines we stopped amid wild strawberries. The ground was white with their blossoms over an area of a hundred square yards. The herbwoman comes here to pick strawberry leaves sometimes. They sell for 20 cents a pound. But she never comes to pick strawberries. By the time they are ripe the rattlers and copperheads that live in the honey-suckle tangle are out and active.

"There's a heap of berries here," she told us, "but you can't get near 'em for snakes."

Once, back in the mountains, she was standing in thick bushes when she heard a buzzing sound and looked down in time to see the brownish body and V-shaped crossbands of a timber rattlesnake slide almost across her foot. The snake, apparently, did not see her. What did she do?

"I made tracks out of there in a hurry."

In the main, however, when she is hunting herbs in the mountains she gives little thought to snakes.

"Hits a wonder," she observed, "I ain't all eat up."

We followed the creek, swollen with spring rains, until we came to the first of the balm of Gilead trees. Under favorable conditions these balsam poplars reach a height of 100 feet. The young twigs are hairy and the cigar-shaped leaf buds are fragrant and shining with yellow wax. Indians used this wax for sealing the seams of their birchbark canoes. Honeybees collect it to stop up cracks in the hives. Pioneers valued the wax so highly as a healing salve that they planted balm of Gileads near their cabins. It was a medicine tree. Today these "balm buds" still form the source of an important ingredient in many manufactured salves.

We pulled down branches and picked off buds. They rattled into the basket. We went from tree to tree. The sun was warm, the air filled with fragrance. Above the roar of the swollen stream, tumbling over the boulders of its bed, the calling of a cardinal carried far from his perch in the top of a willow tree. The ringing "What cheer! What cheer! What cheer!" was repeated over and over again.

"Hits got a big enough mouth," said the herbwoman succinctly.

The farthest she goes into the mountains in her plant collecting is about four miles. This is for the rarer herbs. The most sought-after of the roots grow scarcer every year. There is only one place now in the mountains where she is sure of finding ginseng. Also rapidly disappearing in the region is the "Noah's ark," the yellow lady-slipper. Its roots, collected in autumn, sell for $1 a pound, dried. The mountains of western North Carolina supply a large part of the nation's medicinal plants. Yet even here, where at one time the supply seemed unlimited, uncontrolled collecting is having its effect. Herb hunters have to roam farther and farther into remote regions to make their harvest. Near settled communities, many species have been completely extirpated.

As we walked along, the herbwoman pointed out plants that she would visit later. Horse nettle—apple of Sodom or tread-softly—grew in a sandy place. Its berries, split and dried in autumn, bring 36 cents a pound. The dried roots bring 25 cents. The spindle-shaped roots of the yellow dock sell for only 9 cents a pound. Mullein, that plant of many names—candlewick, blanket leaf, Adam's-flannel, old-man's-flannel, hare's-beard, velvet plant, clown's lungwort—was beginning the production of the thick, felty leaves of a new year. The leaves and tender tops of the mullein, picked and dried, have a market value of 10 cents a pound. Once we passed a mound of pokeweed. This was a wild garden the herbwoman visited annually. Poke-berries bring 15 cents a pound; the roots, which unfortunately "dry up to next to nothing," bring only 10. Nearer the stream, in a boggy stretch, skunk cabbage massed its sappy green leaves. Here harvest days come in early spring. The roots and rootstocks are dug up and dried, after being split to hasten the process. The split, dried roots sell for 20 cents a pound.

One of the few things the herbwoman never collects is mistletoe. These clumps usually grow too high in trees. However, much of the mistletoe that reaches northern states during the holiday season comes from North Carolina, tons being shipped from one county alone. Some modern Daniel Boones, expert with a squirrel rifle, are said to harvest the topmost bunches in their own peculiar way, snipping off the branches with well-directed lead.

Along the creek, as we walked back, willow trees leaned, in clouds of new, pale-green leaves, far out over the rush of the mountain stream.

"I've skinned more willow bark in this place than most people think," the herbwoman volunteered.

In recent years the streamside willows have become a new source of revenue. The catkins have assumed special importance. For willow pollen has gone to market. Each spring Mrs. Miller collects bushels of the staminate catkins, sifting their floral dust through a fine cloth into a dishpan. The best time for harvesting pollen, she has found, is in the morning just after the dawn mist has evaporated.

The fluffy, greenish catkins of the black willows are as long as a little finger. Sometimes the tassels are more than three inches in length. They represent the largest pollen source with which the herbwoman deals. The smallest is the white flower of the plantain. On one of the hottest days of June, the previous year, she had followed the black-top road through Happy Valley, picking plantain flowers on either side. A score of times cars pulled up and people who thought she must be crazy wanted to know what she was doing.

When R. T. Greer, head of the Lenoir company, needs a new kind of pollen, he frequently puts Mrs. Toy Miller on its trail. Her knowledge of local plants is widely respected. Will Rogers once observed that we are all ignorant; we are just ignorant about different things. Our companion that day had had little schooling; she had never been beyond sight of one small part of the Blue Ridge Mountains. Her knowledge was narrow—but it was deep. She was an expert, an authority in her field.

A century and a half before, when André Michaux was wandering through the wilderness of the New World, collecting plants for Old World herbariums, he had recorded in his journal, in the spring of 1795, that he was "herborising in the Bleue Ridges." We too, that day, had been "herborising" in those same mountains.

As we drove away down the red dirt road heading for Statesville, we reflected on how humbling such a trip as ours eventually becomes. I remembered a famous explorer once saying to me: "The main thing I learn on every expedition is my ignorance." Everywhere we went we met new and unfamiliar things. Everywhere we went we encountered people who had spent their lives reading from one particular shelf in nature's library. They knew more about it—more about their area and their particular field—than we could ever hope to know. We could but sample the books they had time to read in detail.

We were near Hickory, North Carolina, in the sunset that evening when we caught the perfume of the first lilacs of our trip. They bloomed in a farmyard close to the road. A little farther on we ran through a great swirl of apple petals carried from a hillside orchard. And all along the way mockingbirds and cardinals sang in the failing light. It was dusk when we reached Statesville.

EDWIN WAY TEALE
[*North with the Spring* (1951)]

Section Three

FASHIONS IN GARDENS

Such gardens are not made
By singing: "Oh, how beautiful!" and sitting in the shade.

KIPLING

My garden is an honest place. Every tree and every vine are incapable of conceal-ment, and tell after two or three months exactly what sort of treatment they have had. The sower may mistake and sow his peas crookedly: the peas make no mistake, but come up and show his line.

EMERSON'S *Journal*

The Elysian Fields

[*Literature contains more descriptions of ideal than of actual gardens. Many of them are either heavenly or earthly paradises—including of course Eden and the Mohammedan, the latter of which includes remarkable roses without thorns as well as the more often remembered Houris. The late Greek romancer and satirist Lucian goes into more detail than either Mohammed or the author of Genesis.*]

IN the Island of the Blessed they have no night nor bright day, but a perpetual twilight; one equal season reigns throughout the year: it is always Spring with them, and no wind blows but Zephyrus; the whole region abounds in sweet flowers, and shrubs of every kind; their vines bear twelve times in the year, yielding fruit every month, their apples, pomegranates, and the rest of our autumnal produce, thirteen times, bearing twice in the month of Minos: instead of corn, the fields bring forth loaves of ready made bread, like mushrooms; there are three hundred and sixty-five fountains of water round the city, as many of honey, and five hundred rather smaller, of sweet scented oil, besides seven rivers of milk, and eight of wine.

Their Symposia are held in a place without the city, which they call the Elysian Field; this is a most beautiful meadow, skirted by a large and thick wood, affording an agreeable shade to the guests, who repose on couches of flowers; the winds attend upon, and bring them everything necessary, except wine, which is otherwise provided, for there are large trees on every side, made of the finest glass, the fruit of

which are cups of various shapes and sizes; whoever comes to the entertainment gathers one or more of these cups, which immediately becomes
full of wine, and so they drink of it, whilst the nightingales, and other
birds of song, with their bills peck the flowers out of the neighbouring
fields, and drop them on their heads; thus are they crowned with perpetual garlands; their manner of perfuming them is this; the clouds suck
up the scented oils from the fountains and rivers, and the winds gently
fanning them, distil it like soft dew on those who are assembled there;
at supper they have music also, and singing, particularly the verses of
Homer, who is himself generally at the feast, and sits next above Ulysses,
with a chorus of youths and virgins: he is led in, accompanied by Euno-
mus the Locrian, Arion of Lesbos, Anacreon and Stesichorus, whom
I saw there along with them, and who at length is reconciled to Helen:
when they have finished their songs, another chorus begins of swans,
swallows, and nightingales, and to these succeeds the sweet rustling of
the Zephyrs, the whistle through the woods, and close the concert. What
most contributes to their happiness is, that near the symposium are two
fountains, the one of milk, the other of pleasure; from the first they drink
at the beginning of the feast, there is nothing afterwards but joy and
festivity.

LUCIAN OF SAMOSATA
[*True History* (2nd century A.D.)]

One of the Seven Wonders

[*If Eden was the most famous garden of ancient times, the Hanging
Gardens of Babylon come next. They are largely legend but here is what
a Greek historian of the first century* A.D. *thought he knew about them.*]

THE hanging Garden of Babylon was not built by Semiramis who
founded the city, but by a later prince called Cyrus for the sake of a
courtezan, who being a Persian, as they say, by birth, and creating
meadows on mountain tops, desired the king, by an artificial plantation,

to imitate the land in Persia. This garden was 400 feet square, and the ascent up to it was to the top of a mountain, and had buildings and apartments out of one into another, like a theatre. Under the steps to the ascent were built arches one above another, rising gently by degrees, which supported the whole plantation. The highest arch, upon which the platform of the garden was laid, was 50 cubits high, and the garden itself was surrounded with battlements and bulwarks. The walls were made very strong, built at no small charge and expense, being 22 feet thick, and every sally port 10 feet wide. Over the several storeys of this fabric were laid beams, and summers of large massy stones, each 16 feet long and 4 broad. The roof over all these was first covered with reeds daubed with abundance of brimstone (or bitumen), then upon them were laid double tiles, joined with a hard and durable mortar, and over them all was a covering with sheets of lead, that the wet, which drained through the earth, might not rot the foundation. Upon all these was laid earth, of a convenient depth, sufficient for the growth of the greatest trees. When the soil was laid even and smooth, it was planted with all sorts of trees, which both for beauty and size might delight the spectators. The arches, which stood one above the other had in them many stately rooms of all kinds, and for all purposes. There was one that had in it certain engines, whereby it drew plenty of water out of the river Euphrates, through certain conduits hid from the spectators, which supplied it to the platform of the garden.

DIODORUS SICULUS
[*The Praise of Gardens* (1st century B.C.)]

In Homer's Day

[*Of the gardens of Homer's day we know precious little. But here is a glimpse into one.*]

AND without the court-yard hard by the door is a great garden, of four plough-gates, and a hedge runs round on either side. And there grow tall trees blossoming, pear-trees and pomegranates, and apple-trees with bright fruit, and sweet figs, and olives in their bloom. . . . There too, skirting the furtherest line, are all manner of garden beds, planted trimly, that are perpetually fresh, and therein are two fountains of water, whereof one scatters his streams all about the garden, and the other runs over against it beneath the threshold of the court-yard, and issues by the lofty house, and thence did the townsfolk draw water. These were the splendid gifts of the gods in the palace of Alcinous.

HOMER
[*The Odyssey,*
TRANSLATED BY BUTCHER AND LANG]

Pliny Trims His Hedges

[*Most prosperous Romans, like their American counterparts, had a country home. Pliny the Younger, whose self-conscious but gossipy letters to his friends give so vivid a picture of life during the early empire, was wealthy enough to boast a pretty elaborate one. Since Romans loved regularity and were not averse to conspicuous expenditure, it is not surprising to discover that Pliny's retreat was more elaborate than cozy. But it is a little surprising to note that he went in for "topiary work"— hedges trimmed into fantastic shapes.*]

MY villa is so advantageously situated, that it commands a full view of all the country round; yet you approach it by so insensible a rise that you find yourself upon an eminence, without perceiving you ascended. Behind, but at a great distance, stand the Apennine Mountains. In the calmest days we are refreshed by the winds that blow from thence, but so spent, as it were, by the long tract of land they travel over, that they are entirely divested of all their strength and violence before they reach us. The exposition of the principal front of the house is full south, and seems to invite the afternoon sun in summer (but somewhat earlier in winter) into a spacious and well-proportioned portico, consisting of several members, particularly a porch built in the ancient manner. In the front of the portico is a sort of terrace, embellished with various figures and bounded with a box-hedge, from whence you descend by an easy slope, adorned with the representation of divers animals in box, answering alternately to each other, into a lawn overspread with the soft—I had almost said the liquid—Acanthus: this is surrounded by a walk enclosed with tonsile evergreens, shaped into a variety of forms. Beyond it is the Gestatio, laid out in the form of a circus, ornamented in the middle with box cut in numberless different figures, together with a plantation of shrubs, prevented by the shears from shooting up too high; the whole is fenced in by a wall covered by box, rising by different ranges to the top. On the outside of the wall lies a meadow that owes as many beauties to nature, as all I have been describing *within* does to art; at the end of which are several other meadows and fields interspersed with thickets. At the extremity of this portico stands a grand dining-room, which opens upon one end of the terrace; as from the windows there is a very extensive prospect over the meadows up into the country, from whence you also have a view of the terrace and such parts of the house which project forward, together with the woods enclosing the adjacent hippodrome. Opposite almost to the centre of the portico stands a square edifice, which encompasses a small area, shaded by four plane-trees, in the midst of which a fountain rises, from whence the water, running over the edges of a marble basin, gently refreshes the surrounding plane-trees and the verdure underneath them. . . . In the front of these agreeable buildings lies a very spacious hippodrome, entirely open in the middle, by which means the eye, upon your first entrance, takes in its whole extent at one glance. It is encompassed on every side with plane-trees covered with ivy, so that while their heads flourish with their own foliage, their bodies enjoy a borrowed verdure; and thus the ivy, twining round the trunk and branches, spreads from tree to tree, and connects them together.

Between each plane-tree are planted box-trees, and behind these, bay-trees, which blend their shade with that of the planes. This plantation, forming a straight boundary on both sides of the hippodrome, bends at the farther end into a semicircle, which, being set round and sheltered with cypress-trees, varies the prospect, and casts a deeper gloom; while the inward circular walks (for there are several), enjoying an open exposure, are perfumed with roses, and correct, by a very pleasing contrast, the coolness of the shade with the warmth of the sun. Having passed through these several winding alleys, you enter a straight walk, which breaks out into a variety of others, divided by box-hedges. In one place you have a little meadow, in another the box is cut into a thousand different forms: sometimes into letters expressing the name of the master; sometimes that of the artificer; whilst here and there little obelisks rise, intermixed alternately with fruit-trees: when, on a sudden, in the midst of this elegant regularity, you are surprised with an imitation of the negligent beauties of rural nature: in the centre of which lies a spot surrounded with a knot of dwarf plane-trees.

Beyond these is a walk planted with the smooth and twining Acanthus, where the trees are also cut into a variety of names and shapes. At the upper end is an alcove of white marble, shaded by vines, supported by four small Carystian pillars. From this bench, the water, gushing through several little pipes, as if it were pressed out by the weight of the persons who repose themselves upon it, falls into a stone cistern underneath, from whence it is received into a fine polished marble basin, so artfully contrived that it is always full without ever overflowing.

When I sup here, this basin serves for a table, the larger sort of dishes being placed round the margin, while the smaller ones swim about in the form of little vessels and water-fowl. Corresponding to this, is a fountain which is incessantly emptying and filling; for the water, which it throws up a great height, falling back into it, is by means of two openings, returned as fast as it is received. Fronting the alcove (reflecting as great an ornament to it, as it borrows from it) stands a summer-house of exquisite marble, the doors whereof project and open into a green enclosure; as from its upper and lower windows the eye is presented with a variety of different verdures. Next to this is a little private recess (which, though it seems distinct, may be laid into the same room) furnished with a couch; and notwithstanding it has windows on every side, yet it enjoys a very agreeable gloominess, by means of a spreading vine which climbs to the top and entirely overshades it. Here you may recline and fancy yourself in a wood; with this difference only—that you are not exposed to the weather. In this place a fountain also rises and instantly disappears; in different quarters are disposed marble seats, which serve, no less than the summer-house, as so many reliefs after one is wearied with walking. Near each seat is a little fountain; and, throughout the whole hippodrome, several small rills run murmuring along, wheresoever the hand of art thought proper to conduct them; watering here and there different spots of verdure, and in their progress refreshing the whole.

PLINY THE YOUNGER
[*Letter to Apollinaris* (1st century A.D.)]

The Gardens of Ancient Mexico

[*At a time when the most advanced of the Indian tribes living in what is now the United States had not progressed beyond simple farming and when some tribes had not yet progressed beyond hunting and the collection of wild plants, their kinsmen in Mexico were cultivating elaborate pleasure gardens.*]

B U T the pride of Iztapalapan, on which its lord had freely lavished his care and his revenues, was its celebrated gardens. They covered an immense tract of land; were laid out in regular squares, and the paths intersecting them were bordered with trellises, supporting creepers and aromatic shrubs that loaded the air with their perfumes. The gardens were stocked with fruit-trees, imported from distant places, and with the gaudy family of flowers which belonged to the Mexican flora, scientifically arranged, and growing luxuriant in the equable temperature of the table-land. The natural dryness of the atmosphere was counteracted by means of aqueducts and canals that carried water into all parts of the grounds.

In one quarter was an aviary, filled with numerous kinds of birds, remarkable in this region both for brilliancy of plumage and of song. The gardens were intersected by a canal communicating with the lake of Tezcuco, and of sufficient size for barges to enter from the latter. But the most elaborate piece of work was a huge reservoir of stone, filled to a considerable height with water well supplied with different sorts of fish. This basin was sixteen hundred paces in circumference, and was surrounded by a walk, made also of stone, wide enough for four persons to go abreast. The sides were curiously sculptured, and a flight of steps led to the water below, which fed the aqueducts above noticed, or, collected into fountains, diffused a perpetual moisture.

Such are the accounts transmitted of these celebrated gardens, at a period when similar horticultural establishments were unknown in Europe; and we might well doubt their existence in this semi-civilized land, were it not a matter of such notoriety at the time and so explicitly attested by the invaders. But a generation had scarcely passed after the Conquest, before a sad change came over these scenes so beautiful. The town itself was deserted, and the shore of the lake was strewed with the wreck of buildings which once were its ornament and its glory. The gardens shared the fate of the city. The retreating waters withdrew the means of nourishment, converting the flourishing plains into a foul and unsightly morass, the haunt of loathsome reptiles; and the water-fowl built her nest in what had once been the palaces of princes!

W. M. PRESCOTT
[*The Conquest of Mexico* (1843)]

Boccaccio's Garden

[*Many of the most familiar flowers of our gardens are, of course, relatively recent introductions, but many others have been in cultivation since very early times. Thus though the so-called African Violet was not brought to Europe until 1890, the Athenians grew the true violet as well as the carnation and the daffodil. The Egyptians had oleander, poppy and jasmine; the gardens of medieval monasteries, foxglove, Madonna lilies, mallows and roses—though the finest of the roses came much later from China.*

Many of the methods used have also changed little. Pliny gives usable directions for grafting, for example. An English book of the seventeenth century contains an illustration which includes pots, cold frames and cloches hardly different from those of today. What has changed most drastically from age to age is the fashionable design and the idea of what a garden should look like. Most striking of these changes is the modern emphasis upon flowering plants and "borders" as against walks, parterres, tubs, statuary, etc. Until the nineteenth century most flower gardens (as opposed to landscaping) would have struck us as stiff and

*formal—even when they were a reaction against an earlier style of for-
mality.*

*If we may trust the evidence of painting, the Renaissance gar-
den was largely a matter of pots and tubs in courtyard or patio. Into such
a thirteenth-century Italian garden we get a delightful glimpse in the
Decameron of Boccaccio. The ladies and gentlemen who tell one another stories (not always entirely proper) had retired to a country estate
to escape the Black Death raging in the cities. One day was spent in a
walled garden.]*

T H E Y were now shown into the garden, which was on one side of
the palace, and walled round about. It seemed so full of beauties at their
first entrance, that they were the more attentive in viewing every part.
All round and through the midst of it were broad straight walks flanked
with vines, which seemed to promise a plenteous vintage; and being all
in blossom, they gave so delicious a scent, joined with other flowers
then blowing in the garden, that they thought themselves amongst the
spiceries of the east. The sides of these walks were closed with white
and red roses and jassamine, in such a manner as to exclude the morning
and even the mid-day sun. What was the variety of plants, and how
elegantly disposed, it would be needless to mention, since there was
nothing belonging to our climate which was not there in great abundance. In the middle of this garden, what seemed more delightful than
anything else, was a plot of ground like a meadow; the grass of a deep
green, spangled with a thousand different flowers, and set round with
orange and cedar trees, whose branches were stored with ripe fruit and
blossoms, at the same time affording a most pleasing object to the eye, as
well as a grateful odour to the smell. In the centre of this meadow was a
fountain of white marble, beautifully carved; and (whether by a natural
or artificial spring I know not) from a figure standing on a column in
the midst of the fountain, a jet of water spouted up, which made a most
agreeable sound in its fall: the water which came thence ran through
the meadow by a secret passage; when, being received into canals, it
appeared again, and was carried to every part of the garden, uniting in
one stream at its going out, and falling with such force into the plain, as
to turn two mills before it got thither. The sight of this garden, its form
and contrivance, with the fountains and the spring proceeding from it,
pleased the gentlemen and ladies so much, that they spared not to say
that if there was a paradise on earth, it could be in no other form, nor

was it possible to add any thing to it. While they were walking about, therefore, diverting themselves with weaving chaplets of flowers, and listening to the various melody of the birds, who seemed to vie with each other, a new beauty presented itself to them, which they had before taken no notice of; they perceived the garden to be full of a hundred different creatures: in one place they saw rabbits issuing forth; from another quarter they saw hares: here were goats lying down, and there were deer grazing, with many others passing backwards and forwards at their pleasure, as though they were tame. When their senses had sufficiently feasted on these several beauties, the table was spread by the side of the fountain, and, after half a dozen songs and some dances, they sat down to eat, being served in a sumptuous manner with everything that was dainty and elegant; and when they had done feasting, they began again to sing and dance, till the queen commanded them to give over, and permitted such as were so disposed to take their ease. Accordingly some departed; and others, charmed with the pleasantness of the place, stayed to read or play at chess. At nine they arose, and went into the meadow at the fountain-side, and being seated there as usual, they waited for the time when they should begin their novels upon the subject which the queen had proposed.

BOCCACCIO
[*The Decameron* (14th century)]

In the Italian Manner

[*Though Renaissance painters introduced into their pictures innumerable glimpses of courtyard gardens, the writers of the time are more likely merely to allude to them in passing. The nineteenth-century essayist "Vernon Lee" (Violet Paget) has reconstructed from various sources an image of what these gardens were like.*]

BOCCACCIO and the Italians more usually employ the word *orto*, which has lost its Latin signification, and is a place, as we learn from the context, planted with fruit-trees and with pot-herbs. . . . But although in this story (of Madonna Dianora) Boccaccio employs the word *giardino*, instead of *orto*, I think we must imagine that magic flower garden rather as a corner—they still exist on every hillside—of orchard connected with the fields of wheat and olives below by the long tunnels of vine trellis, and dying away into them with the great tufts of lavender and rosemary and fennel on the grassy bank under the cherry trees. This piece of terraced ground along which the water—spurted from the dolphin's mouth or the sirens' breasts—runs through walled channels, refreshing impartially violets and salads, lilies and tall flowering onions, under the branches of the peach tree and the pomegranate, to where in the shade of the great pink oleander tufts, it pours out below into the big tank, for the maids to rinse their linen in the evening, and the peasants to fill their cans to water the bedded-out tomatoes and the potted clove-pinks in the shadow of the house. . . .

Now this poverty of flower-beds and richness of pots made it easy and natural for the Italian garden to become, like the Moorish one, a place of mere greenery and water, a palace whose fountains plashed in sunny yards walled in with myrtle and bay, in mysterious chambers roofed over with ilex and box. And this it became. Moderately at first; a few hedges of box and cypress—exhaling its resinous breath in the sunshine—leading up to the long, flat, Tuscan house, with its tower or pillared loggia under the roof to take the air and dry linen; a few quaintly cut trees set here and there, along with the twisted mulberry tree where the family drank its wine and ate its fruit of an evening; a little grove of ilexes to the back, in whose shade you could sleep, while the cicalas buzzed at noon; some cypresses gathered together into a screen, just to separate the garden from the olive yard above; gradually perhaps a balustrade set at the end of the bowling-green, that you might see, even from a distance the shimmery blue valley below—the pale blue distant hills; and if you had it, some antique statue, not good enough for the courtyard of the town house, set on the balustrade or against the tree; also, where water was plentiful, a little grotto scooped out under that semicircular screen of cypresses. A very modest place, but differing essentially from the orchard and kitchen-garden of the mediaeval burgher; and out of which comes something immense and unique—the classic Roman villa.

For your new garden, your real Italian garden, brings in a new element—that of perspective, architecture, decoration; the trees used as building material, the lie of the land as theatre arrangements, the water as the most docile and multiform stage property. . . .

Now go where you may in the outskirts of Rome you are sure

to find ruins—great aqueduct arches, temples half-standing, gigantic terrace works belonging to some baths or palace hidden beneath the earth and vegetation. Here you have naturally an element of architectural ground-plan and decoration which is easily followed: the terraces of quincunxes, the symmetrical groves, the long flights of steps, the triumphal arches, the big ponds, come, as it were, of them—obeying the order of what is below. And from underground, everywhere, issues a legion of statues, headless, armless, in all stages of mutilation, who are charitably mended and take their place, mute sentinels, white and earth-stained, at every intersecting box hedge, under every ilex grove, beneath the cypresses of each sweeping hillside avenue, wherever a tree can make a niche or a bough in a canopy.

VERNON LEE
[*Limbo and Other Essays* (1908)]

Elizabethan Gardens

[*Most writers have had the habit—annoying to future historians—of taking for granted the very details of contemporary life which we are most curious to know about. When, for example, they mention a garden they too often let it go at that, leaving us to imagine, quite erroneously, that we know what the word implied. But it is often possible, as the author of the following account demonstrates, to piece together a more accurate picture.*]

T H E flower-gardens of Shakespeare's time were very different to the flower-gardens of our day; but we have so many good descriptions of them in books and pictures that we have no difficulty in realizing them both in their general form and arrangement. I am now speaking only of the flower-gardens; the kitchen-gardens and orchards were very much like our own, except in the one important difference, that they had necessarily much less glass than our modern gardens can command. In the flower-garden the grand leading principle was uniformity and formality carried out into very minute details. "The garden is best to be square," was Bacon's rule; "the form that men like in general is a square, though roundness be *forma perfectissima*," was Lawson's rule; and this form was chosen because the garden was considered to be a purtenance and continuation of the house, designed so as strictly to harmonize with the architecture of the building. And Parkinson's advice was to the same effect: "The orbicular or round form is held in its own proper existence to be the most absolute form, containing within it all other forms whatsoever; but few, I think, will chuse such a proportion to be joyned to their habitation. The triangular or three-square form is such a form also as is seldom chosen by any that may make another choice. The four-square form is the most usually accepted with all, and doth best agree with any man's dwelling."

This was the shape of the ideal garden—

And whan I had a while goon,
I saugh a gardyn right anoon,
Full long and broad; and every delle
Enclosed was, and walled welle
With high walles embatailled.

. . . . .

I felle fast in a waymenting
By which art, or by what engyne
I might come into that gardyne;
But way I couthe fynd noon
Into that gardyne for to goon.

. . . . .

Tho' gan I go a fulle grete pas,
Environyng evene in compas,
The closing of the square walle,
Tyl that I fonde a wiket smalle
So shett that I ne'er myght in gon,
And other entre was ther noon.

Romaunt of the Rose

This square enclosure was bounded either by a high wall—"circummured with brick," "with high walles embatailled"—or with a thick high hedge—"encompassed on all the four sides with a stately arched hedge." These hedges were made chiefly of Holly or Hornbeam, and we can judge of their size by Evelyn's description of his "impreg-

nable hedge of about 400 ft. in length, 9 ft. high, and 5 ft. in diameter."
Many of these hedges still remain in our old gardens. Within this enclosure the garden was accurately laid out in formal shapes, with paths
either quite straight or in some strictly mathematical figures—

> And all without were walkes and alleyes dight
> With divers trees enrang'd in even rankes;
> And here and there were pleasant arbors pight,
> And shadie seats, and sundry flowring bankes,
> To sit and rest the walkers' wearie shankes.
>
> *F. Q.,* iv. x. 25

The main walks were not, as with us, bounded with the turf,
but they were bounded with trees, which were wrought into hedges,
more or less open at the sides, and arched over at the top. These formed
the "close alleys," "covert alleys," or "thick-pleached alleys," of which
we read in Shakespeare and other writers of that time. Many kinds of
trees and shrubs were used for this purpose; "every one taketh what
liketh him best, as either Privit alone, or Sweet Bryer and White Thorne
interlaced together, and Roses of one, two, or more sorts placed here and
there amongst them. Some also take Lavender, Rosemary, Sage, South-
ern-wood, Lavender Cotton, or some such other thing. Some again plant
Cornel trees, and plash them or keep them low to form them into a
hedge; and some again take a low prickly shrub that abideth always
green, called in Latin Pyracantha" (Parkinson). It was on these hedges
and their adjuncts that the chief labour of the garden was spent. They
were cut and tortured into every imaginable shape, for nothing came
amiss to the fancy of the topiarist. When this topiary art first came into
fashion in England I do not know, but it was probably more or less the
fashion in all gardens of any pretence from very early times, and it
reached its highest point in the sixteenth century, and held its ground as
the perfection of gardening till it was driven out of the field in the last
century by the "picturesque style," though many specimens still remain
in England, as at Levens and Hardwicke on a large scale, and in the
gardens of many ancient English mansions and old farmhouses on a
smaller scale. It was doomed as soon as landscape gardeners aimed at the
natural, for even when it was still at its height Addison described it thus:
"Our British gardeners, instead of humouring Nature, love to deviate
from it as much as possible. Our trees rise in cones, globes, and pyramids;
we see the mark of the scissors upon every plant and bush."

But this is a digression: I must return to the Elizabethan garden,
which I have hitherto only described as a great square, surrounded by

wide, covered, shady walks, and with other similar walks dividing the central square into four or more compartments. But all this was introductory to the great feature of the Elizabethan garden, the formation of the "curious knotted garden." Each of the large compartments was divided into a complication of "knots," by which was meant beds arranged in quaint patterns, formed by rule and compass with mathematical precision, and so numerous that it was a necessary part of the system that the whole square should be fully occupied by them. Lawn there was none; the whole area was nothing but the beds and the paths that divided them. There was Grass in other parts of the pleasure-grounds, and apparently well kept, for Bacon has given his opinion that "nothing is more pleasant to the eye than green Grass kept finely shorn," but it was apparently to be found only in the orchard, the bowling-green, or the "wilderness"; in the flower-garden proper it had no place. The "knots" were generally raised above the surface of the paths, the earth being kept in its place by borders of lead, or tiles, or wood, or even bones; but sometimes the beds and paths were on the same level, and then there were the same edgings that we now use, as Thrift, Box, Ivy, flints, &c. The paths were made of gravel, sand, spar, &c., and sometimes with coloured earths: but against this Bacon made a vigorous protest: "As to the making of knots or figures with divers coloured earths, that they may lie under the windows of the house on that side on which the garden stands they be but toys; you may see as good sights many times in tarts."

The old gardening books are full of designs for these knots; indeed, no gardening book of the date seems to have been considered complete if it did not give the "latest designs," and they seem to have much tried the wit and ingenuity of the gardeners, as they must have also sorely tried their patience to keep them in order; and I doubt not that the efficiency of an Elizabethan gardener was as much tested by his skill and experience in "knot-work," as the efficiency of a modern gardener is tested by his skill in "bedding-out," which is the lineal descendant of "knot-work." In one most essential point, however, the two systems very much differed. In "bedding-out" the whole force of the system is spent in producing masses of colours, the individual flowers being of no importance, except so far as each flower contributes its little share of colour to the general mass; and it is for this reason that so many of us dislike the system, not only because of its monotony, but more especially because it has a tendency "to teach us to think too little about the plants individually, and to look at them chiefly as an assemblage of beautiful colours. It is difficult in those blooming masses to separate one from another; all produce so much the same sort of impression. The consequence is people

see the flowers on the beds without caring to know anything about them
or even to ask their names. It was different in the older gardens, because
there was just variety there; the plants strongly contrasted with each
other, and we were ever passing from the beautiful to the curious. Now
we get little of quaintness or mystery, or of the strange delicious thought
of being lost or embosomed in a tall rich wood of flowers. All is clear,
definite, and classical, the work of a too narrow and exclusive taste."—
FORBES WATSON. The old "knot-work" was not open to this censure,
though no doubt it led the way which ended in "bedding-out." The beginning of the system crept in very shortly after Shakespeare's time.
Parkinson spoke of an arrangement of spring flowers which, when "all
planted in some proportion as near one unto another as is fit for them,
will give such a grace to the garden that the place will seem like a piece
of tapestry of many glorious colours, to encrease every one's delight."
And again—"The Tulipas may be so matched, one colour answering and
setting off another, that the place where they stand may resemble a piece
of curious needlework or piece of painting." But these plants were all
perennial, and remained where they were once planted, and with this
one exception named by Parkinson, the planting of knot-work was as
different as possible from the modern planting of carpet-beds. The beds
were planted inside their thick margins with a great variety of plants,
and apparently set as thick as possible, like Harrison's garden quoted
above, with its 300 separate plants in as many square feet. These were
nearly all hardy perennials, with the addition of a few hardy annuals, and
the great object seems to have been to have had something of interest or
beauty in these gardens at all times of the year. The principle of the old
gardeners was that "Nature abhors a vacuum," and, so far as their gardens went, they did their best to prevent a vacuum occurring at any time.
In this way I think they surpassed us in their practical gardening, for,
even if they did not always succeed, it was surely something for them to
aim (in Bacon's happy words) "to have *ver perpetuum* as the place
affords."

Where the space would allow of it, the garden was further
decorated with statues, fountains, "fair mounts," labyrinths, mazes,
arbours and alcoves, rocks, "great Turkey jars," and "in some corner (or
more) a true Dial or Clock, and some Antick works" (LAWSON). These
things were fitting ornaments in such formal gardens, but the best judges
saw that they were not necessaries, and that the garden was complete
without them. "They be pretty things to look on, but nothing for health
or sweetness." "Such things are for state and magnificence, but nothing
to the true pleasure of a garden."

Such was the Elizabethan garden in its general outlines; the sort of garden which Shakespeare must have often seen both in Warwickshire and in London. According to our present ideas such a garden would be too formal and artificial, and we may consider that the present fashion of our gardens is more according to Milton's idea of Eden, in which there grew—

> Flowers worthy of Paradise, which not nice art,
> In beds and curious knots, but Nature boon
> Poured forth profuse on hill and dale and plaine.
>
> *Paradise Lost*, Book iv

None of us probably would now wish to exchange the straight walks and level terraces of the sixteenth century for our winding walks and undulating lawns, in the laying out of which the motto has been "ars est celare artem"—

> That which all faire workes doth most aggrace,
> The art, which all that wrought, appeareth in no place.
>
> *F. Q.*, ii. xii. 58

Yet it is pleasant to look back upon these old gardens, and to see how they were cherished and beloved by some of the greatest and noblest of Englishmen. Spenser has left on record his judgment on the gardens of his day—

> To the gay gardens his unstaid desire
> Him wholly carried, to refresh his sprights;
> There lavish Nature, in her best attire,
> Poures forth sweete odors and alluring sights:
> And Arte, with her contending, doth aspire
> To excell the naturall with made delights;
> And all, that faire or pleasant may be found,
> In riotous excesse doth there abound.
>
> .   .   .   .   .
>
> There he arriving around about doth flie,
> From bed to bed, from one to other border;
> And takes survey, with curious busie eye,
> Of every flowre and herbe there set in order.
>
> *Muiopotmos*

Clearly in Spenser's eyes the formalities of an Elizabethan garden (for we must suppose he had such in his thoughts) did not exclude nature or beauty.

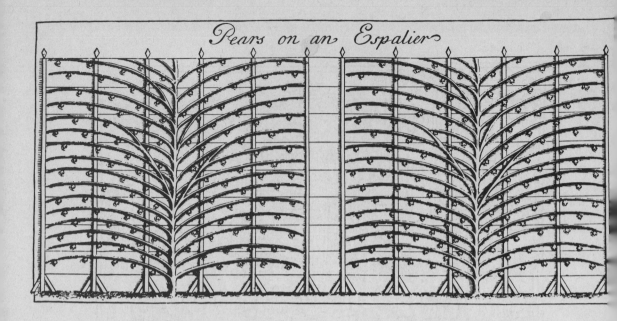

Pears on an Espalier

Habit de Jardinier,

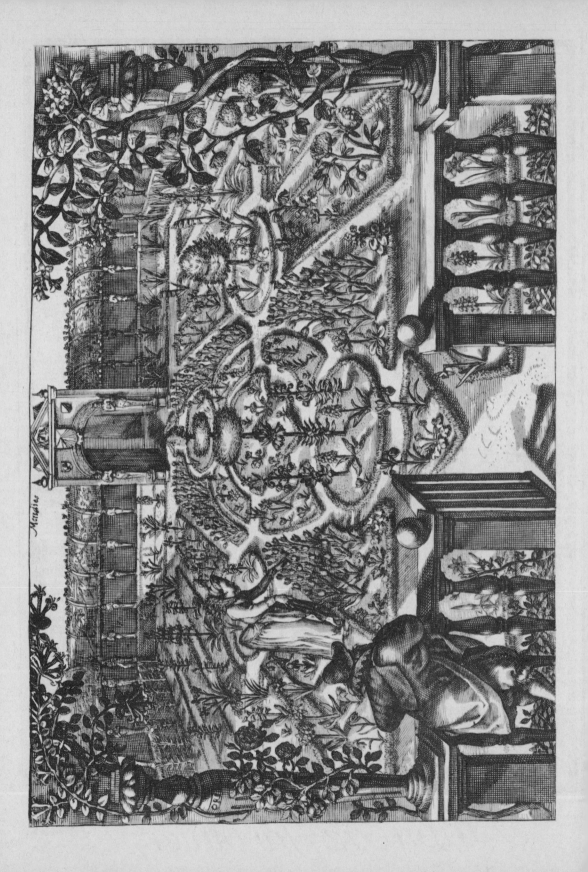

It was also with such formal gardens in his mind and before his eyes that Bacon wrote his "Essay on Gardens," and commenced it with the well-known sentence (for I must quote him once again for the last time), "God Almighty first planted a garden, and indeed it is the purest of all human pleasures; it is the greatest refreshment to the spirits of man, without which buildings and palaces are but gross handiworks; and a man shall ever see, that when ages grow to civility and elegance, men come to build stately sooner than to garden finely, as if gardening were the greater perfection." And, indeed, in spite of their stiffness and unnaturalness, there must have been a great charm in those gardens, and though it would be antiquarian affectation to attempt or wish to restore them, yet there must have been a stateliness about them which our gardens have not, and they must have had many points of real comfort which it seems a pity to have lost. Those long shady "covert alleys," with their "thick-pleached" sides and roof, must have been very pleasant places to walk in, giving shelter in winter, and in summer deep shade, with the pleasant smell of Sweet Brier and Roses. They must have been the very places for a thoughtful student, who desired quiet and retirement for his thoughts—

> And adde to these retired leisure
> That in trim gardens takes his pleasure
> > *Il Penseroso*

and they must have been also "pretty retiring places for conference" for friends in council. The whole fashion of the Elizabethan garden has passed away, and will probably never be revived; but before we condemn it as a ridiculous fashion, unworthy of the science of gardening, we may remember that it held its ground in England for more than two hundred years, and that during that time the gardens of England and the flowers they bore won not the cold admiration, but the warm affection of the greatest names in English history, the affection of such a queen as Elizabeth, of such a grave and wise philosopher as Bacon, of such a grand hero as Raleigh, of such poets as Spenser and Shakespeare.

HENRY N. ELLACOMBE
[*The Plant Lore and Garden Craft of Shakespeare* (1878)]

Advice to an Elizabethan Gardener

[*The Elizabethan pamphleteer Gervase Markham wrote on so many subjects that one suspects him of undertaking whatever he thought would sell. For that very reason his writings about horticulture are excellent evidence of a widespread interest in gardens.*]

I T is a commendable and seemly thing to behold out at a window many acres of ground well-tilled and husbanded; but yet it is much more to behold fair and comely proportions, handsome and pleasant arbors, and, as it were, closets, delightful borders of lavender, rosemary, box and other such-like; to hear the ravishing music of an infinite number of pretty, small birds, which continually, day and night, do chatter and chant their proper and natural branch-songs upon the hedges and trees of the garden; and to smell so sweet a nosegay so near at hand, seeing that this so fragrant a smell cannot but refresh the lord of the farm exceedingly when going out of his bedchamber in the morning after sunrise; and while as yet the clear and pearl-like dew doth perch on to the grass he giveth himself to hear the melodious music of the bees which do fill the air with a most acceptable sweet and pleasant harmony.

Now for the general proportion of gardens. They may at your pleasure carry any of these four shapes: that is to say, either square, round, oval, or diamond. This is but the outward proportion, or the verge and girdle of your garden. As for the inward proportions and shapes of the Quarters, Beds, Banks, Mounts, and such-like, they are to be divided by Alleys, Hedges, Borders, Rails, Pillars and such-like; and by these you may draw your garden unto what form you please, not respecting whatsoever shape the outward verge carrieth. For you may make that garden which is square without to be round within, and that which is round, either square, or oval; that which is oval, either of the former, and that which is diamond any shape at all—and yet all exceedingly comely. You may also, if your ground be naturally so situated, or if your industry please so to bring it to pass, make your garden rise and mount by several degrees, one level ascending above another, in such sort as if you had divers gardens one above another, which is exceedingly beautiful to the eye and very beneficial to your flowers and fruit-trees, especially if such ascents have the benefit of the Sun rising upon them; and thus, if you please, you may have in one level a square plot; in another, a round, in a third a diamond; and in a fourth, an oval; then amongst the ascending banks, which are on either side the stairs, you mount into your several gardens, you shall make your physic garden or places to plant your physic herbs. . . .

The Garden of Pleasure shall be set about and compassed with arbors made of jessamin, rosemarie, box, juniper, cypress-trees, savin, cedars, rose-trees and other dainties first planted and pruned according as the nature of every one doth require, but after brought into some form and order with willow or juniper poles, such as may serve for the making of arbors. The ways and alleys must be covered and sown with fine sand well beat, or with the powder of the sawing of marble, or else paved handsomely with good pit stone.

This garden, by means of a large path of the breadth of six feet, shall be divided into two equal parts; the one shall contain the herbs and flowers used to make nosegays and garlands of, as March violets, Provence gilliflowers, purple gilliflowers, Indian gilliflowers, small pansies, daisies, yellow and white gilliflowers, marigolds, lily connally, daffodils, Canterbury bells, purple velvet flowers, anemones, corn-flag, mugwort, lilies and other such-like; and it may be indeed the Nosegay Garden.

The other part shall have all other sweet-smelling herbs whether they be such as bear no flowers, or, if they bear any, yet they are not put in nosegays alone, but the whole herb be with them, as Southernwood, wormwood, pellitory, rosemary, jessamine, marierom, balmmints, pennyroyal, costmarie, hyssop, lavender, basil, sage, savory, rue, tansy, thyme, camomile, mugwort, bastard marierum, nept, sweet balm, all-good, anis, horehound and other such-like; and this may be called the garden for herbs and good smell.

These sweet herbs and flowers for nosegays shall be set in order upon beds and quarters of such-like length and breadth as those of the kitchen garden; others in mazes made for the pleasing and recreating of the sight, and other some are set in proportions made of beds interlaced and drawn one within another or broken off with borders, or without borders.

. . . .

There is to be required at the hands of every perfect Gardiner three especiall vertues, that is to say, Diligence, Industry and Art: the two first, as namely, Diligence (under which word I comprehend his love, care and delight in the vertue hee professeth) and Industry (under which word I conclude his labour, paine, and study, which are the onely testimonies of his perfection) he must reape from Nature: for if he be not inclined, even from the strength of his blood to this love and labour, it is impossible he should ever prove an absolute Gardiner.

GERVASE MARKHAM
[*Country Farm* (1616)
and *The English Husbandman* (1613)]

Do It Yourself

[*William Lawson's description of what to look for in a gardener seems designed to lead up to his final suggestion—perhaps you had best "do it yourself."*]

⚹

WHOSOEVER desireth and endeavoureth to have a Pleasant and Profitable Orchard, must (if he be able) provide himself of a Fruiterer, Religious, Honest, Skilfull in that facultie, and therwithall painfull: By religious, I mean (because many think religion but a fashion or custome to goe to Church) maintaining, and cherishing things religious; as Schooles of Learning, Churches, Tythes, Church-goods, and rights; and above all thinges, God's word, and the Preachers thereof, so much as hee is able, practising prayers, comfortable conference, mutuall instruction to edifie, almes, and other workes of Charity, and all out of a good conscience.

Honestie in a Gardner, will grace your Garden, and all your house and help to stay unbrideled Serving-men, giving offence to none, not calling your name into question by dishonest acts, nor infecting your family by evill counsell or example. For there is no plague so infectious as Popery and Knavery, hee will not purloin your profite, nor hinder your pleasures.

Concerning his skill, hee must not be a Scholist, to make shew of, or take in hand that, which he cannot performe, especially in so weighty a thing as an Orchard: then the which, there can be no humane thing more excellent, eyther for pleasure or profit. And what an hinderance shall it bee, not only to the owner but to the common good, that the unspeakable benefits of many hundred yeares, shall be lost, by th' audacious attempt of an unskilful Arborist.

The Gardener had not need be an idle or lazy Lubber, for so your Orchard, being a matter of such moment, will not prosper, there will ever be something to do. Weeds are alwaies growing, the great Mother of all living Creatures, the Earth, is full of Seed in her Bowels, and any stirring gives them heat of Sun, and being laid near day, they grow: Moles work daily, though not alwaies alike: Winter Herbs at all times will grow (except in extream Frost). In Winter your Trees and Herbs would be lightened of Snow, and your Allies cleansed: drifts of Snow will set Deer, Hares and Conies, and other noysome Beasts, over your Walls and Hedges into your Orchard. When Summer cloaths your Borders with Green and speckled colours, your Gardener must dress his hedges, and antick works; watch his Bees, and hive them: Distill his Roses and other Herbs. Now begin Summer Fruits to ripen, and crave your hand to pull them. If he have a Garden (as he must needs) to keep, you must needs allow him good help, to end his labours which are endless; for no one man is sufficient for these things.

Such a gardner as will conscionably, quietly and patiently, travell in your Orchard, God shall crowne the labors of his hands with ioyfulnesse, and make the cloudes droppe fatnesse upon your Trees, hee will provoke your love, and earne his Wages, and fees belonging to his place: The house being served, fallen fruict, superfluity of hearbes, and floures, seedes, grasses, sets, and besides all other of that Fruit which your bountifull hand shall award him withall: will much augment his Wages, and the profite of your bees will paye you backe againe.

If you bee not able, nor willing to hyre a gardner, keepe your profites to your selfe, but then you must take all the paines.

WILLIAM LAWSON
[*A New Orchard and Garden* (1618)]

The Formal Garden in England

[*During the seventeenth century English gardens grew steadily more elaborate and more formal until, by the end of the century, the "Dutch style," which favored an intricately geometrical layout of beds, had triumphed and a garden often resembled what we are accustomed to see in a city park.*]

T H E characteristic of the old formal garden, the garden of Markham and Lawson, was its exceeding simplicity.

The primary purpose of a garden as a place of retirement and seclusion, a place for quiet thought and leisurely enjoyment was kept steadily in view. The grass and the yew-trees were trimmed close to gain their full beauty from the sunlight.

Sweet kindly flowers filled the knots and borders. Peacocks and pigeons brightened the terraces and lawns. The paths were straight and ample, the garden-house solidly built and comfortable; everything was reasonable and unaffected. But this simple genuine delight in nature and art became feebler as the seventeenth century grew older.

Gardening became the fashionable art, and this was the golden age for professional gardeners; but the real pleasure of it was gone. Rows of statues were introduced from the French, costly architecture superseded the simple terrace, intricate parterres were laid out from gardeners' pattern-books, and meanwhile the flowers were forgotten. It was well that all this pomp should be swept away. We do not want this extravagant statuary, these absurdities in clipped work, this aggressive prodigality. But though one would admit that in its decay the formal garden became unmanageable and absurd, the abuse is no argument against the use. An attempt has been made in this book to show the essential reasonableness of the principles of Formal Gardening, and the sanity of its method when properly handled. The long yew-hedge is clipped and shorn because we want its firm boundary lines and the plain mass of its colour; the grass bank is formed into a definite slope to attain the beauty of close-shaven turf at varied angles with the light. The broad grass walk, with its paved footpath in the centre, is cool to walk upon in summer and dry on the pavement in winter; and the flower border on either side is planted with every kind of delightful flower, so that the refinements of its colour may be enjoyed all through the summer.

REGINALD BLOMFIELD
AND INIGO THOMAS
[*The Formal Garden in England* (1901)]

The Bourbon Garden

[*The formality of the garden reached its ultimate extreme in France and, specifically, at Versailles and the other royal gardens. Here the parterres were laid out in absurdly intricate geometrical designs which, as pictured in the garden books, look like carpets rather than flower beds. "A parterre," wrote the great contemporary theoretician Dezallier d'Argenville, whose work on the theory and practice of gardening was published under the name of Alexandre Le Blond, "is the first thing that should present itself to the sight"; and for the parterres in the Dauphin's garden Louis XIV ordered, in 1698, 87,000 tulips, 800 tuberoses, 400 lilies and 83,000 narcissus. Le Blond gave many precise rules, such as that the length of the garden should be one and one half times its breadth; that there should be two principal walks at right angles; and that, after the open space directly in front of the house, the remainder of the garden should be laid out with "Designs of tall groves, quincunxes, close-walks, galleries and halls of verdure, green-arbours, labyrinths, bowling-greens, amphitheatres adorned with fountains, canals, figures etc."*

The English never followed the French style to its own extreme, perhaps because it was actually related to the formality of the French court. During the eighteenth century the great English estates turned to a freer form of landscaping instead, though they did borrow from the French what was called in England a "ha-ha"—an invisible ditch serving the purpose of a fence.

Nevertheless, the English must have known all about the theory of the purely formal garden, since "Le Blond's" work was published in a handsome translation in 1712.]

UPON examining most Authors who have writ of Agriculture and Gardening, I found none of them had enlarged upon the Subject I determined to treat of. This, at first, had almost discouraged me from an Undertaking, in which I could hope for no Assistance from others, it being easy to go wrong where no-body has beaten the Way. As I may, then, without Vanity, say, this Work has something New in it, I hope, the Reader will more readily excuse the Faults that shall be found therein: Some more able Hand may possibly come after, and give the finishing Stroke to that which I propose but a Sketch of.

My Design being to write of Gardens, which may properly be called Pleasure-Gardens; that is to say, those that we take care to keep with the greatest Delicacy and Neatness, and where we expect to find Regularity, good Order, and whatever may most please the Eye, as Parterres, Groves, and Grass-Plots, set off with Portico's, and Cabinets of Arbor-work, Figures, Fountains, Cascades, &c. For my Information in this Point, I have neglected nothing, having read a great many *Latin, Italian, French,* and *Spanish* Authors on the Subject of Gardening; the Reading of whom, tho' good in itself, has, however, been of no great Service to me in this Case. Among the *French,* we have but two or three Authors that have spoke of fine Gardens, and they have done no more than lightly touch'd upon them; besides, that the Designs they give at the end of their Books are of very mean Gusto, and such as are now quite out of Use. Other Writers of Agriculture have thought this Matter unworthy of their Pen: Some speaking of the pruning of Fruit-Trees; of the Culture of Kitchen-Gardens; of Botanicks, and the Nature of Simples; of Flower-Gardens, Orange-Trees, &c. Others of Tillage, and Manuring of Ground; of the Duty of a good Housholder, Farmer, and Husbandman; of the Vineyard and Vintage; of Fishing and Hunting; of Cookery, and making all sorts of Sweetmeats; in all which may be seen the Difference between this Work and theirs.

The great Love I always had for Agriculture and Gardening; the Abode I made at *Paris* and *Versailles,* whose neighbouring Parts contain so many Wonders of this Nature; the Satisfaction I found in surveying all those Beauties; and the Pains I have taken in planting several fine Gardens, induced me to make proper Remarks from time to time. Nature, that I have so often consulted; Proofs of Soil; long Experience; and the Conversation of the most Able in the Profession, may be allowed to have given me some Light in this Affair; and the considerable Mistakes and unneccessary Expence I have observ'd in many Gardens, join'd with the Ignorance of most Gardeners, made me, at length, resolve to communicate my Observations to the Publick.

I cannot but admire, that among so many as have written of Fruit and Kitchen-Gardens, there should be none hitherto, that have spoken fully of Pleasure-Gardens, which, without Controversy, are the most beautiful and most noble of all others; notwithstanding what a late Author has said, who strives to give the former the Preference. In truth, nothing can be more pleasant and agreeable than a handsome Garden, rightly disposed, and well kept; no Prospect yields more Delight to the Eye, or gives greater Satisfaction to Persons of a good Taste.

'Tis not my Design, to condemn Fruit and Kitchen-Gardens; they are valuable in their Place, and, I agree, are as necessary to make up a complete Garden, as the finest Groves and Parterres: We have Instances of this, in the most magnificent Gardens that are, where the former are as curious in their Kind, as the latter. Nevertheless, all these Kitchen and Fruit-Gardens, how fine soever, are constantly set in Byplaces, distinct from the other Gardens; an evident Proof that they are rather accounted necessary for the Service of the House, than designed to improve the Beauty and Magnificence. These are Things should be sought after, if one would see them, and ought never to present themselves first to sight in a handsome Garden.

I am very sensible, every one will not join with me in this Opinion; especially those who have written of Fruit, and such as are great Lovers of it: These make the Perfection of the Art of Gardening, and the whole Beauty of a Garden, to consist of a Kitchen-Ground, a Fruit-Garden planted in *Quincunce*, and in long Espaliers, for the Satisfaction of gathering from them a Pear or Peach. 'Tis to this they confine and limit their utmost Desires in the Business of Gardening; and as for Parterres, Groves, and the like, they have no manner of Esteem for them.

These Men conceit too, that because they can prune a Fruit-Tree, and make a Kitchen-Bed, they are perfectly skill'd in what relates to Pleasure-Gardens, whose Disposition and Culture are very different from the other.

I do not suppose this Work can be of any great Service to such Persons; they are wholly ignorant of the Beauties it treats of; and Interest with them is above all other Considerations: They would rather have a Garden, like a Plain Field, stock'd with Apple-Trees, Cherry-Trees, &c. or, like a Marsh, fill'd with Kitchen-Garden Stuff, than enjoy that which is truly beautiful and magnificent. This Spirit of Interest, however, is not general, nor to be charged upon Persons of greater and more elevated Minds; for whose sake, partly, I profess to have written, to further their noble Intentions, and to make way for their good Taste to shew itself in Publick. I flatter myself, this Treatise may be of use to such, and may conduct them aright in the planting of a handsome Garden. This, at least, I am sure of, That such a Garden, as I propose in the following Chapters, shall do a private Man more Credit, than the finest Fruit and Kitchen-Gardens in the World; which, in truth, seem to argue, that their Master has more regard to his Profit, than to any other Consideration.

Supposing, then, that a private Person, wealthy, and curious in the Art of Gardening, would be at the necessary Expence of planting a handsome Garden, I lead him, step by step, from the Choice he ought to make of a good Soil, to the Execution and highest Perfection of his Garden, instructing him in whatever he ought to know, that he be not impos'd upon by the Countrymen and Artificers he shall have occasion to employ.

I shew him the way to know good Plants, and to set and raise them in little time: I instruct him to make Basons, and Fountains with Water-spouts, to convey Water into his Gardens; to dispose the Terrasses, Stairs, &c. and, above all, to form a right Taste of what concerns the general Dispositions of Gardens, and the Designs of Parterres, Grass-Plots, Groves, Arbor-work, Cascades, and other suitable Ornaments. . . .

I purpose likewise to give this Gentleman so full Instructions in the Business of Gardening, that he may be able of himself to make his Ground, and to lay out and trace his Garden with his Domesticks, without being obliged to have recourse to those of the Trade. But to this end, he must be a Lover of the Country, and of Agriculture; a Knowledge so agreeable, and always so much esteem'd by Persons of the greatest Quality, that many Princes have not disdain'd, after the Fatigues of War, to apply themselves to it; and the Ancients, especially, held it in very great Reputation. . . .

Four fundamental Maxims to be observ'd.

Art must give place to Nature.

Gardens should not be made dull and gloomy, by clouding them with Thickets and too much Cover. Fine Openings should be preserved about the Building, and in other places where the Prospect of the Country can be seen to advantage.

Gardens should not lay too open, so that it is needless to go into them to see them; you discover the whole at one View from the Vestibule of the House without troubling yourself to walk in them. The pleasure of a Garden is to have the View stopt in certain places, that you may be led on with Delight to see the more agreeable Parts of it, as fine Groves of Woodwork, Green-Halls adorned with Fountains and Figures etc. Those great flat Parts rob us of the Woods which make the Contrariety and Change in a Garden, and which alone make all the rest valuable.

A Garden should always look bigger than it really is

ALEXANDRE LE BLOND
[*The Theory and Practice of Gardening,*
TRANSLATED BY JOHN JAMES (1712)]

An Englishman in France

[*In France the size, the formality, and the lavishness of the royal gardens exceeded anything attempted in England. John Evelyn, though a true-born Englishman and himself more interested in forests than in either flowers or French elegance, seems nevertheless to have been profoundly impressed by the Tuileries in 1644.*]

I FINISHED this day with a walk in the great garden of the Thuilleries, which is rarely contrived for privacy, shade, or company, by groves, plantations of tall trees, especially that in the middle, being of elmes, another of mulberys. There is a labyrinth of cypresse, noble hedges of pomegranates, fountains, fishponds, and an aviary. Here is an artificial echo, redoubling the words distinctly, and it is never without some faire nymph singing to it. Standing at one of the focus's, which is under a tree, or little cabinet of hedges, the voice seems to descend from the clouds; at another, as if it were underground. This being at the bottom of the garden, we were let into another which being kept with all imaginable accuratenesse as to the orangery, precious shrubes, and rare fruites seem'd a paradise. From a terrace in this place we saw so many coaches, as one would hardly think could be maintained in the whole City, going, late as it was in the year, towards the course, which is a place adjoyning, of neere an English mile long, planted with four rows of trees, making a large circle in the middle. This course is walled about, neere breast high, with squared freestone, and has a stately arch at the entrance, with sculpture and statues about it, built by Mary di Medices. Here it is that the gallants and ladys of the Court take the ayre and divert themselves, as with us in Hide Park, the circle being capable of containing an hundred coaches to turne commodiously, and the larger of the plantations for five or six coaches a brest.

JOHN EVELYN
[*Diary* (1644)]

"The Spectator" Preaches Simplicity

[*We generally think (correctly enough) that in all the arts the ideal of regularity, "correctness" and "decorum" was most clearly triumphant in England during the first two decades of the eighteenth century. Those decades thought of themselves as being—as they have ever since been called—"the Augustan Age." But the romantic revolt was already brewing and a renewed admiration for "simplicity" was one of the elements of romanticism. Though no one was more Augustan than Joseph Addison and the spirit of the age nowhere more characteristically revealed than in the periodical essays which he and Richard Steele presented under the signature of "The Spectator," Addison was among the first to suggest that gardens should imitate what he thought of as "the simplicity of nature." The second of the two following selections from* The Spectator *purports to be a letter to the editor but was written by Addison himself.*]

WRITERS who have given us an account of China, tell us the inhabitants of that country laugh at the plantations of our Europeans, which are laid out by the rule and line; because they say, any one may place trees in equal rows and uniform figures.

They choose rather to shew a genius in works of this nature, and therefore always conceal the art by which they direct themselves. They have a word, it seems, in their language, by which they express the particular beauty of a plantation, that thus strikes the imagination at first sight, without discovering what it is, that has so agreeable an effect.

Our British gardeners, on the contrary, instead of humouring nature, love to deviate from it as much as possible. Our trees rise in cones, globes, and pyramids. We see the marks of the scissors upon every plant and bush. I do not know whether I am singular in my opinion, but for my own part, I would rather look upon a tree in all its luxuriancy and diffusion of boughs and branches, than when it is thus cut and trimmed into a mathematical figure: and cannot but fancy that an orchard in flower looks infinitely more delightful, than all the little labyrinths of the most finished parterre. But as our great modellers of gardens have their magazines of plants to dispose of, it is very natural for them to tear up all the beautiful plantations of fruit trees, and contrive a plan that may most turn to their own profit, in taking off their evergreens, and the like movable plants, with which their shops are plentifully stocked.

I have often looked upon it as a piece of happiness that I have never fallen into any of these fantastical tastes, nor esteemed anything the more for its being uncommon and hard to be met with. For this reason I look upon the whole country in Springtime as a spacious garden, and make as many visits to a spot of daisies, or a bank of violets, as a florist does to his borders or parterres.

There is not a bush in blossom within a mile of me, which I am not acquainted with, nor scarce a daffodil or cowslip that withers away in my neighbourhood without my missing it. I walked home in this temper of mind through several fields and meadows with an unspeakable pleasure, not without reflecting on the bounty of providence, which has made the most pleasing and most beautiful objects the most ordinary and most common.

JOSEPH ADDISON
[*The Spectator*, No. 414 and *The Tatler*, No. 218]

SIR,

Having lately read your essay on the pleasures of the imagination, I was so taken with your thoughts upon some of our English gardens, that I cannot forbear troubling you with a letter upon that subject. I am one, you must know, who am looked upon as an humourist in gardening. I have several acres about my house, which I call my garden, and which a skilful gardener would not know what to call. It is a confusion of kitchen and parterre, orchard and flower-garden, which lie so mixt and interwoven with one another, that if a foreigner, who had seen nothing of our country, should be conveyed into my garden at his first landing, he would look upon it as a natural wilderness, and one of the uncultivated parts of our country. My flowers grow up in several parts of the garden in the greatest luxuriancy and profusion. I am so far from being fond of any particular one, by reason of its rarity, that if I meet with any one in a field which pleases me, I give it a place in my garden. By this means, when a stranger walks with me, he is surprised to see several large spots of ground covered with ten thousand different colours, and has often singled out flowers that he might have met with under a common hedge, in a field or in a meadow, as some of the greatest beauties of the place. The only method I observe in this particular, is to range in the same quarter the products of the same season, that may make their appearance together, and compose a picture of the greatest variety. There is the same irregularity in my plantations, which run into as great a wildness as their nature will permit. I take in none that do not naturally rejoice in the soil, and am pleased when I am walking in a labyrinth of my own raising, not to know whether the next tree I shall meet with is an apple or an oak, an elm or a pear-tree. My kitchen has likewise its particular quarters assigned it; for besides the wholesome luxury which that place abounds with, I have always thought a kitchen-garden a more pleasant sight than the finest orangery or artificial green-house. I love to see every thing in its perfection, and am more pleased to survey my rows of colworts and cabbages, with a thousand nameless pot-herbs, springing up in their full fragrancy and verdure, than to see the tender plants of foreign countries kept alive by artificial heats, or withering in an air and soil that are not adapted to them. I must not omit, that there is a fountain rising in the upper part of my garden, which forms a little wandring rill, and administers to the pleasure as well as the plenty of the place. I have so conducted it, that it visits most of my plantation; and have taken particular care to let it run in the same manner as it would do in an open field, so that it generally passes through banks of violets and primroses, plats of willow, or other plants, that seem to be of its own producing. There is another circumstance in which I am very particular, or as my neighbours call me, very whimsical: As my garden invites into it all the birds of the country, by offering them the conveniency of springs and shades, solitude and shelter, I do not suffer any one to destroy their nests in the spring, or drive them from their usual haunts in fruit-time, I value my garden more for being full of blackbirds than cherries, and very frankly give them fruit for their songs. By this means I have always the music of the season in its perfection, and am highly delighted to see the jay or the thrush hopping about my walks, and shooting before my eyes across the several little glades and alleys that I pass through. I think there are as many kinds of gardening as of poetry: Your makers of parterres and flower-gardens are epigrammatists and sonneteers in this art: contrivers of bowers and grottoes, treillages and cascades, are romance writers. Wise and London are our heroic poets; and if, as a critic, I may single out any passage of their works to commend, I shall take notice of that part in the upper garden, at Kensington, which was at first nothing but a gravel pit. It must have been a fine genius for gardening, that could have thought of forming such an unsightly hollow into so beautiful an area, and to have hit the eye with so uncommon and agreeable a scene as that which it is now wrought into. To give this particular spot of ground the greater effect, they have made a very pleasing contrast; for as on one side of the walk you see this hollow basin, with its several little plantations, lying so conveniently under the eye of the beholder; on the other side of it there appears a seeming mount, made up of trees rising one higher than another in proportion as they approach the center. A spectator who has not heard this account of it, would think this circular mount was not only a real one, but that it had been actually scooped out of that hollow space which I have before mentioned. I never yet met with any one who has walked in this garden, who was not struck with that part of it which I have here mentioned. As for myself, you will find, by the account which I have already given you, that my compositions in gardening are altogether after the *Pindaric* manner, and run into the beautiful wildness of nature, without affecting the nicer elegancies of art. What I am now going to mention, will, perhaps, deserve your attention more than any thing I have yet said. I find that in the discourse which I spoke of at the beginning of my letter, you are against filling an *English* garden with ever-greens; and indeed I am so far of your opinion, that I can by no means think the verdure of an ever green comparable to that which shoots out annually, and clothes our trees in the summer-season. But I have often wondered that those who are like myself, and love to live in gardens, have never thought of contriving a *Winter-garden*, which would consist of such trees only as never cast their leaves. We have very often little comfortable parts of the year, and have frequently several days in November and January that are as agreeable as any in the finest months. At such times, therefore, I think there could not be a greater pleasure, than to walk in such a *Winter-garden* as I have proposed. In the summer-season the whole country blooms, and is a kind of garden, for which reason we are not so sensible of those beauties, that at this time may be every where met with; but when nature is in her desolation, and presents us with nothing but bleak and barren prospects, there is something unspeakably cheerful in a spot of ground which is covered with trees that smile amidst all the rigour of winter, and give us a view of the most gay season in the midst of that which is the most dead and melancholy. I have so far indulged myself in this thought, that I have set apart a whole acre of ground for the executing of it. The walls are covered with ivy instead of vines. The laurel, the horn-beam, and the holly, with many other trees and plants of the same nature, grow so thick in it that you cannot imagine a more lively scene. The glowing redness of the berries with which they are hung at this time, vies with the verdure of their leaves, and are apt to inspire the heart of the beholder with that vernal delight which you have somewhere taken notice of in your former papers. It is very pleasant, at the same time, to see the several kinds of birds retiring into this little green spot, and enjoying themselves among the branches and foliage, when my great garden, which I have before mentioned to you, does not afford a single leaf for their shelter.

You must know, Sir, that I look upon the pleasure which we take in a garden, as one of the most innocent delights in human life. A garden was the habitation of our first parents before the fall. It is naturally apt to fill the mind with calmness and tranquility, and to lay all its turbulent passions at rest. It gives us a great insight into the contrivance and wisdom of Providence, and suggests innumerable subjects for meditation. I cannot but think the very complacency and satisfaction which a man takes in these works of nature, to be a laudable, if not a virtuous habit of mind. For all which reasons I hope you will pardon the length of my present letter.

I am,

SIR, &c.

JOSEPH ADDISON
[*The Spectator*, No. 477 (1712)]

So Does Mr. Pope

[*If any man of letters was more Augustan than Addison it was Alexander Pope. His famous grotto at Twickingham would probably not strike us as notably "natural." But all things are relative and, like Addison, he was beginning to preach simplicity in gardens.*]

H O W contrary to this simplicity (of Homer) is the modern practice of gardening! We seem to make it our study to recede from nature, not only in the various tonsure of greens into the most regular and formal shape, but even in monstrous attempts beyond the reach of the art itself: we run into sculpture, and are yet better pleased to have our trees in the most aukward figures of men and animals, than in the most regular of their own. . . .

A citizen is no sooner proprietor of a couple of yews, but he entertains thoughts of erecting them into giants, like those of Guildhall. I know an eminent cook, who beautified his country-seat with a coronation-dinner in greens, where you see the champion flourishing on horseback at one end of the table, and the Queen in perpetual youth at the other.

For the benefit of all my loving countrymen of this curious taste, I shall here publish a catalogue of greens to be disposed of by an eminent town-gardener, who has lately applied to me upon this head. He represents that for the advancement of a politer sort of ornament in the villas and gardens adjacent to this great city, and in order to distinguish those places from the mere barbarous countries of gross nature, the world stands much in need of a virtuoso gardener, who has a turn to sculpture, and is thereby capable of improving upon the ancients in the imagery of evergreens. I proceed to this catalogue:

Adam and Eve in yew; Adam a little shattered by the fall of the tree of Knowledge in the great storm; Eve and the serpent very flourishing.

Noah's Ark in holly, the ribs a little damaged for want of water.

The tower of Babel not yet finished.

St. George in Box; his arm scarce long enough, but will be in a condition to stick the dragon by next April.

A green dragon of the same, with a tail of ground-ivy for the present.

N.B.—Those two are not to be sold separately.

Edward the Black Prince in Cypress. . . .

A Queen Elizabeth in Phyllirea, a little inclining to the Green sickness, but of full growth. . . .

An old Maid of Honour in wormwood.

A topping Ben Jonson in Laurel.

Divers eminent modern poets in bays, somewhat blighted, to be disposed of a penny worth.

I can afford room for your self and two servants; I have indeed room enough, nothing but myself at home; the kind and hearty house-wife is dead! the agreeable and instructive neighbour is gone! yet my house is inlarg'd, and the gardens extend and flourish, as knowing nothing of the guests they have lost. I have more fruit-trees and kitchen garden than you have any thought of; nay I have good Melons and Pine-apples of my own growth. I am as much a better Gardiner, as I am a worse Poet, than when you saw me: but gardening is near a-kin to Philosophy, for Tully says "Agricultura proxima sapientiae." For God's sake why should not you (that are a step higher than a philosopher, a Divine, yet have too much grace and wit than to be a Bishop) e'en give all you have to the poor of Ireland (for whom you have already done everything else) so quit the place, and live and die with me? And let "Tales Animae Concordes" be our Motto and our Epitaph.

Let the young ladies be assured I make nothing new in my gardens, without wishing to see the print of their fairy steps in every part of them. I have put the last hand to my works of this kind, in happily finishing the subterraneous way and grotto. I there found a spring of the clearest water, which falls in a perpetual rill, that echoes through the Cavern day and night. From the river Thames, you see through my arch up a walk of the wilderness, to a kind of open temple, wholly composed of shells in the rustic manner; and from that distance under the temple, you look down through a sloping arcade of trees, and see the sails on the river passing suddenly and vanishing as through a perspective glass. When you shut the doors of this grotto it becomes on the instant, from a luminous room, a *Camera obscura*, on the walls of which all the objects of the river, hills, woods and boats are forming a moving picture in their visible radiations; and when you have a mind to light it up, it affords you a very different scene. It is finished with shells interspersed with pieces of looking-glass in angular forms; and in the ceiling is a star of the same material, at which when a lamp, of an orbicular figure of thin alabaster, is hung in the middle, a thousand pointed rays glitter, and are reflected over the place. There are connected to this grotto by a narrower passage two porches with niches and seats—one towards the river, of smooth stones, full of light, and open; the other towards the arch of trees, rough with shells, flints and iron-ore. The bottom is paved with simple pebble, as the adjoining walk up the wilderness to the temple is to be cockle-shells, in the natural taste, agreeing not ill with the little dripping murmur, and the acquatic idea of the whole place. It wants nothing to complete it but a good Statue with an inscription, like that beautiful antique one which you know I am so fond of:

Nymph of the Grot, those sacred springs steep,
And to the murmur of these waters sleep;
Ah, spare my slumbers, gently tread the cave!
And drink in silence, or in silence lave.

My Lord Chesterfield tells me your Lordship has got ahead of all the gardening lords; that you have distanced Lord Burlington and Lord Cobham in the true scientific past; but he is studying after you, and has here lying before him those Thesauruses from which he affirms you draw all your knowledge—Miller's Dictionaries; but I informed him better, and told him your chief lights were from Johannes Serlius, whose books he is now enquiring for of Leake, the bookseller, who has wrote for them to his correspondents.

ALEXANDER POPE
[*The Guardian*, No. 173, and Letters to Dean Swift,
Edward Blount, and Lord Marchmont (18th century)]

A Poet's Garden

[*William Shenstone, a minor poet now remembered (if at all) only for his pleasantly sentimental poem "The Schoolmistress," was a man of some wealth who is said to have ruined himself by the expense of his elaborate country estate.*]

HERE entering a gate, you are led, thro' a thicket of many sorts of willows, into a large root-house, inscribed to the Right Honorable the Earl of Stamford. It seems, that worthy peer was present at the first opening of the cascade, which is the principal object from the root-house, where the eye is presented with a fairy vision, consisting of an irregular and romantic fall of water, very unusual, one hundred and fifty yards in continuity, and a very striking scene it affords. Other cascades may possibly have the advantage of a greater descent, and a larger torrent, but a more wild and romantic appearance of water, and at the same time strictly natural, is what I never saw in any place whatever. This scene, though comparatively small, is yet aggrandized with so much art, that we forget the quantity of water which flows through this close and overshaded vally; and are so much transported with the intricacy of scene, and the concealed height from whence it flows, that we, without reflection, add the idea of magnificence to that of beauty. In short, it is not but upon reflection that we find the stream is not a Niagara, but rather a waterfal in miniature; and that the same artifice, upon a larger scale, were there large trees instead of small ones, and a river instead of a rill, it would be capable of forming a scene that would exceed the utmost of our ideas. But I will not dwell longer upon this inimitable scene; those who would admire it properly must view it, as surely as those that view it must admire it beyond almost any thing they ever saw.

WILLIAM SHENSTONE
[*A Description of the Leasowes* (1764)]

Faint Praise

[*Dr. Samuel Johnson had very little sympathy with any of the arts except literature. In his* Lives of the Poets *he damns Shenstone's gardening with very faint praise indeed.*]

MR. DOLMAN, to whose care he was indebted for his ease and leisure, died in 1745, and the care of his own fortune now fell upon him. He tried to escape it awhile, and lived at his house with his tenants, who were distantly related; but finding that imperfect possession inconvenient, he took the whole estate into his own hands, more to the improvement of its beauty, than the increase of its produce.

   Now was excited his delight in rural pleasures, and his ambition of rural elegance: he began, from this time, to point his prospects, to diversify his surface, to entangle his walks, and to wind his waters; which he did with such judgment and such fancy, as made his little domain the envy of the great, and the admiration of the skilful; a place to be visited by travellers, and copied by designers. Whether to plant a walk in undulating curves, and to place a bench at every turn where there is an object to catch the view; to make water run where it will be heard, and to stagnate where it will be seen; to leave intervals where the eye will be pleased, and to thicken the plantation where there is something to be hidden; demands any great powers of mind, I will not inquire: perhaps a surly and sullen speculator may think such performances rather the sport than the business of human reason. But it must be at least confessed, that to embellish the form of nature is an innocent amusement; and some praise must be allowed, by the most supercilious observer, to him who does best what such multitudes are contending to do well.

SAMUEL JOHNSON
[*The Lives of the Poets* (1781)]

Tulip Mania

[*"On our way to Constantinople . . . we were passing through a region where many flowers were offered us—Narcissus, Hyacinths, and those which the Turks call Tulipan. . . . Scent in the Tulipan is either lacking or slight but they are admired for the beauty and variety of their colors. The Turks cultivate flowers with extreme zeal and though they are a careful people they do not hesitate to pay a large sum for an exceptional flower."*

The author of this passage, written in 1554, was one de Busbecq, on his way to Constantinople as ambassador to the Sultan from the Emperor Ferdinand I of Austria, and he was, so far as is known, the first European ever to see a tulip. He brought back a few bulbs which attracted so much attention—partly because of the ease with which new varieties could be produced—that less than three quarters of a century later the speculative "Tulip Mania" was sweeping Holland and before the end of the century 416 named varieties were listed. The "mania" is the setting for Dumas's romance The Black Tulip. *The selection which follows is a vivid modern account of the strange "bubble" which ultimately burst like the South Sea and the Mississippi bubbles which succeeded it.*]

T H E tulip—so named, it is said, from a Turkish word, signifying a turban—was introduced into western Europe about the middle of the sixteenth century. Conrad Gesner, who claims the merit of having brought it into repute—little dreaming of the commotion it was shortly afterwards to make in the world—says that he first saw it in the year 1559, in a garden at Augsburg, belonging to the learned Counsellor Herwart, a man very famous in his day for his collection of rare exotics. The bulbs were sent to this gentleman by a friend at Constantinople, where the flower had long been a favourite. In the course of ten or eleven years after this period, tulips were much sought after by the wealthy, especially in Holland and Germany. Rich people at

Amsterdam sent for the bulbs direct to Constantinople, and paid the most extravagant prices for them. The first roots planted in England were brought from Vienna in 1600. Until the year 1634 the tulip annually increased in reputation, until it was deemed a proof of bad taste in any man of fortune to be without a collection of them. Many learned men, including Pompeius de Angelis, and the celebrated Lipsius of Leyden, the author of the treatise "De Constantia," were passionately fond of tulips. The rage for possessing them soon caught the middle classes of society, and merchants and shopkeepers, even of moderate means, began to vie with each other in the rarity of these flowers and the preposterous prices they paid for them. A trader at Harlaem was known to pay one-half of his fortune for a single root, not with the design of selling it again at a profit, but to keep in his own conservatory for the admiration of his acquaintance.

One would suppose that there must have been some great virtue in this flower to have made it so valuable in the eyes of so prudent a people as the Dutch; but it has neither the beauty nor the perfume of the rose—hardly the beauty of the "sweet, sweet-pea"; neither is it as enduring as either. Cowley, it is true, is loud in its praise. He says—

> The tulip next appeared, all over gay,
> But wanton, full of pride, and full of play;
> The world can't show a dye but here has place;
> Nay, by new mixtures, she can change her face;
> Purple and gold are both beneath her care,
> The richest needlework she loves to wear;
> Her only study is to please the eye,
> And to outshine the rest in finery.

This, though not very poetical, is the description of a poet. Beckmann, in his *History of Inventions*, paints it with more fidelity, and in prose more pleasing than Cowley's poetry. He says, "There are few plants which acquire, through accident, weakness, or disease, so many variegations as the tulip. When uncultivated, and in its natural state, it is almost of one colour, has large leaves, and an extraordinarily long stem. When it has been weakened by cultivation, it becomes more agreeable in the eye of the florist. The petals are then paler, smaller, and more diversified in hue; and the leaves acquire a softer green colour. Thus this masterpiece of culture, the more beautiful it turns, grows so much the weaker, so that, with the greatest skill and most careful attention, it can scarcely be transplanted, or even kept alive."

Many persons grow insensibly attached to that which gives

them a great deal of trouble, as a mother often loves her sick and ever-ailing child better than her more healthy offspring. Upon the same principle we must account for the unmerited encomia lavished upon these fragile blossoms. In 1634, the rage among the Dutch to possess them was so great that the ordinary industry of the country was neglected, and the population, even to its lowest dregs, embarked in the tulip trade. As the mania increased, prices augmented, until, in the year 1635, many persons were known to invest a fortune of 100,-000 florins in the purchase of forty roots. It then became necessary to sell them by their weight in *perits*, a small weight less than a grain. A tulip of the species called *Admiral Liefken*, weighing 400 *perits*, was worth 4400 florins; an *Admiral Van der Eyck*, weighing 446 *perits*, was worth 1260 florins; a *Childer* of 106 *perits*, was worth 1615 florins; a *Viceroy* of 400 *perits*, 3000 florins; and, most precious of all, a *Semper Augustus*, weighing 200 *perits*, was thought to be very cheap at 5500 florins. The latter was much sought after, and even an inferior bulb might command a price of 2000 florins. It is related that, at one time, early in 1636, there were only two roots of this description to be had in all Holland, and those not of the best. One was in the possession of a dealer in Amsterdam, and the other in Harlaem. So anxious were the speculators to obtain them, that one person offered the fee-simple of twelve acres of building-ground for the Harlaem tulip. That of Amsterdam was bought for 4600 florins, a new carriage, two grey horses, and a complete set of harness. Munting, an industrious author of that day, who wrote a folio volume of one thousand pages upon the tulipomania, has preserved the following list of the various articles, and their value, which were delivered for one single root of the rare species called the *Viceroy:*

	florins
Two lasts of wheat	448
Four lasts of rye	558
Four fat oxen	480
Eight fat swine	240
Twelve fat sheep	120
Two Hogsheads of wine	70
Four tuns of beer	32
Two tuns of butter	192
One thousand lbs. of cheese	120
A complete bed	100
A suit of clothes	80
A silver drinking-cup	60
	2500

People who had been absent from Holland, and whose chance it was to return when this folly was at its maximum, were sometimes led into awkward dilemmas by their ignorance. There is an amusing instance of the kind related in Blainville's *Travels*. A wealthy merchant, who prided himself not a little on his rare tulips, received upon one occasion a very valuable consignment of merchandise from the Levant. Intelligence of its arrival was brought him by a sailor, who presented himself for that purpose at the counting-house, among bales of goods of every description. The merchant, to reward him for his news, munificently made him a present of a fine red herring for his breakfast. The sailor had, it appears, a great partiality for onions, and seeing a bulb very like an onion lying upon the counter of this liberal trader, and thinking it, no doubt very much out of its place among silks and velvets, he slily seized an opportunity and slipped it into his pocket, as a relish for his herring. He got clear off with his prize, and proceeded to the quay to eat his breakfast. Hardly was his back turned when the merchant missed his valuable *Semper Augustus*, worth three thousand florins, or about 280 £ sterling. The whole establishment was instantly in an uproar; search was everywhere made for the precious root, but it was not to be found. Great was the merchant's distress of mind. The search was renewed, but again without success. At last some one thought of the sailor.

The unhappy merchant sprang into the street at the bare suggestion. His alarmed household followed him. The sailor, simple soul! had not thought of concealment. He was found quietly sitting on a coil of ropes, masticating the last morsel of his "*onion*." Little did he dream that he had been eating a breakfast whose cost might have regaled a whole ship's crew for a twelvemonth; or, as the plundered merchant himself expressed it, "might have sumptuously feasted the Prince of Orange and the whole court of the Stadtholder." Anthony caused pearls to be dissolved in wine to drink the health of Cleopatra; Sir Richard Whittington was as foolishly magnificent in an entertainment to King Henry V; and Sir Thomas Gresham drank a diamond dissolved in wine to the health of Queen Elizabeth, when she opened the Royal Exchange; but the breakfast of this roguish Dutchman was as splendid as either. He had an advantage, too, over his wasteful predecessors: *their* gems did not improve the taste or the wholesomeness of *their* wine, while *his* tulip was quite delicious with his red herring. The most unfortunate part of the business for him was, that he remained in prison for some months on a charge of felony preferred against him by the merchant.

Another story is told of an English traveller, which is scarcely less ludicrous. This gentleman, an amateur botanist, happened to see a tulip-root lying in the conservatory of a wealthy Dutchman. Being ignorant of its quality, he took out his penknife, and peeled off its coats, with the view of making experiments upon it. When it was by this means reduced to half its size, he cut it into two equal sections, making all the time learned remarks on the singular appearances of the unknown bulb. Suddenly the owner pounced upon him, and, with fury in his eyes, asked him if he knew what he had been doing? "Peeling a most extraordinary onion," replied the philosopher. "*Hundert tausend duyvel!*" said the Dutchman; "it's an *Admiral Van der Eyck.*" "Thank you," replied the traveller, taking out his notebook to make a memorandum of the same; "are these admirals common in your country?" "Death and the Devil!" said the Dutchman, seizing the astonished man of science by the collar; "come before the syndic, and you shall see." In spite of his remonstrances, the traveller was led through the streets followed by a mob of persons. When brought into the presence of the magistrate, he learned, to his consternation, that the root upon which he had been experimentalising was worth four thousand florins; and, notwithstanding all he could urge in extenuation, he was lodged in prison until he found securities for the payment of this sum.

The demand for tulips of a rare species increased so much in the year 1636, that regular marts for their sale were established on the Stock Exchange of Amsterdam, in Rotterdam, Harlaem, Leyden, Alkmar, Hoorn, and other towns. Symptoms of gambling now became, for the first time, apparent. The stock-jobbers, ever on the alert for a new speculation, dealt largely in tulips, making use of all the means they so well knew how to employ to cause fluctuations in prices. At first, as in all these gambling mania, confidence was at its height, and every body gained. The tulip-jobbers speculated in the rise and fall of the tulip stocks, and made large profits by buying when prices fell, and selling out when they rose. Many individuals grew suddenly rich. A golden bait hung temptingly out before the people, and one after the other, they rushed to the tulip marts, like flies around a honey-pot. Every one imagined that the passion for tulips would last for ever, and that the wealthy from every part of the world would send to Holland, and pay whatever prices were asked for them. The riches of Europe would be concentrated on the shores of the Zuyder Zee, and poverty banished from the favoured clime of Holland. Nobles, citizens, farmers, mechanics, seamen, footmen, maid-servants, even chimney-sweeps and old clotheswomen, dabbled in tulips. People of all grades converted their property into cash, and invested it in flowers. Houses and lands were offered for sale at ruinously low prices, or assigned in payment of bargains made at the tulip-mart. Foreigners became smitten with the same frenzy, and money poured into Holland from all directions. The prices of the necessaries of life rose again by degrees: houses and lands, horses and carriages, and luxuries of every sort, rose in value with them, and for some months Holland seemed the very antechamber of Plutus. The operations of the trade became so extensive and so intricate, that it was found necessary to draw up a code of laws for the guidance of the dealers. Notaries and clerks were also appointed, who devoted themselves exclusively to the interests of the trade. The designation of public notary was hardly known in some towns, that of tulip-notary usurping its place. In the smaller towns, where there was no exchange, the principal tavern was usually selected as the "show-place," where high and low traded in tulips, and confirmed their bargains over sumptuous entertainments. These dinners were sometimes attended by two or three hundred persons, and large vases of tulips, in full bloom, were placed at regular intervals upon the tables and side-boards for their gratification during the repast.

At last, however, the more prudent began to see that this folly could not last for ever. Rich people no longer bought the flowers to keep them in their gardens, but to sell them again at cent per cent profit. It was seen that somebody must lose fearfully in the end. As this conviction spread, prices fell, and never rose again. Confidence was destroyed, and a universal panic seized upon the dealers. *A* had agreed to purchase ten *Semper Augustines* from *B*, at four thousand florins each, at six weeks after the signing of the contract. *B* was ready with the flowers at the appointed time; but the price had fallen to three or four hundred florins, and *A* refused either to pay the difference or receive the tulips. Defaulters were announced day after day in all the towns of Holland. Hundreds who, a few months previously, had begun to doubt that there was such a thing as poverty in the land suddenly found themselves the possessors of a few bulbs, which nobody would buy, even though they offered them at one quarter of the sums they had paid for them. The cry of distress resounded every where, and each man accused his neighbour. The few who had contrived to enrich themselves hid their wealth from the knowledge of their fellow-citizens, and invested it in the English or other funds. Many who, for a brief season, had emerged from the humbler walks of life, were cast back into their original obscurity. Substantial merchants were reduced almost to beggary, and many a representative of a noble line saw the fortunes of his house ruined beyond redemption.

When the first alarm subsided, the tulip-holders in the several towns held public meetings to devise what measures were best to be taken to restore public credit. It was generally agreed that deputies should be sent from all parts to Amsterdam, to consult with the government upon some remedy for the evil. The government at first refused to interfere, but advised the tulip-holders to agree to some plan among themselves. Several meetings were held for this purpose; but no measure could be devised likely to give satisfaction to the deluded people, or repair even a slight portion of the mischief that had been done. The language of complaint and reproach was in every body's mouth, and all the meetings were of the most stormy character. At last, however, after much bickering and ill-will, it was agreed, at Amsterdam, by the assembled deputies, that all contracts made in the height of the mania, or prior to the month of November, 1636, should be declared null and void, and that, in those made after that date, purchasers should be freed from their engagements, on paying ten per cent to the vendor. This decision gave no satisfaction. The vendors who had their tulips on hand were, of course, discontented, and those who had pledged themselves to purchase, thought themselves hardly treated. Tulips which had, at one time, been worth six thousand florins, were now to be procured for five hundred; so that the composition of ten per cent was one hundred florins more than the actual value. Actions for breach of contract were threatened in all the courts of the country; but the latter refused to take cognisance of gambling transactions.

The matter was finally referred to the Provincial Council at the Hague, and it was confidently expected that the wisdom of this body would invent some measure by which credit should be restored. Expectation was on the stretch for its decision, but it never came. The members continued to deliberate week after week, and at last, after thinking about it for three months, declared that they could offer no final decision until they had more information. They advised, however, that, in the meantime, every vendor should, in the presence of witnesses, offer the tulips *in natura* to the purchaser for the sums agreed upon. If the latter refused to take them, they might be put up for sale by public auction, and the original contractor held responsible for the difference between the actual and the stipulated price. This was exactly the plan recommended by the deputies, and which was already shown to be of no avail. There was no court in Holland which would enforce payment. The question was raised in Amsterdam, but the judges unanimously refused to interfere, on the ground that debts contracted in gambling were no debts in law.

Thus the matter rested. To find a remedy was beyond the power of the government. Those who were unlucky enough to have had stores of tulips on hand at the time of the sudden reaction were left to bear their ruin as philosophically as they could; those who had made profits were allowed to keep them; but the commerce of the country suffered a severe shock, from which it was many years ere it recovered.

The example of the Dutch was imitated to some extent in England. In the year 1636 tulips were publicly sold in the Exchange of London, and the jobbers exerted themselves to the utmost to raise them to the fictitious value they had acquired in Amsterdam. In Paris also the jobbers strove to create a tulipomania. In both cities they only partially succeeded. However, the force of example brought the flowers into great favour, and amongst a certain class of people tulips have ever since been prized more highly than any other flowers of the field. The Dutch are still notorious for their partiality to them, and continue to pay higher prices for them than any other people. As the rich Englishman boasts of his fine race-horses or his old pictures, so does the wealthy Dutchman vaunt him of his tulips.

In England, in our day, strange as it may appear, a tulip will produce more money than an oak. If one could be found, *rara in terris*, and black as the black swan of Juvenal, its price would equal that of a dozen acres of standing corn. In Scotland, towards the close of the seventeenth century, the highest price for tulips, according to the authority of a writer in the supplement to the third edition of the *Encyclopaedia Britannica*, was ten guineas. Their value appears to have diminished from that time till the year 1769, when the two most valuable species in England were the *Don Quevedo* and the *Valentinier*, the former of which was worth two guineas and the latter two guineas and a half. These prices appear to have been the minimum. In the year 1800, a common price was fifteen guineas for a single bulb. In 1835 a bulb of the species called the Miss Fanny Kemble was sold by public auction in London for seventy-five pounds. Still more remarkable was the price of a tulip in the possession of a gardener in the King's Road, Chelsea—in his catalogues it was labelled at two hundred guineas.

CHARLES MACKAY
[*Memoirs of Extraordinary Popular Delusions* (1841)]

Thomas Fuller Is Not Impressed

[The quaint Thomas Fuller, whose Worthies of England *is a minor classic, despised tulips before he knew what their subsequent history was to be.]*

✠

T H E R E is lately a *Flower* (shal I call it so? in courtesie I will tearme it so, though it deserve not the appelation) a *Toolip*, which hath engrafted the love and affections of most people unto it; and what is this Toolip? a well complexion'd stink, an ill favour wrapt up in pleasant colours; as for the use thereof in *Physick*, no *Physitian* hath honoured it yet with the mention, nor with a *Greek*, or Latin name, so inconsiderable hath it hitherto been accompted; and yet this is that which filleth all Gardens, hundred of pounds being given for the root thereof, whilst I the *Rose*, am neglected and contemned, and conceived beneath the honour of noble hands, and fit only to grow in the gardens of Yeomen. I trust the remainder to your apprehensions, to make out that which grief for such undeserved injuries will not suffer me to expresse.

THOMAS FULLER
*[Antheologia, or The Speech of Flowers:
partly Morall, partly Misticall (1660)]*

Too Many Tulips

[The Tatler missed few contemporary follies and had the following to say about the Tulip Mania.]

✠

I CHANCED to rise very early one particular morning this summer, and took a walk into the Country to divert myself among the fields
and meadows, while the green was new, and the flowers in their bloom.
As at this season of the year every lane is a beautiful walk, and every
hedge full of nosegays; I lost myself with a great deal of pleasure among
several thickets and bushes, that were filled with a great variety of birds,
and an agreeable confusion of notes, which formed the pleasantest scene
in the world to one who had passed a whole winter in noise and smoke.
The freshness of the dews that lay upon every thing about me, with the
cool breath of the morning, which inspired the birds with so many delightful instincts, created in me the same kind of animal pleasure, and
made my heart overflow with such secret emotions of joy and satisfaction as are not to be described or accounted for. On this occasion, I could
not but reflect upon a beautiful simile in Milton.

> As one who long in populous city pent,
> Where houses thick, and sewers annoy the air,
> Forth issuing on a summer's morn, to breathe
> Among the pleasant villages, and farms
> Adjoin'd, from each thing met conceives delight:
> The smell of grain, or tedded grass, or kine,
> Or dairy, each rural sight, each rural sound.

Those, who are conversant in the writings of polite Authors,
receive an additional entertainment from the Country, as it revives in
their memories those charming descriptions, with which such Authors
do frequently abound.

I was thinking of the foregoing beautiful simile in *Milton*, and
applying it to myself, when I observed to the windward of me a black
cloud falling to the earth in long trails of rain, which made me betake
myself for shelter to a house, which I saw at a little distance from the
place where I was walking. As I sat in the porch, I heard the voices of
two or three persons, who seemed very earnest in discourse. My curiosity
was raised when I heard the names of *Alexander* the Great and *Arta-
xerxes*; and as their talk seemed to run on ancient heroes, I concluded
there could not be any secret in it; for which reason I thought I might
very fairly listen to what they said.

After several parallels between great men, which appeared to
me altogether groundless and chimerical, I was surprised to hear one say,
That he valued the *Black Prince* more than the Duke of *Vendosme*. How

the Duke of *Vendosme* should become a rival of the *Black Prince*, I could not conceive: And was more startled when I heard a second affirm with great vehemence, that if the Emperor of *Germany* was not going off, he should like him better than either of them. He added, that though the season was so changeable, the Duke of *Marlborough* was in blooming beauty. I was wondering to myself from whence they had received this odd intelligence; especially when I heard them mention the names of several other great Generals, as the Prince of *Hesse*, and the King of *Sweden*, who, they said, were both running away. To which they added, what I entirely agreed with them in, that the crown of *France* was very weak, but that the Marshal *Villars* still kept his colours. At last one of them told the company, if they would go along with him, he would shew them a chimney-sweeper and a painted lady in the same bed, which he was sure would very much please them. The shower, which had driven them as well as myself into the house, was now over: And as they were passing by me into the garden, I asked them to let me be one of their company.

The Gentleman of the house told me, if I delighted in flowers, it would be worth my while; for that he believed he could shew me such a blow of tulips, as was not to be matched in the whole country.

I accepted the offer, and immediately found that they had been talking in terms of gardening, and that the Kings and Generals they had mentioned were only so many tulips, to which the gardeners, according to their usual custom, had given such high titles and appellations of honour.

I was very much pleased and astonished at the glorious show of these gay vegetables, that arose in great profusion on all the banks about us. Sometimes I considered them with the eye of an ordinary spectator, as so many beautiful objects varnished over with a natural gloss, and stained with such a variety of colours, as are not to be equalled in any artificial dyes or tinctures. Sometimes I considered every leaf as an elaborate piece of tissue, in which the threads and fibres were woven together into different configurations, which gave a different colouring to the light as it glanced on the several parts of the surface. Sometimes I considered the whole bed of tulips, according to the notion of the greatest mathematician and philosopher that ever lived, as a multitude of optic instruments, designed for the separating light into all those various colours of which it is composed.

I was awakened out of these my philosophical speculations, by observing, the company often seemed to laugh at me. I accidentally praised a tulip as one of the finest I ever saw; upon which they told me,

L. Tulipa cinnah: et alb: flamm.

L. Tulipa sanguin:.

Le Jardin de Mr. De Chanteloup rue du Colombier.

avec privilege.

A Bowling green of Grass work only)

A Bowling green environed with Trees & adorned with Cabinets & Palisades

fig. 6.

fig. 1.

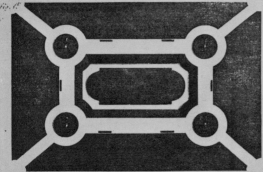

A Bowling green with Edgings of Box.

A Bowling green in a Wood surrounded with a Palisade cut into Arches.

fig. 4.

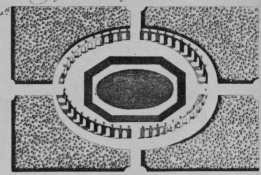

Fathom

M.te Ga. Guchr. Sculp.
Plate D. f.st

A great Hall of Horsechesnuts in a Wood.

A Wood planted in Quincunce with Cabinets

fig. 3.

A great Hall of Horsechesnuts with borders of Grass.

A Little Hall invironed with Palisades & green Borders.

fig. 2.

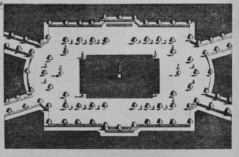

Fathom

Fathom

C.

茉莉
開葉

西番菊

栀子

it was a common Fool's Coat. Upon that I praised a second, which it seems was but another kind of Fool's Coat. I had the same fate with two or three more; for which reason I desired the owner of the garden to let me know, which were the finest of the flowers; for that I was so unskilful in the art, that I thought the most beautiful were the most valuable, and that those which had the gayest colours were the most beautiful. The Gentleman smiled at my ignorance: He seemed a very plain honest man, and a person of good sense, had not his head been touched with that distemper which Hippocrates calls the *Tulippomania;* insomuch, that he would talk very rationally on any subject in the world but a tulip.

He told me, that he valued the bed of flowers which lay before us, and was not above twenty yards in length and two in breadth, more than he would the best hundred acres of land in *England*; and added, that it would have been worth twice the money it is, if a foolish cook-maid of his had not almost ruined him the last winter, by mistaking a handful of tulip-roots for an heap of onions, and by that means, says he, made me a dish of porridge, that cost me above a thousand pounds sterling. He then shewed me what he thought the finest of his tulips, which I found received all their value from their rarity and oddness, and put me in mind of your great fortunes, which are not always the greatest Beauties.

I have often looked upon it as a piece of happiness, that I have never fallen into any of these fantastical tastes, nor esteemed any thing the more for its being uncommon and hard to be met with. For this reason, I look upon the whole Country in spring-time as a spacious garden, and make as many visits to a spot of daisies, or a bank of violets, as a florist does to his borders or parterres. There is not a bush in blossom within a mile of me which I am not acquainted with, nor scarce a daffodil or cowslip that withers away in my neighbourhood without my missing it. I walked home in this temper of mind through several fields and meadows with an unspeakable pleasure, not without reflecting on the bounty of Providence, which has made the most pleasing and most beautiful objects the most ordinary and most common.

JOSEPH ADDISON
[*The Tatler*, No. 218 (1710)]

A Chinese Nursery Garden

[*One of the earliest botanists to explore the riches of China was Robert Fortune, who spent some twenty years in the Orient as an agent of the Royal Horticultural Society. We shall meet him again among the explorers but his description of a Chinese garden belongs here.*]

I LOST no time in visiting the celebrated Fa-tee Gardens, near Canton, the "flowery land," as the name implies, from whence a great number of those fine plants were first procured which now decorate our gardens in England. They are situated two or three miles above the city, on the opposite side of the river, and are, in fact, Chinese nursery gardens, where plants are cultivated for sale.

Here, then, I beheld a specimen of the far-famed system of Chinese gardening, about which we have read so much in European authors: I will, therefore, describe them somewhat fully. The plants are principally kept in large pots arranged in rows along the sides of narrow paved walks, with the houses of the gardeners at the entrance through which the visitors pass to the gardens. There are about a dozen of these gardens, more or less extensive, according to the business or wealth of the proprietor; but they are generally smaller than the smallest of our London nurseries. They have also stock-grounds, where the different plants are planted out in the ground, and where the first process of dwarfing their celebrated trees is put in operation. These contain large collections of Camellias, Azaleas, oranges, roses, and various other well-known plants, which are purchased by the Chinese when in flower. The most striking plant in autumn or winter is the curious fingered Citron, which the Chinese gather and place in their dwellings or on their altars. It is much admired both for its strange form and also for its perfume. The mandarin orange is also much grown at Fa-tee, where the plants are kept in a dwarf state, and flower and fruit most profusely, producing large, flat, dark, red-skinned fruit. The Chinese have a great variety of plants belonging to the orange tribe; and of one which they call the *cum quat*—a small oval-fruited variety—they make a most excellent preserve. The *Murraya exotica*, *Aglaia odorata*, *Ixoras*, and *Lagerstroemias* are very ornamental here in autumn.

But it is of course in spring that the Fa-tee gardens possess the greatest attractions. They are then gay with the tree paeony, azaleas, camellias, roses, and various other plants. The azaleas are splendid, and reminded me of the exhibitions in the gardens of the Horticultural Society at Chiswick, but the Fa-tee exhibitions were on a much larger scale. Every garden was one mass of bloom, and the different colours of red, white, and purple blended together, had a most beautiful and imposing effect. The principal kinds grown were *Azalea indica*, *indica alba*, *phoenicea*, *lateritia*, *variegata*, and the yellow *Azalea sinensis*. I may mention in passing, that I found the latter plant wild on the Ning-po hills, so that there is no doubt of its being a genuine Chinese species. The air at this season around Fa-tee is perfumed with the sweet flowers of *Olea fragrans*, and the *Magnolia fuscata*, both of which are grown extensively in these gardens. Dwarf trees, as may be supposed, occupy a principal station; they are trained into the most grotesque and curious forms. The plants which stand next to dwarf trees in importance with the Chinese are certainly chrysanthemums, which they manage extremely well, perhaps better than they do any other plant. So high do these plants stand in the favour of the Chinese gardener, that he will cultivate them extensively, even against the wishes of his employer; and, in many instances, rather leave his situation than give up the growth of his favourite flower. I was told that the late Mr. Beale used to say that he grew chrysanthemums in his garden for no other purpose than to please his gardener, not having any taste for this particular flower himself.

Tree paeonies are not natives of the south of China, but are brought down in large quantities every year, about the month of January, from the northern provinces. They flower soon after they arrive, and are rapidly bought up by the Chinese to ornament their houses, after which they are thrown away, as they do not thrive well so far south as Canton or Macao, and will not flower a second season. They are sold according to the number of flower-buds they may have upon them, many of them fetching rather high prices.

One of the old gardeners here speaks the English language very well, and carries on a considerable trade in seeds with the English and American residents, but, unfortunately, he has got a bad name, owing to his seeds generally failing to grow when they are sent home. It is now currently reported that the old man boils them, in order that his trade may not be spoiled by some enterprising propagator in England or America. Such, however, is not the case; on the contrary, I am quite certain that he does everything in his power to preserve them, but very likely some may be a year or two old before they are dispatched to Europe. Besides the long voyage round the Cape—during which the seeds have twice to cross the tropics—is very prejudicial to their generation. There is, however, no great loss in these seeds not growing, as there is nothing amongst them new, or of any value, for they are gathered from the plants common in the Fa-tee gardens, the greater part of which have been years ago introduced to our gardens at home. I would therefore, strongly advise my friends in China not to spend their money upon such seeds.

ROBERT FORTUNE
[*Three Years' Wanderings in the Northern
Provinces of China* (1847)]

The Gardens of Japan

[*Lafcadio Hearn, the American journalist and essayist, went to Japan in
1890, became a Japanese citizen and died in Tokyo. He was one of the
first to write sympathetically of the Japanese culture, and his exposition
of the aims of the Japanese gardener is perhaps still the best.*]

A F T E R having learned—merely by seeing, for the practical knowledge of the art requires years of study and experience, besides a natural,
instinctive sense of beauty—something about the Japanese manner of
arranging flowers, one can thereafter consider European ideas of floral
decoration only as vulgarities. This observation is not the result of any
hasty enthusiasm, but a conviction settled by long residence in the interior. I have come to understand the unspeakable loveliness of a solitary
spray of blossoms arranged as only a Japanese expert knows how to
arrange it—not by simply poking the spray into a vase, but by perhaps
one whole hour's labor of trimming and posing and daintiest manipula-

tion—and therefore I cannot think now of what we Occidentals call a "bouquet" as anything but a vulgar murdering of flowers, an outrage upon the color-sense, a brutality, an abomination. Somewhat in the same way, and for similar reasons, after having learned what an old Japanese garden is, I can remember our costliest gardens at home only as ignorant displays of what wealth can accomplish in the creation of incongruities that violate nature.

Now a Japanese garden is not a flower garden; neither is it made for the purpose of cultivating plants. In nine cases out of ten there is nothing in it resembling a flower-bed. Some gardens may contain scarcely a sprig of green; some have nothing green at all, and consist entirely of rocks and pebbles and sand, although these are exceptional. As a rule, a Japanese garden is a landscape garden, yet its existence does not depend upon any fixed allowance of space. It may cover one acre or many acres. It may also be only ten feet square. It may, in extreme cases, be much less; for a certain kind of Japanese garden can be contrived small enough to put in a tokonoma. Such a garden, in a vessel no larger than a fruit-dish, is called koniwa or tokoniwa, and may occasionally be seen in the tokonoma of humble little dwellings so closely squeezed between other structures as to possess no ground in which to cultivate an outdoor garden. (I say "an outdoor garden," because there are indoor gardens, both upstairs and downstairs, in some large Japanese houses.) The tokoniwa is usually made in some curious bowl, or shallow carved box, or quaintly shaped vessel impossible to describe by any English word. Therein are created minuscule hills with minuscule houses upon them, and microscopic ponds and rivulets spanned by tiny humped bridges; and queer wee plants do duty for trees, and curiously formed pebbles stand for rocks, and there are tiny tōrō, perhaps a tiny torii as well—in short, a charming and living model of a Japanese landscape.

Another fact of prime importance to remember is that, in order to comprehend the beauty of a Japanese garden, it is necessary to under-stand—or at least to learn to understand—the beauty of stones. Not of stones quarried by the hand of man, but of stones shaped by nature only. Until you can feel, and keenly feel, that stones have character, that stones have tones and values, the whole artistic meaning of a Japanese garden cannot be revealed to you. In the foreigner, however aesthetic he may be, this feeling needs to be cultivated by study. It is inborn in the Japanese; the soul of the race comprehends Nature infinitely better than we do, at least in her visible forms. But although, being an Occidental, the true sense of the beauty of stones can be reached by you only through long familiarity with the Japanese use and choice of them, the characters of the lessons to be acquired exist everywhere about you, if your life be in the interior. You cannot walk through a street without observing tasks and problems in the aesthetics of stones for you to master. At the approaches to temples, by the side of roads, before holy groves, and in all parks and pleasure-grounds, as well as in all cemeteries, you will notice large, irregular, flat slabs of natural rock—mostly from the river beds and water-worn—sculptured with ideographs, but unhewn. These have been set up as votive tablets, as commemorative monuments, as tombstones, and are much more costly than the ordinary cut-stone columns and haka chiseled with the figures of divinities in relief. Again, you will see before most of the shrines, nay, even in the grounds of nearly all large homesteads, great irregular blocks of granite or other hard rock, worn by the action of torrents, and converted into water-basins (*chodzu-bachi*) by cutting a circular hollow in the top. Such are but common examples of the utilization of stones even in the poorest villages; and if you have any natural artistic sentiment, you cannot fail to discover, sooner or later, how much more beautiful are these natural forms than any shapes from the hand of the stone-cutter. It is probable, too, that you will become so habituated at last to the sight of inscriptions cut upon rock surfaces, especially if you travel much through the country, that you will often find yourself involuntarily looking for texts or other chiselings where there are none, and could not possibly be, as if ideographs belonged by natural law to rock formation. And stones will begin, perhaps, to assume for you a certain individual or physiognomical aspect —to suggest moods and sensations, as they do to the Japanese. Indeed, Japan is particularly a land of suggestive shapes in stone, as high volcanic lands are apt to be; and such shapes doubtless addressed themselves to the imagination of the race at a time long prior to the date of that archaic text which tells of demons in Izumo "who made rocks, and the roots of trees, and leaves, and the foam of the green waters to speak." . . .

No effort to create an impossible or purely ideal landscape is made in the Japanese garden. Its artistic purpose is to copy faithfully the attractions of a veritable landscape, and to convey the real impression that a real landscape communicates. It is therefore at once a picture and a poem; perhaps even more a poem than a picture. For as nature's scenery, in its varying aspects, affects us with sensations of joy or of solemnity, of grimness or of sweetness, of force or of peace, so must the true reflection of it in the labor of the landscape gardener create not merely an impression of beauty, but a mood in the soul. The grand old landscape gardeners, those Buddhist monks who first introduced the art into Japan, and subsequently developed it into an almost occult science, carried their theory yet farther than this. They held it possible to express moral lessons in the design of a garden, and abstract ideas, such as Chastity, Faith, Piety, Content, Calm, and Connubial Bliss. Therefore were gardens contrived according to the character of the owner, whether poet, warrior, philosopher, or priest. In those ancient gardens (the art, alas, is passing away under the withering influence of the utterly commonplace Western taste) there were expressed both a mood of nature and some rare Oriental conception of a mood of man.

I do not know what human sentiment the principal division of my garden was intended to reflect; and there is none to tell me. Those by whom it was made passed away long generations ago, in the eternal transmigration of souls. But as a poem of nature it requires no interpreter. It occupies the front portion of the grounds, facing south; and it also extends west to the verge of the northern division of the garden, from which it is partly separated by a curious screen-fence structure. There are large rocks in it, heavily mossed; and divers fantastic basins of stone for holding water; and stone lamps green with years; and a shachihoko, such as one sees at the peaked angles of castle roofs—a great stone fish, an idealized porpoise, with its nose in the ground and its tail in the air. There are miniature hills, with old trees upon them; and there are long slopes of green, shadowed by flowering shrubs, like river banks; and there are green knolls like islets. All these verdant elevations rise from spaces of pale yellow sand, smooth as a surface of silk and miming the curves and meanderings of a river course. These sanded spaces are not to be trodden upon; they are much too beautiful for that. The least speck of dirt would mar their effect; and it requires the trained skill of an experienced native gardener—a delightful old man he is—to keep them in perfect form. But they are traversed in various directions by lines of flat unhewn rock slabs, placed at slightly irregular distances from one another, exactly like stepping-stones across a brook. The whole effect is that of the shores of a still stream in some lovely, lonesome, drowsy place.

There is nothing to break the illusion, so secluded the garden is. High walls and fences shut out streets and contiguous things; and the shrubs and the trees, heightening and thickening toward the boundaries, conceal from view even the roofs of the neighboring katchiū-yashiki. Softly beautiful are the tremulous shadows of leaves on the sunned sand; and the scent of flowers comes thinly sweet with every waft of tepid air; and there is a humming of bees.

By Buddhism all existences are divided into Hijō, things without desire, such as stones and trees; and Ujō, things having desire, such as men and animals. This division does not, so far as I know, find expression in the written philosophy of gardens; but it is a convenient one. The folk-lore of my little domain relates both to the inanimate and the animate. In natural order, the Hijō may be considered first, beginning with a singular shrub near the entrance of the yashiki, and close to the gate of the first garden.

Within the front gateway of almost every old samurai house, and usually near the entrance of the dwelling itself, there is to be seen a small tree with large and peculiar leaves. The name of this tree in Izumo is tegashiwa, and there is one beside my door. What the scientific name of it is I do not know; nor am I quite sure of the etymology of the Japanese name. However, there is a word tegashi, meaning a bond for the hands; and the shape of the leaves of the tegashiwa somewhat resembles the shape of a hand.

Now, in old days, when the samurai retainer was obliged to leave his home in order to accompany his daimyō to Yedo, it was customary, just before his departure, to set before him a baked tai served up on a tegashiwa leaf. After this farewell repast, the leaf upon which the tai had been served was hung up above the door as a charm to bring the departed knight safely back again. This pretty superstition about the leaves of the tegashiwa had its origin not only in their shape but in their movement. Stirred by a wind they seemed to beckon—not indeed after our Occidental manner, but in the way that a Japanese signs to his friend to come, by gently waving his hand up and down with the palm towards the ground. . . .

The second garden, on the north side, is my favorite. It contains no large growths. It is paved with blue pebbles, and its centre is occupied by a pondlet—a miniature lake fringed with rare plants, and containing a tiny island, with tiny mountains and dwarf peach-trees and pines and azaleas, some of which are perhaps more than a century old, though scarcely more than a foot high. Nevertheless, this work, seen as it was intended to be seen, does not appear to the eye in miniature at all. From a certain angle of the guest-room looking out upon it, the appearance is that of a real lake shore with a real island beyond it, a stone's throw away. So cunning the art of the ancient gardener who contrived all this, and who has been sleeping for a hundred years under the cedars of Gesshoji, that the illusion can be detected only from the zashiki by the presence of an ishidōrō, or stone lamp, upon the island. The size of the ishidōrō betrays the false perspective, and I do not think it was placed there when the garden was made.

Here and there at the edge of the pond, and almost level with the water, are placed large flat stones, on which one may either stand or squat, to watch the lacustrine population or to tend the water-plants. There are beautiful water-lilies, whose bright green leaf-disks float oilily upon the surface (*Nuphar Japonica*), and many lotus plants of two kinds, those which bear pink and those which bear pure white flowers. There are iris plants growing along the bank, whose blossoms are prismatic violet, and there are various ornamental grasses and ferns and mosses. But the pond is essentially a lotus pond; the lotus plants make its greatest charm. It is a delight to watch every phase of their marvelous growth, from the first unrolling of the leaf to the fall of the last flower. On rainy days, especially, the lotus plants are worth observing. Their great cup-shaped leaves, swaying high above the pond, catch the rain and hold it a while; but always after the water in the leaf reaches a certain level the stem bends, and empties the leaf with a loud plash, and then straightens again. Rain-water upon a lotus-leaf is a favorite subject with Japanese metal-workers, and the metal-work only can reproduce the effect, for the motion and color of water moving upon the green oleaginous surface are exactly those of quicksilver.

The third garden, which is very large, extends beyond the inclosure containing the lotus pond to the foot of the wooded hills which form the northern and northeastern boundary of this old samurai quarter. Formerly all this broad level space was occupied by a bamboo grove; but it is now little more than a waste of grasses and wild flowers. In the northeast corner there is a magnificent well, from which ice-cold water is brought into the house through a most ingenious little aqueduct of bamboo pipes; and in the northwestern end, veiled by tall weeds, there stands a very small stone shrine of Inari, with two proportionately small stone foxes sitting before it. Shrine and images are chipped and broken, and thickly patched with dark green moss. But on the east side of the house one little square of soil belonging to this large division of the garden is still cultivated. It is devoted entirely to chrysanthemum plants, which are shielded from heavy rain and strong sun by slanting frames of light wood fashioned like shōji, with panes of white paper, and supported like awnings upon thin posts of bamboo. I can venture to add nothing to what has already been written about these marvelous products of Japanese floriculture considered in themselves; but there is a little story relating to chrysanthemums which I may presume to tell.

There is one place in Japan where it is thought unlucky to cultivate chrysanthemums, for reasons which shall presently appear; and that place is in the pretty little city of Himeji, in the province of Harima. Himeji contains the ruins of a great castle of thirty turrets; and a daimyō used to dwell therein whose revenue was one hundred and fifty-six thousand koku of rice. Now, in the house of one of that daimyō's chief retainers there was a maid-servant, of good family, whose name was O-Kiku; and the name "Kiku" signifies a chrysanthemum flower. Many precious things were intrusted to her charge, and among others ten costly dishes of gold. One of these was suddenly missed, and could not be found; and the girl, being responsible therefor, and knowing not how otherwise to prove her innocence, drowned herself in a well. But ever thereafter her ghost, returning nightly, could be heard counting the dishes slowly, with sobs:

Ichi-mai,	Yo-mai,	Shichi-mai,
Ni-mai,	Go-mai,	Hachi-mai,
San-mai,	Roku-mai,	Ku-mai—

Then would be heard a despairing cry and a loud burst of weeping; and again the girl's voice counting the dishes plaintively: "One—two—three—four—five—six—seven—eight—*nine*—"

Her spirit passed into the body of a strange little insect, whose head faintly resembles that of a ghost with long disheveled hair; and it is called O-Kikumushi, or "the fly of O-Kiku"; and it is found, they say, nowhere save in Himeji. A famous play was written about O-Kiku, which is still acted in all the popular theatres, entitled Banshu-O-Kiku-no-Sara-ya-shiki; or, The Manor of the Dish of O-Kiku of Banshu.

Some declare that Banshu is only the corruption of the name of an ancient quarter of Tōkyō (Yedo), where the story should have been laid. But the people of Himeji say that part of their city now called Go-Ken-Yashiki is identical with the site of the ancient manor. What is certainly true is that to cultivate chrysanthemum flowers in the part of Himeji called Go-Ken-Yashiki is deemed unlucky, because the name of O-Kiku signifies "Chrysanthemum." Therefore, nobody, I am told, ever cultivates chrysanthemums there. . . .

Somewhere among the rocks in the pond lives a small tortoise—left in the garden, probably, by the previous tenants of the house. It is very pretty, but manages to remain invisible for weeks at a time. In popular mythology, the tortoise is the servant of the divinity Kompira; and if a pious fisherman finds a tortoise, he writes upon his back characters signifying "Servant of the Deity Kompira," and then gives it a drink of saké and sets it free. It is supposed to be very fond of saké.

LAFCADIO HEARN
[*Glimpses of Unfamiliar Japan* (1894)]

Section Four

THE LINNAEAN AGE

He esteemed the smallest and most insignificant plant as highly as the fairest sweet-smelling flower, though such were not wanting either in the garden during his lifetime; he always wished for more species than he had.

Prince of Botanists

[*During the eighteenth century, natural history in general and botany in particular first became a subject of general interest and was probably the hobby of a larger proportion of the population than ever before or since. The* Gentleman's Magazine *devoted a good deal of attention to it; many books (often sumptuous) pictured both familiar and rare species; explorers were either botanists themselves or took a botanist along; and wealthy gentlemen took great pride in their collections of new and splendid flowering plants.*

Many things contributed to this explosion of interest, including, of course, the discovery that in little-known corners of the earth thousands of hitherto unknown plants were growing and blooming. But no one *man contributed so much as the first of modern botanists, Carolus Linnaeus, who sent forth book after book from his native Sweden.*

The best known of his contributions is the system of classification and nomenclature which gave to each organism a generic and a specific name in place of the confusing and unrelated descriptive tags in Latin by which the relatively few recognized species could be identified by those who had committed them to memory. Thanks to his system of binomials, similar plants were grouped together, newly discovered species could be assigned to existing categories, and it was possible to construct keys (essentially similar to those still in use) by means of which even a layman could learn to find the name and relationships of any flower he happened to come across. Moreover, Linnaeus's scheme was devised just in the nick of time—just, that is to say, before the flood of newly discovered species began to roll in from the four quarters of the earth.

But Linnaeus did much more than invent the modern system of nomenclature. He generated a new enthusiasm and embodied a new spirit. Plants were still valuable as medicine and as garden ornaments. But they were also much more. Though subjects of scientific study, they were also to him ever-wonderful examples of God's handiwork. Linnaeus was a poet as well as a scientist; he took botany out of the study and the garden into the great world; and in many respects he anticipated that kind of "love of nature" which we associate with Thoreau and Hudson.

Donald Culross Peattie, who belongs to the same line, is peculiarly fitted to introduce him.]

O N this day [May 23] in 1707, in southern Sweden, was born the man we know as Charles Linnaeus. The lad's schoolmasters—who were sure he would never amount to anything—called him Nils Ingermarsson, but that is only a peasant patronymic, and when Nils set off for Upsala University, he took a prouder title. For two hundred years, in a corner of Jonsboda Parish, there had stood a great linden, sacred in family tradition. *Lin*, the linden, furnished him with the name he was looking for.

At Upsala, Linnaeus passed the first year in dire want, putting paper in the soles of his worn shoes. The old botanical gardens, started by Rudbeck, had been allowed to fall into ruins, and the science of botany itself was then like a sleeping, dusty, dead-seeming garden in March, half full of lifeless brushwood—but for the rest secretly quick and budded and only awaiting a warming breath.

The only friend of Linnaeus at this time was Artedi, who would have become the Linnaeus of zoology but for falling into a canal and drowning. This lad was so poor that Linnaeus and he loaned each other money, as only the destitute could do. These boys exchanged the usual wild ideas of young students—in this case nothing less than the principles of classification that ultimately brought order into the hopelessly muddled work of the herbalists struggling to find the plants of northern Europe in their Pliny and Theophrastus.

So like two winter birds, living on weed seeds, and sleeping in the lee of a tree trunk, the ragged hungry lads lived on till spring, when Dean Celsius, himself a naturalist, came to their aid with money, food, shelter, appointments, and gave them grace to think, without danger of turning into fasting visionaries.

In May, 1732 there rode out of the gates of gray old Upsala a thin young man in a light coat of West Gothland linsey without folds, lined with red shaloon, having small cuffs and a collar of shag; he wore

leather breeches, and a round wig topped by a green leather cap, his feet
in a pair of half-boots. On his saddle he carried a small leather bag containing two pairs of false sleeves, two half-shirts and one whole one, an
inkstand, pencase, microscope, a gauze cap to protect him from gnats,
a comb, drying papers for plants, and a few books. A fowling-piece hung
at his side, and a graduated stick for measuring. In his pocket was a passport for Lapland from the governor of Upsala.

Linnaeus was going into the field. In a sense that journey was
the first of its kind ever made. It was the morning, the springtide of
science, after the dark winter of the book-ridden Middle Ages, when
men wrangled over Aristotle and quoted Pliny's authority. Linnaeus was
the first naturalist to whom it occurred to take a great trip to Nature
itself. No wonder that as he rode north, the very larks burst into song.

"*Ecce suum* tirile, tirile, *suum* tirile *tractat!*" they sang, or so he
records it with his quaint blend of Latin and fantasy. "The sky was clear
and warm, while the west wind refreshed one with delicious breath,"
he wrote. "The winter rye stood six inches high, and the barley was
newly come into leaf. The birch was beginning to shoot and all the trees
leafing except the elm and aspen. Though only a few spring flowers were
in bloom it was obvious that the whole land was smiling with the coming
of spring."

When Linnaeus published his great Lapland report, it was
swiftly translated into the languages of Europe. A door had been burst
open, and all men beheld that, outside, the fields were burning with
flowers, the sky ringing with birdsong. Very disturbing, all that, to the
medieval-minded schoolmen, the obscurantists who would have kept
their science to themselves, like alchemists.

Dillenius of Oxford, looking out of his window at the young
Swede walking about in the botanical garden, cried: "There goes a man
who is bringing all botany into confusion!" He locked up the herbarium,
would not give Linnaeus the books he wanted. But in the end, Linnaeus,
patient and tactful, persuaded him to look at his great system of classification. Converted, the delighted Dillenius begged him to stay forever
and share his salary with him. Philip Miller, last of the herbalists, went
over enthusiastically to him. The rich Clifford became his patron.
Gronovius published him at his own expense.

To understand Linnaeus's "Sexual System" as he called it, we
have to cast an eye at the medieval confusion of the past, when a plant
not found in Theophrastus's two thousand year old description of the
Greek flora might be thrown away as heretical. Classification was so

superficial that all prickly plants, for instance, were lumped together—cacti and roses and thistles and even some poppies. What Linnaeus did was to classify by the number of stamens and pistils, every plant as a species and assign it to a genus or clan of related species, and give it two descriptive names in the universal language of Latin. Today all this is commonplace, the sure footing on which we rest—thanks to the boy who would not become a tailor's apprentice.

When once the new system of Linnaeus had swept aside resistance, all Europe was ready to acknowledge him. The King of Spain offered him a princely salary and complete liberty. Clifford wanted never to part with him, and Boerhaave, the rich Dutch scholar, offered him travel in Africa and America.

But Linnaeus was a young man, and a human one, and at heart a bit of a peasant. Sara Morea was waiting for him, and like a bird that does its mating in the north, he flew back to his Sara and made her his wife. For a man of the world it was a great mistake, for the thrifty, cleanly, strapping Sara was no great lady. She thrashed her daughters, spoiled her son, urged her husband toward a lucrative practice as a physician at the cost of science, and told magnificent Gustavus Third to treat his servants better.

And there are other errors of Linnaeus's judgment. To his weak boy he willed his collections and high position at Upsala, so that the vain young man attained to honors he had not earned and responsibilities he was not fitted for.

It must be admitted, too, that Linnaeus's work was hasty; he was never quite a success as a zoologist, and, owing partly to the state of knowledge at that time, he did not quite know what he was doing amongst the lower plants, the fungi, algae, and ferns. His attempt to classify genera and species of metals is entirely untenable, and he was not the equal of Jussieu in grouping genera into natural families. But without his haste, without his lusty courage to undertake an outline of everything—hang the details!—science would have been delayed for decades. Even the faults of his character were human, natural and lovable.

At this season [May] it used to be the custom, and I hope it still may be, for botanists everywhere to do honor to Linnaeus by meeting together for a light-hearted trip afield in search of plants, in the good old style. Formidable has grown that once gentle science of botany—a thing of laboratories and test tubes, of the complex mathematics of the geneticist. For such is the way of a science. It begins in medieval wonder and magic; then a door opens to the fields, it goes forth to its Lapland, to delight and describe and classify. Next come the lens, the laboratory, the investigation of structure, the experiment with function, and at last the mechanical control of the life processes themselves. Sometimes the youngsters of today look back upon the descriptive era as dry, dilettante, unworthy of the name of science.

But more seasoned men, conscious of the history of their science, still hold the name of Linnaeus in reverence. They remember that he did not foist Latin binomials on plants and animals, but pared the latinity down from some twenty words to two! To them the time of Linnaeus is an age of innocence and the true beginnings of modernism. Who would not, if he could, go back today and join Linnaeus and his pupils—so many of whom were to die for him at the ends of the earth— and march afield today to push the moss apart and find the little twin-flowers that he loved above all others, *Linnaea borealis*? Who would not be glad to come back with them, to the fluttering of banners and the piping of hautboys, and unslinging his heavy case of plants, stand with Thunberg and Peter Kalm and Olaf Swartz and give the rousing "*Vivat Scientia! Vivat Linnaeus!*"

DONALD CULROSS PEATTIE
[*An Almanac for Moderns* (1935)]

The Problem of Classification

[*The late Liberty Hyde Bailey spent most of his ninety-odd years in the service of horticulture and was the author of innumerable standard works. In one of his lighter, popular books he gives a clear, simple account of the problem of naming and classification to which Linnaeus addressed himself.*]

THE characters employed by the early herbalists and botanists in making their classifications illustrate the extent of the knowledge of plants at the time, and a comparison of successive methods of classification

L. Clematis altera Purpureo flore.
Ga Viorne
H. Gormadera
Ge. Braeckcruyt, ofte
    Waldrebe

Corona Imperialis
classe duplici florum.

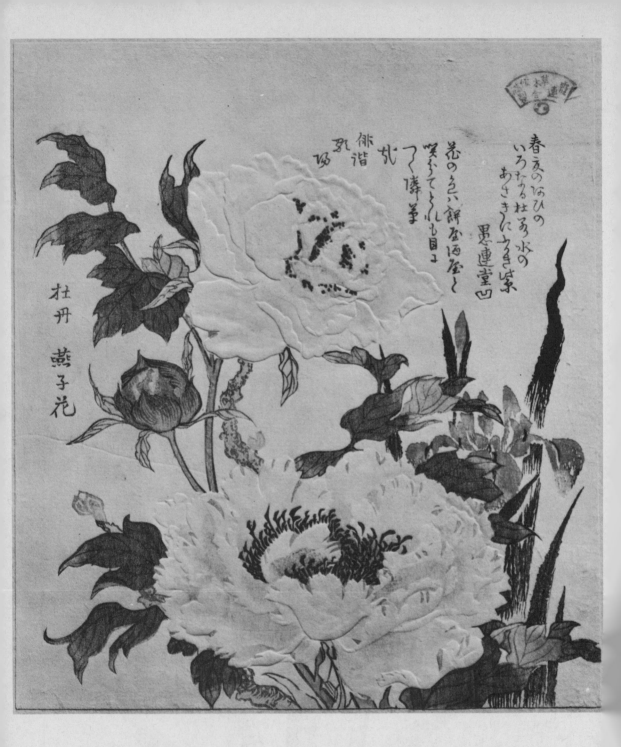

牡丹 燕子花

俳諧
乳房

春戻のなひの
いろなる牡予水の
あさきにうき紫

愚連堂回

花の色八餅を酒金と
咲かてくれも目エ
つ僊筆

indicates the advancement in such knowledge. For instance, upon being told that Dioscorides in the first century divided plants into aromatic, alimentary, medicinal, and vinous, one is at once impressed with the thought that Dioscorides studied plants from a medicinal point of view, and that he understood their medicinal characters better than any other features. A very early classification, and one which denotes a superficial knowledge of plants, was that which recognized the three divisions of trees, shrubs, and herbs, and this classification was not entirely dispelled until Linnaeus rejected it in the middle of last century. It is strange that the forms of flowers did not earlier attract attention. Fuchs, a studious German whose botanical labors are appropriately commemorated in the name Fuchsia, was perhaps the first to define any of the parts of the flower. He called the anthers the apices, and the floral envelope, at least in some cases, the gluma. Fuchs published a botanical work in 1542. Hieronymus Tragus, another German, published an herbal in 1551, in which he associates some of the mints, the mustards, and the sunflowers. The first indication of a general scientific arrangement of plants occurs in the "De Plantis Libri" of Andreas Caesalpinus, published in Florence in 1583. In a vague manner Caesalpinus pointed out ten classes. . . .

Linnaeus is by common consent regarded as the greatest of botanists. He was a Swede, and lived from 1707 till 1778. Linnaeus entered upon his scientific labors at a time when the knowledge of plants and animals was vague and superficial, and when there were no acceptable methods of classifying and arranging either natural objects or the knowledge of them. He entered the field as a reformer. In this capacity he was admirable for his skill, and still more so for the success he won. He brought order out of confusion. His work extended to all kinds of animals and to minerals. Through his exertions a new life was imparted to the pursuit of scientific learning. In this connection we can consider but two of the important reforms instituted by Linnaeus, but these two are among his most conspicuous labors. He made a radical change in the nomenclature of natural objects, and he propounded a new and important system of classification. We will first speak of the reform in nomenclature. Before Linnaeus plants were named in scientific works by a Latin phrase, which was commonly used in the ablative. Thus "Acer foliis palmato-angulatis, florbus subapetalis, sessilibus, fructu pedunculato corymboso" was the name of the red maple. Rendered into English the name reads: "Acer with palmate, angular leaves, sessile and nearly apetalous flowers, and stalked fruit in corymbs." Acer is the generic or general name of all the maples, the same as the word maple is the generic name. The different kinds or species of maples were distinguished from each other by the descriptive phrases. These phrases were unwieldy and inconvenient, and Linnaeus saw what confusion and unpleasantness must come from a multiplication of such names. A very small part of the plants of the world, or even of Europe, were then described. Linnaeus adopted the method of making the name of each plant consist of two words, one a substantive and a generic name, the other an adjective and a specific name. Thus the red maple became in botanical language Acer rubrum. The adoption of this binomial nomenclature, as it is called, meant more than simple convenience to the botanist: it gave a fixedness to genera and to species. The genera of plants were but vaguely defined before this time. We might illustrate a vaguely defined genus by supposing that the term maple might include ashes or other trees besides the true maples, or that one person might apply the name to one set of plants, and another person to a different set. The idea of genus is an important one. This idea is supposed to have originated with Conrad Gessner, an obscure German, who died in 1565; at least most of the merit of the invention is to be ascribed to him. The strictly scientific definition and use of the genus began with Tournefort, however. . . .

The Linnaean System of Classification, although now wholly superseded by the Natural System, was an exceedingly important one, because it first brought strict order into the arrangement of plants and because it recognized the presence and importance of the stamens and pistils.

LIBERTY HYDE BAILEY
[*Talks Afield* (1894)]

On the Naming of Flowers

[*Linnaeus was not the first to realize that some system of nomenclature was desirable. Indeed his own interest was first aroused by the writings of others. Probably he had never heard of the Englishman John Cowell, but just a few years before the Linnaean system was first publicly proposed Cowell published a letter from one P. Belandine with a curious— and not very practical—suggestion.*]

✗

BEFORE I speak of the Management of the choice Sorts of Flowers, such as Tulips, Ranuncula's, &c. I think it necessary to insert the following Letter I receiv'd from a Curious Gentleman, concerning the naming of Flowers, whereby not only they may have pompous Names, as they generally now receive; but the same Names shall likewise express the several Colours in every Flower: so that, without having them painted, one may know by each Name every Colour which is remarkable in each Flower, and which Colour abounds in it.

To Mr. Cowell, Gardener, at Hoxton

Mr. Cowell,

I Have been a Lover of Flowers above twenty Years, the greatest Part of which Time I have lived in *France* and *Flanders:* I am however of *English* Birth, and shall endeavour to explain to you the several Methods we have abroad of naming our Choice Flowers, so that one may know, by seeing any of the pompous Names we give them, what Colours they are of: but 'tis not the way in *England*, I find, to do so; for they give the Flowers Names at random, without considering that every Flower's Name might carry with it a Mark of its Colours.

Abroad our very Curious Flowerists have Lists of all the great Personages, Castles, and Cities by them; and when a good Flower happens to come in their Garden, they give it a Name from them that shall in the two first Letters signify what Colours it is mark'd with: and so when they read their Catalogues over, every Name is, as it were, a Painting of the Flower. The Method is, to make a Table as follows, *viz.*

For White, put the Letter	*W*—or *A* for Argent.
For Yellow put	*Y*.
For Orange	*O*.
For Red	*R*.
For Crimson	*C*.
For Purple of a Reddish Cast	*P*.
For Violet Colour	*V*.
For Blue	*B*.

And if you have any *Black* in a Flower, *that is,* Sable, and may be therefore represented by the Letter *S* because we have *B* already for Blue.

An Example of Naming Flowers after this Manner

A Flower perhaps with White abounding, and mark'd with Crimson, may be called *William the Conqueror;* the *W* in *William* expressing the White abounding, and the *C* the Crimson: or, in a different manner, the same Flower might be named the *Wonder of Constantinople,* where the *W* and the *C* denote the Colours.

A Flower striped with Crimson and Purple, may be called the *Charming Phyllis,* or the *Curious Ptolemy,* the two first Letters denoting the Colours, always understanding that the prevailing Colour is express'd by the first Capital Letter: So in a Flower where the *Violet* prevails, and the other Colour is *Orange,* one may name it *Victorious Orlando,* or the *Virtuous Oreda.* Where the Colours are Blue and Red, the Name may be the *Beautiful Rodolinda,* or the *British Rover:* and for Yellow and Purple, one might name the Flower the *Young Prince;* or White and Purple, the *Wise Prince,* and so on.

The Curious abroad have now, for the most part, this sort of Catalogue; and if they happen to meet with old Flowers that are not named after this manner, they add a Character which expresses their Colour; as in the Flower called *Duchesse d'Avero,* which is *White* streak'd with *Violet,* and which Name singly denotes none of the Colours the Flower bears; but as *Blanc* in *French* signifies *White,* and the *Violet* is the same in *English* as in *French,* so they add to the Name, by way of Distinction of Colour, *Bonne Veuve;* which signifies a *Good Widow,* as herself was allow'd to be: and then *B* in the *French* Word *Blanc,* which is *White,* expresses that Colour; and *Veuve,* whose first Letter signifies *Violet,* is Mark sufficient for the Flowerist to distinguish by. So may we add a Character to any Flower already named in *England;* as for Example, the fine Carnation, which is called the *Princess Amelia,* whose Principal is *White,* and mark'd with *Violet:* To this might be added, the *Worthy Virgin,* taking the Colours of the Flower from the two initial Letters; which shew from the *W* the chief Colour is *White,* and the other in *Virgin* denotes *Violet.* And by this means you will always know the Colours of your Flowers, by writing the Names of each sort on some piece of Wood, &c. and placing them in each Pot: So that whenever you see these Names, you will remember what Colours every Flower carries with it. One might bring many more Examples, which I have from some of the *French* and *Flemish* Catalogues, but I guess these will be sufficient to inform you of the Design; and so I conclude.

JOHN COWELL
[*The Curious and Practical Gardener* (1730)]

The Creed of Linnaeus

[*Linnaeus was quickly famous both at home and abroad. In Europe he was employed both by his government and by noble patrons. A preface to a museum catalogue* (Museum Regis Adolphi Friderici, *1754*) *was translated into English only seven years after his death because it so vividly expressed his spirit.*]

I F therefore the Maker of all things, who had done nothing without design, has furnished this earthly globe, like a museum, with the most admirable proofs of his wisdom and power; if, moreover, this splendid theatre would be adorned in vain without a spectator; and if he placed in it Man, the chief and most perfect of all his works, who is alone capable of duly considering the wonderful œconomy of the whole; it follows, that Man is made for the purpose of studying the Creator's works, that he may observe in them the evident marks of divine wisdom.

Thus we learn, not only from the opinions of moralists and divines, but also from the testimony of nature herself, that this world is destined to the celebration of the Creator's glory, and that man is placed in it to be the publisher and interpreter of the wisdom of God: and indeed he who does not make himself acquainted with God from the consideration of nature, will scarcely acquire knowledge of him from any other source; for "if we have no faith in the things which are seen, how should we believe those things which are not seen?" . . .

For the Author of eternal salvation is also the Lord of nature. He who has destined us for future joys, has at present placed us in this world. Whoever therefore shall regard with contempt the œconomy of the Creator here, is as truly impious as the man who takes no thought of futurity. And in order to lead us toward our duty, the Deity has so closely connected the study of his works with our general convenience and happiness, that the more we examine them, the more we discover for our use and gratification. . . .

The magnificence and beauty, the regularity, convenience, and utility of the works of creation, cannot fail to afford man the highest degree of pleasure; so that he who has seen and examined most of these, must the more perfectly admire and love the world as the work of the great Creator, and must the more readily aquiesce in his wise government. . . .

Can any work be imagined more forcibly to proclaim the majesty of its author, than a little inactive earth rendered capable of contemplating itself as animated by the hand of God? . . .

Man, ever desirous of knowledge, has already explored many things; but more and greater still remain concealed; perhaps reserved for far distant generations, who shall prosecute the examination of their Creator's works in remote countries, and make many discoveries for the pleasure and convenience of life. Posterity shall see its increasing Museums, and the knowledge of the Divine Wisdom, flourish together; and at the same time all the practical sciences, antiquities, history, geography, natural philosophy, natural history, botany, mineralogy, dietetics, pathology, medicine, materia medica, œconomy, and the manual arts, shall be enriched: for we cannot avoid thinking, that what we know of the Divine works are much fewer than those of which we are ignorant.

CAROLUS LINNAEUS
[*Reflections on the Study of Nature* (1785)]

Lapland Journey

[*While still a student and at the age of twenty-five, Linnaeus made his one and only extensive journey—the famous peregrination of Lapland on foot in the year 1732. By comparison with the great voyages of the century it may not seem very impressive, but Lapland was indescribably primitive and little known to Europeans. To journey through it alone and without equipment was a considerable undertaking which, by the way, Linnaeus himself was not inclined to minimize. The account which he wrote has the curious springtime freshness of both his own youth and the youth of field botany. Of it the early nineteenth-century translator James Edward Smith wrote: "We here behold, not the awful preceptor*

of the learned world in his professorial chair but a youthful inexperienced
student full of ardour and curiosity, such as we ourselves have been,
recording his ideas and observations for his own use, not delivering them
forth for the instruction of others."]

HAVING been appointed by the Royal Academy of Sciences to
travel through Lapland, for the purpose of investigating the three kingdoms of Nature in that country, I prepared my wearing apparel and
other necessaries for the journey as follows.

My clothes consisted of a light coat of Westgothland linsey-
woolsey cloth without folds, lined with red shalloon, having small cuffs
and collar of shag; leather breeches: a round wig; a green leather cap,
and a pair of half boots. I carried a small leather bag, half an ell in length,
but somewhat less in breadth furnished on one side with hooks and
eyes, so that it could be opened and shut at pleasure. This bag contained
one shirt; two pair of false sleeves; two half shirts; an inkstand, pencase,
microscope, and spying-glass, a gauze cap to protect me occasionally
from the gnats; a comb; my journal, and a parcel of paper stitched
together for drying plants, both in folio; my manuscript Ornithology,
Flora Uplandica, and *Characteres generici*. I wore a hanger at my side,
and carried a small fowling-piece, as well as an octangular stick, graduated for the purpose of measuring. My pocketbook contained a passport
from the Governor of Upsal, and a recommendation from the Academy.

I set out alone from the city of Upsal on Friday May 12, 1732,
at eleven o'clock, being at that time within half a day of twenty-five years
of age.

At this season Nature wore her most cheerful and delightful
aspect, and Flora celebrated her nuptials with Phoebus.

> *Omnia vere vigent et veris tempore florent*
> *Et totus fervet Veneris dulcedine mundus.*

Spring clothes the fields and decks the flowery grove,
And all creation glows with life and love.

Now the winter corn was half a foot in height, and the barley
had just shot out its blade. The birch, the elm, and the aspen-tree began
to put forth their leaves.

Upsal is the ancient seat of government. Its palace was destroyed by fire in 1702. With respect to situation, and variety of prospects, scarcely any city can be compared with this. For the distance of

a quarter of a Swedish mile it is surrounded with fertile corn-fields, which are bounded by hills, and the view is terminated by spacious forests.

I had no sooner passed the northern gate of the city than I perceived signs of a clay soil, except in the hills, which consist of sand and stones. The road here is level, and for a quarter of a mile destitute of trees. In ditches by the way side the Water Byssus was observable (*Byssus Flos aquae*), particularly in places sheltered from the wind. It greatly resembles the cream of milk, and is called by the peasants *Watnet Blommar*, or Water Flower.

A number of mares with their colts were grazing every where near the road. I remarked the great length of the young animals' legs, which according to common opinion are as long at their birth as they ever will be; therefore if a measure be taken from the hoof up to the knee of a young colt, and so on from the knee to the extremity, it will give the height of the horse when full grown. A similar observation has been made on the size of the bones in the ear of an infant.

I observed the same kind of moss, or rather *Lichenoides terrestre, daedaleis sinubus* (*Lichen nivalis*), which is found on the hill near the palace at Upsal.

Geese were now accompanied by their goslings, which are all uniformly of the same yellow hue when hatched, whatever colour they may acquire afterwards.

I left old Upsal on the right with its three large sepulchral mounds or *tumuli*.

The few plants now in flower were *Taraxacum* (*Leontodon Taraxacum*), which Tournefort erroneously combines with *Pilosella* (*Hieracium Pilosella*) notwithstanding the reflexed leaves of its calyx; *Draba caule nudo* (*D. verna*), which in Smoland is called Rye Flower, because as soon as the husbandman sees it in bloom he is accustomed to sow his Lent Corn; *Myosotis scorpioides; Viola tricolor and odorata; Thlaspi arvense; Lithospermum arvense; Cyperoides* (probably some species of *Carex*); *Juncoides* (*Juncus campestris*); *Salix* (S. *caprea?*); *Primula veris*, as it is called, though neither here nor in other places the first flower of the spring; *Caltha palustris*, known by the name of Swedish Caper, as many people are said to eat it instead of the true Caper; the report of its giving a colour to butter is certainly false.

The lark was my companion all the way, flying before me quivering in the air.

Ecce suum tirile, tirile, suum tirile tractat.

The weather was warm and serene. Now and then a refreshing breeze sprang up from the west, and a rising cloud was observable in that quarter.

Okstad (more properly Högsta) is a mile and a quarter from Upsal. Here the forests began to thicken. The charming lark, which had till now attended my steps, here left me; but another bird welcomed my approach to the forest, the Red-wing or *Turdus iliacus*, whose amorous warblings from the tops of the Spruce Fir were no less delightful. Its lofty and varied notes rival those of the nightingale herself.

In the forest innumerable dwarf Firs are to be seen, whose diminutive height bears no proportion to their thick trunks, their lowermost branches being on a level with the uppermost, and the leading shoot entirely wanting. It seems as if all the branches came from one centre, like those of a palm, and that the top had been cut off. I attribute this to the soil, and could not but admire it as the pruning of Nature. This form of the Fir has been called *Pinus plicata*.

Läby is a mile and a quarter further. Here the forest abounds with the Red Spanish Whortle-berry (*Arbutus Uva Ursi*), which was now in blossom, and of which, as it had not been scientifically described, I made a description (see *Flora Lapponica*; and *Engl. Bot.* t. 714). . . .

We pursued our journey by water with considerable labour and difficulty all night long, if it might be called night, which was as light as the day, the sun disappearing for about half an hour only, and the temperature of the air being rather cold. The colonist who was my companion was obliged sometimes to wade along in the river, dragging the boat after him, for half a mile together. His feet and legs were protected by shoes made of birch bark. In the morning we went on shore, in order to inquire for a native Laplander, who would undertake to be my guide further on. Finding only an empty hut at the spot where we landed, we proceeded as fast as we could to the next hut, a quarter of a mile distant, which likewise proved unoccupied. At length we arrived at a third hut, half a mile further, but met with as little success as at the two former, it being quite empty. Upon which I dispatched my fellow-traveller to a fourth hut, at some distance, to see if he could find any person fit for my purpose, and I betook myself to the contemplation of the wild scenes of Nature around me.

The soil here was extremely sterile, consisting of barren sand (*Arena Glarea*) without any large stones or rocks, which are only seen near the shores of the waters. Fir trees were rather thinly scattered, but they were extremely lofty, towering up to the clouds. Here were spacious tracts producing the finest timber I ever beheld. The ground was clothed with Ling, Red Whortle-berries (*Vaccinium Vitis Idaea*) and mosses. In such parts as were rather low grew smaller firs, amongst abundance of birch, the ground there also producing Red Whortle-berries, as well as the common black kind (*Vaccinium Myrtillus*), with *Polytrichum* (*commune*). On the dry hills, which most abounded with large pines, the finest timber was strewed around, felled by the force of the tempests, lying in all directions, so as to render the country in some places almost impenetrable. I seemed to have reached the residence of Pan himself, and shall now describe the huts in which his subjects the Laplanders contrive to resist the rigours of their native climate.

The *Kodda*, or hut, is formed of double timbers, lying one upon another, and has mostly six sides, rarely but four. It is supported within by four inclining posts, as thick as one's arm, crossing each other in pairs at the top, upon which is laid a transverse beam, four ells in length. On each side lower down is another cross piece of wood, serving to hang pipes on. The walls are formed of beams of a similar thickness, but differing in length, leaving a hole at the top to serve as a chimney, and a door at the side. . . . These are covered with a layer of bark, either of Spruce Fir or Birch, and over that is another layer of wood like the first. In the centre, the fire is made on the ground, and the inhabitants lie round it. In the middle of the chimney hangs a pole, on which the pot is suspended over the fire.

The height of the hut is three ells, its greatest breadth at the base two fathoms.

They always construct their huts in places where they have ready access to clear cold springs.

The inhabitants sleep quite naked on skins of reindeer, spread over a layer of branches of Dwarf Birch (*Betula nana*), with similar skins spread over them. The sexes rise from this simple couch, and dress themselves promiscuously without any shame or concealment.

When, as occasionally happens in the course of the summer, they cannot procure fresh water, and are necessitated to drink the warm sea water, they are infallibly tormented with griping pains, with strong spasms in the region of the stomach, and pain in the lower part of the abdomen, accompanied with bloody urine. This is a species of colic, and is called *ullem*. It generally lasts but one day, rarely two. The same thing happens if they drink before they have broke their fast in a morning.

Every where around the huts I observed horns of reindeer lying neglected, and it is remarkable that they were gnawed, and sometimes half devoured, by squirrels. . . .

The forest here was full of the noblest pine trees, growing to no purpose with respect to the inhabitants, as the wood is not used even for building huts, nor the bark for food, as it is in some other parts. I wonder they have not contrived to turn these trees to some account, by burning them for tar or pitch.

The colonists who reside among the Laplanders are beloved by them, and treated with great kindness. These good people willingly point out to the strangers where they may fix their abode so as to have access to moist meadows affording good hay, which they themselves do not want, their herds of reindeer preferring the driest pastures. They expect in return that the colonists should supply them with milk and flour.

Ovid's description of the silver age is still applicable to the native inhabitants of Lapland. Their soil is not wounded by the plough, nor is the iron din of arms to be heard; neither have mankind found their way to the bowels of the earth, nor do they engage in wars to define its boundaries. They perpetually change their abode, live in tents, and follow a pastoral life, just like the patriarchs of old.

Among these people the men are employed in the business of cookery, so that the master of a family has no occasion to speak a good word to his wife, when he wishes to give a hospitable entertainment to his guests.

The dress of these Laplanders is as follows.

On the head they wear a small cap, like those used at my native place of Stenbrohult, made with eight seams covered with strips of brown cloth, the cap itself being of a greyish colour. This reaches no lower than the tips of the ears.

Their outer garment, or jacket, is open in front half way down the bosom, below which part it is fastened with hooks, as far as the pit of the stomach. Consequently the neck is bare, and from the effects of the sun abroad and the smoke at home, approaches the complexion of a toad. The jacket when loose reaches below the knees; but it is usually tied up with a girdle, so as scarcely to reach so far, and is sloped off at the bottom. The collar is of four fingers' breadth, thick, and stitched with thread.

All the needle-work is performed by the women. They make their thread of the sinews in the legs of the reindeer, separating them, while fresh, with their teeth, into slender strings, which they twist together. A kind of cord is also made of the roots of spruce fir. . . .

We waited till about two'oclock in the afternoon for the Laplander I had sent on the expedition above mentioned, who at length returned quite spent with fatigue. He had made the requisite inquiries at many of the huts, but in vain. He was accompanied by a person whose appearance was such that at first I did not know whether I beheld a man or a woman. I scarcely believe that any poetical description of a fury could come up to the idea, which this Lapland fair-one excited. It might well be imagined that she was truly of Stygian origin. Her stature was very diminutive. Her face of the darkest brown from the effects of smoke. Her eyes dark and sparkling. Her eyebrows black. Her pitchy-coloured hair hung loose about her head, and on it she wore a flat red cap. She had a grey petticoat; and from her neck, which resembled the skin of a frog, were suspended a pair of large loose breasts of the same brown complexion, but encompassed, by way of ornament, with brass rings. Round her waist she wore a girdle, and on her feet a pair of half boots.

Her first aspect really struck me with dread; but though a fury in appearance, she addressed me, with mingled pity and reserve, in the following terms:

"O thou poor man! what hard destiny can have brought thee hither, to a place never visited by any one before? This is the first time I ever beheld a stranger. Thou miserable creature! How didst thou come, and whither wilt thou go? Dost thou not perceive what houses and habitations we have, and with how much difficulty we go to church?"

I entreated her to point out some way by which I might continue my journey in any direction, so as not to be forced to return the way I came.

"Nay, man," said she, "thou hast only to go the same way back again; for the river overflows so much, it is not possible for thee to proceed further in this direction. From us thou hast no assistance to expect in the prosecution of thy journey, as my husband, who might have helped thee, is ill. Thou mayst inquire for our next neighbour, who lives about a mile off, and perhaps, if thou shouldst meet with him, he may give thee some assistance, but I really believe it will scarcely be in his power."

I inquired how far it was to Sorsele. "That we do not know," replied she; "but in the present state of the roads it is at least seven days journey from hence, as my husband had told me."

My health and strength being by this time materially impaired by wading through such an extent of marshes, laden with my apparel and luggage, for the Laplander had enough to do to carry the boat; by walking for whole nights together; by not having for a long time tasted any boiled meat; by drinking a great quantity of water, as nothing else

was to be had; and by eating nothing but fish, unsalted and crawling with
vermin, I must have perished but for a piece of dried and salted reindeer's
flesh, given me by my kind hostess the clergyman's wife at Lycksele.
This food, however, without bread, proved unwholesome and indigestible. How I longed once more to meet with people who feed on spoon-
meat! I inquired of this woman whether she could give me any thing to
eat. She replied, "Nothing but fish." I looked at the fresh fish, as it was
called, but perceiving its mouth to be full of maggots, I had no appetite
to touch it; but though it thus abated my hunger, it did not recruit my
strength. I asked if I could have any reindeer tongues, which are commonly dried for sale, and served up even at the tables of the great; but
was answered in the negative. "Have you no cheese made of reindeer's
milk?" said I. "Yes," replied she, "but it is a mile off."

"If it were here, would you allow me to buy some?" "I have
no desire," answered the good woman, "that thou shouldst die in my
country for want of food."

On arriving at her hut, I perceived three cheeses lying under a
shed without walls, and took the smallest of them, which she, after some
consultation, allowed me to purchase.

The cap of my hostess, like that of all the Lapland women, was
very remarkable. It was made of double red cloth, as is usually the case,
of a round flat form. The upper side was flat, a foot broad, and stitched
round the edge, where the lining was turned over. At the under side was
a hole to receive the head with a projecting border round it. The lining
being loose, the cap covers the head more or less, at the pleasure of the
wearer.

As to shift, she, like all her country-women, was destitute of
any such garment. She wore a collar or tippet of the breadth of two
fingers, stitched with thread, and bordered next the skin with brass rings.
Over this she wore two grey jackets, both alike, which reached to her
knees, just like those worn by the men.

I was at last obliged to return the way I came, though very unwillingly, heartily wishing it might never be my fate to see this place
again. It was as bad as a visit to Acheron. If I could have run up the bed
of a river like a Laplander, I might have gone on, but that was impossible. . . .

Chamaedaphne of Buxbaum (*Andromeda polifolia*) was at this
time in its highest beauty, decorating the marshy grounds in a most
agreeable manner. The flowers are quite blood-red before they expand,
but when full-grown the corolla is of a flesh-colour. Scarcely any paint-

er's art can so happily imitate the beauty of a fine female complexion; still less could any artificial colour upon the face itself bear a comparison with this lovely blossom. As I contemplated it I could not help thinking of Andromeda as described by the poets; and the more I meditated upon their descriptions, the more applicable they seemed to the little plant before me, so that if these writers had had it in view, they could scarcely have contrived a more apposite fable. Andromeda is represented by them as a virgin of most exquisite and unrivalled charms; but these charms remain in perfection only so long as she retains her virgin purity, which is also applicable to the plant, now preparing to celebrate its nuptials. This plant is always fixed on some little turfy hillock in the midst of the swamps, as Andromeda herself was chained to a rock in the sea, which bathed her feet, as the fresh water does the roots of the plant. Dragons and venomous serpents surrounded her, as toads and other reptiles frequent the abode of her vegetable prototype, and, when they pair in the spring, throw mud and water over its leaves and branches. As the distressed virgin cast down her blushing face through excessive affliction, so does the rosy-coloured flower hang its head, growing paler and paler till it withers away. Hence, as this plant forms a new genus, I have chosen for it the name of *Andromeda*. . . .

The clergyman of Jockmock, Mr. Malming, who is the schoolmaster, and Mr. Hogling the curate, tormented me with their consummate and most pertinacious ignorance. I could not but wonder how so much pride and ambition, such scandalous want of information, with such incorrigible stupidity, could exist in persons of their profession, who are commonly expected to be men of knowledge; yet any schoolboy twelve years of age might be better informed. No man will deny the propriety of such people as these, at least, being placed as far as possible from civilized society.

The learned curate began his conversation with remarks on the clouds in this country, setting forth how they strike the mountains as they pass, carrying away stones, trees and cattle. I ventured to suggest that such accidents were rather to be attributed to the force of the wind, for that the clouds could not of themselves lift, or carry away, anything. He laughed at me, saying surely I had never seen any clouds. For my part, it seemed to me that he could have never been any where but in the clouds. I replied, that whenever the weather is foggy I walk in clouds, and when the fog is condensed, and no longer supported in the air, it immediately rains beneath my feet. At all such reasoning, being above his comprehension, he only laughed with a sardonic smile. Still less was he satisfied with my explanation how watery bubbles may be lifted up into the air, as he told me the clouds were solid bodies. On my denying this, he reinforced his assertion with a text of scripture, silencing me by authority, and then laughing at my ignorance. He next condescended to inform me that after rain a phlegm is always to be found on the mountains, where the clouds have touched them. Upon my replying that this phlegm is a vegetable called *Nostoc*, I was, like St. Paul, judged to be mad, and that too much learning had turned my brain. This philosopher, who was as fully persuaded of his own complete knowledge of nature, as Sturmius was of being able to fly by means of hollow globes, was pleased to be very facetious at my expense. At length he graciously advised me to pay some regard to the opinions of people skilled in these abstruse matters, and not, at my return home, to expose myself by publishing such absurd and preposterous opinions as I had now advanced.

The other, the pedagogue, lamented that people should bestow so much attention upon temporal vanities, and consequently, alas! neglect their spiritual good; and he remarked that many a man had been ruined by too great application to study.

CAROLUS LINNAEUS
[*Lachesis Lapponica,*
TRANSLATED BY JAMES SMITH (1811)]

Linnaean Names

[*Of Linnaeus it may be said that no other man since Adam has had the privilege of bestowing so many names, and many of those he chose are still in official use. Specimens poured in to him from all corners of the world and he either christened them or confirmed the names some of them already bore. Addicted as he was to a kind of fancy half-serious, half-playful he would, on occasion, justify by some quaint analogy the application to a plant of the family name of an individual—as in the few examples which follow.*]

Commelina has flowers of three petals—two distinct, the third hardly conspicuous. Named after the two botanists whose name was Commelin, the third having died before achieving anything in botany.

Hernandia is an American tree with beautiful leaves but less remarkable flowers. Named after a botanist who had extraordinary good luck and was paid well for his research into American natural history. Would that the fruits of his labors had equalled the expenditure.

Dillenia has of all plants the most magnificent flower and fruits, as Dillenius is a magnificent specimen among botanists.

Pisonia is a somber tree because of its thorns. Named according to a tradition concerning Piso who is somber indeed if what a relative of Marcgraf accuses him of is true—namely that he got all his knowledge from Marcgraf after the death of the latter.

Gronovia is a creeper embracing all other plants within its reach. Named after a man who was equalled by few as an embracer and collector of plants.

Linnaea was given its name by Gronovius. It is a Lapland plant of short growth, insignificant, disregarded, and flowering for a short time. It was named for Linnaeus who resembles it.

Hymenaea Courbaril. When the small leaves are young they close together at night so that they look like one leaf. The name "wedding night" is therefore given it.

CAROLUS LINNAEUS
[*Critica Botanica* (1737)]

The First Great American Plant Man as Seen by an Admirer

[*The first great American botanists—and they are in the Linnaean tradition—were John Bartram and his son William of Philadelphia. We shall meet them again as noted explorers for plants but here is an account of the first Bartram by that pseudo "American Farmer" Michel de Crève-coeur, in the form of a letter purportedly from a "Russian gentleman."*

Some of the biographical details are suspected of being more picturesque than strictly accurate.]

I N order to convince you that I have not bestowed undeserved praises, in my former letters on this celebrated government; and that either nature or the climate seems to be more favourable here to the arts and sciences, than to any other American province; let us together, agreeable to your desire, pay a visit to Mr. John Bertram, the first botanist, in this new hemisphere: become such by a native impulse of disposition. It is to this simple man that America is indebted for several useful discoveries, and the knowledge of many new plants. I had been greatly prepossessed in his favour by the extensive correspondence which I knew he held with the most eminent Scotch and French botanists; I knew also that he had been honored with that of Queen Ulrica of Sweden.

His house is small, but decent; there was something peculiar in its first appearance, which seemed to distinguish it from those of his neighbours: a small tower in the middle of it, not only helped to strengthen it but afforded convenient room for a staircase. Every disposition of the fields, fences, and trees, seemed to bear the marks of perfect order and regularity, which in rural affairs, always indicate a prosperous industry.

I was received at the door by a woman dressed extremely neat and simple, who without courtesying, or any other ceremonial, asked me, with an air of benignity, who I wanted? I answered, I should be glad to see Mr. Bertram. If thee wilt step in and take a chair, I will send for him. No, I said, I had rather have the pleasure of walking through his farm, I shall easily find him out, with your directions. After a little time I perceived the Schuylkill, winding through delightful meadows, and soon cast my eyes on a new-made bank, which seemed greatly to confine its stream. After having walked on its top a considerable way I at last reached the place where ten men were at work. I asked, if any of them could tell me where Mr. Bertram was? An elderly looking man, with wide trowsers and a large leather apron on, looking at me said, "My name is Bertram, dost thee want me?" Sir, I am come on purpose to converse with you, if you can be spared from your labour. "Very easily (he answered) I direct and advise more than I work." We walked toward the house, where he made me take a chair while he went to put on clean clothes, after which he returned and sat down by me. The fame of your knowledge, said I, in American botany, and your well-known hospitality, have induced me to pay you a visit, which I hope you will not think troublesome: I should be glad to spend a few hours in your garden. "The greatest advantage (replied he) which I receive from what thee callest my botanical fame, is the pleasure which it often procureth me in receiving the visits of friends and foreigners: but our jaunt into the garden must be postponed for the present, as the bell is ringing for dinner." We entered into a large hall, where there was a long table full of victuals; at the lowest part sat his negroes, his hired men were next, then the family and myself; and at the head, the venerable father and his wife presided. Each reclined his head and said his prayers, divested of the tedious cant of some, and of the ostentatious stile of others. "After the luxuries of our cities, (observed he) this plain fare must appear to thee a severe fast." By no means, Mr. Bertram, this honest country dinner convinces me, that you receive me as a friend and an old acquaintance. "I am glad of it, for thee art heartily welcome. I never knew how to use ceremonies; they are insufficient proofs of sincerity; our society, besides, are utterly strangers to what the world calleth polite expressions. We treat others as we treat ourselves. I received yesterday a letter from Philadelphia, by which I understand thee art a Russian; what motives can possibly have induced thee to quit thy native country and to come so far in quest of knowledge or pleasure? Verily, it is a great compliment thee payest to this our young province, to think that any thing it exhibiteth may be worthy thy attention.". . .

Our walks and botanical observations engrossed so much of our time, that the sun was almost down ere I thought of returning to Philadelphia; I regretted that the day had been so short, as I had not spent so rational a one for a long time before. I wanted to stay, yet was doubtful whether it would not appear improper, being an utter stranger. Knowing however, that I was visiting the least ceremonious people in the world, I bluntly informed him of the pleasure I had enjoyed, and with the desire I had of staying a few days with him. "Thee art as welcome as if I was thy father; thee art no stranger; thy desire of knowledge, thy being a foreigner besides, entitleth thee to consider my house as thine own, as long as thee pleaseth: use thy time with the most perfect freedom; I too shall do so myself." I thankfully accepted the kind invitation.

We went to view his favourite bank; he shewed me the principles and method on which it was erected; and we walked over the grounds which had been already drained. The whole store of nature's kind luxuriance seemed to have been exhausted on these beautiful meadows; he made me count the amazing number of cattle and horses now feeding on solid bottoms, which but a few years before had been covered with water. Thence we rambled through his fields, where the right-angular fences, the heaps of pitched stones, the flourishing clover, announced the best husbandry, as well as the most assiduous attention. His cows were then returning home, deep bellied, short legged, having udders ready to burst; seeking with seeming toil, to be delivered from the great exuberance they contained: he next shewed me his orchard, formerly planted on a barren sandy soil, but long since converted into one of the richest spots in that vicinage.

"This (said he) is altogether the fruit of my own contrivance; I purchased some years ago the privilege of a small spring, about a mile and a half from hence, which at a considerable expence I have brought to this reservoir; therein I throw old lime, ashes, horse-dung, &c. and twice a week I let it run, thus impregnated; I regularly spread on this ground in the fall, old hay, straw, and whatever damaged fodder I have about my barn. By these simple means I mow, one year with another, fifty-three hundreds of excellent hay per acre, from a soil, which scarcely produced five-fingers (a small plant resembling strawberries) some years before." This is, Sir, a miracle in husbandry; happy the country which is cultivated by a society of men, whose application and taste lead them to prosecute and accomplish useful works. "I am not the only person who do these things (he said) wherever water can be had it is always turned to that important use; wherever a farmer can water his meadows, the greatest crops of the best hay and excellent after-grass, are the sure rewards of his labours. With the banks of my meadow ditches, I have greatly enriched my upland fields, those which I intend to rest for a few years, I constantly sow with red clover, which is the greatest meliorator of our lands. For three years after, they yield abundant pasture; when I want to break up my clover fields, I give them a good coat of mud, which hath been exposed to the severities of three or four of our winters. This is the reason that I commonly reap from twenty-eight to thirty-six bushels of wheat an acre; my flax, oats, and Indian corn, I raise in the same proportion. Wouldst thee inform me whether the inhabitants of thy country follow the same methods of husbandry?" No, Sir; in the neighbourhood of our towns, there are indeed some intelligent farmers, who prosecute their rural schemes with attention; but we should be too numerous, too happy, too powerful a people, if it were possible for the whole Russian Empire to be cultivated like the province of Pennsylvania. Our lands are so unequally divided, and so few of our farmers are possessors of the soil they till, that they cannot execute plans of husbandry with the same vigor as you do, who hold yours, as it were from the Master of nature, unincumbered and free. Oh, America! exclaimed I, thou knowest not as yet the whole extent of thy happiness: the foundation of thy civil polity must lead thee in a few years to a degree of population and power which Europe little thinks of! "Long before this happen (answered the good man) we shall rest beneath the turf; it is vain for mortals to be presumptuous in their conjectures: our country, is, no doubt, the cradle of an extensive future population; the old world is growing weary of its inhabitants, they must come here to flee from the tyranny of the great. But doth not thee imagine, that the great will, in the course of years, come over here also; for it is the misfortune of all societies every where to hear of great men, great rulers, and of great tyrants." My dear Sir, I replied, tyranny never can take a strong hold in this country, the land is too widely distributed: it is poverty in Europe that makes slaves. "Friend Iwan, as I make no doubt that thee understandest the Latin tongue, read this kind epistle which the good Queen of Sweden, Ulrica, sent me a few years ago. Good woman! that she should think in her palace at Stockholm of poor John Bertram, on the banks of the Schuylkill; appeareth to me very strange." Not in the least, dear Sir; you are the first man whose name as a botanist hath done honour to America; it is very natural at the same time to imagine, that so extensive a continent must contain many curious plants and trees: is it then surprising to see a princess, fond of useful knowledge, descend sometimes from the throne, to walk in the gardens of Linnaeus? "Tis to the directions of that learned man (said Mr. Bertram) that I am indebted for the method which has led me to the knowledge I now possess; the science of botany is so diffusive, that a proper thread is absolutely wanted to conduct the beginner." Pray, Mr. Bertram, when did you imbibe the first wish to cultivate the science of botany; was you regularly bred to it in Philadelphia? "I have never received any other education than barely reading and writing; this small farm was all the patrimony my father left me, certain debts and the want of meadows kept me rather low in the beginning of my life; my wife brought me nothing in money, all her riches consisted in her good temper and great knowledge of housewifery. I scarcely know how to trace my steps in the botanical career; they appear to me now like unto a dream: but thee mayest rely on what I shall relate, though I know that some of our friends have laughed at it." I am not one of those people, Mr. Bertram, who aim at finding out the ridiculous in what is sincerely and honestly averred. "Well, then, I'll tell thee: One day I was very busy in holding my plough (for thee seest that I am but a ploughman) and being weary I ran under the shade of a tree to repose myself. I cast my eyes on a daisy, I plucked it mechanically and viewed it with more curiosity than common country farmers are wont to do; and observed therein very many distinct parts, some perpendicular, some horizontal. What a shame, said my mind, or something that inspired my mind, that thee shouldest have employed so many years in tilling the earth and destroying so many flowers and plants, without being acquainted with their structures and their uses! This seeming inspiration suddenly awakened my curiosity, for these were not thoughts to which I had been accustomed. I returned to my team, but this new desire did not quit my mind; I mentioned it to my wife, who greatly discouraged me from prosecuting my new scheme, as she called it; I was not opulent enough, she said, to dedicate much of my time to studies and labours which might rob me of that portion of it which is the only wealth of the American farmer. However her prudent caution did not discourage me; I thought about it continually, at supper, in bed, and wherever I went. At last I could not resist the impulse; for on the fourth day of the following week, I hired a man to plough for me, and went to Philadelphia. Though I knew not what book to call for, I ingeniously told the bookseller my errand, who provided me with such as he thought best, and a Latin grammar beside. Next I applied to a neighbouring schoolmaster, who in three months taught me Latin enough to understand Linnaeus, which I purchased afterward. Then I began to botanize all over my farm; in a little time I became acquainted with every vegetable that grew in my neighbourhood; and next ventured into Maryland, living among the Friends: in proportion as I thought myself more learned I proceeded farther, and by a steady application of several years I have acquired a pretty general knowledge of every plant and tree to be found in our continent. In process of time I was applied to from the old countries, whither I every year send many collections. Being now made easy in my circumstances, I have ceased to labour, and am never so happy as when I see and converse with my friends. If among the many plants or shrubs I am acquainted with, there are any thee wantest to send to thy native country, I will chearfully procure them, and give thee moreover whatever directions thee mayest want."

MICHEL DE CRÈVECOEUR
[*Letters from an American Farmer* (1782)]

Section Five

EXPLORING FOR PLANTS

Gardening is civil and social, but it wants the vigor and freedom of the forest and the outlaw. . . . There are other, savager and more primitive aspects of nature than our poets have sung.

THOREAU

Some men go into the wilderness to slay, and they come home bearing their burdens of fish and game. Others—the gentle hunters—go armed with basket and trowel, for the quarry they would track are green growing things that they hope to keep alive—ferns and flowers and the tender roots that will grow to lusty shrubs. . . . The gentle hunter has always his quarry beside him in his garden. In spring he awaits its awakening, watches its burgeoning in summer, sees its leaves turn and fall in the shortening days of autumn and in winter can rest content in the certainty that the cycle will start afresh when spring comes again.

RICHARDSON WRIGHT

Plant Introduction

[The father of Benjamin Disraeli was an antiquarian who compiled a still-useful collection of curious historical facts. Here he pays tribute to the introducers of new plants.]

T H E R E has been a class of men whose patriotic affection, or whose general benevolence, have been usually defrauded of the gratitude their country owes them: these have been the introducers of new flowers, new plants, and new roots into Europe; the greater part which we now enjoy was drawn from the luxuriant climates of Asia, and the profusion which now covers our land originated in the most anxious nursing, and were the gifts of individuals. Monuments are reared, and medals struck, to commemorate events and names, which are less deserving our regard than those who have transplanted into the colder gardens of the North the rich fruits, the beautiful flowers, and the succulent pulse and roots of more favoured spots; and carrying into their own country, as it were, another Nature, they have, as old Gerard well expresses it, "laboured with the soil to make it fit for the plants, and with the plants to make them delight in the soil.". . .

There was a period when the spirit of plantation was prevalent in this kingdom; it probably originated from the ravages of the soldiery during the civil wars. A man, whose retired modesty has perhaps obscured his claims on our regard, the intimate friend of the great spirits of that age, by birth a Pole, but whose mother had probably been an English woman, SAMUEL HARTLIB, to whom Milton addressed his tract on education, published every manuscript he collected on the subjects of horticulture and agriculture. The public good he effected attracted the notice of Cromwell, who rewarded him with a pension, which after the restoration of Charles II was suffered to lapse, and Hartlib died in utter neglect and poverty. One of his tracts is "A design for plenty by an universal planting of fruit-trees." The project consisted in enclosing the waste lands and commons, and appointing officers, whom he calls fruiterers, or wood-wards, to see the plantations were duly attended to. The writer of this project observes on fruits, that it is a sort of provisions so natural to the taste, that the poor man and even the child will prefer it before better food, "as the story goeth," which he has preserved in these ancient and simple lines.

> The poor man child invited was to dine,
> With flesh of oxen, sheep, and fatted swine,
> (Far better cheer than he at home could find),
> And yet this child to stay had little minde.
> You have, quoth he, no apple, froise, nor pie,
> Stew'd pairs, with bread and milk, and walnuts by.

The enthusiasm of these transplanters inspired their labours. They have watched the tender infant of their planting, till the leaf and the flowers and the fruit expanded under their hand; often indeed they have even ameliorated the quality, increased the size, and even created a new species. The apricot, drawn from America, was first known in Europe in the sixteenth century: an old French writer has remarked, that it was originally not larger than a damson; our gardeners, he says, have improved it to the perfection of its present size and richness. One of these enthusiasts is noticed by Evelyn, who for forty years had in vain tried by a graft to bequeath his name to a new fruit; but persisting on wrong principles, this votary of Pomona has died without a name. We sympathise with Sir William Temple when he exultingly acquaints us with the size of his orange-trees, and with the flavour of his peaches and grapes, confessed by Frenchmen to have equalled those of Fontaine-bleau and Gascony, while the Italians agreed that his white figs were as good as any of that sort in Italy: and of his "having had the honour" to naturalize in this country four kinds of grapes, with his liberal distributions of cuttings from them, because "he ever thought all things of this kind the commoner they are the better."

The greater number of our exotic flowers and fruits were carefully transported into this country by many of our travelled nobility and gentry; some names have been casually preserved. The learned Linacre first brought, on his return from Italy, the damask-rose; and Thomas Lord Cromwell, in the reign of Henry VIII, enriched our fruit-gardens with three different plums. In the reign of Elizabeth, Edward Grindal, afterwards Archbishop of Canterbury, returning from exile, transported here the medicinal plant of the tamerisk: the first oranges appear to have been brought into England by one of the Carew family; for a century after, they still flourished at the family seat at Beddington, in Surrey. The cherry orchards of Kent were first planted about Sittingbourne, by a gardener of Henry VIII; and the currant-bush was transplanted when our commerce with the island of Zante was first opened in the same reign. The elder Tradescant in 1620 entered himself on board of a privateer, armed against Morocco, solely with a view of finding an opportunity of stealing apricots into Britain: and it appears that he succeeded in his design. To Sir Walter Rawleigh we have not been indebted solely for the luxury of the tobacco-plant, but for that infinitely useful root, which forms a part of our daily meal, and often the entire meal of the poor man—the potatoe, which deserved to have been called a *Rawleigh*. Sir Anthony Ashley first planted cabbages in this country, and a cabbage at his feet appears on his monument. Sir Richard Weston first brought clover grass into England from Flanders, in 1645; and the figs planted by Cardinal Pole at Lambeth, so far back as the reign of Henry VIII, are said to be still remaining there: nor is this surprising, for Spilman, who set up the first paper-mill in England, at Dartford, in 1590, is said to have brought over in his portmanteau the two first lime-trees, which he planted here, and which are still growing. The Lombardy poplar was introduced into England by the Earl of Rochford in 1758. The first mulberry-trees in this country are now standing at Sion-house. By an Harleian MS. it is mentioned that the first general planting of mulberries and making of silk in England was by William Stallenge, comptroller of the custom-house, and Monsieur Verton, in 1608. It is probable that Monsieur Verton transplanted this novelty from his own country, where we have seen De Serres's great attempt. Here the mulberries have succeeded better than the silk-worms.

The very names of many of our vegetable kingdom indicate their locality: from the majestic cedar of Lebanon, to the small Cos-lettuce, which came from the isle of Cos; the cherries from Cerasuntis, a city of Pontus; the peach, or *persicum*, or *mala Persica*, Persican apples, from Persia; the pistachio, or *psittacia*, is the Syrian word for that nut. The chestnut, or *chataigne*, in French, and *castagna* in Italian, from Castagna, a town of Magnesia. Our plums coming chiefly from Syria and

Damascus, the damson, or damascene plum, gives us a recollection of its distant origin.

It is somewhat curious to observe on this subject that there exists an unsuspected intercourse between nations, in the propagation of exotic plants, &c. Lucullus, after the war with Mithridates, introduced cherries from Pontus into Italy; and the newly-imported fruit was found so pleasing that it was rapidly propagated, and six and twenty years afterwards, as Pliny testifies, the cherry-tree passed over into Britain. Thus a victory obtained by a Roman consul over a king of Pontus, with which it would seem that Britain could have no concern, was the real occasion of our countrymen possessing cherry-orchards. Yet to our shame must it be told, that these cherries from the king of Pontus's city of Cerasuntis are not the cherries we are now eating; for the whole race of cherry-trees was lost in the Saxon period, and was only restored by a gardener of Henry VIII, who brought them from Flanders—without a word to enhance his own merits, concerning the *bellum Mithridaticum*!

A calculating political economist will little sympathise with the peaceful triumphs of those active and generous spirits, who have thus propagated the truest wealth, and the most innocent luxuries of the people. The project of a new tax, or an additional consumption of ardent spirits, or an act of parliament to put a convenient stop to population by forbidding the banns of some happy couple, would be more congenial to their researches; and they would leave without regret the names of those, whom we have held out to the grateful recollections of their country. The Romans, who with all their errors were at least patriots, entertained very different notions of these introducers into their country of exotic fruits and flowers. Sir William Temple has elegantly noticed the fact. "The great captains, and even consular men, who first brought them over, took pride in giving them their own names, by which they ran a great while in Rome, as in memory of some great service or pleasure they had done their country; so that not only laws and battles, but several sorts of apples and pears were called Manlian and Claudian, Pompeyan and Tiberian, and by several other such noble names." Pliny has paid his tribute of applause to Lucullus, for bringing cherry and nut-trees from Pontus into Italy. And we have several modern instances, where the name of the transplanter, or rearer, has been preserved in this sort of creation. Peter Collinson, the botanist, to "whom the English gardens are indebted for many new and curious species which he acquired by means of an extensive correspondence in America," was highly gratified when Linnaeus baptised a plant with his name; and with great spirit asserts his honourable claim: "Something, I think, was due to me for the great number of plants and seeds I have annually procured from abroad, and you have been so good as to pay it, by giving me a species of eternity, botanically speaking; that is, a name as long as men and books endure." Such is the true animating language of these patriotic enthusiasts!

Some lines at the close of Peacham's Emblems give an idea of an English fruit-garden in 1612. He mentions that cherries were not long known, and gives an origin to the name of filbert.

> The Persian Peach, and fruitful Quince;
> And there the forward Almond grew,
> With cherries knowne no long time since;
> The Winter Warden, orchard's pride;
> The *Philibert* that loves the vale,
> And red queen-apple, so envide
> Of school-boies, passing by the pale.

ISAAC D'ISRAELI
[*Curiosities of Literature* (1834)]

First Glimpse of a New World

[*The earliest visitors to the North American continent were for the most part interested only in what promised to be useful, but Captain John Smith recognized at least that the Englishmen who were thinking of coming to Virginia as colonists would want to know what things grew or could be made to grow there.*]

VIRGINIA doth afford many excellent vegitables and liuing Creatures, yet grasse there is little or none but what groweth in lowe Marishes: for all the Countrey is overgrowne with trees, whose droppings continually turneth their grasse to weedes, by reason of the rancknesse of the ground; which would soone be amended by good husbandry. The wood that is most common is Oke and Walnut: many of their Okes are so tall and straight, that they will beare two foot and a halfe square of good timber for 20 yards long. Of this wood there is 2 or 3 seuerall kinds. The Acornes of one kind, whose barke is more white then the other, is somewhat sweetish; which being boyled halfe a day in severall waters, at last afford a sweet oyle, which they keep in goards to annoint their heads and ioints. The fruit they eate, made in bread or otherwise.

There is also some Elme, some black walnut tree, and some Ash: of Ash and Elme they make sope Ashes. If the trees be very great, the ashes will be good, and melt to hard lumps: but if they be small, it will be but powder, and not so good as the other.

Of walnuts there is 2 or 3 kindes: there is a kinde of wood we called Cypres, because both the wood, the fruit, and leafe did most resemble it; and of those trees there are some neere 3 fadome about at the root, very straight, and 50, 60, or 80 foot without a braunch.

By the dwelling of the *Savages* are some great Mulbery trees; and in some parts of the Countrey, they are found growing naturally in prettie groues. There was an assay made to make silke, and surely the wormes prospered excellent well, till the master workeman fell sicke: during which time, they are eaten with rats.

In some parts, were found some Chestnuts whose wild fruit equalize the best in *France, Spaine, Germany,* or *Italy,* to their tastes that had tasted them all.

Plumbs there are of 3 sorts. The red and white are like our hedge plumbs: but the other, which they call Putchamins, grow as high as a Palmeta. The fruit is like a medler; it is first greene, then yellow, and red when it is ripe: if it be not ripe it will drawe a mans mouth awrie with much torment; but when it is ripe, it is as delicious as an Apricock.

They haue Cherries, and those are much like a Damsen; but for their tastes and colour, we called them Cherries. We see some few Crabs, but very small and bitter.

Of vines, [there is] great abundance in many parts, that climbe the toppes of the highest trees in some places, but these beare but fewe grapes. But by the riuers and Savages habitations where they are not overshadowed from the sunne, they are covered with fruit, though never pruined nor manured. Of those hedge grapes, wee made neere 20 gallons of wine, which was neare as good as your French Brittish wine, but certainely they would proue good were they well manured.

There is another sort of grape neere as great as a Cherry, this they call *Messaminnes;* they bee fatte, and the iuyce thicke: neither doth the tast so well please when they are made in wine.

They haue a small fruit growing on little trees, husked like a

Chesnut, but the fruit most like a very small acorne. This they call Chechinquamins, which they esteeme a great daintie. They haue a berry much like our gooseberry, in greatnesse, colour, and tast; those they call *Rawcomenes*, and doe eat them raw or boyled.

Of these naturall fruits, they liue a great part of the yeare, which they vse in this manner. *The walnuts, Chesnuts, Acornes, and Chechinquamens* are dryed to keepe. When they need them, they breake them betweene two stones, yet some part of the walnut shels will cleaue to the fruit. Then doe they dry them againe vpon a mat ouer a hurdle. After, they put it into a morter of wood, and beat it very small: that done, they mix it with water, that the shels may sinke to the bottome. This water will be coloured as milke; which they cal *Pawcohiscora*, and keepe it for their vse.

The fruit like medlers, they call *Putchamins*, they cast vppon hurdles on a mat, and preserue them as Pruines. *Of their Chesnuts* and *Chechinquamens* boyled 4 houres, they make both broath and bread for their chiefe men, or at their greatest feasts.

Besides those fruit trees, there is *a white populer*, and another tree like vnto it, that yeeldeth a very cleere and an odoriferous *Gumme like Turpentine, which some called Balsom*. There are also *Cedars* and *Saxafras trees*. They also yeeld gummes in a small proportion of themselues. Wee tryed conclusions to extract it out of the wood, but nature afforded more then our arts.

In the watery valleyes groweth *a berry*, which they call *Ocoughtanamnis*, very much like vnto Capers. These they dry in summer. When they will eat them, they boile them neare halfe a day; for otherwise they differ not much from poyson. *Mattoume* groweth as our bents do in meddows. The seede is not much vnlike to rie, though much smaller. This they vse for a dainty bread buttered with deare suet.

During Somer there are either *strawberries* which ripen in April; or mulberries which ripen in May and Iune. Raspises hurres; or a fruit that the Inhabitants call Maracocks, which is a pleasant wholsome fruit much like a lemond.

Many hearbes in the spring time there are commonly dispersed throughout the woods, good for brothes and sallets, as Violets, Purslin, Sorrell, &c. Besides many we vsed whose names we know not.

The chiefe roote they haue for foode is called *Tockawhoughe*. It groweth like a flagge in low muddy freshes. In one day a *Savage* will gather sufficient for a weeke. These rootes are much of the greatnes and taste of *Potatoes*. They vse to couer a great many of them with oke leaues and ferne, and then couer all with earth in the manner of a colepit; over it, on each side, they continue a great fire 24 houres before they dare eat it. Raw it is no better then poison, and being roasted, except it be tender and the heat abated, or sliced and dried in the sun, mixed with sorrell and meale or such like, it will prickle and torment the throat extreamely, and yet in sommer they vse this ordinarily for bread.

They haue an other roote which they call *wighsacan:* as the other feedeth the body, so this cureth their hurts and diseases. It is a small root which they bruise and apply to the wound. *Pocones* is a small roote that groweth in the mountaines, which being dryed and beate in powder turneth red: and this they vse for swellings, aches, annointing their ioints, painting their heads and garments. They account it very pretious and of much worth. *Musquaspenne* is a roote of the bignesse of a finger, and as red as bloud. In drying, it will wither almost to nothing. This they vse to paint their Mattes, Targets, and such like.

There is also *Pellitory of Spaine, Sasafrage,* and diuers other simples, which the Apothecaries gathered, and commended to be good and medicinable.

In the low Marishes, *growe plots of Onyons* containing an acre of ground or more in many places; but they are small, not past the bignesse of the Toppe of ones Thumbe.

CAPTAIN JOHN SMITH
[*A Description of New England* (1616)]

The Naturalist-Pirate

[*The great age of exploration which opened with the first voyage of Columbus reached its climax in the eighteenth century. Columbus himself took some note of the possibly useful animals and plants he or his men came across, and so did many of the early explorers. Before the eighteenth century was over, it had become a regular practice to take a naturalist along on most important expeditions; and exploration for the express purpose of discovering new "natural products" had become not unusual. But it has been said that the first voyager ever to take a detached, non-*

*utilitarian interest in the animals and plants he encountered was the
extraordinary English pirate William Dampier.*

     *To read his A New Voyage Round the World (1697) is to be
convinced that he might, under different circumstances, have been a
naturalist rather than a pirate, but pirate he was—morally, practically and
by legal definition. For something like eighteen years he sailed the Pacific
and took part in various piratical raids upon the South American coast.
He was an officer on board the ship which put Alexander Selkirk ashore
on "Robinson Crusoe's Island," and though it is not quite clear how he
escaped hanging he returned to England in 1691 to become a highly
respected citizen as well as the author of a best seller. His lively, essentially scientific description of the kapok tree and of such important
tropical fruits as the avocado, the mammee, and the star apple gives a
surprising glimpse into the mind of a pirate.*]

T H E R E are two sorts of Cotton-trees, one is called the Red, the other
the White Cotton-tree. The White Cotton-tree grows like an Oak, but
generally much bigger and taller than our Oaks: The body is straight
and clear from knots or boughs to the very head: there it spreads forth
many great limbs just like an Oak. The Bark is smooth and of a grey
colour: the Leaves are as big as a large Plumb-Leaf, jagged at the edge;
they are oval, smooth, and of a dark green colour. Some of these Trees
have their bodies much bigger, 18 or 20 foot high, than nearer the
Ground, being big-bellied like Nine-pins. They bear a very fine sort of
Cotton, called Silk-Cotton. When this Cotton is ripe, the trees appear
like our Apple-trees in England, when full of Blossoms. If I do not mistake, the Cotton falls down in November, or December: then the
Ground is covered white with it. This is not substantial and continuous,
like that which grows upon the Cotton-shrubs, in Plantations, but like
the Down of Thistles; so that I did never know any use made of it in
the West-Indies, because it is not worth the Labour of gathering it: but
in the East-Indies the Natives gather and use it for Pillows. It hath a
small black Seed among it. The Leaves of this Tree fall off the beginning
of April; while the old Leaves are falling off, the young ones spring out,
and in a weeks time the Tree casts off her old Robes, and is cloathed in
a new pleasant Garb. The red Cotton-tree is like the other, but hardly
so big: it bears no Cotton, but its Wood is somewhat harder of the two,
yet both sorts are soft spungy Wood, fit for no use that I know, but only
for Canoas, which being strait and tall they are very good for; but they

will not last long, especially if not drawn ashore often and tarred; otherwise the Worm and the Water soon rot them. They are the biggest Trees, or perhaps Weeds rather, in the West-Indies. They are common in the East and West-Indies in good fat Land.

As the Cotton is the biggest Tree in the Woods, so the Cabbage-tree is the tallest: The Body is not very big, but very high and strait. I have measured one in the Bay of Campeachy 120 feet long as it lay on the Ground, and there are some much higher. It has no Limbs nor Boughs, but at the head there are many Branches bigger than a Man's Arm. These Branches are not covered, but flat, with sharp edges; they are 12 or 14 foot long. About two foot from the Trunk, the Branches shoot forth small long Leaves, about an Inch broad, which grow so regularly on both sides of the Branch, that the whole Branch seems to be but one Leaf, made up of many small ones. The Cabbage Fruit shoots out in the midst of these Branches, from the top of the Tree; it is invested with many young Leaves or Branches which are ready to spread abroad, as the old Branches drop and fall down. The Cabbage it self, when it is taken out of the leaves which it seems to be folded in, is as big as the small of a Man's Leg, and a foot long; it is as white as Milk, and as sweet as a Nut, if eaten raw, and it is very sweet and wholesom if boiled. Besides, the Cabbage it self, there grow out between the Cabbage and the large Branches, small Twigs, as of a Shrub, about two foot long from their Stump. At the end of those Twigs (which grow very thick together) there hang Berries hard and round, and as big as a Cherry. These the Tree sheds every year, and they are very good for Hogs: for this reason the Spaniards fine any who shall cut down any of these in their Woods. The body of the Tree is full of rings round it, half a foot asunder from the Bottom to the top. The Bark is thin and brittle; the Wood is black and very hard, the heart or middle of the Tree is white Pith. They do not climb to get the Cabbage, but cut them down; for should they gather it off the Tree as it stands, yet its head being gone, it soon dies. These Trees are much used by Planters in Jamaica, to board the sides of the Houses, for it is but splitting the Trunk into four parts with an Axe, and there are so many Planks. Those Trees appear very pleasant, and they beautifie the whole Wood, spreading their green Branches above all other Trees.

Chepelio is the pleasantest Island in the Bay of Panama: It is but 7 leagues from the City of Panama, and a league from the Main. This Island is about a mile long, and almost so broad; it is low on the North-side, and riseth by a small ascent towards the South-side. The soil is yellow, a kind of Clay. The high side is stony; the low Land is planted with all sorts of delicate Fruits, viz. Sapadilloes, Avogato-pears, Mammees, Mammee-Sappota's, Star-apples, &c. The middle of the Island is planted with Plantain-Trees, which are not very large, but the Fruit extraordinary sweet.

The Sapadillo-Tree is as big as a large Pear-tree, the Fruit much like a Bergamot-pear, both in colour, shape and size; but on some Trees the Fruit is a little longer. When it is green or first gathered, the Juice is white and clammy, and it will stick like glew; then the Fruit is hard, but after it hath been gathered 2 or 3 days, it grows soft and juicy, and then the juice is clear as Spring-Water, and very sweet; in the midst of the Fruit are 2 or 3 black Stones or Seeds, about the bigness of a Pumpkin-seed: This is an excellent Fruit.

The Avogato Pear-tree is as big as most Pear-trees, and is commonly pretty high; the skin or bark black, and pretty smooth; the leaves large, of an oval shape, and the Fruit as big as a large Lemon. It is of a green colour, till it is ripe, and then it is a little yellowish. They are seldom fit to eat till they have been gathered 2 or 3 days; then they become soft, and the Skin or Rind will peel off. The substance in the inside is green, or a little yellowish, and as soft as Butter. Within the substance there is a stone as big as a Horse-Plumb. This Fruit hath no taste of it self, and therefore 'tis usually mixt with Sugar and Lime-juice, and beaten together in a Plate; and this is an excellent dish. The ordinary way is to eat it with a little Salt and a roasted Plantain; and thus a Man that's hungry, may make a good meal of it. It is very wholesome eaten any way. It is reported that this Fruit provokes to Lust, and therefore is said to be much esteemed by the Spaniards: and I do believe they are much esteemed by them, for I have met with plenty of them in many places in the North Seas, where the Spaniards are settled, as in the Bay of Campeachy, on the Coast of Cartagena, and the Coast of Caraccos; and there are some in Jamaica, which were planted by the Spaniards when they possessed that Island.

The Mammee-Sappota Tree is different from the Mammee described at the Island Tabago in this Chapter. It is not so big or so tall, neither is the Fruit so big or so round. The Rind of the Fruit is thin and brittle; the inside is a deep red, and it has a rough flat long stone. This is accounted the principal Fruit of the West-Indies. It is very pleasant and wholesome. I have not seen any of these on Jamaica; but in many places in the West-Indies among the Spaniards. There is another sort of Mammee-tree, which is called the Wild Mammee: This bears a Fruit which is of no value, but the Tree is straight, tall, and very tough, and therefore principally used for making Masts.

The Star Apple-tree grows much like the Quince Tree, but much bigger. It is full of leaves, and the leaf is broad, of an oval shape, and of a very dark green colour. The Fruit is as big as a large Apple, which is commonly so covered with leaves, that a Man can hardly see it. They say this is a good Fruit; I did never taste any, but have seen both of the Trees and Fruit in many places on the Main, on the North side of the Continent, and in Jamaica. When the Spaniards possess'd that Island, they planted this and other sorts of Fruit, as the Sapadillo, Avogato-Pear, and the like; and of these Fruits there is still in Jamaica in those Planta-tions that were first settled by the Spaniards as at the Angels, at 7 Mile Walk, and 16 Mile Walk. There I have seen these Trees which were planted by the Spaniards, but I did never see any improvement made by the English, who seem in that little curious.

WILLIAM DAMPIER
[*A New Voyage Round the World* (1697)]

A Naturalist Sees Tahiti

[*The first great voyages of which scientific discovery was a major objec-tive were those made by Captain James Cook during the second half of the eighteenth century. When in 1772 his second expedition set sail it included a nineteen-year-old naturalist of German birth named Georg Forster. Though almost unknown at the time and destined to die young, he published in two handsome folios an account of his journey around the world which is perhaps the first really modern travel book and one in which, as Prof. N. J. Berrill has said, "we can see the world of the late eighteenth century through the wonderfully clear eyes of a highly intel-ligent, highly educated youth, old enough to have both comprehension and sympathy, and young enough not to be stuffed full of blinding doctrine."*]

I T was one of those beautiful mornings which the poets of all nations have attempted to describe, when we saw the isle of O-Taheite, within two miles before us. The east-wind which had carried us so far was entirely vanished and a faint breeze only wafted a delicious perfume from the land, and curled the surface of the sea. The mountains, clothed with forests, rose majestic in various spiry forms, on which we already perceived the light of the rising sun: nearer to the eye a lower range of hills, easier of ascent, appeared, wooded like the former, and coloured with several pleasing hues of green, soberly mixed with autumnal browns. At their foot lay the plain, crowned with its fertile bread-fruit trees, over which rose innumerable palms, the princes of the grove. Here every thing seemed as yet asleep, the morning scarce dawned, and a peaceful shade still rested on the landscape. We discerned however, a number of houses among the trees, and many canoes hauled up along the sandy beaches. About half a mile from the shore a ledge of rocks level with the water, extended parallel to the land, on which the surf broke, leaving a smooth and secure harbour within. The sun beginning to illuminate the plain, its inhabitants arose, and enlivened the scene. Having perceived the large vessels on their coast, several of them hastened to the beach, launched their canoes, and paddled towards us, who were highly de- lighted in watching all their occupations.

The canoes soon passed through the openings in the reef, and one of them approached within hale. In it were two men almost naked, with a kind of turban on the head, and a sash round their waist. They waved a large green leaf, and accosted us with the repeated exclamation of *tayo* which even without the help of vocabularies, we could easily translate into the expression of proffered friendship. The canoe now came under our stern, and we let down a present of beads, nails, and medals to the men. In return, they handed up to us a green stem of a plantane, which was their symbol of peace, with a desire that it might be fixed in a conspicuous part of the vessel. It was accordingly stuck up in the main shrouds, upon which our new friends immediately returned towards the land. In a short time we saw great crouds of people on the seashore gazing at us, while numbers in consequence of this treaty of peace, which was now firmly established, launched their canoes, and loaded them with various productions of their country. In less than an hour we were surrounded by an hundred canoes each of which carried one, two, three, and sometimes four persons, who placed a perfect confi- dence in us, and had no arms whatsoever. The welcome sound of *tayo* resounded on all sides, and we returned it with a degree of heart-felt pleasure, on this favourable change of our situation. Coco-nuts, and plantanes in great quantity, bread-fruit and several other vegetables, besides some fresh fish were offered to us and eagerly exchanged for transparent beads and small nails. Pieces of cloth, fish-hooks, hatchets of stone, and a number of tools, were likewise brought for sale and readily disposed of; and many canoes kept plying between us and the shore, exhibiting a picture of a new kind of fair. I immediately began to trade for natural productions through the cabin-windows, and in half an hour had got together two or three species of unknown birds and a great number of new fishes, whose colours while alive were exquisitely beautiful. I therefore employed the morning in sketching their outlines, and laying on the vivid hues, before they disappeared in the dying objects.

The people around us had mild features, and a pleasing countenance; they were about our size, of a pale mahogany brown, had fine black hair and eyes, and wore a piece of cloth round their middle of their own manufacture, and another wrapped about the head in various picturesque shapes like a turban. Among them were several females, pretty enough to attract the attention of Europeans, who had not seen their own country-women for twelve long months past. These wore a piece of cloth with a hole in the middle, through which they had passed the head, so that one part of the garment hung down behind, and the other before, to the knees; a fine white cloth like a muslin, was passed over this in various elegant turns round the body, a little below the breast, forming a kind of tunic, of which one turn sometimes fell gracefully across the shoulder. If this dress had not entirely that perfect form so justly admired in the draperies of the ancient Greek statues, it was however infinitely superior to our expectations, and much more advantageous to the human figure, than any modern fashions we had hitherto seen. Both sexes were adorned, or rather disfigured, by those singular black stains occasioned by puncturing the skin, and rubbing a black colour into the wounds, which are mentioned by former voyagers. They were particularly visible on the loins of the common men, who went almost naked, and exhibited a proof how little the ideas of ornament of different nations agree, and yet how generally they all have adopted such aids to their personal perfection. It was not long before some of these good people came aboard. That peculiar gentleness of disposition, which is their general characteristic, immediately manifested itself in all their looks and actions, and gave full employment to those, who made the human heart their study. They expressed several marks of affection in their countenance, took hold of our hands, leaned on our shoulder, or embraced us. They admired the whiteness of our bodies, and frequently pushed aside our clothes from the breast, as if to convince themselves that we were made like them. . . .

The next morning we resumed our course towards the shore, and stood in along the north part of the lesser peninsula. We were in a short time surrounded, as the day before, by the natives, who in a great number of canoes brought us an abundance of vegetable, but no animal food, and whose clamours were sometimes loud enough to stun our ears. These canoes very frequently overset, but the natives were not much discomposed by such accidents, as both sexes were expert swimmers, and re-established themselves in a moment. Seeing that I enquired for plants, and other natural curiosities, they brought off several, though sometimes only the leaves without the flowers, and vice versa; however among them we saw the common species of black night-shade, and a beautiful *erythrius*, or coral-flower; I also collected by these means many shells, coralines, birds, &c.

About eleven o'clock we anchored in a little harbour called O-Aitepeha, on the north-east end of the southern or lesser peninsula of Taheitee, named Tiarraboo. Here the concourse of natives still increased, and we saw their canoes coming towards us from all parts. They were eager to obtain our beads, nails and knives, for which an immense quantity of their mats, blankets, and various tools, as well as abundance of coco-nuts, bread-fruit, yams and bananas were exchanged. Many of them came on deck, and took the opportunity of conveying away a number of trifles; nay, some went so far as privately to throw over board the coco-nuts, which we had already purchased, to their comrades, who immediately picked them up, and sold them to our people again. To prevent our being imposed upon for the future in this manner, the thieves were turned out of the vessel, and punished with a whip, which they bore very patiently.

The heat was as great as it had been the day before, the thermometer standing at 90° in the shade, when the sky was covered with clouds; the wind likewise dying away again at noon to a perfect calm. Notwithstanding the waste of fluids which the weather occasioned, we could not say that we found the climate affected us too much, or was very disagreeable. On the contrary, allowing for the violent exercise we had undergone at the striking of the ship, we found ourselves more refreshed by the bare proximity of the shore, than we could have expected. The bread-fruit and yams proved a luxurious and most welcome substitute for worm-eaten biscuit; while plantanes, and a fruit of the shape of an apple, called *e-vee* by the natives, furnished out a delicious desert. . . .

In the afternoon the captains, accompanied by several gentlemen, went ashore the first time, in order to visit O-Aheatua, whom all the natives thereabouts acknowledged as *aree*, or king. Numbers of canoes in the mean while surrounded us, carrying on a brisk trade with vegetables, but chiefly with great quantities of the cloth made in the island. The decks were likewise crouded with natives, among whom were several women who yielded without difficulty to the ardent sollicitations of our sailors. Some of the females who came on board for this purpose, seemed not to be above nine or ten years old, and had not the least marks of puberty. So early an acquaintance with the world seems to argue an uncommon degree of voluptuousness, and cannot fail of affecting the nation in general. The effect, which was immediately obvious to me, was the low stature of the common class of people, to which all these prostitutes belonged. Among this whole order we saw few persons above the middle size, and many below it; an observation which confirms what M. de Buffon has very judiciously said on the subject of early connections of the sexes (see his Histoire Naturelle). Their features were very irregular, and in general very ordinary, except the eyes, which were always large and full of vivacity; but a natural smile, and a constant endeavour to please, had so well replaced the want of beauty, that our sailors were perfectly captivated, and carelessly disposed of their shirts and cloaths to gratify their mistresses. The simplicity of a dress which exposed to view a well proportioned bosom and delicate hands, might also contribute to fan their amorous fire; and the view of several of these nymphs swimming nimbly all round the sloop, such as nature had formed them, was perhaps more than sufficient entirely to subvert the little reason which a mariner might have left to govern his passions. A trifling circumstance had given cause to their taking the water. One of the officers on the quarter-deck intended to drop a bead into a canoe for a little boy about six years old; by accident it missed the boat and fell into the sea; but the child immediately leaped overboard, and diving after it brought it up again. To reward his performance we dropped some more beads to him, which so tempted a number of men and women, that they amused us with amazing feats of agility in the water, and not only fetched up several beads scattered at once, but likewise large nails, which, on account of their weight, descended quickly to a considerable depth. Some of them continued a long while under water, and the velocity with which we saw them go down, the water being perfectly clear, was very surprising. The frequent ablutions of these people already mentioned in Captain Cook's former voyage seem to make swimming familiar to them from their earliest childhood; and indeed their easy position in the water, and the pliancy of their limbs, gave us reason to look on them almost as amphibious creatures. They continued this sport, and their other occupations about us, till sun-set, when they all withdrew by degrees to the shore. . . .

Our first care was to leave the dry sandy beach, which could afford us no discoveries in our science, and to examine the plantations, which from the ships had an enchanting appearance, notwithstanding the brownish cast which the time of the year had given. We found them indeed to answer the expectations we had formed of a country described as an elysium by M. de Bougainville. We entered a grove of bread-trees, on most of which we saw no fruit at this season of winter, and followed a neat but narrow path, which led to different habitations, half hid under various bushes. Tall coco-palms nodded to each other, and rose over the rest of the trees; the bananas displayed their beautiful large leaves, and now and then one of them still appeared loaded with its clustering fruit. A sort of shady trees, covered with a dark-green foliage, bore golden apples, which resembled the anana in juiciness and flavour. Betwixt these the intermediate space was filled with young mulberry-trees (*morus papyrifera*) of which the bark is employed by the natives in the manufacture of their cloth; with several species of arum or eddies, with yams, sugar-canes, and other useful plants.

We found the cottages of the natives scattered at short distances, in the shade of fruit-trees, and surrounded by various odoriferous shrubs, such as the gardenia, guettarda, and calophyllum. The neat simplicity of their structure gave us no less pleasure than the artless beauty of the grove which encompassed them. The pandang or palm-nut tree had given its long prickly leaves to thatch the roofs of the buildings, and these were supported by a few pillars made of the bread-tree, which is thus useful in more respects than one. As a roof is sufficient to shelter the natives from rains and nightly dews, and as the climate of this island is perhaps one of the happiest in the world, the houses seldom have any walls, but are open on all sides. We saw, however, a few dwellings constructed for greater privacy, which were entirely enclosed in walls of reeds, connected together by transverse pieces of wood, so as to give us the idea of large bird-cages. In these there was commonly a hole left for the entrance, which could be closed up with a board. Before every hut, on the green turf or on dry grass, we observed groups of inhabitants lying down or sitting in the eastern stile, and passing their happy hours away in conversation or repose. Some of them got up at our approach, and joined the croud that followed us; but great numbers, especially those of a mature age, remained in their attitude, and only pronounced a kind *tayo* as we passed by them. Our attendant croud seeing us gather plants, were very ready to pluck and offer the same sorts to us, which they found attracted our notice. Indeed a variety of wild species sprung up amidst the plantations, in that beautiful disorder of nature, which is so truly admirable when checked by the hand of industry, and infinitely surpasses the trimness of regular gardens. Among them we found several species of grasses, which though thinner than in our northern countries, yet by growing always in the shade, looked fresh and formed a soft bed of verdure. The soil was by their means kept sufficiently moist to give nourishment to the trees, and both were in a thriving state, owing to the reciprocal assistance which they gave each other. Various little birds dwelt in the shade of the bread-fruit and other trees, and had a very agreeable note, though common report among Europeans has denied the powers of harmony (I know not on what grounds) to the birds of warm climates. The heads of the tallest coco-trees were the usual residence of a kind of very small perroquets of a beautiful sapphirine blue, while another sort of a greenish colour, with a few red spots, were more common among the bananas, and appeared frequently tame in the houses of the natives, who seemed to value them for their red feathers. A king's fisher, of a dark-green, with a collar of the same hue round his white throat, a large cuckoo, and several sorts of pigeons or doves, were frequently seen hopping from branch to branch, and a bluish heron gravely stalked along the sea side, picking up shell-fish and worms. . . .

We proceeded a little farther up in a narrow valley, where a well-looking man invited us to sit down in the shade before his house. There was a little area paved with broadish stones, on which he spread banana leaves for us, and brought out a little stool made of the bread-tree-wood, cut out of one piece, on which he desired one of us to sit down, whom he took to be the principal person. Seeing us all seated he ran into his house, and brought out a quantity of bread-fruit baked, which he laid before us on fresh banana leaves. To this he added a matted basket full of the vee, or Taheitee apples, a fruit of the *Spondias* genus, which resembles the anana, or pine-apple in the taste, and entreated us to partake of these refreshments. We breakfasted with a hearty appetite, sharpened by the exercise we had taken, the fine air of the morning, and the excellence of the provisions. We found the Taheitee method of dressing bread-fruit and other victuals, with heated stones under ground, infinitely superior to our usual way of boiling them; in the former all the juices remained, and were concentrated by the heat; but in the latter, the fruit imbibed many watery particles, and lost a great deal of its fine flavour and mealiness. To conclude this treat our host brought us five fresh coco-nuts, which he opened by pulling the fibres off with his teeth. The cool limpid liquor contained in them he poured into a clean cup, made of a ripe coco-nut-shell, and offered that to each of us in our turns. The people in this country had on all occasions been good-natured and friendly, and for beads sometimes sold us coco-nuts and fruit, if we called for them; but we had not yet seen an instance of hospitality exercised in so complete a manner during our short stay. We therefore thought it our duty to recompense our friend as much as lay in our power, and presented him with a number of transparent beads and iron nails, with which he was highly satisfied and contented.

We continued our walk into the country from this seat of patriarchal hospitality, notwithstanding the uneasiness which many of the natives expressed, among the croud that followed us. When they saw us persist in our expedition, the greatest part of them dispersed to their different habitations, and only a few of them attended us, who made it their business to act as our guides. We came to the foot of the first hills, where we left the huts and plantations of the natives behind us, and ascended on a beaten path, passing through an uncultivated shrubbery mixed with several tall timber-trees. Here we searched the most intricate parts, and found several plants and birds hitherto unknown to natural historians. With these little acquisitions we returned towards the sea, at which our friends the natives expressed their satisfaction. We found a vast concourse of inhabitants on the beach at our trading-place, and saw that our people had brought a great quantity of large eddies and other roots, but few bread-fruits, which were now very scarce, only a few trees bearing them so late in the season, while most of the others were already shooting forth the embryo of a new crop. The excessive heat of the sun, now tempted us to bathe in a branch of the adjacent river, which formed a deep pond of some extent; and being refreshed with this bath we returned on board to dinner. In the afternoon we had heavy rains, attended with wind, during which the Adventure drove from her moorings, but was brought up again by a timely manoeuvre. This bad weather confined us on board, where we arranged the plants and animals which we had hitherto collected, and made drawings of such as were not known before. Our three days excursions had supplied us only with a small number of species, which in an island so flourishing as Taheitee, gave a convincing proof of its high cultivation; for a few individual plants occupied that space, which in a country entirely left to itself, would have teemed with several hundred different kinds in wild disorder. The small size of the island, together with its vast distance from either the eastern or western continent, did not admit of a great variety of animals. We saw no other species of quadrupeds than hogs, and dogs which were domestic, and incredible numbers of rats, which the natives suffered to run about at pleasure, without ever trying to destroy them. We found however a tolerable number of birds, and when the natives gave themselves the trouble to fish, we commonly purchased a considerable variety of species, as this class of creatures can easily roam from one part of the ocean to the other, and particularly in the torrid zone, where certain sorts are general all round the world.

If the scarcity of spontaneous plants was unfavourable to the botanist, still it had the most salutary effects with regard to the whole company on board of both our vessels, since their place was occupied by great quantities of wholesome vegetables. We daily bought abundance of yams, eddies, and Taheitee apples; together with some bananas and bread-fruit, which, on account of the season, were grown very scarce. The wholesome regimen which we had by this means been able to keep, had visibly, and I might almost say miraculously, operated to restore to their health, all those who were ill of the scurvy at our arrival; and the only inconvenience we felt from it was a kind of flux, owing to the sudden change of diet, with which a few of the people were afflicted. . . .

We were now able to breathe a little, after the continual hurry which had been the necessary consequence of the multiplicity of new objects around us, and of the short space of time which we had to observe them. This interval of repose was the more acceptable, as it gave us leisure to indulge the reflections which had crouded upon us during our stay. The result of these was a conviction, that this island is indeed one of the happiest spots on the globe. The rocks of New Zeeland appeared at first in a favourable light to our eyes, long tired with the constant view of sea, and ice, and sky; but time served to undeceive us, and gave us daily cause of dislike, till we formed a just conception of that rude chaotic country. But O-Taheitee, which had presented a pleasing prospect at a distance, and displayed its beauty as we approached, became more enchanting to us at every excursion which we made on its plains.

GEORG FORSTER
[*A Voyage Round the World* (1777)]

Hands Across the Sea

[*John Bartram's son William surpassed his father as collector and natu-
ralizer of American plants. While still quite young he partly financed
his collecting trips by supplying "curiosities" to eager English collectors.
Most unfortunately his best patron, the young Lord Petre, died young,
but he maintained for many years a correspondence with one Peter
Collinson, a Quaker merchant who had a consuming passion, not only
for living plants, but also for all the "natural productions" of the New
World. The letters which passed between the two still glow with the
eager curiosity of both men and reveal the excitement, so general at the
time, created by a realization that "the wonders of God's creation" were
far more numerous and varied than those who had been confined to
Europe had ever imagined. Bartram's letter to his father was written at
the end of the first stage of his great expedition into the South—of which
we shall hear more later.*]

THEE writes for some botanical books; and indeed I am at a loss
which to recommend, for, as I have observed, a complete history of
plants is not to be found in any author. For the present, I am persuaded
the gentlemen of the Library Company, at my request, will endulge thee
the library, when thee comes to town, to peruse their botanical books;
there is Miller's *Dictionary*, and some others.

Please to remember those Solomon's Seals, that escaped thee
last year.

The great and small Hellebore are great rarities here, so pray
send a root or two of each next year. Please to remember all sorts of
lilies, as they happen in thy way; and your spotted Martagons will be
very acceptable.

The Devil's Bit, or Blazing Star, pray add a root or two, and
any of the Lady's Slippers.

My dear friend, I only mention these plants; but I beg thee not to neglect thy more material affairs to oblige me. A great many may be put in a box 20 inches or 2 feet square, and 15 or 16 inches high; and a foot in earth is enough. This may be put under the captain's bed, or set in the cabin, if it is sent in October or November. Nail a few small narrow laths across it to keep the cats from scratching it. . . .

I hope thee had mine, per Captain Davis, with a box with seeds in sand, and two parcels of seeds per my good friend Isaac Norris, Jr. . . .

Pray what is your Sarsaparilla? The May apple, a pretty plant, is what I have had for some years sent me per Doctor Witt. It flowers well with us; but our summers are not hot long enough to perfect the fruit. . . .

The Ground Cypress is a singular pretty plant. If it bears berries or seeds, pray send some; and if it bears flowers or seeds pray send some specimens in both states.

Pray send me a good specimen or two of the shrub, 3 feet high, that grows by the water courses.

The shrub that grows out of the sides of rocks, sometimes five or six feet high, bearing red berries hanging by the husks, is called Euonymous, or Spindle tree. We have the same plant, with a small difference; grows plenty in England.

Your wild Senna, with yellow flowers, is a pretty plant. Send seeds of both this and Mountain Goat's Rue.

Thee need not collect any more of the White Thorn berries, that has prodigious long, sharp, thorns. It is what we call Cock-spur Thorn. I had a tree last year, that had at least a bushel of berries. But haws of any other sort of Thorns will be acceptable.

Pray send me a root or two of cluster-bearing Solomon's Seal. It is in all appearances a very rare plant—as is the *Panax*. . . .

When it happens in thy way, send me a root or two of the little tuberous root called Devil's Bit, which produces one or two leaves yearly.

I only barely mention these plants; not that I expect thee to send them. I don't expect or desire them, but as they happen to be found accidentally: and what is not to be met with one year, may be another. . . .

Send a quantity of seed of the Birch or Black Beech; it seems to be new. Send me a good root of Swallow-wort, with the narrow leaves and orange colored flowers; and of the pretty shrub called Red Root, and of the Cotton-weed or Life-everlasting, and some more seeds of the Perannual Pea, that grows by rivers; this year, or next, as it happens.

Pray send me a walking-cane, of the Cane-wood.

PETER COLLINSON to JOHN BARTRAM
London, January 20, 1734–5

I have thine of August 12th, which gives me both pleasure and pain. I dreaded to go on board to see the disaster, and so much labor and pain thrown away by such a swarm of pestilent beetles. As we say by a fine old woman, "There's the ruins of a fine face," and such as I never saw before. Pray next time divide the precious from the vile; I will send thee boxes enough. Keep the butterflies, or day-flies, by themselves, and these devouring beetles by themselves, but drown them in rum, or heat them in a gentle oven will stop all their further progress. Moths are sometimes subject to breed insects which will eat up their bodies, but the heat of a very slack oven kills them. Butterflies are not liable to these accidents, but at the proper time of sending, they may be collected all in one box, and desire the captain to set it in any dry place in the cabin; for the last, being put in the Lazaretto, under the cabin, narrowly escaped all being spoilt by a bag or barrel of salt being put over them, which came through the box. . . . As thee intends to repair that loss, which is very obliging, I only just give this hint, that I prefer butterflies and moths before beetles; and good reason, for there is ten times the beauty and variety in one as the other.

I shall now tell thee something which very much pleased me, and will surprise thee. The box of turtle eggs (which was an ingenious thought of thine to send), on the day I brought it from on board ship, being the 20th of October, I took off the lid, having a mind to see the eggs, and on peeping about I saw a little head just above ground, and while I was looking, I saw the ground move in a place or two more. In short, in the space of three or four hours, eight tortoises were hatched. It was very well worth observing how artfully they disengaged themselves from the shell, and then with their fore feet scratched their eyes open. They have had many visitors; such a thing never happened, I dare say, in England before.

PETER COLLINSON to JOHN BARTRAM
London, Dec. 20 (?), 1737

DEAR FRIEND JOHN:

Lord Petre has ordered me to give thee two guineas, for thy extraordinary trouble about the specimens. The Laurels are perfectly fine. That and the White Cedar are very acceptable. Thee shall not lose thy reward.

Dear friend, I must beg the favor of thee to remember what I have formerly requested, in behalf of a curious naturalist who, to engage thy memory, sends thee a specimen of his performance. He neglected, when in Virginia, to draw the Papaw; and as this is a curious plant, in flower and fruit, and not figured by anybody, now there is no way to convey to us perfect ideas of this plant but by gathering the blossoms and leaves and drying them between paper; but as the color and figure of the flower is liable to change, then he begs a short description of its colors; or else, to prevent further trouble, if some of the flowers growing on a small twig were put into some rum, one small twig would be enough; but thee may put several loose flowers in the jar of spirits, and then a couple of fruit, full ripe; and if it was not too remote, a couple of half ripe—for I am informed they grow in couples.

It is observed that spirits do very little to alter the color of fruits. If they do before thee sends it, pray give a little description of its color. Now, by these helps, my ingenious friend will be able to delineate the plant and fruit: and if thee will further assist him in the height of its growth, and the size of its stem, and what soil and place is most natural to it—we shall all be much obliged to thee. Pray fail not, and thee will oblige thine,

PETER COLLINSON
(To John Bartram, not dated; Dec. 10, 1738?)

DEAR FRIEND

I am exceedingly pleased with thy long letters, as thee calls them; but I wish they had been as long again. I shall make my observations on them, as follows: *December the 10th.* I am almost overjoyed in reading the contents of this letter—wherein thee acknowledges thy satisfaction of my remarks on the Locusts, Caterpillars, Pigeons, and Snakes. I am very thankful to thee, and the Royal Society, for taking so much notice of my poor performances. It is a great encouragement for me to continue my observations of natural phenomena. If I see any Locusts this year, I shall be very particular in my remarks; as also the Papaw, to gratify the curious friend who, thee says, will send me a specimen of his performances; which will be very acceptable. *December the 14th.* I am glad my map of the Schuylkill pleases thee and Lord Petre. . . .

In thy letter of December 20th thee supposes me to spend five or six weeks in collections for thee, and that ten pounds will defray all my annual expenses; but I assure thee, I spend more than twice that time, annually; and ten pounds will not, at any moderate expense, defray my charges abroad—beside my neglect of business at home, in fallowing, harvest, and seed time. Indeed, I was more than two weeks' time in gathering the small acorns of the Willow-leafed Oak, which are very scarce, and falling with the leaves—so that daily I had to rake up the leaves and shake the acorns out, before they were devoured by the squirrels and hogs; and I reckoned it good luck if I could gather twenty under one tree—hardly one in twenty bore any. Yet I don't begrudge my labor; but would do anything reasonable to serve you. But by the sequel of thy letter, you are not sensible of the fourth part of the pains I take to oblige thee. . . .

JOHN BARTRAM to PETER COLLINSON
May, 1738

DEAR PETER,

I have now my dear, worthy Peter's letter before me of February the 10th. I am very sorry that the seeds was damaged by the rotten squash. It seemed when I put it in the box to be ripe enough and I thought to oblige my dear friend with the best sort I ever ate. But I believe misfortune will pursue me to the grave, let my intention and care be ever so good. . . .

I have received the laurel berries and arbutus in good order. The acorns was every one rotten. The packet of seeds was good. I sowed them directly after receiving, which was a week in June.

The seed thee sent last fall was choice good and most of them come up. The ranunculus and anemone root grows finely and several bore fine flowers. The flags—iris—grow well and two of the bulbous is ready to flower. Many aconites is come up and the polianthus by hundreds. Balm of Gilead and a pretty annual linaria hath been long in flower, sowed last February.

I hope the yellow digitalis and double-blossom celandine is come up. But how glad, glad should I be if the doronicum gentian and laurels would come up which I sowed carefully last winter under shelter. All these are very acceptable. Above thirty carnations grows finely. Several of the bulbous roots and polianthus flowered pretty, as my wife told me, while I was gone.

Dear friend, I am going to build a green house. Stone is got and [I] hope, as soon as harvest is over, to begin to build it—to put some pretty flowering winter shrubs and plants for winter's diversion;—not

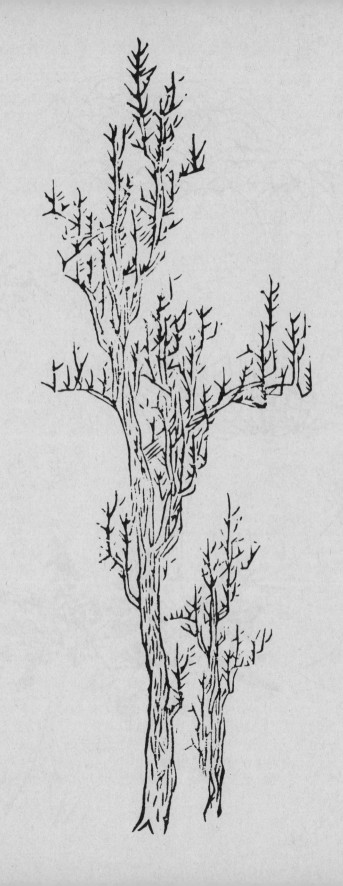

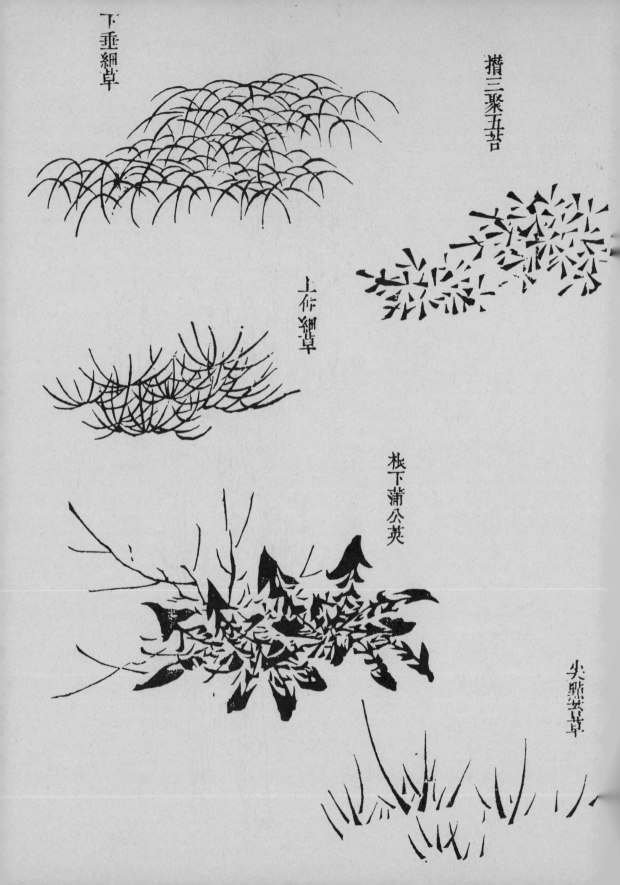

下垂細草

攢三聚五苔

上作細草

根下蒲公英

尖點莠草

to be crowded with orange trees or those natural to the torrid zone but such as will do being protected from frost.

The pretty little flower rudbeckia is a charming flower but difficult to raise by seed. I have often sent it. It improves prodigiously being in a garden. In the woods commonly it sends up but one stalk to a root and but one (or two) flower on it. But one I have hath now about 100 stalks on one root so I transplanted a pretty oenothera out of a meadow and it hath now shot up thirty-six stalks, each being full of flowers, and [I] hope these will continue to flower till frost. My aconite that I brought from James River last fall, if it be it grows finely and though in its native place sends forth but one stalk from one root, yet mine hath now five stalks and by its forward growth it may flower two month sooner than it did last fall, yet I hope to continue it in flower till frost if I don't let it seed to send to you. . . .

JOHN BARTRAM to PETER COLLINSON
June the 24th, 1760

HONORED AND BENEVOLENT FATHER:

I am happy, by the blessings of the Almighty God by whose care I have been protected and led safe through a pilgrimage these three and twenty months till my return to Charleston two days since. I am now lodged most kindly in the family of your deceased friend Lambol. His daughter, Mrs. Thomas, excellent in goodness beyond her sex, with expressions of the same affable and cordial friendship so particular in the character of her ancient, excellent parent, asked me to her house while I stay in this province, which [I] believe will be but a few days.

I wrote to my father soon after my return to Savannah from Tugaloo River, which letter gives an account of my proceedings there in that journey, which I traveled upwards of 300 miles. I collected a large number of specimens I sent to Doctor Fothergill with some drawings, in answer to which the doctor was pleased to send me a list of the new and non-described, which I was glad to find were many, and here he was pleased to express his satisfaction with the success of my labors and his willingness that I should continue my researches. This packet I received in East Florida soon after my return to Savannah, in order to forward my collections to Doctor Fothergill.

I intended to go back into the Cherokee and Creek countries, when the alarm from the frontiers of hostilities commencing between the Indians and the whites put a stop to that scheme. I then turned my views towards East Florida and prepared for it. I put my baggage on board a vessel bound from Savannah to Mr. Spalding's Store on the St. John's, intending to go by land there and set off accordingly. Got safe to the Altamaha, where I was taken ill of a fever of which I did not recover so as to be able to travel for near two months, when I set off again but was turned back again by expresses from East Florida that the Indians were up in arms against us in that province, having killed and captured several white people, and the inhabitants were flying in to Augustine, and all the Indian stores except one were robbed and broken up. So I stayed in the south part of Georgia, waiting for a favorable turn, and here I discovered and collected many valuable and new vegetables.

Hearing that the Lower Creeks were dealing with the governor of St. Augustine for peace, I resolved to make the second attempt. I left my horse in Georgia and went down the Altamaha to Frederica on the Island St. Simon. Waited on Mr. Spalding, who was pleased to give me letters to his agent in East Florida, and in a few days went on board his vessel bound to his store on St. John's. Two days after we left Frederica we met another of his vessels. We came too, went on board. This vessel was returned from the Store, having on board numbers of traders returning from the Indian country, being drove away by the Indians. They brought very bad tales and had on board the vessel all the goods of the trading houses except a few which the governor of Florida purchased of Mr. Spalding's agent, at the request of the Seminole Indians, they being desirous to have the Lower Store kept up. These goods were landed on an island a few miles below the Store in the river St. John's, where my chest and baggage was with them. The vessel returned back to Frederica and I prevailed on them to set me on Amelia Island near the mouth of St. Mary's, being determined to pursue my journey into Florida at all events, and having some papers and books in my chest which I stood in need of; I walked the beach until I came to a plantation where I was friendly received by Lord Egmont's agent.

I stayed with him three or four days on his promising me a passage to St. John's in a boat. He going to St. Augustine, [we] went on board a boat rowed by five Negroes and in about thirty hours arrived at St. John's near the Cowford, and here I was again put to my shift, being once more left alone. However, this gentleman sent me to a plantation, in his boat, higher up the river where I purchased a small canoe. I, having furnished myself with a sail and paddle, set off on my voyage up the river St. John's and got safe to the island, where I found my chest. Went to the Store, where I heard much more favorable accounts of the Indian affairs, and on confering with Mr. Spalding's agent, he encouraged me to stay a while until the Indians were quiet. A short time after this, some of the traders thought fit to risk a journey out to Alachua in quest of horses which they had amongst the Indians. I, having an inclination to see the Seminole Indian town of Cuscoela on the great Alachua savannah, went with them.

The savannah is vast and beautiful beyond description. The chief of the town received us most friendly, assured us of his protection, and gave the traders liberty to hunt up their horses. I rode with them near fifty miles round the green verge of this beautiful savannah and went to the sink, or vortex, where the waters are discharged. The savannah is surrounded by hammocks of rich land planted with orange groves, palm trees, Morus, Magnolia grandiflora, Tilia, Laurus ocra, Laurus coeasus and a variety of other trees and shrubs.

After a week or ten days, returned from Alachua to the Store. Continued my excursions about the country. Took a trip in my canoe up the St. John's about 100 miles above the Store to the uppermost plantation. Returned down to the Store and after some time an opportunity offered to an Indian town on Little St. Juan's River at the Bay of Apalache, about 100 miles west from the Store across the isthmus. This was a pleasant journey and afforded me many curiosities. The face and condition of this country is Indian, new and pleasing.

The Indians of the town received us with the complaisance and good breeding peculiar to them, treated us with the best they had, and offered us their protection whilst with them.

Returned to the Store and took another voyage up the St. John's. Returned with some fine roots and seeds which, together with my former collections, made up three large boxes of roots and one of seeds, which I carried up with me to Sunbury in Georgia; there I put them on board a vessel to London for Doctor Fothergill, having collected a number of curious roots in Georgia.

Dear Father, it is the greatest pleasure that I hear by my worthy Doctor Chalmers that you are alive and well, with my dear Mother, which I pray may continue. I beg leave to acquaint my benevolent parents that I am resolved, with the concurrence of Doctor Chalmers, to continue my travels another year; intend to go through the Cherokee countries to Pensacola, where I shall send my necessary baggage, and if it please God to spare my life and health, I may go to the Mississippi River. I have been often with the Doctor concerning it, and he promises to assist me with proper recommendatory letters through the Nations. Please to excuse this long, tedious letter.

I am ever your faithful son,

WILLIAM BARTRAM
(Letter to his father, 1735)

David Douglas Has a Narrow Escape

[*Hundreds know the Douglas fir for each one who knows David Douglas, the extraordinary Scots gardener, of whom it has been said that no other collector reaped such a harvest in America or is associated with so many useful plants. Sent out in 1823 by the Royal Horticultural Society, he ranged the West from Hudson Bay to California and is credited with collecting more than three hundred hitherto unknown species, of which at least two hundred have been introduced into gardens —including* Clarkia elegans, *the flowering currant* (Ribes sanguinea) *and the scarlet monkey flower* (Mimulus cardinalis). *In 1833 he sailed for Hawaii where he lost his young life* (aetat. 36) *under the hoofs of a wild bull. From his diary comes the following account of the ticklish circumstances under which he first collected the huge cones of the Sugar Pine which are now so familiar as winter decorations.*]

THURSDAY, 26th. I left my camp this morning at daylight. . . . About an hour's walk from my camp I was met by an Indian, who on discovering me strung his bow and placed on his left arm a sleeve of racoon-skin and stood ready on the defence. As I was well convinced this was prompted through fear, he never before having seen such a being, I laid my gun at my feet on the ground and waved my hand for him to come to me, which he did with great caution. I made him place his bow and quiver beside my gun, and then struck a light and gave him to smoke and a few beads. With a pencil I made a rough sketch of the cone and Pine I wanted and showed him it, when he instantly pointed to the hills about 15 or 20 miles to the south. As I wanted to go in that direction, he seemingly with much good-will went with me. At midday I reached my long-wished *Pinus* (called by the Umpqua tribe *Natele*), and lost no time in examining and endeavouring to collect specimens and seeds. New or strange things seldom fail to make great impressions, and often at first we are liable to over-rate them; and lest I should never see my friends to tell them verbally of this most beautiful and immensely large tree, I now state the dimensions of the largest one I could find that was blown down by the wind: Three feet from the ground, 57 feet 9 inches in circumference; 134 feet from the ground, 17 feet 5 inches; extreme length 215 feet. The trees are remarkably straight; bark uncommonly smooth for such large timber, of a whitish or light brown colour, and yields a great quantity of gum of a bright amber colour. The large trees are destitute of branches, generally two-thirds the length of the tree; branches pendulous, and the cones hanging from their points like small sugar-loaves in a grocer's shop. . . . Being unable to climb or hew down any, I took my gun and was busy clipping them from the branches with ball when eight Indians came at the report of my gun. They were all painted with red earth, armed with bows, arrows, spears of bone, and flint knives, and seemed to be anything but friendly. I endeavoured to explain to them what I wanted and they seemed satisfied and sat down to smoke, but had no sooner done so than I perceived one string his bow and another sharpen his flint knife with a pair of wooden pincers and hang it on the wrist of the right hand, which gave me ample testimony of their inclination. To save myself I could not do by flight, and without any hesitation I went backwards six paces and cocked my gun, and then pulled from my belt one of my pistols, which I held in my left hand. I was determined to fight for life. As I as much as possible endeavoured to preserve my coolness and perhaps did so, I stood eight or ten minutes looking at them and they at me without a word passing, till one at last, who seemed to be the leader, made a sign for tobacco, which I said they should get on condition of going and fetching me some cones. They went, and as soon as out of sight I picked up my three cones and a few twigs, and made a quick retreat to my camp, which I gained at dusk. . . . The position I am now in is lying on the grass with my gun beside me, writing by the light of my Columbian candle—namely a piece of wood containing rosin.

DAVID DOUGLAS
[Diary (1826)]

Bartram in Florida

[William Bartram we have already met, first as the son of that John Bartram described by Crèvecoeur and then as a supplier of curiosities to the ardent London collector Peter Collinson. In April 1773 he set out from Philadelphia by boat for Charleston and from there proceeded on horseback, by boat, and on foot through Georgia and Florida, collecting plants as he went. His Travels, *published in Philadelphia in 1791 and in London next year, was one of the first American books to be widely admired in England. Wordsworth and Coleridge both drew images from it—the latter notably in "Kubla Khan"—and, later, Carlyle wrote enthusiastically to Emerson about its "wonderful kind of floundering eloquence." The passage which follows describes Bartram's delight in subtropical Florida where only a few white planters and traders were beginning to intrude.]*

T H I S morning the winds on the great river were high and against me; I was therefore obliged to keep in port a great part of the day, which I employed in little excursions round about my encampment. The Live Oaks are of an astonishing magnitude, and one tree contains a prodigious quantity of timber; yet, comparatively, they are not tall, even in these forests, where growing on strong land, in company with others of great altitude (such as Fagus sylvatica, Liquidambar, Magnolia grandiflora, and the high Palm tree) they strive while young to be upon an equality with their neighbours, and to enjoy the influence of the sun-beams, and of the pure animating air. But the others at last prevail, and their proud heads are seen at a great distance, towering far above the rest of the forest, which consists chiefly of this species of oak, Fraxinus, Ulmus, Acer rubrum, Laurus Borbonia, Quercus dentate, Ilex aquafolium, Olea Americana, Morus, Gleditsia triacanthus, and, I believe, a species of Sapindus. But the latter spreads abroad his brawny arms, to a great distance. The trunk of the Live Oak is generally from twelve to eighteen feet in girt, and rises ten or twelve feet erect from the earth, some I have seen eighteen or twenty; then divides itself into three, four, or five great limbs, which continue to grow in nearly an horizontal direction, each limb forming a gentle curve, or arch, from its base to its extremity. I have stepped above fifty paces, on a straight line, from the trunk of one of these trees, to the extremity of the limbs. It is evergreen, and the wood almost incorruptible, even in the open air. It bears a prodigious quantity of fruit; the acorn is small, but sweet and agreeable to the taste when roasted, and is food for almost all animals. The Indians obtain from it a sweet oil, which they use in the cooking of hommony, rice etc; and they also roast it in hot embers, eating it as we do chesnuts.

The wind being fair in the evening, I sat sail again, and crossing the river, made a good harbour on the East shore, where I pitched my tent for the night. The bank of the river was about twelve or fifteen feet perpendicular from its surface, but the ascent gentle. Although I arrived here early in the evening, I found sufficient attractions to choose it for my lodging-place, and an ample field for botanical employment. It was a high, airy situation, and commanded an extensive and varied prospect of the river and its shores, up and down.

Behold yon promontory, projecting far into the great river, beyond the still lagoon, half a mile distant from me: what a magnificent grove arises on its banks! how glorious the Palm! how majestically stands the Laurel, its head forming a perfect cone! its dark green foliage seems silvered over with milk-white flowers. They are so large, as to be distinctly visible at the distance of a mile or more. The Laurel Magnolias, which grow on this river, are the most beautiful and tall that I have any where seen, unless we except those, which stand on the banks of the Mississippi; yet even these must yield to those of St. Juan, in neatness of form, beauty of foliage, and, I think, in largeness and fragrance of flower. Their usual height is about one hundred feet, and some greatly exceed that. The trunk is perfectly erect, rising in the form of a beautiful column, and supporting a head like an obtuse cone. The flowers are on the extremities of the subdivisions of the branches, in the center of a coronet of dark green, shining, ovate pointed entire leaves: they are large, perfectly white, and expanded like a full blown Rose. They are polypetalous, consisting of fifteen, twenty, or twenty-five petals: these are of a thick coriaceous texture, and deeply concave, their edges being somewhat reflex, when mature. In the center stands the young cone; which is large, of a flesh colour, and elegantly studded with a gold coloured stigma, that by the end of summer is greatly enlarged, and in the autumn ripens to a large crimson cone or strobile, disclosing multitudes of large coral red berries, which for a time hang down from them, suspended by a fine, white, silky thread, four, six or even nine inches in length. The flowers of this tree are the largest and most complete of any yet known: when fully expanded, they are of six, eight, and nine inches diameter. The pericarpium and berries possess an agreeable spicy scent, and an aromatic bitter taste. The wood when seasoned is of a straw colour, compact, and harder and firmer than that of the poplar.

It is really astonishing to behold the Grape-Vines in this place. From their bulk and strength, one would imagine they were combined to pull down these mighty trees to the earth; when, in fact, amongst other good purposes, they serve to uphold them. They are frequently nine, ten, and twelve inches in diameter, and twine round the trunks of the trees, climb to their very tops, and then spread along their limbs, from tree to tree, throughout the forest: the fruit is but small and ill tasted. The Grape vines, with the Rhamnus volubilis, Bignonia crucigera, and another rambling shrubby vine, which seems allied to the Rhamnus, perhaps Zizyphus scandens, seem to tie the trees together with garlands and festoons, and form enchanting shades. The long moss, so called (Tilландsea usneaoides), is a singular and surprising vegetable production: it grows from the limbs and twigs of all trees in these southern regions, from N. lat. 35 down as far as 28, and I believe every where within the tropics. Wherever it fixes itself, on a limb, or branch, it spreads into short and intricate divarications; these in time collect dust, wafted by the wind, which, probably by the moisture it absorbs, softens the bark and sappy part of the tree, about the roots of the plant, and renders it more fit for it to establish itself; and from this small beginning, it increases, by sending downwards and obliquely, on all sides, long pendant branches, which divide and subdivide themselves ad infinitum. It is common to find the spaces betwixt the limbs of large trees, almost occupied by this plant: it also hangs waving in the wind, like streamers, from the lower limbs, to the length of fifteen or twenty feet, and of bulk and weight, more than several men together could carry; and in some places, cart loads of it are lying on the ground, torn off by the violence of the wind. Any part of the living plant, torn off and caught in the limbs of a tree, will presently take root, grow, and increase, in the same degree of perfection as if it had sprung up from the seed. When fresh, cattle and deer will eat it in the winter season. It seems particularly adapted to the purpose of stuffing mattresses, chairs, saddles, collars, etc.; and for these purposes, nothing yet known equals it. The Spaniards in South America and the West-Indies, work it into cables, that are said to be very strong and durable;

but, in order to render it useful, it ought to be thrown into shallow ponds of water, and exposed to the sun, where it soon rots, and the outside furry substance is dissolved. It is then taken out of the water, and spread to dry; when, after a little beating and shaking, it is sufficiently clean, nothing remaining but the interior, hard, black, elastic filament, entangled together, and greatly resembling horse-hair.

The Zanthoxylum clava Herculis also grows here. It is a beautiful spreading tree, and much like a well grown apple-tree. Its aromatic berry is delicious food for the little turtle dove; and epicures say, that it gives their flesh a fine flavour.

Having finished my observations, I betook myself to rest; and when the plunging and roaring of the crocodiles, and the croaking of the frogs, had ceased, I slept very well during the remainder of the night; as a breeze from the river had scattered the clouds of musquitoes that at first infested me.

It being a fine cool morning, and fair wind, I sat sail early, and saw, this day, vast quantities of the Pistia stratiotes, a very singular aquatic plant. It associates in large communities, or floating islands, some of them a quarter of a mile in extent, which are impelled to and fro, as the wind and current may direct. They are first produced on, or close to, the shore, in eddy water, where they gradually spread themselves into the river, forming most delightful green plains, several miles in length, and in some places a quarter of a mile in breadth. These plants are nourished and kept in their proper horizontal situation, by means of long fibrous roots, which descend from the nether center, downwards, towards the muddy bottom. Each plant, when full grown, bears a general resemblance to a well grown plant of garden lettuce, though the leaves are more nervous, of a firmer contexture, and of a full green colour, inclining to yellow. It vegetates on the surface of the still stagnant water; and in its natural situation, is propogated from seed only. In great storms of wind and rain, when the river is suddenly raised, large masses of these floating plains are broken loose, and driven from the shores, into the wide water, where they have the appearance of islets, and float about, until broken to pieces by the winds and waves; or driven again to shore, on some distant coast of the river, where they again find footing, and there, forming new colonies, spread and extend themselves again, until again broken up and dispersed as before. These floating islands present a very entertaining prospect: for although we behold an assemblage of the primary productions of nature only, yet the imagination seems to remain in suspense and doubt; as in order to enliven the delusion, and form a most picturesque appearance, we see not only flowery plants, clumps of shrubs, old weather-beaten trees, hoary and barbed, with the long moss waving from their snags, but we also see them completely inhabited, and alive, with crocodiles, serpents, frogs, otters, crows, herons, curlews, jackdaws, etc. There seems, in short, nothing wanted but the appearance of a wigwam and a canoe to complete the scene.

Keeping along the west or Indian shore, I saw basking, on the sedgy banks, numbers of alligators, some of them of an enormous size.

The high forests on this coast now wore a grand and sublime appearance; the earth rising gradually from the river westward, by easy swelling ridges, behind one another, lifting the distant groves up into the skies. The trees are of the lofty kind, as the grand laurel magnolia, palma elata, liquidambar styraciflua, fagus sylvatica, querci, juglans hiccory, fraxinus, and others.

On my doubling a long point of land, the river appeared surprisingly widened, forming a large bay, of an oval form, and several miles in extent. On the West side it was bordered round with low marshes, and invested with a swamp of Cypress, the trees so lofty, as to preclude the sight of the high-land forests beyond them; and these trees, having flat tops, and all of equal height, seemed to be a green plain, lifted up and supported upon columns in the air, round the West side of the bay.

The Cupressus disticha stands in the first order of North American trees. Its majestic stature is surprising; and on approaching it, we are struck with a kind of awe, at beholding the stateliness of the trunk, lifting its cumbrous top towards the skies, and casting a wide shade upon the ground, as a dark intervening cloud, which, for a time, excludes the rays of the sun. The delicacy of its colour, and texture of its leaves, exceed every thing in vegetation. It generally grows in the water, or in low flat lands, near the banks of great rivers and lakes, that are covered, great part of the year, with two or three feet depth of water; and that part of the trunk which is subject to be under water, and four or five feet higher up, is greatly enlarged by prodigious buttresses, or pilasters, which, in full grown trees, project out on every side, to such a distance, that several men might easily hide themselves in the hollows between. Each pilaster terminates under ground, in a very large, strong, serpentine root, which strikes off, and branches every way, just under the surface of the earth: and from these roots grow woody cones, called cypress knees, four, five, and six inches high, and from six to eighteen inches and two feet in diameter at their bases. The large ones are hollow, and serve very well for bee-hives; a small space of the tree itself is hollow, nearly as high as the buttresses already mentioned. From this place, the tree, as it were, takes another beginning, forming a grand straight column eighty or ninety feet high, when it divides every way around into an extensive flat horizontal top, like an umbrella, where eagles have their secure nests, and cranes and storks their temporary resting-places; and what adds to the magnificence of their appearance is the streamers of long moss that hang from the lofty limbs and float in the winds. This is their majestic appearance when standing alone, in large rice plantations, or thinly planted on the banks of great rivers.

Paroquets are commonly seen hovering and fluttering on their tops: they delight to shell the balls, its seed being their favourite food. The trunks of these trees, when hollowed out, make large and durable pettiaugers and canoes, and afford excellent shingles, boards, and other timber, adapted to every purpose in frame buildings. When the planters fell these mighty trees, they raise a stage round them, as high as to reach above the buttresses; on this stage, eight or ten negroes ascend with their axes, and fall to work round its trunk. I have seen trunks of these trees that would measure eight, ten, and twelve feet in diameter, and forty and fifty feet straight shaft.

As I continued coasting the Indian shore of this bay, on doubling a promontory, I suddenly saw before me an Indian settlement, or village. It was a fine situation, the bank rising gradually from the water. There were eight or ten habitations, in a row, or street, fronting the water, and about fifty yards distance from it. Some of the youth were naked, up to their hips in the water, fishing with rods and lines; whilst others, younger, were diverting themselves in shooting frogs with bows and arrows. On my near approach, the little children took to their heels, and ran to some women who were hoeing corn; but the stouter youth stood their ground, and, smiling, called to me. As I passed along, I observed some elderly people reclined on skins spread on the ground, under the cool shade of spreading Oaks and Palms that were ranged in front of their houses: they arose, and eyed me as I passed, but perceiving that I kept on without stopping, they resumed their former position. They were civil, and appeared happy in their situation.

There was a large Orange grove at the upper end of their village; the trees were large, carefully pruned, and the ground under them clean, open, and airy. There seemed to be several hundred acres of cleared land about the village; a considerable portion of which was planted, chiefly with corn (Zea), Batatas, Beans, Pompions, Squashes (Cucurbita verrucosa), Melons (Cucurbita citrullus), Tobacco (Nicotiana), etc. abundantly sufficient for the inhabitants of the village.

After leaving this village, and coasting a considerable cove of the lake, I perceived the river before me much contracted within its late bounds, but still retaining the appearance of a wide and deep river, both coasts bordered for several miles with rich deep swamps, well timbered with Cypress, Ash, Elm, Oak, Hiccory, Scarlet Maple, Nyssa aquatica, Nyssa tupilo, Gordonia lasianthus, Corypha palma, Corypha pumila, Laurus Borbonia, etc. The river gradually narrowing, I came in sight of Charlotia, where it is not above half a mile wide, but deep; and as there was a considerable current against me, I came here to an anchor. This town was founded by Den. Rolle, esq. and is situated on a high bluff, on the east coast, fifteen or twenty feet perpendicular from the river, and is in length half a mile, or more, upon its banks. The upper stratum of the earth consists entirely of several species of fresh water Cochleae, as Coch. helix, Coch. labyrinthus, and Coch. voluta; the second, of marine shells, as Concha mytulus, Conc. ostrea, Conc. peeton, Haliotus auris marina, Hal. patella, etc. mixed with sea sand; and the third, or lower stratum, which was a little above the common level of the river, of horizontal masses of a pretty hard rock, composed almost entirely of the above shell, generally whole, and lying in every direction, petrified or cemented together, with fine white sand; and these rocks were bedded in a stratum of clay. I saw many fragments of the earthen ware of the ancient inhabitants, and bones of animals, amongst the shells, and mixed with the earth, to a great depth. This high shelly bank continues, by gentle parallel ridges, near a quarter of a mile back from the river, gradually diminishing to the level of the sandy plains, which widen before and on each side eastward, to a seemingly unlimited distance, and appear green and delightful, being covered with grass and the corypha repens, and thinly planted with trees of the long-leaved, or Broom Pine and decorated with clumps, or coppices, of floriferous, evergreen, and aromatic shrubs, and enamelled with patches of the beautiful little Kalmea ciliata. These shelly ridges have a vegetable surface of loose black mould, very fertile, which naturally produces Orange groves, Live Oak, Laurus Borbonia, Palma elata, Carica papaya, Sapindus, Liquidambar, Fraxinus excelsior, Morus rubra, Ulmus, Tilia, Sambucus, Ptelea, Tallow-nut or Wild Lime, and many others.

Mr. Rolle obtained from the crown a grant of forty thousand acres of land, in any part of East Florida, where the land was unlocated. It seems, his views were to take up his grant near St. Mark's, in the bay of Apalatchi; and he sat sail from England, with about one hundred families, for that place; but by contrary winds, and stress of weather, he missed his aim; and being obliged to put into St. Juan's, he, with some of the principal of his adherents, ascended the river in a boat, and being struck with its majesty, the grand situations of its banks, and fertility of its lands, and at the same time considering the extensive navigation of the river, and its near vicinity to St. Augustine, the capital and seat of government, he altered his views on St. Mark's, and suddenly determined on this place, where he landed his first little colony. But it seems, from an ill-concerted plan in its infant establishment, negligence, or extreme parsimony in sending proper recruits and other necessaries, together with a bad choice of citizens, the settlement by degrees grew weaker, and at length totally fell to the ground. Those of them who escaped the constant contagious fevers, fled the dreaded place, betaking themselves for subsistence to the more fruitful and populous regions of Georgia and Carolina.

The remaining old habitations are mouldering to earth, except the mansion house, which is a large frame building, of cypress wood, yet in tolerable repair, and inhabited by an overseer and his family. There is also a blacksmith with his shop and family, at a small distance from it. The most valuable district belonging to Mr. Rolle's grant, lies on Dun's lake, and on a little river, which runs from it into St. Juan. This district consists of a vast body of rich swamp land, fit for the growth of rice, and some very excellent high land surrounding it. Large swamps of excellent rice land are also situated on the west shore of the river, opposite to Charlotia.

The aborigines of America had a very great town in this place, as appears from the great tumuli, and conical mounts of earth and shells, and other traces of a settlement which yet remain. There grew in the old fields on these heights, great quantities of callicarpa, and of the beautiful shrub annona: the flowers of the latter are large, white, and sweet scented.

WILLIAM BARTRAM
[*Travels* (1791)]

A Botanist in China

[*The richest of all treasure houses from which new flowering plants—especially trees and shrubs—have been brought to enrich western gardens is China. From the middle of the nineteenth century down to our own day a succession of intrepid explorers have braved the hardships and very real dangers of the primitive and bandit-infested interior in search of new beauties. One of the earliest was Robert Fortune, who was sent there first in 1843 by the Royal Horticultural Society and spent in all some twenty years in the Orient. Often in danger of his life, he fought off pirates on the river and when forbidden to penetrate the interior went disguised as a native beggar. His reward was innumerable plants new to European gardens, including such now omnipresent favorites as For-sythia and the Bleeding Heart as well as Japanese anemones, the large-flowered Clematis, and the yellow tea rose.* He was also the first Englishman to study the cultivation and manufacture of tea and was thus ultimately responsible for the British tea industry of India. His Three Years' Wanderings in the Northern Provinces of China *is so rich that selection might be made almost at random but chosen here are some adventures with wily Chinese nurserymen; an account of his first glimpse of the yellow tea rose and (from another of his books) a "ramble" in the course of which he found a new ornamental evergreen.*]

A T this period the Chinese were making great preparations for the celebration of New Year's Day, which then fell on the 18th of February. Flowers of all kinds were in great demand amongst the inhabitants, who employ them in the decoration of their houses and temples. In going up the river towards the Fa-tee Gardens, I met boats in great numbers loaded with branches of peach and plum trees in bloom, *Enkianthus quinqueflorus,* camellias, cockscombs, magnolias, and various other plants which flower at this season. The Enkianthus is brought down from the hills with the buds just expanding; and after being placed in water for a day or two, the flowers come out as healthy and fresh as if the branches had not been removed from the parent tree. This plant is a great favourite amongst the Chinese. The common jonquil too comes in for a very extensive share of patronage; and in the streets of Canton one meets with thousands of bulbs growing in small pans amongst water and a few white stones. In this case the Chinese exhibit their peculiar propensity for dwarf and monstrous growth, by planting the bulbs upside down, and making the plants and flowers assume curious twisted forms, which appear to be so agreeable to the eyes of a Chinaman. Large quantities of all these flowers are exposed for sale in many of the shops and in the corners of the streets in Canton, where they seem to be eagerly bought up by the Chinese, who consider them quite indispensable at this particular season. Not only are the houses and temples decorated with them, but the boats on the river also come in for a most extensive share. Indeed, these boats are only floating houses, for a very great part of the population of Canton lives upon the river. The flower-boats, as they are commonly called, are particularly gay at new-year time with flowers of all hues, and gaudy flags streaming from each mast and stern. Crackers or fireworks, of which the Chinaman is so fond, are let off in large quantities for several days in all parts of the town, and form part of their religious ceremonies or offerings to their gods. Their shops are closed on New Year's Day, and for two or three days afterwards. The greater part of the natives wear their holiday clothes, and tramp about amongst their relations and friends to *chin-chin* them, and wish them a happy new year, as we do at home. Large parties are made at this season to go up to the gardens at Fa-tee; and on particular days you find there hundreds of these flower-boats crowded with young Chinese of the better classes, enjoying themselves as our own population do at Richmond or Hampton Court. Great numbers of well dressed ladies also go over to Fa-tee in the flower-boats, and walk about in the gardens; and this is the only season when they are visible at Canton. . . .

My first business, when I reached Ning-po, was to make inquiries regarding the gardens of the Mandarins, which I had heard something of from the officers who were there when the city was taken by the English troops, during the war. I had the same difficulties to encounter as I had at Amoy, owing to the jealousy of the Chinese. Ultimately, however, these too were overcome, and I obtained access to several Mandarins' gardens and nurseries, out of which several new plants were procured, which proved very valuable additions to my collections. Here, as at other places, I made many inquiries after the supposed yellow camellia, and offered ten dollars to any Chinaman who would bring me one. Anything can be had in China for dollars! and it was not long before two plants were brought to me, one of which was said to be light yellow, and the other as deep a colour as the double yellow rose. Both had flower-buds upon them, but neither were in bloom. I felt quite certain that the Chinaman was deceiving me, and it seemed foolish to pay such a sum for plants which I should in all probability have to throw away afterwards; and yet I could not make up my mind to lose the chance, slight as it was, of possessing the *yellow camellia*. And the rogue did his business so well. He had a written label stuck in each pot, and *apparently* the writing and labels had been there for some years. I fancied I was as cunning as he was, and requested him to leave the plants and return on the following morning, when he should have an answer. In the meantime I asked a respectable Chinese merchant to read the writing upon the labels. All was correct; the writing agreed with what the man had told me; namely, that one of the plants produced light yellow blooms, and the other deep yellow. "Did you ever see a camellia with yellow flowers?" I inquired of my friend the merchant. "No," said he, in his broken English. "*My never have seen he, my thinkie no have got.*" On the following morning the owner of the plant presented himself, and asked me if I had made up my mind upon the subject. I told him that I would take the plants to Hong-kong, where I was going at the time; that they would soon flower there; and that, if they proved *yellow*, he should have his money. This, however, he would not consent to; and at last we compromised the matter, I agreeing to pay half the money down, and the other half when the plants flowered, providing they were "true." On these conditions I got the camellias, and took them with me to Hong-kong. It is almost needless to say that when they flowered there was nothing yellow about them but the stamens, for they were both semi-double worthless kinds.

The gardens of the Mandarins in the city of Ning-po are very pretty and unique; they contain a choice selection of the ornamental trees and shrubs of China, and generally a considerable number of dwarf trees. Many of the latter are really curious, and afford another example of the patience and ingenuity of this people. Some of the specimens are only a few inches high, and yet seem hoary with age. Not only are they trained to represent old trees in miniature, but some are made to resemble the fashionable pagodas of the country, and others different kinds of animals, amongst which the deer seems to be the favourite. Junipers are generally chosen for the latter purpose, as they can be more readily bent into the desired form; the eyes and tongue are added afterwards, and the representation altogether is really good. One of the Mandarins of Nin-po, anxious, I suppose, to confer some mark of especial favour upon me, presented me with one of these animals—plants, I should say; but as it was of no real use to me, and as my collections of other things were large, I was obliged to decline his present, which he evidently considered of great value, and no doubt wondered at my want of taste.

Another example will show the passion which exists amongst the Chinese for things of this kind. When I was travelling on the hills of Hong-kong, a few days after my first arrival in China, I met with a most curious dwarf *Lycopodium*, which I dug up and carried down to Messrs. Dent's garden, where my other plants were at the time. "Hai-yah," said the old compradore, when he saw it, and was quite in raptures of delight. All the other coolies and servants gathered round the basket to admire this curious little plant. I had not seem them evince so much gratification since I showed them the "old man Cactus" (*Cereus senilis*), which I took out from England, and presented to a Chinese nurseryman at Canton. On asking them why they prized the Lycopodium so much, they replied, in Canton English, "*Oh, he too muchia handsome; he grow only a leete and a leete every year; and suppose he be one hundred year oula, he only so high*," holding up their hands an inch or two higher than the plant. This little plant is really very pretty, and often naturally takes the very form of a dwarf tree in miniature, which is doubtless the reason of its being such a favourite with the Chinese.

The dwarfed trees of the Chinese and Japanese have been noticed by every author who has written upon these countries, and all have attempted to give some description of the method by which the effect is produced. The process is in reality a very simple one, and is based upon one of the commonest principles of vegetable physiology. We all know that any thing which retards in any way the free circulation of the sap, also prevents to a certain extent the formation of wood and leaves. This may be done by grafting, by confining the roots, withholding water, bending the branches, or in a hundred other ways which all proceed upon the same principle. This principle is perfectly understood by the Chinese, and they make nature subservient to this particular whim of theirs. We are told that the first part of the process is to select the very smallest seeds from the smallest plants, which is not at all unlikely, but I cannot speak to the fact from my own observation. I have, however, often seen Chinese gardeners selecting suckers and plants for this purpose from the other plants which were growing in their garden. Stunted varieties were generally chosen, particularly if they had the side branches opposite or regular, for much depends upon this; a one-sided dwarf tree is of no value in the eyes of the Chinese. The main stem was then in most cases twisted in a zigzag form, which process checked the flow of the sap, and at the same time encouraged the production of side branches at those parts of the stem where they were most desired. When these suckers had formed roots in the open ground, or kind of nursery where they were planted, they were looked over and the best taken up for potting. The same principles, which I have already noticed, were still kept in view, the pots used being narrow and shallow, so that they held but a small quantity of soil compared with the wants of the plants, and no more water being given than what was barely sufficient to keep them alive. Whilst the branches were forming, they were tied down and twisted in various ways; the points of the leaders and strong growing

ones were generally nipped out, and every means were taken to discourage the production of young shoots which were possessed of any
degree of vigour. Nature generally struggles against this treatment for a
while, until her powers seem in a great measure exhausted, when she
quietly yields to the power of art. The Chinese gardener, however, must
be ever on the watch, for should the roots of his plants get through the
pots into the ground, or happen to be liberally supplied with moisture, or
should the young shoots be allowed to grow in their natural position for
a short time, the vigour of the plant which has so long been lost will be
restored, and the fairest specimen of Chinese dwarfing destroyed. Sometimes, as in the case of peach and plum trees, which are often dwarfed,
the plants are thrown into a flowering state, and then, as they flower
freely year after year, they have little inclination to make vigorous
growth. The plants generally used in dwarfing are pines, junipers, cypresses, bamboos, peach and plum trees, and a species of small-leaved elm.

Amongst the Mandarins' gardens, in the city of Ning-po, there
is one in particular which is generally visited by all strangers, and is much
admired. It is situated near the lake in the centre of the city. The old
man to whom it belongs has long retired from trade with an independent
fortune, and he now enjoys his declining years in the peaceful pursuits
of gardening, and is passionately fond of flowers. Both his house and
garden are unique in their way, but they are most difficult to describe,
and must be seen to be appreciated. In this part of the country the building of artificial rockwork is so well understood, that the resemblance to
nature is perfect, and it forms a principal feature in every garden. This
old gentleman has the different parts of his house joined together by
rude-looking caverns, and what at first sight appears to be a subterraneous
passage, leading from room to room, through which the visitor passes to
the garden, which lies behind the house. The small courts, of which a
glimpse is caught in passing through, are fitted up with this rockwork;
dwarf trees are planted here and there in various places, and creepers
hang down naturally and gracefully until their ends touch the little ponds
of water which are always placed in front of the rockwork. These small
places being passed, we are again led through passages like those already
noticed, when the garden, with its dwarf trees, vases, rockwork, ornamental windows, and beautiful flowering shrubs, is suddenly opened to
the view.

It must be understood, however, that all which I have now described is very limited in extent, but the most is made of it by windings
and glimpses through rockwork, and arches in the walls, as well as by
hiding the boundary with a mass of shrubs and trees.

Here old Dr. Chang—I believe that was his name—was spending the evening of his days in peaceful retirement. When I called upon him he was extremely polite, and, after making a great many very low bows, requested me to take the seat of honour by his side. The servants were then ordered to bring tea, a beverage which is offered to every stranger, and which was of the very finest description. Messengers were sent round to all the old man's particular friends, who each hurried to see the foreigner. One by one they dropt in, until the room was nearly full. The servants, who seemed to think themselves quite as good as their masters, mixed with the company, and made their remarks upon me with the greatest freedom. Every thing about me was examined and criticised most minutely, particularly my watch, which they seemed to admire very much. I was frequently requested, as a great favour, to allow them to see the works, and to hold it to their ears, in order that they might hear the sound which it made. The old mandarin now led me round his house, and showed me all the curiosities which it contained, and of which he was a great collector. Old bronzes, carved woods, specimens of porcelain, and other articles of that kind, were arranged with great taste in several of the rooms. From the house we proceeded to the garden, but as it was winter, and the trees leafless, I could form but little idea of the rarity or beauty of the plants which it contained. I took my leave, after drinking some more tea, promising to visit the old man again whenever I returned to Ning-po.

I visited also at this time several other Mandarins who had gardens, and from all of them I received the greatest civility. Some small articles which I brought out with me as presents were of the greatest use, not only in procuring me a civil reception, but also in enabling me to get plants or cuttings of rare species which were only found in the gardens of the rich, and which, of course, were not for sale. . . .

The gardens of the mandarins were extremely gay; particularly during the early months of the year; and, what was of more importance to me, contained a number of new plants of great beauty and interest. On entering one of the gardens on a fine morning in May, I was struck with a mass of yellow flowers which completely covered a distant part of the wall. The colour was not a common yellow, but had something of buff in it, which gave the flowers a striking and uncommon appearance. I immediately ran up to the place, and, to my surprise and delight, found that it was a most beautiful *new double yellow climbing rose*. I have no doubt, from what I afterwards learned, that this rose is from the more northern districts of the empire, and will prove perfectly hardy in

Europe. Another rose, which the Chinese call the *"five coloured,"* was also found in one of these gardens at this time. It belongs to the section commonly called China roses in this country, but grows in a very strange and beautiful manner. Sometimes it produces self-coloured blooms—being either red or French white, and frequently having flowers of both on one plant at the same time—while at other times the flowers are striped with the two colours. This will also be as hardy as our common China rose. *Glycine sinensis* is often grown on a flat trellis in front of the summer-house, or forms a kind of portico, which affords a pleasing shade. Entwined with one of these trees, I found another variety, having very long racemes of pure white flowers, which contrasted well with the light blue of the other. I obtained permission from the old Chinese gentleman to whom it belonged (my old friend Dr. Chang) to make some layers of this fine plant, and I am happy to say that one of these is now alive in the garden at Chiswick.

ROBERT FORTUNE
[*Three Years' Wanderings in the Northern*
Provinces of China (1847)]

A B O U T ten or twelve miles above Yen-chow the country appears more fertile; the hills are covered again with low pines, and the lowlands abound in tallow-trees, camphor-trees, and bamboos. Large quantities of Indian corn and millet are grown in this part of the country, which is, for the most part, too hilly for rice crops.

Our progress upwards was now very slow, owing to the great rapidity of the river. Every now and then we came to rapids, which it took us hours to get over, notwithstanding that fifteen men, with long ropes fastened to the mast of our boat, were tracking along the shore, and five or six more were poling with long bamboos. Nothing shows so much as this the indefatigable perseverance of the Chinese. When looking upon a river such as this is, one would think it quite impossible to navigate it, yet even this difficulty is overcome by hard labour and perseverance.

The slow progress which we necessarily made suited my purposes exactly, and enabled me to explore the botanical riches of the country with convenience and ease. I used to rise at break of day, and spend the morning inspecting the hills and valleys near the sides of the river, and then return to the boat in time for breakfast. Breakfast over, I generally went on shore again, accompanied by my men, who carried the seeds, plants or flowers we might discover during our rambles. The first thing we did on these occasions was to ascend the nearest hill and take

a survey of the windings of the river, with the number of rapids, in order
that we might form some idea of the progress our boat would make
during our absence. If the rapids were numerous we knew that she
would progress slowly, and that we might wander to a considerable
distance with perfect safety; if, on the other hand, the river seemed
smooth, and its bed comparatively level, we were obliged to keep within
a short distance of the banks.

During these rambles I met with many plants growing wild
on the hills, which I had never seen before, except in gardens. Here the
curious and much-prized *Edgworthia chrysantha* was growing in great
abundance. Reeves's Spiræa and *Spiræa prunifolia* were found in great
profusion. Several species of the *Chimonanthus* or Japan allspice, *For-
sythia viridissima, Buddlea Lindleyana,* and numerous Daphnes, Garde-
nias, and Azaleas, were also met with. Many kinds of mosses and
Lycopods were growing out of the crevices of the moist rock; amongst
the latter, and very abundant, was a fine species named *Lycopodium
Willdenorii.* . . .

Limestone rock is very plentiful in this district, and there are a
great number of kilns for burning it, constructed exactly like those we
see at home. Large quantities of water-fowl, such as geese, ducks, teal,
and several fine varieties of the kingfisher, were common about the river.
Inland, on the hill-sides, pheasants, woodcocks, and partridges were most
abundant. I believe deer are also plentiful, but I did not see any.

Thus day after day passed pleasantly by; the weather was delightful, the natives quiet and inoffensive, and the scenery picturesque
in the highest degree. My Chinamen and myself, often footsore and
weary, used to sit down on the hill-top and survey and enjoy the beautiful scenery around us. The noble river, clear and shining, was seen
winding amongst the hills; here it was smooth as glass, deep and still, and
there shallow, and running rapidly over its rocky bed. At some places
trees and bushes hung over its sides, and dipped their branches into the
water, while at others rocks reared their heads high above the stream,
and bade defiance to its rapid current.

The whole country was hilly, and the distant mountains, varying in height from three hundred to three thousand feet, were peaked,
ridged, and furrowed in a most remarkable manner. Altogether the views
were most charming, and will long remain vividly impressed upon my
memory.

On the 29th and 30th of October we passed the towns of Tsa-
yuen, Tsasa-poo, Kang-koo, and Shang-i-yuen, all places of considerable
note, particularly the last, which must contain at least 100,000 inhabit-

ants. Opposite to the town of Tsa-yuen there is a curious shaped hill, which is composed chiefly of granite of a beautiful greenish colour, much prized by the Chinese. The slabs which are quarried out of the hill are used for various ornamental purposes, but they are more particularly in demand for the building of tombs. Large quantities are taken down the river to Yen-chow and Hang-chow for this purpose.

The tea-plant was now frequently seen in cultivation on the hill-sides, this being the outskirt of the great green-tree country to which I was bound. Large camphor-trees were frequently seen in the valleys, particularly near the villages. Tallow-trees were still in extensive cultivation, and at this season of the year, being clothed in their autumnal hues, they produced a striking effect upon the varied landscape. The leaves had changed from a light-green to a dark blood-red colour. Another tree, a species of maple, called by the Chinese the fung-gze, was also most picturesque from the same cause. These two trees formed a striking contrast with the dark-green foliage of the pine tribe.

But the most beautiful tree found in this district is a species of weeping cypress, which I had never met with in any other part of China, and which was quite new to me. It was during one of my daily rambles that I saw the first specimen. About half a mile distant from where I was I observed a noble-looking fir-tree, about sixty feet in height, having a stem as straight as the Norfolk Island pine, and weeping branches like the willow of St. Helena. Its branches grew at first at right angles to the main stem, then described a graceful curve upwards, and bent again at their points. From these main branches others long and slender hung down perpendicularly, and gave the whole tree a weeping and graceful form. It reminded me of some of those large and gorgeous chandeliers, sometimes seen in theatres and public halls in Europe.

What could it be? It evidently belonged to the pine tribe, and was more handsome and ornamental than them all. I walked, no—to tell the plain truth, I ran up to the place where it grew, much to the surprise of my attendants, who evidently thought I had gone crazy. When I reached the spot where it grew it appeared more beautiful even than it had done in the distance. Its stem was perfectly straight, like *Cryptomeria*, and its leaves were formed like those of the well-known arborvitæ, only much more slender and graceful.

This specimen was fortunately covered with a quantity of ripe fruit, a portion of which I was most anxious to secure. The tree was growing in some grounds belonging to a country inn, and was the property of the innkeeper. A wall intervened between us and it, which I confess I felt very much inclined to get over; but remembering that I was acting Chinaman, and that such a proceeding would have been very indecorous, to say the least of it, I immediately gave up the idea. We now walked into the inn, and, seating ourselves quietly down at one of the tables, ordered some dinner to be brought to us. When we had taken our meal we lighted our Chinese pipes, and sauntered out, accompanied by our polite host, into the garden where the real attraction lay. "What a fine tree this of yours is! we have never seen it in the countries near the sea where we come from; pray give us some of its seeds." "It is a fine tree," said the man, who was evidently much pleased with our admiration of it, and readily complied with our request. These seeds were carefully treasured; and as they got home safely, and are now growing in England, we may expect in a few years to see a new and striking feature produced upon our landscape by this lovely tree. Afterwards, as we journeyed westward, it became more common, and was frequently to be seen in clumps on the sides of the hills.

This tree has been named the FUNEREAL CYPRESS. Professor Lindley—to whom I sent one of the dried specimens procured during this journey—pronounces it "an acquisition of the highest interest"; and adds, "We have received a specimen of it, which enables us to say that it must be a plant of the greatest beauty. It may be best described as a tree like the weeping willow in growth, with the foliage of the savin, but of a brighter green; it is, however, not a juniper, as the savin is, but a genuine cypress. It has long been a subject of regret that the Italian cypress cannot be made to endure our climate, and to decorate our burial-places; but we have now a finer tree, still better adapted for the purpose."

ROBERT FORTUNE
[*A Journey to the Tea Country of China* (1852)]

A Missionary Scientist

[*Exploration is likely to be nowadays a matter of groups and of organization. The Abbé Armand David was one of the last representatives of the heroic age and made long journeys into the remote parts of China often alone, on foot and in danger of his life. Deeply religious and also passionately interested in natural history, he joined the missionary order of St. Vincent de Paul and while stationed in China from 1862 to 1874 managed to combine his official duties with a fruitful search for plants and animals. Among the hundreds of ornamental plants he introduced were new rhododendrons, roses, ranunculuses, primulas and gentians, as well as magnolias and firs. "All the sciences concerned with the works of creation," he wrote, "increase the glory of their Author. They are praise-worthy in themselves and holy in their objective, for to know the truth is to know God."]*

I T is really a pity the education of the human species did not develop in time to save the irremediable destruction of so many species which the Creator placed on our earth to live beside man, not merely for beauty, but to fulfill a useful role necessary for the economy of the whole. A selfish and blind preoccupation with material interests has caused us to reduce this cosmos, so marvelous to him with eyes to see it, to a hard, matter-of-fact place. Soon the horse and the pig on one hand and wheat and potatoes on the other will replace hundreds of thousands of animals and plants given us by God. . . .

June 30 (1866)   My baggage is no longer carried by a donkey, but by a big, robust camel. There are three of us in this expedition: Sambdatchiemda, who acquires the titles of camel-driver, guide, cook, and interpreter; Brother Chévrier, as a hunter; and I, who walk ahead carrying my gun, boxes, and a net for insects. Our mixed Chinese and European costume contrasts with our exotic beards.

We expect to be gone fifteen to twenty days and consequently have taken along sufficient supplies—that is to say, forty pounds of small millet, twenty pounds of *tsamba*, and three pounds of pork fat, with a bottle of Chinese brandy for each of us. In addition, we have some hard rolls in case of great necessity. . . .

Finally everything is ready and we start off gaily at about seven in the morning. The road is muddy but the intense heat dries it quickly. Two days of intermittent rain have sufficed to give the mountains and meadows a lush appearance which they have not had for a long time. We proceed straight to the west toward Paotow, the last town on the northern bank of the Yellow River and the commercial center of this region. The road we take is traveled by many carts, loaded mostly with cereals and cloth going either to central Mongolia or toward Kansu, which has been ravaged by the bandits.

As we approach the town, located eighteen miles from Saratsi, where I received such a discouraging welcome a month ago, we are pre-occupied with the thought that they may not permit us to pass. In fact, we see a horseman pass us at full gallop, whom we suppose, and with good reason, to have been sent from Saratsi to warn the authorities at Paotow of our journey, and, undoubtedly, to make us retrace our steps. Hence before reaching the city we decide to go around it by turning southward, although there also we risk finding pickets of soldiers; but there is no other way. By noon we are in sight of the town and about three miles away from it. We ford a little stream, where I collect a curious plant, new to me.

Meanwhile it has become stormy; large black clouds have gathered and are rolling over the whole sky; thunder rumbles almost uinterruptedly from afar; the wind becomes violent and it begins to rain.

We hasten our steps over the salty fields, where we flush lap-wings, *Lobivanellus* (*Microsarcops cinereus*), and curlews, and we seek refuge in an isolated house. A nobleman standing in front of the door offers us provisional shelter; the populace runs to see us and looks at us indifferently without saying a word. Since we are hungry and above all very thirsty we beg them to have a little millet cooked for us, offering to pay for it. They refuse. They even refuse us water, and let us remain soaking wet at the door, like our baggage, which is on the camel's back. The camel, happier than we, browses peacefully in front of the house.

Finally the weather improves and we are able to leave this inhospitable shelter and continue on our way. By evening we arrive at a little inn at Gartchin-yao. We set up our tent in the middle of the high-way, and to save our provisions we each eat a bowl of buckwheat meal at the inn. The night is quite cool; we sleep little because of the numerous passers-by, including Tartar horsemen who come on patrol, undoubtedly in order to look us over. These stupid soldiers continue to follow us, though it is easy for them to see that we have no intention of going to reinforce the rebel armies.

July 1   Last night the people of the inn agreeably prepared our modest repast, and they do the same this morning for our breakfast. This house is also a place where opium is smoked. There is a little lighted lamp beside a pipe to invite travelers to smoke the debilitating drug. The smokers sleep and snore and their faces are unusually red.

The morning is fine as usual. At Ning-hsia we leave the main road leading to the Yellow River and Ordos, and go westward across a plain covered with yellow *Statice* and a kind of *Lycium* with white flowers. The curlews and pratincoles can be heard near by.

Toward evening we camp south of Hatamel near a Mongol tent, whence they bring us a little milk and dung in exchange for four cups of millet.

July 2   Departing at eight o'clock, we intend to cover as much ground as yesterday; we quicken our steps, and the camel holds his pace well. The weather is boiling hot and we advance in a sandy desert plain covered with licorice, which we use in abundance to refresh ourselves for lack of water: thus Providence provides the remedy alongside the evil. The principal plants in this plain are blue *Iris* and a coarse grass, on which I catch in quantities a new species of *Hoplia*, reddish and glazed with blue underneath. I also find there numerous little grasshoppers and a few cockchafers. The only birds we see are the field pipit, the lark, and, near the hills, the crested lark.

After a while we pass a group of Mongol tents, and after walking an hour and a half we find ourselves opposite the Merghen-gol lamasery, near which we plan to camp; we are certain to find water and fuel there. This large lamasery resembles a village. It is watered by a rushing stream, which loses itself later amid pebbles of granite with large crystals.

We have difficulty finding enough dung to cook our millet; but since the head of the valley appears to be cool and wooded we decide to go there after our meal. It is truly beautiful. . . .

July 3   The whole day is spent collecting plants, birds, and insects. I flush a woodcock from some damp copses of large-leaved willows. This bird is exceedingly rare in northern China and Mongolia. The other birds are not different from those encountered elsewhere, but in vain we exhaust ourselves looking for the blue pheasant. The only varieties known here are the *Phasianus torquatus*, the *Pucrasia xanthospila*, and the rock partridge, which is abundant everywhere but has retired to the high mountains since it began to rain.

The valley we are exploring is well wooded but large trees are scarce. Again I see the common pine, the *Thuya*, two species of juniper, two elms, two willows, the *Coylopsis*, the *Craegus oxycantha*, a *Phyllanthus* ten to thirteen feet high, the common aspen, the poplar with leathery leaves, the large *Hydrangea* with white but not very decorative flowers, the *Cornus sanguinea*, the *Prunus pasus*, and two varieties of mulberry. It is here that Brother Chévrier brings me four or five silkworms, ancestors of the cultivated species. He has found them on a mulberry growing amid almost inaccessible rocks.

July 4   It has rained during the night but we are able nevertheless to go out in the morning and enrich our collection with two

new satyr butterflies and a *Vanessa polychloros* which I have not seen
before. A large, pretty caddisfly that could be easily mistaken for a
butterfly abounds in the willows. We shoot, but in vain, at a roe buck
and at a *ching-yang,* or *Naemorhedus goral candatus.*

The apricot tree is very common here, as are two other species
of *Amygdalus* with inedible fruits. But these trees are leafless. A multitude of hairy caterpillars has entirely despoiled them, as well as the
willows, the cotoneasters, and even the pines. There are quantities of
yellow rose bushes now in flower, but fewer of the pink-flowered rose.
I also find the *Rhamnus saxatilis* and a buckthorn with long linear leaves,
which I also collected at Saratsi. Several large *Umbelliferae* border the
stream, as well as a kind of tassel flower, *Cacalia,* with yellow blossoms.
The ubiquitous Chinese carnation is found everywhere, mixed with
Spiraea shrubs, *Euphrasia officinalis* (or a related species), *Galium verum,*
and so on.

At about five o'clock in the evening there is a violent storm
with frightening thunderclaps echoing in the thousand valleys surrounding us. It would be magnificent if there were no danger, but the lightning
strikes exceedingly close and hits several near-by rocks. . . .

July 6   It rained again last night, accompanied by bursts
of thunder. The vegetation is regaining lost time and is becoming truly
splendid. But we cannot prolong our stay in this pretty valley. We must
visit the more westerly mountains, where we have been promised large
forests and treasures of natural history.

We strike our tent at ten o'clock and go northward up the
brook. First we go through a cool, leafy thicket where some old rotten
willows have fallen. I see many species of *Limenitis* and *Vanessa,* including *V. antiopa.* Soon the water disappears and with it the trees, which
become scarcer and scarcer except along the bottom of the valleys, where
we hear the roe deer bellowing, awakened by our approach.

After one or two hours' climbing we take a westerly direction
along a path that follows the crest of the mountains. We are not the only
travelers in these solitudes, for from afar we see a mandarin whose silk
garments glisten in the sunlight, and who is accompanied by two lamas
dressed in red.

While walking along, I find in the thickets and the highest
meadows an *Anemone* with rose-white petals, whose rounded, cottony
receptable is filled with seeds symmetrically placed on this bowl of white
down. I also find another new species of *Anemone* with fine-toothed
leaves but already faded flowers; I collect ripe seeds of it.

The wooded mountains we traverse have growths of aspen,

birch, white poplar, and pines of medium height. The peony with large, fragrant white or rose flowers (*Paeonia albiflora*) is abundant there, as is also *Clematis florida*, whose large double flowers are sometimes blue, sometimes purple, and sometimes a pale slate gray. We also find *Polemonium*, rose-colored valerian, *Trollius asiatica* with large golden flowers, the large geranium with violet flowers, *Meconopsis cambrica* or the yellow poppy of the Alps, etc. Three woody *Potentilla* abound and form thickets on the granitic rocks crowning the heights. I see and kill a new species of *Saxicola* very difficult to approach. This bird is rare here and reminds me of the European *Saxicola hispanica*, but differs in the pure ash color of its back.

For one or two hours we fear that a storm may force us to stop where there will be no forage for our camel and no place to set up our tent, but suddenly our path leads us to a series of rounded hills covered with the loveliest meadows. It is magnificent; one might take it for the cool sub-alpine mountains of Europe. It is only necessary now to find water. The indications are not propitious, and our guide has already searched most of the valley when I have the good fortune to find a clear and plentiful spring escaping suddenly from enormous granite rocks, hidden in a depression in the meadow under some large willows. We quickly call our camel-driver and set up our tent on this delightful site.

We find ourselves here in a truly alpine region that dominates all the surrounding country. We are on a very high mammillated plateau covered with green herbs and wooded ravines. To the south, north, and west we see the plain, which is crossed by a broad band of yellowish sand called Huang-sha (yellow sand) in the land of the Ordos. A parallel band of the same kind extends from west to east in the northern plain situated between the mountains of Wu-la-t'o and Mao-mingan. . . .

July 12   The night is a bad one. Camping in a damp place gives me rheumatism and a toothache. We are frequently disturbed by the raucous cries of the roe deer, repeated and prolonged by echoes in the valley.

The vegetation, with the exception of a gentian with large blue flowers, does not offer any striking novelties; it is composed of the same plants seen elsewhere. I notice a *Xylosteum* (*Lonicera*) with many red fruits that look like cherries.

Since yesterday morning we have met no one and we are a little uncertain of the direction to take in order to reach Barou-taba. But we are undoubtedly following one of the northern entrances. We ascend the ravine, first toward the southeast, then south. The trail soon becomes very poor—narrow and very steep. We meet a young Mongol with round red cheeks like a European mountaineer, who dispels our doubts and tells us we are on the right road. But we proceed with difficulty on this path strewn with fallen ancient tree-trunks. It is even worse when we reach the top of the gorge, where we have to make a rapid and dangerous descent; and once again we are obliged to hold back on our camel's load with a rope, which two of us pull with all our strength. It is certain that a camel loaded like ours has never passed this way; but I notice that, like a donkey, our large ruminant is stubborn, and on difficult descents where he should slow his steps he hurries, especially when he feels himself held strongly from behind. Brother Chévrier has also discovered this bad habit and exploits it to his benefit; where the road is flat, or almost so, he lets himself be dragged by the good beast to spare himself fatigue. I am almost sorry for our quadruped, already weary with his load and with my daily increasing collections, but fortunately I do not dare protest. At a moment when Brother Chévrier unintentionally pulls the rope harder than usual it suddenly breaks and my comrade falls over backwards, grumbling under his breath. The sight of my dear hunter stretched on the ground, his four limbs in the air, makes us laugh the rest of the day.

As we descend and advance southward the valley broadens, and the mountains seem to rise from the plain and are exceedingly steep. We are told that the *Naemorhedus goral candatus* is abundant here, as well as the *Pucrasia*, called *sung-chi* by the Chinese, which means "fowl of the pines."

Everywhere the forests are almost completely destroyed. Large, old pines are not seen in numbers except on high summits and in inaccessible valleys. Lower down, trees are numerous, but are not allowed time to reach their full development. The prohibition against destroying the forests of Wu-la-t'o is beginning to be no longer effective. The principal species are the *Pinus thunbergii*, the *Thuya orientalis*, a juniper with very pointed foliage peculiar to Wu-la-t'o, another large, very abundant dioecious juniper with fragrant wood which is cultivated in Pekin (undoubtedly brought from here), a white birch, the *Populus tremula*, another poplar, and, finally, *Ulmus montana* and *Ulmus pumila*.

July 13   We spend the night about six miles above the lamasery bearing the name of this valley, in a place where a clear, abundant stream has its source. However, the country is very dry; schists of granite or gneiss cut into enormous slabs form the inaccessible sides of most of the mountains, the highest peaks of which may rise at most four thousand feet.

We have been told that these districts are infested with brigands, but during the night we are awakened only by passers-by who come to look at us. Luckily the sight of our beards, and especially of our firearms, immediately inspires a salutary respect in these inquisitive people.

All morning we pass Mongols dragging trunks of pine trees toward the plain. I learn that opposite the valley to the south is the dwelling of the *Ouang-ye*, or prince of western Wu-la-t'o, who is now at war in Kansu. He is having a flotilla of boats constructed, for which this wood is destined. . . .

July 14   Naturally we have not been able to sleep. We are numb with cold and dampness, but day comes, and, after our usual prayers, which are always our first and last acts of the day, we try to straighten ourselves out. The weather is still uncertain; but it is not raining, though the sky is dark and heavy clouds cover not only the peaks, but also the mountainsides.

The moisture has brought the insects out of the ground, and they fly and buzz around us. They are *Ateuchus*, *Gymnopleurus*, and other *Lamellicornia*. I catch a large black *Necrophorus*. Since we have neither water nor fire here and we fear that another storm may cut our journey short, we start early on empty stomachs. Our tent, heavy with moisture, is folded as usual and loaded with the baggage on the camel, who is somewhat refreshed by the rain. We cover about twenty miles thus without stopping, but my camel-driver is in a bad humor and mal-treats the beast unreasonably.

Toward ten o'clock I send Sambdatchiemda to a near-by tent to buy water and dung in order to prepare our breakfast. We are fam-ished, having eaten nothing this morning and only very poorly and very little yesterday. But the Mongol lingers with his compatriots and does not return for half an hour, meanwhile undoubtedly having eaten and drunk. This is a petty vengeance against me for having decided not to take a road past some Mongol friends of his because it would have been too far out of the way. So we are obliged to continue without eating as far as Hatamel, and do not reach the two Mongol habitations there until fairly late.

It rains somewhat and thunders; nevertheless we are able to make the fire we need to cook our millet. We add to it two partridges killed yesterday morning along the road by Brother Chévrier, which have turned a little gamy from the muggy heat. A well of yellow water and some roots of a partly dried coarse grass furnish us with the means required to cook our meal.

Fifteen days earlier we had camped on this same spot. Today the rains have made the grass grow, and the camel contents himself with goosefoot and *Salsola*, which he likes. Birds, which are very scarce in the dry western plain, are more common here; we see many short-toed larks, crested larks, *Anthus campestris*, and swallows.

July 15   The day is fine and we cover considerable ground. At seven in the evening we set up camp in a plain near a deep stream not far from the ruins of a fort called Charbaté, destroyed at least two years ago like the one at Biljukaé.

The evening is equally fine; a fresh north wind fills our lungs and the air is so clear that the mountains appear bluish. We can see most of the highest summits of the Wu-la-t'o chain, west of the valley of Merghen-gol. On their northern slopes are the high meadows where we spent three days so pleasantly. The highest peaks may be three thousand to forty-five hundred feet above the plain.

July 16   The night is fine, though we are disturbed for a moment by a suspicious visitor. Toward midnight a man comes to ask Sambdatchiemda, snoring under the stars, how many there are of us, and other equally irrelevant banalities. But the unexpected sight of a European beard seen in the light of our dung fire soon causes the importunate visitor to disappear. Resting under our covers, spread out over thick turf composed of *Salsola*, we need fear only the visit of indiscreet frogs that swarm in a near-by pool.

At half past five we are already on our way, after having downed the remains of our *tsamba*. We go directly east toward Paotow in fine weather with a north wind. Today we no longer fear annoyances from the many Tartar soldiers we meet on the road, for they seem to be reassured about us. Herds of their horses are grazing in the meadows. We pass with dignity through the town of Paotow followed by a crowd attracted by the sight of two Europeans. They do try to stop us again in the name of the mandarin; but with a little firmness I prevent them from causing us loss of time, and by night we arrive at an inn only nine miles from Saratsi. Today was free from any untoward events, but tiring, because we traveled thirty-six or more miles under a hot sun, in a sandy plain where the whitish earth reflected the heat.

July 17   At nine o'clock in the morning we return to our dwelling, where we find everything peaceful, thanks to God!

Saratsi and the near-by villages look festive. We meet carts filled with women and girls going to the celebration, dressed in brilliantly colored clothes, red, green, blue, etc. This rejoicing is occasioned by the rain which has just fallen.

We have walked from Barou-taba to here in an almost straight line. I reckon the distance to be more than one hundred and twenty-five miles. If I add forty-five miles from Barou-taba to the mountains I reach a total of close to one hundred and seventy-five miles from Saratsi to the end of the Wu-la-t'o range.

July 19–23   These past five days of extreme heat have been spent here arranging our collections and completing our notes, and in taking small outings in the neighborhood. The birds have disappeared, and there are no insects except near the mountains, although we can always catch cockchafers, as well as satyrs.

The harvest is fairly good at Saratsi. Every morning we see a large number of people in the poppy fields gathering opium, which exudes in brown tears from an incision made in the fruit capsule. The barley has been harvested, the wheat is ripening. However, provisions are fairly expensive because of the great quantity of flour being exported to the soldiers of Kansu.

We are preparing an expedition toward the north, a country I do not know at all.

ABBÉ ARMAND DAVID
[Diary,
TRANSLATED BY HELEN M. FOX (1949)]

Discovering the Regal Lily

[One of the most spectacular introductions from China is the Regal Lily, brought back as recently as 1910 and now one of the most beautiful as well as one of the most widely cultivated of bulbous plants. Its discoverer, the late Ernest H. Wilson, nearly lost his life in the service of this particular plant but fortunately he survived to write a thrilling account of the whole adventure.

Wilson was at the time employed by the Arnold Arboretum of which Wilson himself was later to become Keeper but, like Robert Fortune and James Douglas before him, he had begun as a gardener, entering at sixteen the Birmingham Botanical Garden. Later he became a student worker at Kew and in 1899 (aged twenty-five) he was sent on his first trip to China by James Veitch, the great English plant dealer.

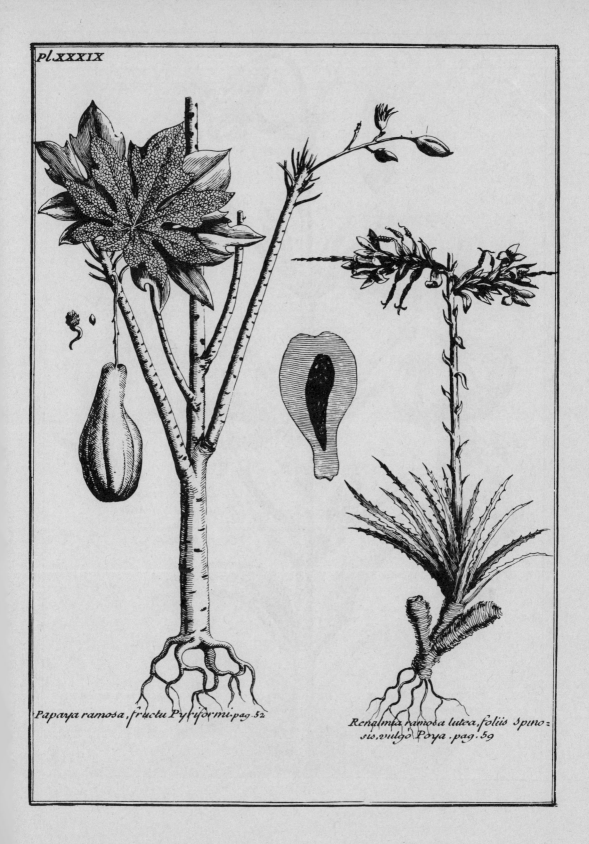

Pl. XXXIX

Papaya ramosa, fructu Pyriformi. pag. 52.

Renalmia ramosa lutea, foliis spino=
sis, vulgo Poya. pag. 59

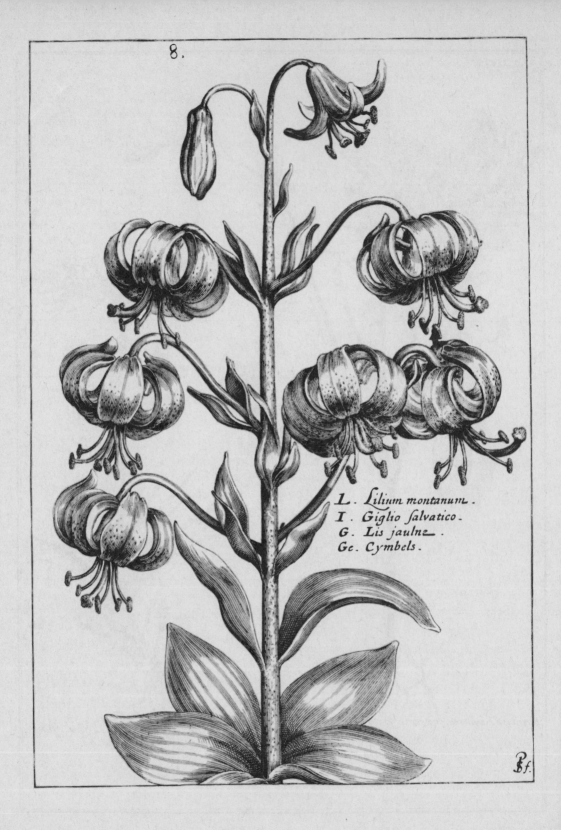

L. Lilium montanum.
I. Giglio salvatico.
G. Lis jaulne.
Ge. Cymbels.

Pf.

Returning after three years he set forth again in 1903 and is credited with having brought back from these two trips two thousand different plants and seed. After coming to the United States he made four more trips for the Arboretum and included Japan, Formosa, New Zealand and Africa in his explorations. All in all, he is credited with introducing more than a thousand species, many very popular, into cultivation.

Though China covers an area only about two-thirds the size of the United States, though it is densely populated and so thoroughly cultivated that one might expect much of the native flora to have been destroyed, yet more than twenty thousand species of plants have been found there and it is said to have the richest temperate flora in the world.

If one asks why, the answer is one which throws light also on the fact that North America, though less rich than China, is richer than Europe. When the great ice age pushed down from the north it gradually swept vegetation before it. Much of what had once flourished in Europe was pushed finally against the Alps and perished. But in North America the mountain ranges run north–south rather than east–west; hence the retreating plants could escape down the valleys and, when the ice receded, move northward again. But China was never glaciated during the tertiary period. Had North America similarly escaped it might have been equally rich, since the actual flora of China is closely related to our own. But—as it may be at least presumed—many species which failed to survive the ice here did survive in Asia to be reintroduced into America by such intrepid adventurers as Wilson.]

HOW many people know the size of a mule's hoof? Quite a number have felt the strength of a mule's leg and the sharpness of his teeth; his obstinacy is a proverb. But the size of his hoof is another matter. Frankly, I do not know with mathematical exactness but as I lay on the ground and more than forty of these animals stepped over my prostrate form the hoof seemed enormous, blotting out my view of the heavens. The instinctive surefootedness of the mule is well-known and I realized it with my gratitude as these animals one by one passed over me and not one even frayed my clothing.

It happened in the No-man's land of the Chino-Thibetan borderland and my predicament had been brought about by a rockslide, a common occurrence in that part of the world. I had left Boston, Massachusetts, at the end of March, 1910, and having crossed to Europe reached Peking by way of the Trans-Siberian Railway early in May. From Peking I travelled by devious routes across China to Sungpang Ting, in the extreme west-northwest, which was reached toward the end of August. My quest was the Regal Lily which I had discovered some years earlier but had failed to successfully introduce into American gardens. Its beauty of blossom and richness of fragrance had won my heart and I was determined that it should grace the gardens of the western world. That such a rare jewel should have its home in so remote and arid region of the world seemed like a joke on Nature's part. However, there it was and my business in life was to effect its transference to lands where its beauty would find proper recognition.

Throughout an indefinite past generations of the Regal Lily had lived unsung and unseen save by the rude peasants of a rude land. But few white men had passed that way when first I made discovery and none had noted my royal lady. This had been preserved for me. And what of the Regal Lily? Journey in thought with me for a moment or two, westward, until "west" becomes "east," although we still chase the setting sun. Across the broad American continent, across that wide ocean misnamed "Pacific" to Shanghai, gate of Far Cathay; onward and westward up the mighty Yangtsze River for 1800 miles, then northward up its tributary the Min, some 250 miles to the confines of mysterious Thibet; to that little-known hinterland which separates China proper from the hierarchy of Lhassa; to a wild and mountainous country peopled mainly by strange tribesfolks of unknown origin; to a land where Lama-ism, Buddhism and Phallism strive for mastery of men's souls; to a region where mighty empires meet. There in narrow, semi-arid valleys, down which torrents thunder, and encompassed by mountains composed of mud-shales and granites whose peaks are clothed with snow eternal, the Regal Lily has her home. In summer the heat is terrific, in winter the cold is intense, and at all seasons these valleys are subject to sudden and violent wind-storms against which neither man nor beast can make headway. There in June, by the way side, in rock-crevice by the torrent's edge and high up on the mountainside and precipice this Lily in full bloom greets the weary wayfarer. Not in twos and threes but in hundreds, in thousands, aye, in tens of thousands. Its slender stems, each from 2 to 4 feet tall, flexible and tense as steel, overtop the coarse grasses and scrub and are crowned with one to several large funnel-shaped flowers, each more or less wine-colored without, pure white and lustrous on the face, clear canary-yellow within the tube and each stamen filament tipped with a golden anther. The air in the cool of the morning and in the evening is laden with delicious perfume exhaled from every blossom.

For a brief season this Lily transforms a lonely, semi-desert region into a veritable fairyland.

Sungpang Ting is a military town situated on the head-waters of the Min River on the very edge of the grasslands of northeastern Thibet. It is a very important outpost of Chinese civilization and a trade entreport of considerable magnitude. Medicines in great variety, including the famous Rhubarb and Musk, are brought in by tribesfolk from the neighboring mountains and bartered to Chinese merchants. I knew the town well and on former occasions had rested within its walls and beneath the clear blue skies it enjoys had recuperated after arduous journeys. So, too, on this occasion. Rested and re-provisioned I and my followers sallied forth and for seven consecutive days plunged down the seemingly interminable gorge of the Min River. The mountains on either side are so high that the summits were usually hidden from view. Here and there where some tributary stream flows in a glimpse of snow eternal met our gaze. Habitations are few and far between but wherever possible patches of the mountainside are under agriculture. It was frightfully hot and travelling was most fatiguing. In many places the narrow track is hewn and blasted from the solid rock and here and there tunnelling has been necessary. In several places Chinese characters of huge size carved in the rocks warn those who can interpret them of the dangers of the road and urge all not to tarry in particular places. This road, difficult and narrow as it is, is the artery of ingress and egress to Sungpang Ting from and to the cities of wealthy Szechuan. There was in consequence much traffic, largely coolies, but several mule-trains taking up brick-tea and cotton cloth in particular, and various merchandise in general and bringing down medicines, hides and deer horns. The road is narrow, sometimes it skirts the edge of the river's turbulent waters but more usually ribbon-like it winds along from fifty to 300 feet above. The passing of mule-trains is a difficult business, often possible only at particular places when one caravan comes to a standstill and allows the other to pass.

I travelled mostly on foot but had with me a light sedan chair made of rattan and my Boy or principal servant was similarly favored. A sedan chair is an outward and visible sign of respectability without which no traveller is properly equipped. In those days it was of far more importance than a passport, for it inspired confidence and insured the respect of the people. Whether one rode in it or walked was immaterial; the important thing was its presence.

On the seventh day we were down to 5500 feet altitude and the following extract from my diary seems worth recording: "A bad

road through barren, desolate country and abnormally long miles sums
up the day's journey. Barring absolute desert no more barren and repel-
ling country could be imagined than that traversed today. But it is really
only the narrow valley and precipitous mountainsides that are so desertlike. On the upper slopes trees and cultivation occur and small villages
and farmhouses are frequent. In the valley houses are far between and
what few there are are in ruinous condition. A fierce up-river wind blows
regularly from about eleven o'clock in the morning and it is difficult to
make headway against it. The leaves on the Maize plants are torn to
shreds by the wind's violence. The houses are of mud and flat-roofed, as
protection against the winds. The Regal Lily occurs here and there in
abundance on the well-nigh stark slate and mudstone cliffs."

The eighth day I camped and for several days was busy arranging to secure in October, the proper season of the year, some six or seven
thousand bulbs of the Regal Lily. Plans completed we set out for
Chengtu Fu, the capital city of Szechuan. The hardship of a four months'
journey were beginning to tell on me and dysentery in a mild form had
troubled me for days. Yet it was with a light heart and a satisfied mind
that I rode in my chair. Soon after starting we passed a mule-train breaking camp and bound our way. With the thoughts of the flesh pots of
Chengtu Fu only four days' distance, all were in a cheerful mood. We
were making good progress, my chair leading, with personal attendants
and man carrying my large camera immediately behind; my black spaniel
dog wagging his tail ahead of us all. The Chinese characters of warning
carved in the rocks did not afright us, we had seen so many and passed
all well. Song was in our hearts, when I noticed my dog suddenly cease
wagging his tail, cringe and rush forward and a small piece of rock hit
the path and rebounded into the river some 300 feet below us. I shouted
an order and the bearers put down the chair. The two front bearers ran
forward and I essayed to follow suit. Just as I cleared the chair-handles
a large boulder crashed into the body of the chair and down to the river
it was hurled. I ran, instinctively ducked as something whisked over my
head and my sun hat blew off. Again I ran, a few yards more and I would
be under the lea of some hard rocks. Then feeling as if a hot wire passed
through my leg, I was bowled over, tried to jump up, found my right
leg was useless, so crawled forward to the shelter of the cliff, where the
two scared chair-bearers were huddled.

It was only a small slide and our lives had had a providential
escape. The man carrying my camera could not run back so fast as
others and suffered a bad scalp wound. I was the biggest sufferer but,
fortunately, was not knocked unconscious. If I had been the men would

probably have deserted from fright, as it was they behaved well. The pigskin puttee on my right leg was cut slantingly as with a knife and forced round my leg, the toe cap of my boot was torn off and with it the nail of my big toe; the right leg was broken in two places below the knee and the side of my calf was badly lacerated. Not a pleasant situation to find oneself in alone with Chinese and four days from the nearest medical assistance!

As soon as it was safe to do so the men came along, terrified and solicitous. My Boy with his chair also came soon afterward but was quite ignorant of the whole affair. With the legs of my camera tripod I improvised splints and while these were being bandaged to my leg the mule-caravan passed in the morning loomed into view. The road was too narrow for them to turn back and they dare not stand still until I could be moved forward, since we knew not when the rock slide would re-commence. There was only one thing to do. I lay across the road and the mules stepped over my body. Then it was that I realized the size of the mule's hoof. There were nearer fifty than forty of them and each stepped clearly over me as if accustomed to such obstacles. Nevertheless, I breathed freely when the last was over!

My own chair being smashed I requisitioned the Boy's, had a piece of wood laid cross-wise and lashed the leg in splints to the right pole. At considerable risk to themselves the men salvaged my wrecked chair and we started on our journey to Chengtu Fu. We made it in three days, marching early and late, and three agonizing days they were for me. At Chengtu Fu I was carried to the house of Dr. Davidson of the Friends' Presbyterian Mission and all that could be done was done. The leg had become infected. In spite of every care, at the end of six weeks there was no signs of the bones uniting. The question of amputation was pressed but somehow I never felt this would be necessary. Other doctors were called in, including a French army surgeon named Dr. Mouillac. Some cutting and slitting was done and the infection stayed. At the end of three months I was out on crutches. Soon afterward I hired a boat and started down the river toward Ichang, where steamers were available for Shanghai and thence for America. At every place on the river where there was medical missionaries I received attention. On crutches I crossed the Pacific Ocean and the American continent to spend a couple of weeks in a hospital in Boston, Massachusetts. Afterward, fitted with a special boot I was able to limp about with a cane and in just a year from the date of the accident walked freely once again. Owing to the infection it was impossible to fit the leg in a cast and so the bones just grew together. The leg is crooked, fifteen-sixteenths of an inch short but is strong and sound and has since carried me many, many thousands of miles.

The accident notwithstanding, I got my Regal Lily and brought the bulbs safely to Boston. The arrangements I had made with the local peasantry to dig the bulbs were carried out under the supervision of my trained collectors. The bulbs were encased in clay, packed in charcoal, shipped at silk rates, and reached Boston a few days after myself. Planted in a garden in Roslindale, Massachusetts, they flowered freely in the June following and some even ripened seeds. From this stock has sprung the millions now happily acclimated in American gardens and other gardens across the seas. Its beauty captured all hearts at sight. Mrs. Francis King, the well-known enthusiast, wrote to me saying, "Nothing so fair or so beautiful has ever before blossomed in my garden." A poem on the Regal Lily was published in the "Boston Transcript," Gouverneur Morris wrote of it aptly as the "Incandescent Lily" in the "Saturday Evening Post." Its merits have been lauded far and wide by many scribes. It loves this country and the climate and from the Atlantic to the Pacific is grown wherever gardens are loved. Each year it adds to the pleasure of millions of folk. The price I paid has been stated. The Regal Lily was worth it and more.

Royal is this Lily and regally it has taken its place and added lustre to gardens. Proud am I to have discovered, introduced and christened the Regal Lily. Did what?

God forgive me! No, I didn't.
'Tis God's present to our gardens.
Anybody might have found it but—
His whisper came to me!
(With apologies to Kipling.)

ERNEST H. WILSON
[*Plant Hunting* (1927)]

Section Six

ROMANTICISM AND THE LANDSCAPE GARDEN

We have given the true model of gardening to the world; let other countries mimic or corrupt our taste; but let it reign here on its verdant throne, original by its elegant simplicity, and proud of no other art than that of softening Nature's harshness and copying her graceful touch.

HORACE WALPOLE

"Mr. Brown, I very earnestly desire that I may die before you."
"Why so?"
"Because I should like to see heaven before you have improved it."—

Anonymous anecdote told of "Capability" Brown,
most famous eighteenth-century
landscape gardener.

Walpole on Gardening

[*During much of the eighteenth century "gardening" was likely to mean what we call "landscape gardening"—which was practiced most elaborately at the great country estates. Herbaceous plants and flowers played a very minor role in this sort of gardening which was largely a matter of trees, lawns, vistas, ornamental buildings, and the like, the great aim being to achieve that balance between nature and the arrangement of nature which represented the ideal of the century. In its extreme form the attempt was sometimes to re-create the idealized landscape of the romantic painters. Indeed, such gardening was obviously a part of the incipient Romantic Movement with its renewed interest in the grand aspects of nature and its revolt against both the coziness of the oldest fashion of garden and the artificiality of the parterre.*

Who originated the new fashion is a matter for argument, but two facts are indisputable. During the earlier period at least the most active designer was Mr. "Capability" Brown. The most literate and articulate historian-defender was Horace Walpole, whose "An Essay on Modern Gardening" (1770) undertook to sketch the rise and explain the aims of the new art.]

GARDENING was probably one of the first arts that succeeded to that of building houses, and naturally attended property and individual possession. Culinary, and afterwards medicinal herbs, were the objects of every head of a family: it became convenient to have them within reach, without seeking them at random in woods, in meadows, and on mountains, as often as they were wanted. When the earth ceased to furnish spontaneously all these primitive luxuries, and culture became requisite, separate inclosures for rearing herbs grew expedient. Fruits were in the same predicament, and those most in use or that demand attention, must have entered into and extended the domestic inclosure. The good man Noah, we are told, planted a vineyard, drank of the wine, and was drunken, and every body knows the consequences. Thus we acquired kitchen-gardens, orchards, and vineyards. I am apprized that the proto-type of all these sorts was the garden of Eden, but as that Paradise was a good deal larger than any we read of afterwards, being inclosed by the rivers Pison, Gihon, Hiddekel, and Euphrates, as every tree that was pleasant to the sight and good for food grew in it, and as two other trees were likewise found there, of which not a slip or sucker remains, it does not belong to the present discussion. After the fall no man living was suffered to enter into the garden; and the poverty and necessities of our first ancestors hardly allowed them time *to make improvements on their estates* in imitation of it, supposing any plan had been preserved. A cottage and a slip of ground for a cabbage and a gooseberry-bush, such as we see by the side of a common, were in all probability the earliest seats and gardens: a well and bucket succeeded to the Pison and Eu-phrates. As settlements increased, the orchard and the vineyard followed; and the earliest princes of tribes possessed just the necessaries of a modern farmer.

Matters, we may well believe, remained long in this situation; and though the generality of mankind form their ideas from the import of words in their own age, we have no reason to think that for many centuries the term *garden* implied more than a kitchen-garden or orchard. When a Frenchman reads of the garden of Eden, I do not doubt but he concludes it was something approaching to that of Versailles, with clip hedges, berceaus, and trellis-work. If his devotion humbles him so far as to allow that, considering who designed it, there might be a labyrinth full of Aesop's fables, yet he does not conceive that four of the largest rivers in the world were half so magnificent as an hundred fountains full of statues by Girardon. It is thus that the word *garden* has at all times passed for whatever was understood by that term in different Countries. But that it meant no more than a kitchen-garden or orchard for several centuries, is evident from those few descriptions that are preserved of the most famous gardens of antiquity. . . .

On his Tuscan villa [Pliny] is more diffuse, the garden makes a considerable part of the description—and what was the principal beauty of that pleasure-ground? Exactly what was the admiration of this country about three score years ago; box-trees cut into monsters, animals, letters, and the names of the master and the artificer. In an age when architecture displayed all its grandeur, all its purity, and all its taste; when arose Vespasian's amphitheater, the temple of Peace, Trajan's forum, Domitian's baths, and Adrian's villa, the ruins and vestiges of which still excite our astonishment and curiosity; a Roman consul, a polished emperor's friend, and a man of elegant litterature and taste, delighted in what the mob now scarce admire in a college-garden. All the ingredients of Pliny's corresponded exactly with those laid out by London and Wise on Dutch principles. He talks of slopes, terrasses, a wilderness, shrubs methodically trimmed, a marble bason, pipes spouting water, a cascade falling into the bason, bay-tress, alternately planted with planes, and a strait walk, from whence issued others parted off by hedges of box, and apple-trees, with obelisks placed between every two. There wants nothing but the embroidery of a parterre, to make a garden in the reign of Trajan serve for a description of one in that of king William. . . .

Yet though these and such preposterous inconveniences prevailed from age to age, good sense in this country had perceived the want of something at once more grand and more natural. These reflections and the bounds set to the waste made by royal spoilers, gave origine to parks. They were contracted forests, and extended gardens. Hentzner says, that according to Rous of Warwick the first park was that at Woodstock. If so, it might be the foundation of a legend that Henry II. secured his mistress in a labyrinth: it was no doubt more difficult to find her in a park than in a palace, when the intricacy of the woods and various lodges buried in covert might conceal her actual habitation.

It is more extraordinary that having so long ago stumbled on the principle of modern gardening, we should have persisted in retaining its reverse, symmetrical and unnatural gardens. That parks were rare in other countries, Hentzner, who travelled over great part of Europe, leads us to suppose by observing that they were common in England. In France they retain the name, but nothing is more different both in compass and disposition. Their parks are usually square or oblong inclosures, regularly planted with walks of chesnuts or limes, and generally every large town has one for its public recreation. They are exactly like Burton's court at Chelsea-college, and rarely larger.

One man, one great man we had, on whom nor education nor custom could impose their prejudices; who, *on evil days though fallen, and with darkness and solitude compassed round*, judged that the mistaken and fantastic ornaments he had seen in gardens, were unworthy of the almighty hand that planted the delights of paradise. He seems with the prophetic eye of taste (as I have heard taste well defined) to have conceived, to have foreseen modern gardening; as lord Bacon announced the discoveries since made by experimental philosophy. The description of Eden is a warmer and more just picture of the present style than Claud Lorrain could have painted from Hagley or Stourhead. The first lines I shall quote exhibit Stourhead on a more magnificent scale.

> Thro Eden went a river large
> Nor chang'd his course, but thro the shaggy hill,
> Pass'd underneath ingulph'd, for God has thrown
> That mountain as his garden-mound, high rais'd
> Upon the rapid current—

Hagley seems pictured in what follows,

> which thro' veins
> Of porous earth with kindly thirst updrawn,
> Rose a fresh fountain, and with many a rill
> Water'd the garden—

What colouring, what freedom of pencil, what landscape in these lines,

> —from that saphire fount the crisped brooks,
> Rolling on orient pearl and sands of gold,
> With mazy error under pendent shades
> Ran nectar, visiting each plant, and fed
> Flow'rs worthy of Paradise, which not *nice art*
> In beds and curious knots, but *nature* boon
> Pour'd forth profuse on hill and dale and plain,
> Both where the morning sun first warmly smote
> The *open field*, and where the unpierc'd shade
> Imbrown'd the noon-tide bow'rs.—*Thus was this place*
> *A happy rural seat of various view.* . . .

Now let us turn to an admired writer, posterior to Milton, and see how cold, how insipid, how tasteless is his account of what he pronounced a perfect garden. I speak not of his style, which it was not necessary for him to animate with the colouring and glow of poetry. It is his want of ideas, of imagination, of taste, that I censure, when he dictated on a subject that is capable of all the graces that a knowledge of beautiful nature can bestow. Sir William Temple was an excellent man; Milton, a genius of the first order.

We cannot wonder that sir William declares in favour of parterres, fountains and statues, as necessary to break the sameness of large grass-plats, which he thinks have an ill effect upon the eye, when he acknowledges that he discovers fancy in the gardens of Alcinous. Milton studied the ancients with equal enthusiasm, but no bigotry, and had judgment to distinguish between the want of invention and the beauties of poetry. Compare his Paradise with Homer's garden, both ascribed to a celestial design. For sir William, it is just to observe, that his ideas centred in a fruit-garden. He had the honour of giving to his country many delicate fruits, and he thought of little else than disposing them to the best advantage. Here is the passage I proposed to quote; it is long, but I need not make an apology to the reader for entertaining him with any other words instead of my own.

"The best figure of a garden is either a square or an oblong, and either upon a flat or a descent: they have all their beauties, but the best I esteem an oblong upon a descent. The beauty, the air, the view makes amends for the expence, which is very great in finishing and supporting the terras-walks, in levelling the parterres, and in the stone-stairs that are necessary from one to the other.

"The perfectest figure of a garden I ever saw, either at home or abroad, was that of Moor-park in Hertfordshire, when I knew it about thirty years ago. It was made by the countess of Bedford, esteemed among the greatest wits of her time, and celebrated by doctor Donne; and with very great care, excellent contrivance, and much cost; but greater sums may be thrown away without effect or honour, if there want sense in proportion to money, or *if nature be not followed*, which I take to be the great rule in this, and perhaps in every thing else, as far as the conduct not only of our lives, but our governments." (We shall see how *natural* that admired garden was.)

"Because I take the garden I have named to have been in all kinds the most beautiful and perfect, at least in the figure and disposition that I have ever seen, I will describe it for a model to those that meet with such a situation, and are above the regards of common expence. It lies on the side of a hill, upon which the house stands, but not very steep. The length of the house, where the best rooms and of most use or pleasure are, lies upon the breadth of the garden; the great parlour opens into the middle of a terras gravel-walk that lies even with it, and which may lie, as I remember, about three hundred paces long, and broad in proportion; the border set with standard laurels and at large distances, which have the beauty of orange-trees out of flower and fruit. From this walk are three descents by many stone steps, in the middle and at each end, into a very large parterre. This is divided into quarters by gravel-walks, and adorned with two fountains and eight statues in the several quarters. At the end of the terras-walk are two summer-houses, and the sides of the parterre are ranged with two large cloisters open to the garden, upon arches of stone, and ending with two other summer-houses even with the cloisters, which are paved with stone, and designed for walks of shade, there being none other in the whole parterre. Over these two cloisters are two terrasses covered with lead and fenced with balusters; and the passage into these airy walks is out of the two summer-houses at the end of the first terras-walk. The cloister facing the south is covered with vines, and would have been proper for an orange-house, and the other for myrtles or other more common greens, and had, I doubt not, been cast for that purpose, if this piece of gardening had been then in as much vogue as it is now.

"From the middle of this parterre is a descent by many steps flying on each side of a grotto that lies between them, covered with lead and flat, into the lower garden which is all fruit-trees ranged about the several quarters of a wilderness which is very shady; the walks here are all green, the grotto embellished with figures of shell-rock-work, fountains, and water-works. If the hill had not ended with the lower garden, and the wall were not bounded by a common way that goes through the park, they might have added a third quarter of all greens; but this want is supplied by a garden on the other side the house, which is all of that sort, very wild, shady, and adorned with rough rock-work and fountains.

"This was Moor-park, when I was acquainted with it, and the sweetest place, I think, that I have seen in my life, either before or since, at home or abroad."—

I will make no farther remarks on this description. Any man might design and *build* as sweet a garden, who had been born in and never stirred out of Holbourn. It was not peculiar to sir William Temple to think in that manner. How many Frenchmen are there who have seen *our* gardens, and still prefer *natural* flights of steps and shady cloisters covered with lead! Le Nautre, the architect of the groves and grottoes at Versailles, came hither on a mission to improve our taste. He planted St. James's and Greenwich parks—no great monuments of his invention. . . .

Fortunately Kent and a few others were not quite so timid, or we might still be going up and down stairs in the open air. . . .

Having thus cleared my way by ascertaining what have been

the ideas on gardening in all ages, as far as we have materials to judge by, it remains to show to what degree Mr. Kent invented the new style, and what hints he had received to suggest and conduct his undertaking.

We have seen what Moor-park was, when pronounced a standard. But as no succeeding generation in an opulent and luxurious country contents itself with the perfection established by its ancestors, more perfect perfection was still sought; and improvements had gone on, till London and Wise had stocked our gardens with giants, animals, monsters, coats of arms and mottoes in yew, box and holly. Absurdity could go no farther, and the tide turned. Bridgman, the next fashionable designer of gardens, was far more chaste; and whether from good sense, or that the nation had been struck and reformed by the admirable paper in the Guardian, No 173, he banished verdant sculpture, and did not even revert to the square precision of the foregoing age. He enlarged his plans, disdained to make every division tally to its opposite, and though he still adhered much to strait walks with high clipped hedges, they were only his great lines; the rest he diversified by wilderness, and with loose groves of oak, though still within surrounding hedges. I have observed in the garden at Gubbins in Hertfordshire many detached thoughts, that strongly indicate the dawn of modern taste. As his reformation gained footing, he ventured farther, and in the royal garden at Richmond dared to introduce cultivated fields, and even morsels of a forest appearance, by the sides of those endless and tiresome walks, that stretched out of one into another without intermission. But this was not till other innovators had broke loose too from rigid symmetry.

But the capital stroke, the leading step to all that has followed, was (I believe the first though was Bridgman's) the destruction of walls for boundaries, and the invention of fossès—an attempt then deemed so astonishing, that the common people called them Ha! Ha's! to express their surprise at finding a sudden and unperceived check to their walk.

One of the first gardens planted in this simple though still formal style, was my father's at Houghton. It was laid out by Mr. Eyre, an imitator of Bridgman. It contains three-and-twenty acres, then reckoned a considerable portion.

I call a sunk fence the leading step, for these reasons. No sooner was this simple enchantment made, than levelling, mowing and rolling, followed. The contiguous ground of the park without the sunk fence was to be harmonized with the lawn within; and the garden in its turn was to be set free from its prim regularity, that it might assort with the wilder country without. The sunk fence ascertained the specific garden, but that it might not draw too obvious a line of distinction between the neat and the rude, the contiguous out-lying parts came to be included in a kind of general design: and when nature was taken into the plan, under improvements, every step that was made, pointed out new beauties and inspired new ideas. At that moment appeared Kent, painter enough to taste the charms of landscape, bold and opinionative enough to dare and to dictate, and born with a genius to strike out a great system from the twilight of imperfect essays. He leaped the fence, and saw that all nature was a garden. He felt the delicious contrast of hill and valley changing imperceptibly into each other, tasted the beauty of the gentle swell, or concave scoop, and remarked how loose groves crowned an easy eminence with happy ornament, and while they called in the distant view between their graceful stems, removed and extended the perspective by delusive comparison.

Thus the pencil of his imagination bestowed all the arts of landscape on the scenes he handled. The great principles on which he worked were perspective, and light and shade. Groupes of trees broke too uniform or too extensive a lawn; evergreens and woods were opposed to the glare of the champain, and where the view was less fortunate, or so much exposed as to be beheld at once, he blotted out some parts by thick shades, to divide it into variety, or to make the richest scene more enchanting by reserving it to a farther advance of the spectator's step. Thus selecting favourite objects, and veiling deformities by screens of plantation, sometimes allowing the rudest waste to add its foil to the richest theatre, he realised the compositions of the greatest masters in painting. Where objects were wanting to animate his horizon, his taste as an architect could bestow immediate termination. His buildings, his seats, his temples, were more the works of his pencil than of his compasses. We owe the restoration of Greece and the diffusion of architecture to his skill in landscape.

But of all the beauties he added to the face of this beautiful country, none surpassed his management of water. Adieu to canals, circular basons, and cascades tumbling down marble steps, that last absurd magnificence of Italian and French villas. The forced elevation of cataracts was no more. The gentle stream was taught to serpentize seemingly at its pleasure, and where discontinued by different levels, its course appeared to be concealed by thickets properly interspersed, and glittered again at a distance where it might be supposed naturally to arrive. Its borders were smoothed, but preserved their waving irregularity. A few trees scattered here and there on its edges sprinkled the tame bank that accompanied its maeanders; and when it disappeared among the hills, shades descending from the heights leaned towards its progress, and framed the distant point of light under which it was lost, as it turned aside to either hand of the blue horizon.

Thus dealing in none but the colours of nature, and catching its most favourable features, men saw a new creation opening before their eyes. The living landscape was chastened or polished, not transformed. Freedom was given to the forms of trees; they extended their branches unrestricted, and where any eminent oak, or master beech had escaped maiming and survived the forest, bush and bramble was removed, and all its honours were restored to distinguish and shade the plain. Where the united plumage of an ancient wood extended wide its undulating canopy, and stood venerable in its darkness, Kent thinned the foremost ranks, and left but so many detached and scattered trees, as softened the approach of gloom and blended a chequered light with the thus lengthened shadows of the remaining columns.

HORACE WALPOLE
["An Essay on Modern Gardening" (1770)]

The English Country House

[*English love of country life existed before the heyday of landscape gardening and has continued through the present. It is, indeed, one of the great constants of the English character, as Washington Irving realized when he undertook to describe the atmosphere of life in England. His own fellow citizens were likely to be either urban or rustic, and even today, despite all our summer homes (to say nothing of suburbia and exurbia), the cultivated and prosperous American is less likely than his English counterpart to accept country living as the norm.*]

THE stranger who would form a correct opinion of the English character must not confine his observations to the metropolis. He must go forth into the country; he must sojourn in villages and hamlets; he must visit castles, villas, farmhouses, cottages; he must wander through parks and gardens; along hedges and green lanes; he must loiter about country churches; attend wakes and fairs, and other rural festivals; and cope with the people in all their conditions, and all their habits and humors.

In some countries the large cities absorb the wealth and fashion of the nation; they are the only fixed abodes of elegant and intelligent society, and the country is inhabited almost entirely by boorish peasantry. In England, on the contrary, the metropolis is a mere gathering-place, or general rendezvous, of the polite classes, where they devote a small portion of the year to a hurry of gayety and dissipation, and, having indulged this kind of carnival, return again to the apparently more congenial habits of rural life. The various orders of society are therefore diffused over the whole surface of the kingdom, and the most retired neighborhoods afford specimens of the different ranks.

The English, in fact, are strongly gifted with the rural feeling. They possess a quick sensibility to the beauties of nature, and a keen relish for the pleasures and employments of the country. This passion seems inherent in them. Even the inhabitants of cities, born and brought up among brick walls and bustling streets, enter with facility into rural habits, and evince a taste for rural occupation. The merchant has his snug retreat in the vicinity of the metropolis, where he often displays as much pride and zeal in the cultivation of his flower garden, and the maturing of his fruits, as he does in the conduct of his business, and the success of a commercial enterprise. Even those less fortunate individuals, who are doomed to pass their lives in the midst of din and traffic, contrive to have something that shall remind them of the green aspect of nature. In the most dark and dingy quarters of the city, the drawing-room window resembles frequently a bank of flowers; every spot capable of vegetation has its grassplot and flower bed; and every square its mimic park, laid out with picturesque taste, and gleaming with refreshing verdure.

Those who see the Englishman only in town are apt to form an unfavorable opinion of his social character. He is either absorbed in business, or distracted by the thousand engagements that dissipate time, thought, and feeling, in this huge metropolis. He has, therefore, too commonly a look of hurry and abstraction. Wherever he happens to be, he is on the point of going somewhere else; at the moment he is talking on one subject, his mind is wandering to another; and while paying a friendly visit, he is calculating how he shall economize time so as to pay the other visits allotted to the morning. An immense metropolis, like London, is calculated to make men selfish and uninteresting. In their casual and transient meetings, they can but deal briefly in commonplaces. They present but the cold superficies of character—its rich and genial qualities have no time to be warmed into a flow.

It is in the country that the Englishman gives scope to his natural feelings. He breaks loose gladly from the cold formalities and negative civilities of town; throws off his habits of shy reserve, and becomes joyous and free-hearted. He manages to collect round him all the conveniences and elegancies of polite life, and to banish its restraints. His country-seat abounds with every requisite, either for studious retirement, tasteful gratification, or rural exercise. Books, paintings, music, horses, dogs, and sporting implements of all kinds, are at hand. He puts no constraint either upon his guests or himself, but in the true spirit of hospitality provides the means of enjoyment, and leaves every one to partake according to his inclination.

The taste of the English in the cultivation of land, and in what is called landscape gardening, is unrivalled. They have studied nature intently, and discover an exquisite sense of her beautiful forms and harmonious combinations. Those charms, which in other countries she lavishes in wild solitudes, are here assembled round the haunts of domestic life. They seem to have caught her coy and furtive graces, and spread them, like witchery, about their rural abodes.

Nothing can be more imposing than the magnificence of English park scenery. Vast lawns that extend like sheets of vivid green, with here and there clumps of gigantic trees, heaping up rich piles of foliage: the solemn pomp of groves and woodland glades, with the deer trooping in silent herds across them; the hare, bounding away to the covert; or the pheasant, suddenly bursting upon the wing: the brook, taught to wind in natural meanderings or expand into a glassy lake: the sequestered pool, reflecting the quivering trees, with the yellow leaf sleeping on its bosom, and the trout roaming fearlessly about its limpid waters; while some rustic temple or sylvan statue, grown green and dank with age, gives an air of classic sanctity to the seclusion.

These are but a few of the features of park scenery; but what most delights me, is the creative talent with which the English decorate the unostentatious abodes of middle life. The rudest habitation, the most unpromising and scanty portion of land, in the hands of an Englishman of taste, becomes a little paradise. With a nicely discriminating eye, he seizes at once upon its capabilities, and pictures in his mind the future landscape. The sterile spot grows into loveliness under his hand; and yet the operations of art which produce the effect are scarcely to be perceived. The cherishing and training of some trees; the cautious pruning of others; the nice distribution of flowers and plants of tender and graceful foliage; the introduction of a green slope of velvet turf; the partial opening to a peep of blue distance, or silver gleam of water: all these are managed with a delicate tact, a pervading yet quiet assiduity, like the magic touchings with which a painter finishes up a favorite picture.

The residence of people of fortune and refinement in the country has diffused a degree of taste and elegance in rural economy, that descends to the lowest class. The very laborer, with his thatched cottage and narrow slip of ground, attends to their embellishment. The trim hedge, the grassplot before the door, the little flower bed bordered with snug box, the woodbine trained up against the wall, and hanging its blossoms about the lattice, the pot of flowers in the window, the holly, providently planted about the house, to cheat winter of its dreariness, and to throw in a semblance of green summer to cheer the fireside: all these bespeak the influence of taste, flowing down from high sources, and pervading the lowest levels of the public mind. If ever Love, as poets sing, delights to visit a cottage, it must be the cottage of an English peasant.

The fondness for rural life among the higher classes of the English has had a great and salutary effect upon the national character. I do not know a finer race of men than the English gentlemen. Instead of the softness and effeminacy which characterize the men of rank in most countries, they exhibit a union of elegance and strength, a robustness of frame and freshness of complexion, which I am inclined to attribute to their living so much in the open air, and pursuing so eagerly the invigorating recreations of the country. These hardy exercises produce also a healthful tone of mind and spirits, and a manliness and simplicity of manners, which even the follies and dissipations of the town cannot easily pervert, and can never entirely destroy. In the country, too, the different orders of society seem to approach more freely, to be more disposed to blend and operate favorably upon each other. The distinctions between them do not appear to be so marked and impassable as in the cities. The manner in which property has been distributed into small estates and farms has established a regular gradation from the nobleman, through the classes of gentry, small landed proprietors, and substantial farmers, down to the laboring peasantry; and while it has thus banded the extremes of society together, has infused into each intermediate rank a spirit of independence. This, it must be confessed, is not so universally the case at present as it was formerly; the larger estates having, in late years of distress, absorbed the smaller, and, in some parts of the country, almost annihilated the sturdy race of small farmers. These, however, I believe, are but casual breaks in the general system I have mentioned.

In rural occupation there is nothing mean and debasing. It leads a man forth among scenes of natural grandeur and beauty; it leaves him to the workings of his own mind, operated upon by the purest and most elevating of external influences. Such a man may be simple and rough, but he cannot be vulgar. The man of refinement, therefore, finds nothing revolting in an intercourse with the lower orders in rural life, as he does when he casually mingles with the lower orders of cities. He lays aside his distance and reserve, and is glad to waive the distinctions of rank, and to enter into the honest, heartfelt enjoyments of common life. Indeed the very amusements of the country bring men more and more together; and the sound of hound and horn blend all feelings into harmony. I believe this is one great reason why the nobility and gentry are more popular among the inferior orders in England than they are in any other country; and why the latter have endured so many excessive pressures and extremities, without repining more generally at the unequal distribution of fortune and privilege.

To this mingling of cultivated and rustic society may also be attributed the rural feeling that runs through British literature; the frequent use of illustrations from rural life; those incomparable descriptions of nature that abound in the British poets, that have continued down from *The Flower and the Leaf* of Chaucer, and have brought into our closets all the freshness and fragrance of the dewy landscape. The pastoral writers of other countries appear as if they had paid nature an occasional visit, and become acquainted with her general charms; but the British poets have lived and revelled with her—they have wooed her in her most secret haunts—they have watched her minutest caprices. A spray could not tremble in the breeze—a leaf could not rustle to the ground—a diamond drop could not patter in the stream—a fragrance could not exhale from the humble violet, nor a daisy unfold its crimson tints to the morning, but it has been noticed by these impassioned and delicate observers, and wrought up into some beautiful morality.

WASHINGTON IRVING
[*The Sketch Book* (1820)]

How to Build a Ruin

[*During the eighteenth century mountains ceased to be "horrid" and became "sublime." Simultaneously an ancient ruin became "romantic" instead of "dismal." Those who happened to have one on their land-*

scaped estates were lucky. Those who did not were not only advised to
build a picturesque ruin but told how dilapidation should be designed.]

I N a garden, where objects are intended only to adorn, every species of
architecture may be admitted, from the Grecian down to the Chinese;
and the choice is so free, that the mischief most to be apprehended, is
an abuse of this latitude in the multiplicity of buildings. Few scenes can
bear more than two or three; in some a single one has a greater effect than
any number; and a careless glimpse here and there, of such as belong
immediately to different parts, frequently enliven the landskip with
more spirit than those which are industriously shewn. If the effect of a
partial sight, or a distant view, were more attended to, many scenes might
be filled, without being crouded; a greater number of buildings would
be tolerated, when they seemed to be casual, not forced; and the animation, and the richness of objects, might be had without pretence or display. . . .

To this great variety must be added the many changes which
may be made by the means of *ruins;* they are a class by themselves, beautiful as objects, expressive as characters, and peculiarly calculated to
connect with their appendages into elegant groupes: they may be accom-
modated with ease to irregularity of ground, and their disorder is improved by it; they may be intimately blended with trees and with
thickets, and the interruption is an advantage; for imperfection and
obscurity are their properties; and to carry the imagination to something
greater than is seen, their effect. They may for any of these purposes be
separated into detached pieces; contiguity is not necessary, nor even the
appearance of it, if the relation be preserved; but straggling ruins have
a bad effect, when the several parts are equally considerable. There
should be one large mass to raise an idea of greatness, to attract the others
about it, and to be a common center of union to all: the smaller pieces
then mark the original dimensions of one extensive structure; and no
longer appear to be the remains of several little buildings.

All remains excite an enquiry into the former state of the edifice, and fix the mind in a contemplation on the use it was applied to;
besides the characters expressed by their style and position, they suggest
ideas which would not arise from the buildings, if entire. The purposes
of many have ceased; an abbey, or a castle, if complete, can now be no
more than a dwelling; the memory of the times, and of the manners, to
which they were adapted, is preserved only in history, and in ruins; and
certain sensations of regret, of veneration, or compassion, attend the

recollection: nor are these confined to the remains of buildings which are now in disuse; those of an old mansion raise reflections on the domestic comforts once enjoyed, and the ancient hospitality which reigned there. Whatever building we see in decay, we naturally contrast its present to its former state, and delight to ruminate on the comparison. It is true that such effects properly belong to real ruins; but they are produced in a certain degree by those which are fictitious; the impressions are not so strong, but they are exactly similar; and the representation, though it does not present facts to the memory, yet suggests subjects to the imagination: but in order to affect the fancy, the supposed original design should be clear, the use obvious, and the form easy to trace; no fragments should be hazarded without a precise meaning, and an evident connection; none should be perplexed in their construction, or uncertain as to their application. Conjectures about the form, raise doubts about the existence of the ancient structure; the mind must not be allowed to hesitate; it must be hurried away from examining into the reality, by the exactness and the force of the resemblance.

In the ruins of Tintern abbey, the original construction of the church is perfectly marked; and it is principally from this circumstance that they are celebrated as a subject of curiosity and contemplation. The walls are almost entire; the roof only is fallen in; but most of the columns which divided the isles are still standing; of those which have dropped down, the bases remain, every one exactly in its place; and in the middle of the nave, four lofty arches, which once supported the steeple, rise high in the air above all the rest, each reduced now to a narrow rim of stone, but completely preserving its form. The shapes even of the windows are little altered; but some of them are quite obscured, others partially shaded, by tufts of ivy, and those which are most clear, are edged with its slender tindrils, and lighter foliage, wreathing about the sides and the divisions; it winds round the pillars; it clings to the walls; and in one of the isles, clusters at the top in bunches so thick and so large, as to darken the space below. The other isles, and the great nave, are exposed to the sky; the floor is entirely overspread with turf; and to keep it clear from weeds and bushes, is now its highest preservation. Monkish tomb-stones, and the monuments of benefactors long since forgotten, appear above the greenswerd; the bases of the pillars which have fallen, rise out of it; and maimed effigies, and sculpture worn with age and weather, Gothic capitals, carved cornices, and various fragments, are scattered about, or lie in heaps piled up together. Other shattered pieces, though disjointed and mouldering, still occupy their original places; and a stair-case much impaired, which led to a tower now no more, is suspended at a great heighth, uncovered and inaccessible. Nothing is perfect; but memorials of every part still subsist; all certain, but all in decay; and suggesting, at once, every idea which can occur in a seat of devotion, solitude, and desolation. Upon such models, fictitious ruins should be formed; and if any parts are entirely lost, they should be such as the imagination can easily supply from those which are still remaining. Distinct traces of the building which is supposed to have existed, are less liable to the suspicion of artifice, than an unmeaning heap of confusion. Precision is always satisfactory; but in the reality it is only agreable; in the copy, it is essential to the imitation.

A material circumstance to the truth of the imitation, is, that the ruin appear to be very old; the idea is besides interesting in itself; a monument of antiquity is never seen with indifference; and a semblance of age may be given to the representation, by the hue of the materials; the growth of ivy, and other plants; and cracks and fragments seemingly occasioned rather by decay, than by destruction. An appendage evidently more modern than the principal structure will sometimes corroborate the effect; the shed of a cottager amidst the remains of a temple, is a contrast both to the former and the present state of the building; and a tree flourishing among ruins, shews the length of time they have lain neglected. No circumstance so forcibly marks the desolation of a spot once inhabited, as the prevalence of nature over it.

Campos ubi Troja fuit

is a sentence which conveys a stronger idea of a city totally overthrown, than a description of its remains; but in a representation to the eye, some remains must appear; and then the perversion of them to an ordinary use, or an intermixture of a vigorous vegetation, intimates a settled despair of their restoration.

J. WHATELY
[*Observations on Modern Gardening* (1770)]

Chinese Wisdom

[*Oliver Goldsmith's "Citizen of the World" was a mythical Chinese who contrasted the good sense of a purely imaginary China with the less sensible opinions and institutions of a real England.*]

T H E English have not yet brought the art of gardening to the same perfection with the Chinese, but have lately begun to imitate them: nature is now followed with greater assiduity than formerly; the trees are suffered to shoot out into the utmost luxuriance; the streams, no longer forced from their native beds, are permitted to wind along the valleys; spontaneous flowers take place of the finished parterre, and the enamelled meadow of the shaven green.

Yet still the English are far behind us in this charming art; their designers have not yet attained a power of uniting instruction with beauty. An European will scarcely conceive my meaning when I say there is scarce a garden in China which does not contain some fine moral, couched under the general design, where one is not taught wisdom as he walks, and feels the force of some noble truth, or delicate precept, resulting from the disposition of the groves, streams, or grottoes. Permit me to illustrate what I mean by a description of my gardens at Quamsi. My heart still hovers round those scenes of former happiness with pleasure; and I find a satisfaction in enjoying them at this distance, though but in imagination.

You descended from the house between two groves of trees, planted in such a manner that they were impenetrable to the eye; while on each hand the way was adorned with all that was beautiful in porcelain, statuary, and painting. This passage from the house opened into an area surrounded with rocks, flowers, trees, and shrubs, but all so disposed as if each was the spontaneous production of nature. As you proceeded forward on this lawn, to your right and left hand were two gates opposite each other, of very different architecture and design; and before you lay a temple, built rather with minute elegance than ostentation.

The right-hand gate was planned with the utmost simplicity, or rather rudeness; ivy clasped round the pillars, the baleful cypress hung over it; time seemed to have destroyed all the smoothness and regularity of the stone; two champions with lifted clubs appeared in the act of guarding its access; dragons and serpents were seen in the most hideous attitudes, to deter the spectator from approaching; and the perspective view that lay behind seemed dark and gloomy to the last degree; the stranger was tempted to enter only from the motto—*Pervia Virtuti*.

The opposite gate was formed in a very different manner; the architecture was light, elegant, and inviting; flowers hung in wreaths round the pillars; all was finished in the most exact and masterly manner; the very stone of which it was built still preserved its polish; nymphs, wrought by the hand of a master, in the most alluring attitudes, beckoned the stranger to approach; while all that lay behind, as far as the eye could reach, seemed gay, luxuriant, and capable of affording endless pleasure. The motto itself contributed to invite him, for over the gate were written these words: *Facilis Descensus*.

By this time I fancy you begin to perceive that the gloomy gate was designed to represent the road to Virtue; the opposite, the more agreeable passage to Vice. It is but natural to suppose that the spectator was always tempted to enter by the gate which offered him so many allurements. I always in these cases left him to his choice; but generally found that he took to the left, which promised most entertainment.

Immediately upon his entering the gate of Vice, the trees and flowers were disposed in such a manner as to make the most pleasing impression; but as he walked farther on, he insensibly found the garden assume the air of a wilderness: the landscapes began to darken, the paths grew more intricate, he appeared to go downwards; frightful rocks seemed to hang over his head; gloomy caverns, unexpected precipices, awful ruins, heaps of unburied bones, and terrifying sounds caused by unseen waters began to take place of what at first appeared so lovely; it was in vain to attempt returning—the labyrinth was too much perplexed for any but myself to find the way back. In short, when sufficiently impressed with the horrors of what he saw, and the imprudence of his choice, I brought him by a hidden door a shorter way back into the area from whence at first he had strayed.

The gloomy gate now presented itself before the stranger; and though there seemed little in its appearance to tempt his curiosity, yet, encouraged by the motto, he gradually proceeded. The darkness of the entrance, the frightful figures that seemed to obstruct his way, the trees of a mournful green, conspired at first to disgust him; as he went forward, however, all began to open and wear a more pleasing appearance; beautiful cascades, beds of flowers, trees loaded with fruit or blossoms, and unexpected brooks improved the scene; he now found that he was ascending, and, as he proceeded, all nature grew more beautiful; the prospect widened as he went higher, even the air itself seemed to become more pure. Thus pleased and happy from unexpected beauties, I at last led him to an arbour from whence he could view the garden, and the whole country around, and where he might own that the road to Virtue terminated in Happiness.

Though from this description you may imagine that a vast tract of ground was necessary to exhibit such a pleasing variety in, yet be assured I have seen several gardens in England take ten times the space which mine did, without half the beauty. A very small extent of ground is enough for an elegant taste; the greater room is required if magnificence is in view. There is no spot, though ever so little, which a skilful designer might not thus improve, so as to convey a delicate allegory, and impress the mind with truths the most useful and necessary. Adieu.

OLIVER GOLDSMITH
[*The Citizen of the World*, Letter XXXI (1762)]

Overimproved

[*Not everyone thought that "improvement" always improved. Two of the innumerable protests follow. The wit Sydney Smith was, surprisingly enough, quite matter-of-fact for once. The fantastic novelist Thomas Love Peacock, on the other hand, let himself go.*]

I WENT for the first time in my life, some years ago, to stay at a very grand and beautiful place in the country, where the grounds are said to be laid out with consummate taste. For the first three or four days I was perfectly enchanted; it seemed something so much better than nature, that I really began to wish the earth had been laid out according to the latest principles of improvement, and that the whole face of nature were a little more the appearance of a park. In three days' time I was tired to death; a thistle, a nettle, a heap of dead bushes, anything that wore the appearance of accident and want of intention, was quite a relief. I used to escape from the made grounds, and walk upon an adjacent goose-common, where the cart-ruts, gravel-pits, bumps, irregularities, coarse ungentlemanlike grass, and all the varieties produced by neglect, were a thousand times more gratifying than the monotony of beauties the result of design, and crowded into narrow confines with a luxuriance and abundance utterly unknown to nature.

SYDNEY SMITH
[*Letters*]

"I PERCEIVE" said Mr. Milestone, after they had walked a few paces, "these grounds have never been touched by the finger of taste."

"The place is quite a wilderness," said Squire Headlong: "for, during the latter part of my father's life, while I was finishing my education, he troubled himself about nothing but the cellar, and suffered everything else to go to rack and ruin. A mere wilderness, as you see, even now in December; but in summer a complete nursery of briers, a forest of thistles, a plantation of nettles, without any live-stock but goats, that have eaten up all the bark of the trees. Here you see is the pedestal of a statue, with only half a leg and four toes remaining: there were many here once. When I was a boy, I used to sit every day on the shoulders of Hercules: what became of him I have never been able to ascertain. Neptune has been lying these seven years in the dust-hole; Atlas had his head knocked off to fit him for propping a shed; and only the day before yesterday we fished Bacchus out of the horse-pond."

"My dear sir," said Mr. Milestone, "accord me your permission to wave the wand of enchantment over your grounds. The rocks shall be blown up, the trees shall be cut down, the wilderness and all its goats shall vanish like mist. Pagodas and Chinese bridges, gravel walks and shrubberies, bowling-greens, canals, and clumps of larch, shall rise upon its ruins. One age, sir, has brought to light the treasures of ancient learning; a second has penetrated into the depths of metaphysics; a third has brought to perfection the science of astronomy; but it was reserved for the exclusive genius of the present times, to invent the noble art of picturesque gardening, which has given, as it were, a new tint to the complexion of nature, and a new outline to the physiognomy of the universe!"

"Give me leave," said Sir Patrick O'Prism, "to take an exception to that same. Your system of levelling, and trimming, and clipping, and docking, and clumping, and polishing, and cropping, and shaving, destroys all the beautiful intricacies of natural luxuriance, and all the graduated harmonies of light and shade, melting into one another, as you see them on that rock over yonder. I never saw one of your improved places, as you call them, and which are nothing but big bowling-greens, like sheets of green paper, with a parcel of round clumps scattered over them, like so many spots of ink, flicked at random out of a pen, and a solitary animal here and there looking as if it were lost, that I did not think it was for all the world like Hounslow Heath, thinly sprinkled over with bushes and highwaymen."

"Sir," said Mr. Milestone, "you will have the goodness to make a distinction between the picturesque and the beautiful."

"Will I?" said Sir Patrick: "och! but I won't. For what is beautiful? That which pleases the eye. And what pleases the eye? Tints variously broken and blended. Now, tints variously broken and blended constitute the picturesque."

"Allow me," said Mr. Gall: "I distinguish the picturesque and the beautiful, and I add to them, in the laying out of grounds, a third and distinct character, which I call unexpectedness."

"Pray, sir," said Mr. Milestone, "by what name do you distinguish this character, when a person walks round the grounds for the second time?"

Mr. Gall bit his lips, and inwardly vowed to revenge himself on Milestone, by cutting up his next publication.

A long controversy now ensued concerning the picturesque and the beautiful, highly edifying to Squire Headlong.

THOMAS LOVE PEACOCK
[*Headlong Hall* (1816)]

A Most Romantic Ruin

[Inasmuch as it was William Cowper who wrote "God made the country, and man made the town," it is hardly surprising that he looked without great enthusiasm at man's effort to make the country also.]

THERE was not, at that time, much to be seen in the Isle of Thanet, besides the beauty of the country, and the fine prospects of the sea, which are no where surpassed except in the Isle of Wight, or upon some parts of the coast of Hampshire. One sight, however, I remember, engaged my curiosity, and I went to see it: a fine piece of ruins, built by the late Lord Holland, at a great expense, which, the day after I saw it, tumbled down for nothing. Perhaps, therefore, it is still a ruin; and if it is, I would advise you by all means to visit it, as it must have been much improved by this fortunate incident. It is hardly possible to put stones together with that air of wild and magnificent disorder which they are sure to acquire by falling of their own accord.

WILLIAM COWPER
[Letter to the Rev. William Unwin]

Section Seven

MYTHS, FANTASIES
AND HOAXES

Certain wild trees there bear wool instead of sheep; and the Indians make their clothing from these trees.

HERODOTUS

Yet mark'd I where the bolt of Cupid fell:
It fell upon a little western flower,
Before milk-white, now purple with love's wound,
And maidens call it, Love-in-idleness.
Fetch me that flower; the herb I show'd thee once:
The juice of it on sleeping eyelids laid
Will make or man or woman madly dote
Upon the next live creature that it sees.

SHAKESPEARE
A Midsummer-Night's Dream

Roman Superstition

[In Pliny the Elder's voluminous compilation called Natural History *a great deal of nonsense is mingled with a good deal of sound information. Here is a bit of the former.]*

ANOTHER kind of prodigy, too, is the springing up of a tree in some extraordinary and unusual place, the head of a statue, for instance, or an altar, or upon another tree even. A fig-tree shot forth from a laurel at Cyzicus, just before the siege of that city; and so in like manner, at Tralles, a palm issued from the pedestal of the statue of the Dictator Caesar, at the period of his civil wars. So, too, at Rome, in the Capitol there, in the time of the wars against Perseus, a palm-tree grew from the head of the statue of Jupiter, a presage of impending victory and triumphs. This palm, however, having been destroyed by a tempest, a fig-tree sprang up in the very same place, at the period of the lustration made by the censors M. Messala and C. Cassius, a time at which, according to Piso, an author of high authority, all sense of shame had been utterly banished. Above all the prodigies, however, that have ever been heard of, we ought to place the one that was seen in our own time, at the period of the fall of the Emperor Nero, in the territory of Marrucinum; a plantation of olives, belonging to Vectius Marcellus, one of the principal members of the Equestrian order, bodily crossed the public highway, while the fields that lay on the opposite side of the road passed over to supply the place which had been thus vacated by the olive-yard.

PLINY THE ELDER
[Natural History (1st century A.D.)]

The Magic Seed

[*The tale of Jack and the Beanstalk combines three motifs: the seemingly foolish bargain, the magic seed, and the slaying of a giant who guards a treasure. All three are of nearly world-wide currency and occur separately as well as in various combinations. This is the version current among the Seneca Indians.*]

SEED-MARKED boy was living at Cottonwood with his grandmother. He used to go out hunting. He said to his grandmother, "Grandmother, do not go out when I have gone out hunting." Grandmother thought to herself, "I wonder why my grandchild does not want me to go out. I will go out today." So she left off grinding and went out. When she went out, a giant came to her. He had a basket water jar and he told the old woman to get into it. He closed the mouth of the jar and carried the old woman on his back to his house. The giant lived far up in the mountain where nobody could go. When the boy came back from hunting, his grandmother did not come out to meet him. He thought to himself, "I wonder why my grandmother does not come running out to meet me." He threw down the deer and ran into the house and did not find his grandmother. The meal she was grinding was left there. Then he followed the tracks of the giant to *takutuna* (wood spoon). Wood Spoon called him and asked, "Where are you going?" He said, "I am going to look for my grandmother." Wood Spoon gave him a spruce seed (*k'uowaxona*). "This will help you to get there," he said. "Cover this seed and it will grow." He took it and went on. He came to Spider old woman. She said, "Seed-marked boy, why are you around while you are living well at Cottonwood, with your grandmother? A good hunter, why are you around here now?"—"Yes, I live there well and happily with my grandmother and bring deer to her all the time. But now the giant has taken her away, so I have to look for her." Spider old woman said, "Your grandmother is far up in the mountain where nobody can go. I know that Wood Spoon gave you the spruce seed and now I will give something that will help you when you get up there." She gave him some medicine and told him to put it in his mouth and over his body so the giant would not kill him. Then Seed-marked boy went to the foot of the mountain and he dug a hole and, while he was putting in the seed, Squirrel came to him. Squirrel said, "I will help you to make this tree grow fast." While the tree was growing, he ran up and down the tree until the tree reached the top of the mountain. Then he ran down and told the boy the tree was close to his grandmother. So the boy climbed the tree and came to his grandmother. She said to him, "Grandchild, why do you come here? I am living with the giant. I know he will eat you up." As they talked together the earth was shaking because the giant was coming. Grandmother hid him underneath the thatch of the hatch. Then the giant came in and said, "I smell the blood of an Indian." Grandmother said, "Who would come here? Nobody can come here."—"Yes, I smell, I smell!" And he began to search. She said, "Yes, my grandchild came."—"He thinks he is one to tame me; but he is not." Then he pulled him out of the thatch. He did not cry, he hollered, "Hip! Hip! Hip! Hip!" Then the giant dug a fire and the giant put him there to roast. The giant lay beside the fire waiting for him to roast. "He is so small, I think it won't take long for him to roast," said the giant. The giant took down his wheel and rolled it so the ashes would disclose the boy. Then the boy jumped out hollering, "Hip! Hip! Hip! Hip!" The boy took the wheel and rolled it to the giant and killed him. He had the people and the *tachin* tied up (that is why it did not rain). So then the boy went and untied them. He went to another place where there were piles of human bones and he put medicine on them and they all turned to life. The women had the jars that they were carrying to get water when the giant caught them and the men had on their backs the ropes which they used when they were going to get wood. "Now you go back to your homes," he said. When the *tachina* were set free, it began to rain, too. He took his grandmother home and they lived happily.

ELSIE CLEWS PARSONS
[Taos Tales (1940)]

The Origin of the Hyacinth

[*Just how lightly "sophisticated" Greeks came to take what had once been their religion is pleasantly illustrated by this flip retelling of the story of the origin of the Hyacinth or, as Milton called it, "that ensanguined flower marked with woe."*]

MERCURY. Why so sad, Apollo?

APOLLO. Because I am crossed in my amours.

MERCURY. That indeed is reason enough. But may one ask what it is at present that causes you to repine at your fate in love? Is the story of Daphne still running in your head?

APOLLO. No; I lament my favourite, the son of Oebalus, Laconia.

MERCURY. How? the amiable Hyacinthus is dead?

APOLLO. Alas!

MERCURY. But of what then? Who could be so great a foe to every thing that is lovely, as to kill so beautiful a boy?

APOLLO. It was I myself that did it.

MERCURY. Are you mad, Apollo?

APOLLO. No. My misfortune made me his murderer against my will.

MERCURY. I should like to know how it happened.

APOLLO. He was learning by practice to throw the discus, and I was his companion. Now the most detested of all the winds, Zephyrus, had long been fond of the boy as well as myself; but because he could not gain his attachment, he watched for an opportunity to be revenged. Now, when I threw the discus, as we had many times done before, high up in the air, this cursed Zephyr gave a blast downwards from Taygetus, and drove it falling with such force against the boy's head, that the blood gushed in torrents from the wound, and the boy died on the spot. Boiling with rage, I pursued Zephyrus quite to the mountain, and shot all my arrows after him; but in vain. I afterwards erected a high tomb to the boy, at Amyclae, on the place where the unlucky discus laid him low; and from his blood, Hermes, I caused the earth to produce the fairest and loveliest of all flowers, and I marked it with the letters of the lamentation for the dead. Have I not reason to be melancholy?

MERCURY. No. Since you knew that you had chose a mortal for your favourite, how can you take it amiss that he is dead?

LUCIAN OF SAMOSATA
[*Dialogues* (2nd century A.D.)]

The Garden City in Utopia

[*Sir Thomas More's* Utopia, *published originally in Latin in 1516 and in English in 1551, became so famous that its title is now the generic name for any unrealizable scheme to improve the human lot. Many of Sir Thomas's proposals are a little too austere for modern taste, but his garden cities sound very much like what one may find in any modern plea for "decentralization."*]

T H E R E are fifty-four cities in the island, all large and well built: the manners, customs, and laws of which are the same, and they are all contrived as near in the same manner as the ground on which they stand will allow. The nearest lie at least twenty-four miles distant from one another, and the most remote are not so far distant, but that a man can go on foot in one day from it, to that which lies next it. Every city sends three of their wisest senators once a year to Amaurot, to consult about their common concerns; for that is the chief town of the island, being situated near the centre of it, so that it is the most convenient place for their assemblies. The jurisdiction of every city extends at least twenty miles: and where the town desires to enlarge its bounds, for the people consider themselves rather as tenants than landlords. They have built

over all the country, farmhouses for husbandmen, which are well contrived, and are furnished with all things necessary for country labor.
Inhabitants are sent by turns from the cities to dwell in them; no country
family has fewer than forty men and women in it, besides two slaves.
There is a master and a mistress set over every family; and over thirty
families there is a magistrate. Every year twenty of this family come
back to the town, after they have stayed two years in the country; and
in their room there are other twenty sent from the town, that they may
learn country work from those that have been already one year in the
country, as they must teach those that come to them the next from the
town. By this means such as dwell in those country farms are never
ignorant of agriculture, and so commit no errors, which might otherwise
be fatal, and bring them under a scarcity of corn. But though there is
every year such a shifting of the husbandmen, to prevent any man being
forced against his will to follow that hard course of life too long; yet
many among them take such pleasure in it, that they desire leave to continue in it many years. These husbandmen till the ground, breed cattle,
hew wood, and convey it to the towns, either by land or water, as is
most convenient. They breed an infinite multitude of chickens in a very
curious manner; for the hens do not sit and hatch them, but vast number
of eggs are laid in a gentle and equal heat, in order to be hatched, and
they are no sooner out of the shell, and able to stir about, but they seem
to consider those that feed them as their mothers, and follow them as
other chickens do the hen that hatched them. They breed very few
horses, but those they have are full of mettle, and are kept only for
exercising their youth in the art of sitting and riding them; for they do
not put them to any work, either of plowing or carriage, in which they
employ oxen; for though their horses are stronger, yet they find oxen
can hold out longer; and as they are not subject to so many diseases, so
they are kept upon a less charge, and with less trouble; and even when
they are so worn out, that they are no more fit for labor, they are good
meat at last. They sow no corn, but that which is to be their bread; for
they drink either wine, cider, or perry, and often water, sometimes
boiled with honey or licorice, with which they abound; and though
they know exactly how much corn will serve every town, and all that
tract of country which belongs to it, yet they sow much more, and
breed more cattle than are necessary for their consumption; and they
give that overplus of which they make no use to their neighbors. When
they want anything in the country which it does not produce, they fetch
that from the town, without carrying anything in exchange for it. And
the magistrates of the town take care to see it given them; for they meet

generally in the town once a month, upon a festival day. When the time of harvest comes, the magistrates in the country send to those in the towns, and let them know how many hands they will need for reaping the harvest; and the number they call for being sent to them, they commonly dispatch it all in one day.

He that knows one of their towns, knows them all, they are so like one another, except where the situation makes some difference. I shall therefore describe one of them; and none is so proper as Amaurot; for as none is more eminent, all the rest yielding in precedence to this, because it is the seat of their supreme council; so there was none of them better known to me, I having lived five years altogether in it.

It lies upon the side of a hill, or rather a rising ground: its figure is almost square, for from the one side of it, which shoots up almost to the top of the hill, it runs down in a descent for two miles to the river Anider; but it is a little broader the other way that runs along the bank of that river. The Anider rises about eighty miles above Amaurot in a small spring at first; but other brooks falling into it, of which two are more considerable than the rest. As it runs by Amaurot, it is grown half a mile broad; but it still grows larger and larger, till after sixty miles' course below it, it is lost in the ocean, between the town and the sea, and for some miles above the town, it ebbs and flows every six hours, with a strong current. The tide comes up for about thirty miles so full, that there is nothing but salt water in the river, the fresh water being driven back with its force; and above that, for some miles, the water is brackish; but a little higher, as it runs by the town, it is quite fresh; and when the tide ebbs, it continues fresh all along to the sea. There is a bridge cast over the river, not of timber, but of fair stone, consisting of many stately arches; it lies at that part of the town which is farthest from the sea, so that ships without any hindrance lie all along the side of the town. There is likewise another river that runs by it, which though it is not great, yet it runs pleasantly, for it rises out of the same hill on which the town stands, and so runs down through it, and falls into the Anider. The inhabitants have fortified the fountain head of this river, which springs a little without the towns; that so if they should happen to be besieged, the enemy might not be able to stop or divert the course of the water, nor poison it; from thence it is carried in earthen pipes to the lower streets; and for those places of the town to which the water of that small river cannot be conveyed, they have great cisterns for receiving the rain water, which supplies the want of the other. The town is compassed with a high and thick wall, in which there are many towers and forts; there is also a broad and deep dry ditch, set thick with thorns, cast round three sides of the town, and the river is instead of a ditch on the fourth side. The streets are very convenient for all carriage, and are well sheltered from the winds. Their buildings are good, and are so uniform, that a whole side of a street looks like one house. The streets are twenty feet broad; there lie gardens behind all their houses; these are large but inclosed with buildings, that on all hands face the streets; so that every house has both a door to the street, and a back door to the garden. Their doors have all two leaves, which, as they are easily opened, so they shut of their own accord; and there being no property among them, every man may freely enter into any house whatsoever. At every ten years' end they shift their houses by lots. They cultivate their gardens with great care, so that they have both vines, fruits, herbs, and flowers in them; and all is so well ordered, and so finely kept, that I never saw gardens anywhere that were both so fruitful and so beautiful as theirs. And this humor of ordering their gardens so well, is not only kept up by the pleasure they find in it, but also by an emulation between the inhabitants of the several streets, who vie with each other; and there is indeed nothing belonging to the whole town that is both more useful and more pleasant. So that he who founded the town, seems to have taken care of nothing more than of their gardens; for they say, the whole scheme of the town was designed at first by Utopus, but he left all that belonged to the ornament and improvement of it, to be added by those that should come after him, that being too much for one man to bring to perfection. Their records, that contain the history of their town and state, are preserved with an exact care, and run back 1,760 years. From these it appears that their houses were at first low and mean, like cottages, made of any sort of timber, and were built with mud walls and thatched with straw. But now their houses are three stories high; the fronts of them are faced either with stone, plastering, or brick; and between the facings of their walls they throw in their rubbish. Their roofs are flat, and on them they lay a sort of plaster, which costs very little, and yet is so tempered that it is not apt to take fire, and yet resists the weather more than lead. They have great quantities of glass among them, with which they glaze their windows. They use also in their windows a thin linen cloth, that is so oiled or gummed that it both keeps out the wind and gives free admission to the light.

SIR THOMAS MORE
[*Utopia* (1516)]

Some Plants of the Bible

[Despite much learned argument the identity of most of the plants men-
tioned in the Bible is still uncertain though it is generally agreed, for
instance, that the "rose of Sharon" was neither a rose nor the shrubby
member of the mallow family now commonly so called; also that "the
lilies of the field" were not lilies. Sir Thomas Browne, that extraordinary
man and extraordinary writer who was so curiously poised between the
ancient and the modern, was already considering the question in the
mid-seventeenth century.]

MANY Plants are mention'd in Scripture which are not distinctly
known in our Countries, or under such Names in the Original, as they
are fain to be rendred by analogy, or by the name of Vegetables of good
affinity unto them. . . .

What Fruit that was which our first Parents tasted in Paradise,
from the disputes of learned men seems yet indeterminable. More clear
it is that they cover'd their nakedness or secret parts with Figg Leaves;
which when I reade, I cannot but call to mind the several considerations
which Antiquity had of the Figg Tree, in reference unto those parts,
particularly how Figg Leaves by sundry Authours are described to have
some resemblance unto the Genitals, and so were aptly formed for such
contection of those parts; how also in that famous Statua of *Praxiteles*,
concerning *Alexander* and *Bucephalus*, the Secret Parts are veil'd with
Figg Leaves; how this Tree was sacred unto *Priapus*, and how the Diseases of the Secret Parts have derived their Name from Figgs.

That the good Samaritan coming from *Jericho* used any of the
Judean Balsam upon the wounded Traveller, is not to be made out, and
we are unwilling to disparage his charitable Surgery in pouring Oil into
a green Wound; and therefore when 'tis said he used Oil and Wine, may
rather conceive that he made an *Oineloeum* or medicine of Oil and Wine
beaten up and mixed together, which was no improper Medicine, and

is an Art now lately studied by some so to incorporate Wine and Oil that they may lastingly hold together, which some pretend to have, and call it *Oleum Samaritanum*, or Samaritans Oil. . . .

Whether in the Sermon of the Mount, the *Lilies of the Field* did point at the proper Lilies, or whether those Flowers grew wild in the place where our Saviour preached, some doubt may be made: because κρίνον the word in that place is accounted of the same signification with λείριον, and that in *Homer* is taken for all manner of specious Flowers: so received by *Eustachius*, *Hesychius*, and the Scholiast upon *Apollonius Rhodius*, καθόλου τὰ ἄνθη λείρια λέγεται. And κρίνον is also received in the same latitude, not signifying onely Lilies, but applied unto Daffodils, Hyacinths, Iris's, and the Flowers of *Colocynthis*.

Under the like latitude of acception, are many expressions in the *Canticles* to be received. And when it is said *he feedeth among the Lilies*, therein may be also implied other specious Flowers, not excluding the proper Lilies. But in that expression, *the Lilies drop forth Myrrhe*, neither proper Lilies nor proper Myrrhe can be apprehended, the one not proceeding from the other, but may be received in a Metaphorical sense: and in some latitude may be also made out from the roscid and honey drops observable in the Flowers of Martagon, and inverted flowred Lilies, and, 'tis like, is the standing sweet Dew on the white eyes of the Crown Imperial, now common among us.

And the proper Lily may be intended in that expression of 1 *Kings* 7. that the brazen Sea was of the thickness of a hand breadth, and the brim like a Lily. For the figure of that Flower being round at the bottom, and somewhat repandous, or inverted at the top, doth handsomely illustrate the comparison.

But that the Lily of the Valley, mention'd in the *Canticles*, *I am the Rose of Sharon, and the Lily of the Valleys*, is that Vegetable which passeth under the same name with us, that is *Lilium convallium*, or the *May* Lily, you will more hardly believe, who know with what insatisfaction the most learned Botanists reduce that Plant unto any described by the Ancients; that *Anguillara* will have it to be the *Oenanthe* of *Athenoeus*, *Cordus* the *Pothos* of *Theophrastus*; and *Lobelius* that the Greeks had not described it; who find not six Leaves in the Flower agreeably to all Lilies, but only six small divisions in the Flower, who find it also to have a single, and no bulbous Root, nor Leaves shooting about the bottom, nor the Stalk round, but angular. And that the learned *Bauhinus* hath not placed it in the Classis of Lilies, but nervifolious Plants.

·   ·   ·   ·   ·   ·

That the Forbidden fruit of Paradise was an Apple, is commonly believed, confirmed by Tradition, perpetuated by Writings, Verses, Pictures; and some have been so bad *Prosodians*, as from thence to derive the Latine word *malum*, because that fruit was the first occasion of evil; wherein notwithstanding determinations are presumptuous, and many I perceive are of another belief. For some have conceived it a Vine; in the mystery of whose fruit lay the expiation of the transgression: *Goropius Becanus* reviving the conceit of *Barcephas*, peremptorily concludeth it to be the *Indian* Fig-tree; and by a witty Allegory labours to confirm the same. Again, some fruits pass under the name of *Adams* apples, which in common acception admit not that appellation; the one described by Mathiolus under the name of *Pomum Adami*, a very fair fruit, and not unlike a Citron, but somewhat rougher, chopt and cranied, vulgarly conceived the marks of *Adams* teeth. Another, the fruit of that plant which *Serapion* termeth *Musa*, but the Eastern Christians commonly the Apples of Paradise; not resembling an apple in figure, and in taste a Melon or Cowcomber. Which fruits although they have received appellations suitable unto the tradition, yet can we not from thence infer they were this fruit in question: No more then *Arbor vitae*, so commonly called, to obtain its name from the tree of life in Paradise, or *Arbor Judae*, to be the same which supplied the gibbet unto *Judas*.

Again, There is no determination in the Text; wherein is only particulared that it was the fruit of a tree good for food, and pleasant unto the eye, in which regards many excell the Apple; and therefore learned men do wisely conceive it inexplicable; and *Philo* puts determination unto despair, when he affirmeth the same kind of fruit was never produced since. Surely were it not requisite to have been concealed, it had not passed unspecified; nor the tree revealed which concealed their nakedness, and that concealed which revealed it; for in the same chapter mention is made of fig-leaves. And the like particulars, although they seem uncircumstantial, are oft set down in holy Scripture; so is it specified that *Elias* sat under a juniper tree, *Absolom* hanged by an Oak, and *Zacheus* got up into a Sycomore. . . .

Since therefore after this fruit, curiosity fruitlessly exquireth, and confidence blindly determineth, we shall surcease our Inquisition; rather troubled that it was tasted, then troubling our selves in its decision; this only we observe, when things are left uncertain, men will assure them by determination. Which is not only verified concerning the fruit, but the Serpent that perswaded; many defining the kind or species thereof. So *Bonaventure* and *Comestor* affirm it was a Dragon, *Eugubinus* a Basilisk, *Delrio* a Viper, and others a common snake. Wherein men still continue the delusion of the Serpent, who having deceived *Eve* in the main, sets her posterity on work to mistake in the circumstance, and endeavours to propagate errors at any hand. And those he surely most desireth which concern either God or himself; for they dishonour God who is absolute truth and goodness; but for himself, who is extreamly evil, and the worst we can conceive, by aberration of conceit they may extenuate his depravity, and ascribe some goodness unto him.

SIR THOMAS BROWNE
["Observations upon Several Plants Mentioned in Scripture"
and *Pseudodoxia Epidemica* (1646)]

Buffon Looks Down His Nose

[*Of all the myths of unnatural history none persisted longer or was more often repeated, not only in popular books of wonder but in serious treatises, than the myth of the little wool-bearing sheep which grew on a bush and the myth of the barnacles which turned into geese. Both were probably mistakes rather than deliberate inventions. The vegetable wool was probably an attempt to interpret ancient accounts of the cotton plant; the barnacle goose a result of the fact, first, that its nesting ground was not known and, second, that an expanded barnacle does vaguely suggest at least a goose's neck. In any event, the Comte de Buffon, naturalist and great courtier, undertook to dispose of the myth once and for all.*]

O F the marvellous productions which ignorance, ever credulous, has so long substituted for the simple and truly wonderful operations of nature, the most absurd perhaps, and yet the most celebrated, is the growth of Barnacles and scoters in certain trees on the coasts of Scotland and the Orknies, or even on the rotten timbers of old ships.

I shall transcribe, for the entertainment of my reader, an account of this wonderful transformation, from our old Botanist, Gerard:

"But what our eyes have seene, and hands have touched, we shall declare. There is a small island in Lancashir called the *Pile of*

Foulders, wherein are found broken pieces of old and bruised ships, some whereof have been cast thither by shipwracke, and also the trunks and bodies with the branches of old and rotten trees, cast up there likewise; whereon is found a certain spume or froth that in time breedeth into certain shells, in shape like those of the Muskle, but sharper pointed, and of a whitish colour, wherein is contained a thing in form like a lace of silke finely woven as it were together, of a whitish colour; one end whereof is fastened unto the inside of the shell, even as the fish of Oisters and Muskles are; the other end is made fast into the belly of a rude masse or lumpe, which in time commeth to the shape and form of a bird: when it is perfectly formed, the shell gapeth open, and the first thing that appeareth is the foresaid lace or string; next come the legs of the bird hanging out, and as it groweth greater it openeth the shell by degrees, till at length it has all come forth and hangeth only by the bill; in short space after it cometh to full maturities, and falleth into the sea, where it gathereth feathers, and groweth to a fowle bigger than a Mallard and lesser than a Goose, having black legs, and bill or beake, and feathers black and white, spotted in such manner as our Mag-Pie, called in some places *Pie-Annet*. . . . For the truth hereof, if any doubt, may it please them to repair to me, and I shall satisfy them by the testimonies of good witnesses."

We need not remark the absurdity of such a notion: Aeneas Silvius relates, that chancing to be in Scotland, he inquired particularly for the place of the wonderful metamorphosis of the Barnacle, but was referred to the remote Hebridies and the Orknies; and he adds pleasantly, that as he sought to advance, the miracle retired from him.

COMTE DE BUFFON
[*Natural History of Birds* (1793)]

A Cure for Rupture

[*Gilbert White was an obscure country clergyman who became famous after his death as one of the founders of that school of amateur writers and observers to which Thoreau belongs. Here he reports on a superstition which no doubt went back to pre-Christian times.*]

✚

I T is the hardest thing in the world to shake off superstitious prejudices: they are sucked in as it were with our mother's milk; and, growing up with us at a time when they take the fastest hold and make the most lasting impressions, become so interwoven into our very constitutions, that the strongest good sense is required to disengage ourselves from them. No wonder therefore that the lower people retain them their whole lives through, since their minds are not invigorated by a liberal education, and therefore not enabled to make any efforts adequate to the occasion.

Such a preamble seems to be necessary before we enter on the superstitions of this district, lest we should be suspected of exaggeration in a recital of practices too gross for this enlightened age.

But the people of Tring, in Hertfordshire, would do well to remember, that no longer ago than the year 1751, and within twenty miles of the capital, they seized on two superannuated wretches, crazed with age, and overwhelmed with infirmities, on a suspicion of witchcraft; and, by trying experiments, drowned them in a horse-pond.

In a farm-yard near the middle of this village stands, at this day, a row of pollard-ashes, which, by the seams and long cicatrices down their sides, manifestly show that, in former times, they have been cleft asunder. These trees, when young and flexible, were severed and held open by wedges, while ruptured children, stripped naked, were pushed through the apertures, under a persuasion that, by such a process, the poor babes would be cured of their infirmity. As soon as the operation was over, the tree, in the suffering part, was plastered with loam, and carefully swathed up. If the parts coalesced and soldered together, as usually fell out, where the feat was performed with any adroitness at all, the party was cured; but, where the cleft continued to gape, the operation, it was supposed, would prove ineffectual. Having occasion to enlarge my garden not long since, I cut down two or three such trees, one of which did not grow together.

We have several persons now living in the village, who, in their childhood, were supposed to be healed by this superstitious ceremony, derived down perhaps from our Saxon ancestors, who practised it before their conversion to Christianity.

At the south corner of the *Plestor*, or area, near the church, there stood, about twenty years ago, a very old grotesque hollow pollard-ash, which for ages had been looked on with no small veneration as a shrew-ash. Now a shrew-ash is an ash whose twigs or branches, when gently applied to the limbs of cattle, will immediately relieve the pains which a beast suffers from the running of a shrew-mouse over the part affected: for it is supposed that a shrew-mouse is of so baneful and deleterious a nature, that wherever it creeps over a beast, be it horse, cow, or sheep, the suffering animal is afflicted with cruel anguish, and threatened with the loss of the use of the limb. Against this accident, to which they were continually liable, our provident forefathers always kept a shrew-ash at hand, which, when once medicated, would maintain its virtue for ever. A shrew-ash was made thus: Into the body of the tree a deep hole was bored with an auger, and a poor devoted shrew-mouse was thrust in alive, and plugged in, no doubt, with several quaint incantations long since forgotten. As the ceremonies necessary for such a consecration are no longer understood, all succession is at an end, and no such tree is known to subsist in the manor, or hundred.

GILBERT WHITE
[*The Natural History of Selborne* (1789)]

The Smoke Nuisance in 1661

[*John Evelyn's* Garden Calendar *was a very practical book. His proposal for dealing with the smoke nuisance in London sounds, on the contrary, a bit Utopian.*]

IT is this horrid smoake which obscures our Churches, and makes our Palaces look old, which fouls our Clothes, and corrupts the Waters, so as the very Rain, and refreshing Dews which fall in the several Seasons, precipitate this impure vapour, which, with its black and tenacious quality, spots and contaminates whatever is exposed to it. . . . London . . . is yet never clear of this Smoake which is a Plague so many other ways, and indeed intolerable; because it kills not at once, but always, since still to languish, is worse than even Death itself. For is there under Heaven such *Coughing* and *Snuffing* to be heard, as in *London* Churches and Assemblies of People, where the Barking and the Spitting is uncessant and most importunate. . . .

The *Remedy* which I would provide [requires] only the Removal of such *Trades*, as are manifest *Nuisances* to the City, which, I would have placed at farther distances; especially, such as in their Works and Fournaces use great quantities of *Sea-Coale*. . . .

      There is yet another expedient, which I have here to offer . . . by which the *City* and environs about it, might be rendred one of the most pleasant and agreeable places in the world. In order to this I propose, That all low-grounds circumjacent to the City, especially *East* and *South-west*, be cast and contriv'd into square plots, or Fields of twenty, thirty, and forty *Akers*, or more, separated from each other by Fences of double *Palisads*, or *Contr'spaliers*, which should enclose a Plantation of an hundred and fifty, or more, feet deep, about each Field. . . . That these *Palisads* be elegantly planted, diligently kept and supply'd, with such *Shrubs*, as yield the most fragrant and odoriferous *Flowers*, and are aptest to tinge the *Aer* upon every gentle emission at a great distance.

JOHN EVELYN
[*Fumifugium: or, The Inconvenience of the Aer and Smoake
of London Dissipated* (1661)]

The Man-Eating Tree

[*Few true believers in vegetable wool, barnacles that turn into geese, or in the efficacy of shrew-trees now remain, but one still occasionally meets sober-faced accounts of both the poison tree which is fatal to anyone foolish enough to sleep under it and of the man-eating tree which seizes human beings in its tentacles much as the little sundew actually does seize small insects. Willy Ley, naturalist and rocketeer, found this really hair-raising account presented as fact in a book published less than forty years ago.*]

THE Mkodos, of Madagascar, are a very primitive race, going entirely naked, having only faint vestiges of tribal relations, and no religion beyond that of the awful reverence which they pay to the sacred tree.

They dwell entirely in caves hollowed out of the limestone rocks in their hills, and are one of the smallest races, the men seldom exceeding fifty-six inches in height. At the bottom of a valley (I had no barometer, but should not think it over four hundred feet above the level of the sea), and near its eastern extremity, we came to a deep tarn-like lake about a mile in diameter, the sluggish oily water of which overflowed into a tortuous reedy canal that went unwillingly into the recesses of a black forest composed of jungle below and palms above. A path diverging from its southern side struck boldy for the heart of the forbidding and seemingly impenetrable forest. Hendrick led the way along this path, I following closely, and behind me a curious rabble of Mkodos, men, women and children. Suddenly all the natives began to cry "Tepe! Tepe!" and Hendrick, stopping short, said, "Look!" The sluggish canal-like stream here wound slowly by, and in a bare spot in its bend was the most singular of trees. I have called it "Crinoida," because when its leaves are in action it bears a striking resemblance to that well-known fossil the crinoid lily-stone or St. Cuthbert's head. It was now at rest, however, and I will try to describe it to you. If you can imagine a pineapple eight feet high and thick in proportion resting upon its base and denuded of leaves, you will have a good idea of the trunk of the tree, which, however, was not the color of an anana, but a dark dingy brown, and apparently as hard as iron. From the apex of this truncated cone (at least two feet in diameter) eight leaves hung sheer to the ground, like doors swung back on their hinges. These leaves, which were joined at the top of the tree at regular intervals, were about eleven or twelve feet long, and shaped very much like the leaves of the American agave or century plant. They were two feet through at their thickest point and three feet wide, tapering to a sharp point that looked like a cow's horn, very convex on the outer (but now under surface), and on the under (now upper) surface slightly concave. This concave face was thickly set with strong thorny hooks like those on the head of the teazle. These leaves hanging thus limp and lifeless, dead green in color, had in appearance the massive strength of oak fibre. The apex of the cone was a round white concave figure like a smaller plate set within a larger one. This was not a flower but a receptacle, and there exuded into it a clear treacly liquid, honey sweet, and possessed of violent intoxicating and soporific properties. From underneath the rim (so to speak) of the undermost plate a series of long hairy green tendrils stretched out in every direction towards the horizon. These were seven or eight feet long, and tapered from four inches to a half inch in diameter, yet they stretched out stiffly as iron rods. Above these (from between the upper and under cup) six

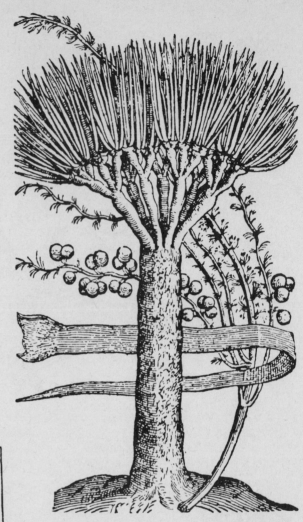

ORIGINAL
FREE. HAND
PEN. DRAWINGS
BY COTTIE

BARBANT

white almost transparent palpi reared themselves towards the sky, twirling and twisting with a marvelous incessant motion, yet constantly reaching upwards. Thin as reeds and frail as quills, apparently they were yet five or six feet tall, and were so constantly and vigorously in motion, with such a subtle, sinuous, silent throbbing against the air, that they made me shudder in spite of myself, with their suggestion of serpents flayed, yet dancing upon their tails. The description I am giving you now is partly made up from a subsequent careful inspection of the plant. My observations on this occasion were suddenly interrupted by the natives, who had been shrieking around the tree with their shrill voices, and chanting what Hendrick told me were propitiatory hymns to the great tree devil. With still wilder shrieks and chants they now surrounded one of the women, and urged her with the points of their javelins, until slowly, and with despairing face, she climbed up the stalk of the tree and stood on the summit of the cone, the palpi swirling all about her. "Tsik! Tsik!" ("Drink, drink!") cried the men. Stooping, she drank of the viscid fluid in the cup, rising instantly again, with wild frenzy in her face and convulsive cords in her limbs. But she did not jump down, as she seemed to intend to do. Oh, no! The atrocious cannibal tree that had been so inert and dead came to sudden savage life. The slender delicate palpi, with the fury of starved serpents, quivered a moment over her head, then as if instinct with demoniac intelligence fastened upon her in sudden coils round and round her neck and arms; then while her awful screams and yet more awful laughter rose wildly to be instantly strangled down again into a gurgling moan, the tendrils one after another, like green serpents, with brutal energy and infernal rapidity, rose, retracted themselves, and wrapped her about in fold after fold, ever tightening with cruel swiftness and the savage tenacity of anacondas fastening upon their prey. It was the barbarity of the Laocoon without its beauty—this strange horrible murder. And now the great leaves slowly rose and stiffly, like the arms of a derrick, erected themselves in the air, approached one another and closed about the dead and hampered victim with the silent force of a hydraulic press and the ruthless purpose of a thumb screw. A moment more, and while I could see the bases of these great levers pressing more tightly towards each other, from their interstices there trickled down the stalk of the tree great streams of the viscid honey-like fluid mingled horribly with the blood and oozing viscera of the victim. At sight of this the savage hordes around me, yelling madly, bounded forward, crowded to the tree, clasped it, and with cups, leaves, hands and tongues each one obtained enough of the liquor to send him mad and frantic. Then ensued a grotesque and indescribably hideous orgy, from which even while its convulsive madness was turning rapidly into delirium and insensibility, Hendrick dragged me hurriedly away into the recesses of the forest, hiding me from the dangerous brutes. May I never see such a sight again.

The retracted leaves of the great tree kept their upright position during ten days, then when I came one morning they were prone again, the tendrils stretched, the palpi floating, and nothing but a white skull at the foot of the tree to remind me of the sacrifice that had taken place there. I climbed into a neighboring tree, and saw that all trace of the victim had disappeared and the cup was again supplied with the viscid fluid.

CHASE SALMON OSBORN
[*Madagascar, Land of the Man-Eating Tree* (1924)]

The Poison Tree of Java

[*As late as 1957 a British newspaper printed with a straight face the tale of the man-eating plant. Also still alive is the horrendous legend of the fatal upas tree of Java, a member of the fig family so venomous that its mere exhalations are fatal to all life, either animal or vegetable, for miles about. This tale has been going for more than two centuries at least. Erasmus Darwin has a solemn footnote about it in* The Botanical Garden *and Pushkin describes it in a poem. In another version, an East Indian chief gives condemned criminals a slim chance at life by sending them to collect the poison.*

The truth is that the juice of the upas tree (Antiaris toxicaria) *is a powerful poison though hardly capable of working at a distance! The nineteenth-century traveler Henry Forbes gives a reasonably sober account of both the tree itself and of the awe in which natives hold it.*]

BENEATH the shady canopy of this tall fig no native will, if he knows it, dare to rest, nor will he pass between its stem and the wind, so strong is his belief in its evil influence.

In the centre of a tea estate not far off from my encampment stood, because no one could be found daring enough to cut it down, an immense specimen, which had long been a nuisance to the proprietor on account of the lightning every now and then striking off, to the damage of the shrubs below, large branches, which none of his servants could be induced to remove. One day, having been pitchforked together and burned, they were considered disposed of; but next morning the whole of his labourers in the adjacent village awoke, to their intense alarm, afflicted with a painful eruption, wherever their bodies were usually uncovered. It was then remembered that the smoke of the burning branches had been blown by the wind through the village; this undoubtedly accounted for the epidemic; but it did not allay their fears that they were all as good as dead men, for the potency of the sap as a poison is but too well known to them.

To prevent a general flight of the workmen it became necessary to get rid of the tree altogether, but the difficulty was to find any one willing to lay the axe to its root. At last a couple of Chinamen, after much persuasion and the offer of a high fee, agreed to perform the hazardous task of cutting up and carting it away. To the surprise of everybody they accomplished their task without experiencing the least harm. They pocketed their fee and departed in silence, without, however, saying that they had at intervals during their work, artfully smeared their bodies with cocoa-nut oil.

The sap of the bark alone is hurtful, for the logs into which the stripped trunk was cut were made into furniture for the owner's dining-room, without ill effects to the carpenters. The bark of another denizen of the same forest—*Gluta benghas*, one of the Anacardiaceae—contains a sap even more noxious, for, falling on the skin, it produces stubborn ulcers which, on the woodcutters—who often get splashed on their arms and body—require months to heal; but its sap is not used by them for poison, as the *antiarin* is. It is curious to reflect how acute native ingenuity has been in elaborating a pharmacopoeia abounding in subtle articles to waste or take away life, while it contains hardly one to preserve it. The action of some of these preparations, whose effects I had heard of as well as seen, astonished me vastly, but no bribe that I could offer was tempting enough to induce their old *dukuns* to disclose their composition.

HENRY O. FORBES
[*A Naturalist's Wanderings in the Eastern Archipelago* (1885)]

The Pot of Basil

[*In a previous section some note was taken of the fact that Italians of the Renaissance made extensive use of potted plants. It is to be hoped that they were not often fertilized by the method employed in the following story from Boccaccio's* Decameron. *Keats retold it in his narrative poem* Isabella.]

ELIZA having concluded her novel, which was commended by the king, Filomena was then ordered to begin. Full of pity for the two unhappy lovers last mentioned, she heaved a deep sigh, and said: My novel will not be concerning people of such high rank as those of whom Eliza has spoken, but perhaps it may be equally moving; and I am led to it from her mentioning Messina, where the thing happened.

  There lived at Messina, three young merchants, who were brothers, and left very rich by their father: they had an only sister, named Isabella, a lady of worth and beauty, who, whatever was the reason, was yet unmarried. Now they had in their employ a young man of Pisa, called Lorenzo, who managed all their affairs. He was a young man of very agreeable person and manners, and being often in Isabella's company, she loved him, and he forsook all others for her sake; nor was it long before their mutual desires were consummated. This affair was carried on between them for a considerable time, without the least suspicion; till one night it happened, as Isabella was going to Lorenzo's chamber, that the eldest brother saw her, without her knowing it. This afflicted him greatly; yet, being a prudent man, he made no discovery, but lay considering with himself till morning, what course was best to take. He then related to his brothers what he had seen, with regard to their sister and Lorenzo, and, after a long debate, it was resolved to seem to take no notice of it for the present, but to make away with him privately, the first opportunity, that they might remove all cause of

reproach both to their sister and themselves. Continuing in this resolution, they behaved with the same freedom and civility to Lorenzo as ever,
till at length, under a pretence of going out of the city, upon a party of
pleasure, they carried him along with them, and arriving at a lonesome
place, fit for their purpose, they slew him, unprepared as he was to make
any defence, and buried him on the spot. Then, returning to Messina,
they gave it out, that they had sent him on a journey of business, which
was easily believed, because they frequently did so.

After some time, Isabella, thinking that Lorenzo made a long
stay, began to inquire earnestly of her brothers concerning him, and
this she did so often, that at last one of them said to her, "What have
you to do with Lorenzo, that you are continually teasing us about him?
If you inquire any more, you shall receive such an answer as you will
by no means like." This grieved her exceedingly, and fearing, she knew
not why, she remained without asking any more questions; yet all the
night would she lament and complain of his long stay; and thus she spent
her life in a tedious and anxious waiting for his return; till one night it
happened, that, having wept herself to sleep, he appeared to her in a
dream, all pale and ghastly, with his clothes rent in pieces, and she
thought that he spoke to her thus: "My dearest Isabel, thou grievest
incessantly for my absence, and art continually calling upon me; but
know that I can return no more to thee, for the last day that thou sawest
me, thy brothers put me to death." And, describing the place where
they had buried him, he bade her call no more upon him, nor ever expect
to see him again; and disappeared.

Isabella woke up, implicitly believing the vision, and wept
bitterly. In the morning, not daring to say anything to her brothers, she
resolved to go to the place mentioned in the dream, to be convinced of
the reality. Accordingly, having leave to go a little way into the country,
along with a companion of hers, who was acquainted with all her affairs,
she went thither, and clearing the ground of the dried leaves, with which
it was covered, she observed where the earth seemed to be lightest, and
dug there. She had not searched far before she came to her lover's body,
which she found in no degree wasted; this informed her of the truth of
her vision, and she was in the utmost concern on that account; but, as
that was not a fit place for lamentation, she would willingly have taken
the corpse away with her, to give it a more decent interment; but, finding
herself unable to do that, she cut off the head, which she put into a
handkerchief, and, covering the trunk again with mould, she gave the
head to her maid to carry, and returned home without being perceived.
She then shut herself up in her chamber, and lamented over her lover's

head till she had washed it with her tears, and then she put it into a flower-pot, having folded it in a fine napkin, and covering it with earth, she planted sweet herbs therein, which she watered with nothing but rose or orange water, or else with her tears, accustoming herself to sit always before it, and devoting her whole heart unto it, as containing her dear Lorenzo.

The sweet herbs, what with her continual bathing, and the moisture arising from the putrefied head, flourished exceedingly, and sent forth a most agreeable odour. Continuing this manner of life, she was observed by some of the neighbours, and they related her conduct to her brothers, who had before remarked with surprise the decay of her beauty. Accordingly, they both reprimanded her for it, and, finding that ineffectual, stole the pot from her. She, perceiving that it was taken away, begged earnestly of them to restore it, which they refusing, she fell sick. The young men wondered much why she should have so great a fancy for it, and were resolved to see what it contained: turning out the earth, therefore, they saw the napkin, and in it the head, not so much consumed, but that, by the curled locks, they knew it to be Lorenzo's, which threw them into the utmost astonishment, and fearing lest it should be known, they buried it privately, and withdrew themselves thence to Naples. The young lady never ceased weeping, and calling for her pot of flowers, till she died: and thus terminated her unfortunate love. But, in some time afterwards, the thing became public, which gave rise to this song—

Most cruel and unkind was he,
That of my flowers deprived me, etc.

BOCCACCIO
[*The Decameron* (14th century)]

Moon Flowers

[*The early "science fiction" of H. G. Wells keeps much closer than that of Jules Verne to the remotely possible. Here he imagines for the plant life of the moon an ingenious solution to the difficulty created by the fact that on that satellite burning-hot days alternate with fantastically cold nights. Every day these plants grow from seed and ripen new seeds which survive the nightly winter. His account begins at the first hint of sunrise.*]

✷

T H E harsh emphasis, the pitiless black and white of the scenery had altogether disappeared. The glare of the sun had taken upon itself a faint tinge of amber; the shadows upon the cliff of the crater wall were deeply purple. To the eastward a dark bank of fog still crouched and sheltered from the sunrise, but to the westward the sky was blue and clear. I began to realise the length of my insensibility.

We were no longer in a void. An atmosphere had risen about us. The outline of things had gained in character, had grown acute and varied; save for a shadowed space of white substance here and there, white substance that was no longer air but snow, the Arctic appearance had gone altogether. Everywhere broad, rusty-brown spaces of bare and tumbled earth spread to the blaze of the sun. Here and there at the edge of the snowdrifts were transient little pools and eddies of water, the only things stirring in that expanse of barrenness. The sunlight inundated the upper two-thirds of our sphere and turned our climate to high summer, but our feet were still in shadow and the sphere was lying upon a drift of snow.

And scattered here and there upon the slope, and emphasised by little white threads of unthawed snow upon their shady sides, were shapes like sticks—dry, twisted sticks of the same rusty hue as the rock upon which they lay. That caught one's thoughts sharply. Sticks! On a lifeless world? Then as my eye grew more accustomed to the texture of their substance I perceived that almost all this surface had a fibrous texture, like the carpet of brown needles one finds beneath the shade of pine-trees.

"Cavor!" I said.

"Yes?"

"It may be a dead world now—but once—"

Something arrested my attention. I had discovered among these needles a number of little round objects. It seemed to me that one of these had moved.

"Cavor," I whispered.

"What?"

But I did not answer at once. I stared incredulous. For an instant I could not believe my eyes. I gave an inarticulate cry. I gripped his arm. I pointed. "Look!" I cried, finding my tongue. "There! Yes! And there!"

His eyes followed my pointing finger. "Eh?" he said.

How can I describe the thing I saw? It is so petty a thing to state, and yet it seems so wonderful, so pregnant with emotion. I have said that amidst the stick-like litter were these round bodies, these little oval bodies that might have passed as very small pebbles. And now first one and then another had stirred, had rolled over and cracked, and down the crack of each of them showed a minute line of yellowish green, thrusting outward to meet the hot encouragement of the newly risen sun. For a moment that was all, and then there stirred and burst a third!

"It is a seed," said Cavor. And then I heard him whisper, very softly: *"Life!"*

"Life!" and immediately it poured upon us that our vast journey had not been in vain, that we had come to no arid waste of minerals, but to a world that lived and moved! We watched intensely. I remember I kept rubbing the glass before me with my sleeve, jealous of the faintest suspicion of mist.

The picture was clear and vivid only in the middle of the field. All about that centre the dead fibres and seeds were magnified and distorted by the curvature of the glass. But we could see enough! One after another all down the sunlit slope these miraculous little brown bodies burst and gaped apart, like seed-pods, like the husks of fruits; opened eager mouths that drank in the heat and light pouring in a cascade from the newly risen sun.

Every moment more of these seed-coats ruptured, and even as they did so the swelling pioneers overflowed their rent distended seed-cases and passed into the second stage of growth. With a steady assurance, a swift deliberation, these amazing seeds thrust a rootlet downward to the earth and a queer bundle-like bud into the air. In a little while the whole slope was dotted with minute plantlets standing at attention in the blaze of the sun.

They did not stand for long. The bundle-like buds swelled and strained and opened with a jerk, thrusting out a coronet of red sharp tips, spreading a whorl of tiny, spiky, brownish leaves, that lengthened rapidly, lengthened visibly even as we watched. The movement was slower than any animal's, swifter than any plant's I have ever seen before. How can I suggest it to you—the way that growth went on? The leaf tips grew so that they moved onward even while we looked at them. The brown seed-case shrivelled and was absorbed with an equal rapidity. Have you ever on a cold day taken a thermometer into your warm hand and watched the little thread of mercury creep up the tube? These moon-plants grew like that.

In a few minutes, as it seemed, the buds of the more forward of these plants had lengthened into a stem, and were even putting forth a second whorl of leaves, and all the slope that had seemed so recently a lifeless stretch of litter was now dark with the stunted, olive-green herbage of bristling spikes that swayed with the vigour of their growing.

I turned about, and behold! along the upper edge of a rock to the eastward a similar fringe, in a scarcely less forward condition, swayed and bent, dark against the blinding glare of the sun. And beyond this fringe was the silhouette of a plant mass, branching clumsily like a cactus and swelling visibly, swelling like a bladder that fills with air.

Then to the westward also I discovered another such distended form was rising over the scrub. But here the light fell upon its sleek sides, and I could see that its colour was a vivid orange. It rose as one watched it; if one looked away from it for a minute and then back, its outline had changed: it thrust out blunt, congested branches, until in a little time it rose a coralline shape of many feet in height. Compared with such a growth the terrestrial puff-ball which will sometimes swell a foot in diameter in a single night, would be a hopeless laggard. But then the puff-ball grows against a gravitational pull of six times that of the moon. Beyond, out of gullies and flats that had been hidden from us but not from the quickening sun, over reefs and banks of shining rock, a bristling beard of spiky and fleshy vegetation was straining into view, hurrying tumultuously to take advantage of the brief day in which it must flower and fruit and seed again and die. It was like a miracle, that growth. So, one must imagine, the trees and plants arose at the Creation, and covered the desolation of the new-made earth.

Imagine it! Imagine that dawn! The resurrection of the frozen air, the stirring and quickening of the soil, and then this silent uprising of vegetation, this unearthly ascent of fleshliness and spikes. Conceive it all lit by a blaze that would make the intensest sunlight of earth seem watery and weak. And still amidst this stirring jungle wherever there was shadow lingered banks of bluish snow. And to have the picture of our impression complete you must bear in mind that we saw it all through a thick bent glass, distorting it as things are distorted by a lens, acute only in the centre of the picture and very bright there, and towards the edges magnified and unreal.

H. G. WELLS
[*First Men in the Moon* (1901)]

A Garden of Talking Flowers

[*The adventures of Lewis Carroll's Alice were more often zoological than botanical. But she met a few queer plants too.*]

"I SHOULD see the garden far better," said Alice to herself, "if I could get to the top of that hill: and here's a path that leads straight to it —at least; no, it doesn't do that" (after going a few yards along the path, and turning several sharp corners), "but I suppose it will at last. But how curiously it twists! It's more like a corkscrew than a path! Well, *this* turn goes to the hill, I suppose—no, it doesn't! This goes straight back to the house! Well then, I'll try it the other way."

And so she did: wandering up and down and trying turn after turn, but always coming back to the house, do what she would. Indeed, once, when she turned a corner rather more quickly than usual, she ran against it before she could stop herself.

"It's no use talking about it," Alice said, looking up at the house and pretending it was arguing with her. "I'm *not* going in again yet. I know I should have to get through the looking-glass again—back into the old room—and there'd be an end of all my adventures!"

So, resolutely turning her back upon the house, she set out once more down the path, determined to keep straight on till she got to the hill. For a few minutes all went on well, and she was just saying, "I really *shall* do it this time—" when the path gave a sudden twist and shook itself (as she described it afterward), and the next moment she found herself actually walking in at the door.

"Oh, it's too bad!" she cried. "I never saw such a house for getting in the way! Never!"

However, there was the hill full in sight, so there was nothing to be done but start again. This time she came upon a large flower-bed, with a border of daisies, and a willow-tree growing in the middle.

"O Tiger-lily," said Alice, addressing herself to one that was waving gracefully about in the wind, "I *wish* you could talk!"

"We *can* talk," said the Tiger-lily: "when there's anybody worth talking to."

Alice was so astonished that she couldn't speak for a minute: it quite seemed to take her breath away. At length, as the Tiger-lily only went on waving about, she spoke again, in a timid voice—almost in a whisper. "And *can* all the flowers talk?"

"As well as *you* can," said the Tiger-lily. "And a great deal louder."

"It isn't manners for us to begin, you know," said the Rose, "and I really was wondering when you'd speak! Said I to myself, 'Her face has got *some* sense in it, though it's not a clever one!' Still you're the right color, and that goes a long way."

"I don't care about the color," the Tiger-lily remarked. "If only her petals curled up a little more, she'd be all right."

Alice didn't like being criticized, so she began asking questions. "Aren't you sometimes frightened at being planted out here, with nobody to take care of you?"

"There's the tree in the middle," said the Rose: "what else is it good for?"

"But what could it do, if any danger came?" Alice asked.

"It could bark," said the Rose.

"It says 'Bough-wough'!" cried a Daisy, "that's why its branches are called boughs!"

"Didn't you know *that*?" cried another Daisy, and here they all began shouting together, till the air seemed quite full of little shrill voices. "Silence, every one of you!" cried the Tiger-lily, waving itself passionately from side to side, and trembling with excitement. "They know I can't get at them!" it panted, bending its quivering head toward Alice, "or they wouldn't dare to do it!"

"Never mind!" Alice said in a soothing tone, and stooping down to the daisies, who were just beginning again, she whispered, "If you don't hold your tongues, I'll pick you!"

There was silence in a moment, and several of the pink daisies turned white.

"That's right!" said the Tiger-lily. "The daisies are worst of all. When one speaks, they all begin together, and it's enough to make one wither to hear the way they go on!"

"How is it you can all talk so nicely?" Alice said, hoping to get it into a better temper by a compliment. "I've been in many gardens before, but none of the flowers could talk."

"Put your hand down and feel the ground," said the Tiger-lily. "Then you'll know why."

Alice did so. "It's very hard," she said, "but I don't see what that has to do with it."

"In most gardens," the Tiger-lily said, "they make the beds too soft—so that the flowers are always asleep."

This sounded a very good reason, and Alice was quite pleased to know it. "I never thought of that before!" she said.

"It's *my* opinion that you never think *at all*," the Rose said in a rather severe tone.

"I never saw anybody that looked stupider," a Violet said, so suddenly, that Alice quite jumped: for it hadn't spoken before.

"Hold *your* tongue!" cried the Tiger-lily. "As if *you* ever saw anybody! You keep your head under the leaves, and snore away there, till you know no more what's going on in the world, than if you were a bud!"

"Are there any more people in the garden beside me?" Alice said, not choosing to notice the Rose's last remark.

"There's one other flower in the garden that can move about like you," said the Rose. "I wonder how you do it" ("You're always wondering," said the Tiger-lily), "but she's more bushy than you are."

"Is she like me?" Alice asked eagerly, for the thought crossed her mind, "There's another little girl in the garden, somewhere!"

"Well, she has the same awkward shape as you," the Rose said. "But she's redder—and her petals are shorter, I think."

"Her petals are done up close, almost like a dahlia," the Tiger-lily interrupted; "not tumbled about anyhow, like yours."

"But that's not *your* fault," the Rose added kindly: "you're beginning to fade, you know—and then one can't help one's petals getting a little untidy."

Alice didn't like this idea at all: so, to change the subject, she asked, "Does she ever come out here?"

"I dare say you'll see her soon," said the Rose. "She's one of the thorny kind."

"Where does she wear the thorns?" Alice asked with some curiosity.

"Why, all round her head, of course," the Rose replied. "I was wondering *you* hadn't got some too. I thought it was the regular rule."

"She's coming!" cried the Larkspur. "I hear her footstep, thump, thump, along the gravel-walk!"

Alice looked round eagerly, and found that it was the Red

Queen. "She's grown a good deal!" was her first remark. She had indeed: when Alice first found her in the ashes, she had been only three inches high—and here she was, half a head taller than Alice herself!

"It's the fresh air that does it," said the Rose: "wonderfully fine air it is, out here."

"I think I'll go and meet her," said Alice, for though the flowers were interesting enough, she felt that it would be far grander to have a talk with a real Queen.

LEWIS CARROLL
[*Through the Looking Glass* (1871)]

Section Eight

GARDENS
WITHOUT GARDENERS

To me the meanest flower that blows can give
Thoughts that do often lie too deep for tears.

WORDSWORTH

For us of the minority the opportunity to see geese is more important than tele-
vision, and the chance to find a pasqueflower is a right as inalienable as free speech.

ALDO LEOPOLD

A Calvinist on Flowers

[To some it may come as a surprise that Jonathan Edwards did not spend all his time describing "Sinners in the Hands of an Angry God" but could echo John Ray in insisting that an appreciation of the beauties of nature is part of our duty to the Creator of them.]

S O that, when we are delighted with flowers, meadows, and gentle breezes of wind, we may consider that we see only the emanation of the sweet benevolence of Jesus Christ. When we behold the fragrant rose and lily, we see His love and purity. So the green trees and fields, and singing of birds, are the emanation of His infinite joy and benignity. The easiness and naturalness of trees and vines are shadows of His beauty and loveliness. The crystal rivers and murmuring streams are the footsteps of His favor, grace, and beauty. When we behold the light and brightness of the sun, the golden edges of an evening cloud, or the beauteous bow, we behold the adumbrations of His glory and goodness; and in the blue sky, of His mildness and gentleness. There are also many things wherein we may behold His awful majesty: in the sun in his strength, in comets, in thunder, in the hovering thunder-cloud, in rugged rocks, and the brows of mountains.

JONATHAN EDWARDS
[Quoted from Ms. in *Jonathan Edwards* by U. G. Allen]

Linnaeus Meets a Toadstool

[*Linnaeus was a little too early to be a romantic but his love of nature and her simplicity brings him close to romantic feeling.*]

I W A S also shown the Agaric [mushroom] of the Willow, which has a very fragrant scent. The people assured me it was formerly the fashion for young men, when going to visit their mistresses, to use this fungus as a perfume, in order to render themselves more agreeable. . . . O whimsical Venus! in other regions you must be treated with coffee and chocolate, preserves and sweetmeats, wines and dainties, jewels and pearls, gold and silver, silks and cosmetics, balls and assemblies, music and theatrical exhibitions: here you are satisfied with a little withered fungus!

CAROLUS LINNAEUS
[*Lachesis Lapponica,*
TRANSLATED BY JAMES SMITH (1811)]

Mrs. Trollope Finds One Thing to Praise

[*The mother of Anthony Trollope visited the United States in the eighteen thirties and achieved a huge success by writing a book in which she disapproved of nearly everything she saw. Perhaps she would not have spoken so favorably of our wild flowers had it not given her an opportunity to suggest in the last sentence of this selection that we were unworthy of them.*]

O U R summer in Maryland [1830] was delightful. The thermometer stood at 94, but the heat was by no means so oppressive as what we had felt in the West. In no part of North America are the natural productions of the soil more various, or more beautiful. Strawberries of the richest flavour sprung beneath our feet; and when these passed away, every grove, every lane, every field looked like a cherry orchard, offering an inexhaustible profusion of fruit to all who would take the trouble to gather it. Then followed the peaches; every hedge-row was planted with them, and though the fruit did not equal in size or flavour those ripened on our garden walls, we often found them good enough to afford a delicious refreshment on our long rambles. But it was the flowers, and the flowering shrubs that, beyond all else, rendered this region the most beautiful I had ever seen (the Alleghany always excepted). No description can give an idea of the variety, the profusion, the luxuriance of them. If I talk of wild roses, the English reader will fancy I mean the pale ephemeral blossoms of our bramble hedges; but the wild roses of Maryland and Virginia might be the choicest favourites of the flower-garden. They are rarely very double, but the brilliant eye atones for this. They are of all shades, from the deepest crimson to the tenderest pink. The scent is rich and delicate; in size they exceed any single roses I ever saw, often measuring above four inches in diameter. The leaf greatly resembles that of the china rose; it is large, dark, firm, and brilliant. The sweetbrier grows wild, and blossoms abundantly; both leaves and flowers are considerably larger than with us. The acacia, or as it is there called the locust, blooms with great richness and profusion; I have gathered a branch less than a foot long, and counted twelve full bunches of flowers on it. The scent is equal to the orange-flower. The dogwood is another of the splendid white blossoms that adorn the woods. Its lateral branches are flat, like a fan, and dotted all over with star-like blossoms, as large as those of the gum-cistus. Another pretty shrub, of smaller size, is the poison alder. It is well that its noxious qualities are very generally known, for it is most tempting to the eye by its delicate fringe-like bunches of white flowers. Even the touch of this shrub is poisonous, and produces violent swelling. The arbor judae is abundant in every wood, and its bright and delicate pink is the earliest harbinger of the American spring. Azaleas, white, yellow, and pink; kalmias of every variety, the too sweet magnolia, and the stately rhododendron, all grow in wild abundance there. The plant known in England as the Virginia creeper, is often seen climbing to the top of the highest forest trees, and bearing a large trumpet-shaped blossom of a rich scarlet. The sassafras is a beautiful shrub, and I cannot imagine why it has not been naturalised in England, for it has every appearance of being extremely hardy. The leaves grow in tufts, and every tuft contains leaves of five or six different forms. The fruit is singularly beautiful; it resembles in form a small acorn, and is jet black; the cup and stem looking as if they were made of red coral. The graceful and fantastic grapevine is a feature of great beauty, and its wandering festoons bear no more resemblance to our well-trained vines, than our stunted azaleas, and tiny magnolias, to their thriving American kindred.

There is another charm that haunts the summer wanderer in America, and it is perhaps the only one found in greatest perfection in the West: but it is beautiful every where. In a bright day, during any of the summer months, your walk is through an atmosphere of butterflies, so gaudy in hue, and so varied in form, that I often thought they looked like flowers on the wing. Some of them are very large, measuring three or four inches across the wings; but many, and I think the most beautiful, are smaller than ours. Some have wings of the most dainty lavender colour, and bodies of black; others are fawn and rose colour; and others again are orange and bright blue. But pretty as they are, it is their number, even more than their beauty, that delights the eye. Their gay and noise-less movement as they glance through the air, crossing each other in chequered maze, is very beautiful. The humming-bird is another pretty summer toy; but they are not sufficiently numerous, nor do they live enough on the wing to render them so important a feature in the trans-atlantic show, as the rainbow-tinted butterflies. The fire-fly was a far more brilliant novelty. In moist situations, or before a storm, they are very numerous, and in the dark sultry evening of a burning day, when all employment was impossible, I have often found it a pastime to watch their glancing light, now here, now there; now seen, now gone: shooting past with the rapidity of lightning, and looking like a shower of falling stars, blown about in the breeze of evening. . . .

I never saw so many autumn flowers as grow in the woods and sheep-walks of Maryland; a second spring seemed to clothe the fields; but with grief and shame I confess, that of these precious blossoms I scarcely knew a single name. I think the Michaelmas daisy, in wonderful variety of form and colour, and the prickly pear were almost my only acquaintance: let no one visit America without having first studied botany; it is an amusement, as a clever friend of mine once told me, that helps one wonderfully up and down hill, and must be superlatively valuable in America, both from the plentiful lack of other amusements, and the plentiful material for enjoyment in this; besides if one is dying to know the name of any of these lovely strangers, it is a thousand to one against his finding any one who can tell it.

FRANCES TROLLOPE
[*Domestic Manners of the Americans* (1832)]

An Aesthete's Eden

[*Hamlet described an "unweeded garden" as one where "things rank and gross by nature possess it merely." Théophile Gautier, being an aesthete and a decadent, could permit himself to imagine, most unrealistically, that it would be a sort of Eden.*]

S O M E time ago we dreamed to plan a garden wherein Nature should have full liberty. Never should the bill-hook cut one branch in it, nor shears trim a hedge or a border. The twigs would have been quite free to interlace themselves according to their own fancy: the plants, to creep and climb; the mosses, to cover with their patches the trunks of trees; the lichens, to make the statues white with their grey bands; the brambles, to bar the walks and arrest you with their thorns; the wild poppy, to raise its dark red spark near the untrained rose; the ivy, to shoot its roving wreaths, and hang over the balustrades of terraces. Full license would have been granted to the nettle, the thistle, the celandine, the cleavers, which cling to you like a burr; to the burdock, the nightshade, the quitch—to all the gipsy host of undisciplined plants—to grow, multiply, invade, obliterate every trace of cultivation, and to turn the flower-garden into a miniature forest.

This forsaken paradise, we should, besides, have liked to see surrounded with walls green with moss, clothed with mural plants, and crowned with stocks, iris, gilliflowers, and seagreens, in place of the broken glass, wherewith it is usual to deter the intruding urchins; and over the rain-washed gate, bare of paint, and having no trace of that green colour beloved by Rousseau, we would have written this inscription in black letters, stone-like in shape, and threatening of aspect: "Gardeners are prohibited from entering here."

THÉOPHILE GAUTIER
[*Nature at Home* (1891)]

The Great Forests of North America

[*Of the thousands who left Europe for the Americas a small but not unimportant minority came to admire and study, rather than to exploit, the natural richness of a new land. None of such was more enthusiastic than the self-taught Yorkshire printer Thomas Nuttall who immigrated to Philadelphia in 1808 and managed to support himself—no one knows quite how—while ranging the continent in search of plants, as far south as Florida, as far north as the Columbia River, and as far west as the Hawaiian Islands. With his own hands he set most of the type for his* Genera of North American Plants *and a* Catalogue of Species *(1818) and he added two new volumes to* The North American Sylva *composed by the earlier French visitor André Michaux. After thirty-four years of residence in the New World he returned to Yorkshire to take possession of a small estate left him on the condition that he spend nine months of the year there. In a farewell to the New World he paid eloquent tribute to the majesty of its forests.*]

THIRTY-FOUR years ago, I left England to explore the natural history of the United States. In the ship Halcyon I arrived at the shores of the New World; and after a boisterous and dangerous passage, our dismasted vessel entered the Capes of the Delaware in the month of April. The beautiful robing of forest scenery, now bursting into vernal life, was exchanged for the monotony of the dreary ocean, and the sad sickness of the sea. As we sailed up the Delaware my eyes were rivetted on the landscape with intense admiration. All was new!—and life, like that season, was then full of hope and enthusiasm. The forests, apparently unbroken, in their primeval solitude and repose, spread themselves on either hand as we passed placidly along. The extending vista of dark pines gave an air of deep sadness to the wilderness.

> . . . these lonely regions, where, retired
> From little scenes of art, great Nature dwells
> In awful solitude, and nought is seen
> But the wild herds that own no master's stall.

The deer brought to bay, or plunging into the flood from the pursuit of the Indian, armed with bow and arrow, alone seemed wanting to realize the savage landscape as it appeared to the first settlers of the country.

Scenes like these have little attraction for ordinary life, but to the naturalist it is far otherwise; privations to him are cheaply purchased, if he may but roam over the wild domain of primeval nature, and behold

> Another *Flora* there, of bolder hues,
> And richer sweets, beyond our garden's pride.

How often have I realized the poet's buoyant hopes amidst these solitary rambles through interminable forests. For thousands of miles my chief converse has been in the wilderness with the spontaneous productions of Nature; and the study of these objects and their contemplation has been to me a source of constant delight.

This fervid curiosity led me to the banks of the Ohio, through the dark forests and brakes of the Mississippi, to the distant lakes of the northern frontier; through the wilds of Florida; far up the Red River and the Missouri, and through the territory of Arkansas; at last over the

> Vast savannahs, where the wandering eye
> Unfixt, is in a verdant ocean lost.

And now across the arid plains of the far west, beyond the steppes of the Rocky Mountains, down the Oregon to the extended shores of the Pacific, across the distant ocean to that famous group of islands where Cook at length fell a sacrifice to his temerity. And here for the first time, I beheld the beauties of a tropical vegetation; a season that knows no change; but that of perpetual spring and summer: an elysian land, where Nature offers spontaneous food to man. The region of the Bread fruit; the Tarrow (*Colocasia esculenta*) which feeds the indigent mass of the population; the Broussonetia, a kind of Mulberry tree, whose inner rind, called tapa, affords an universal clothing. The low groves produce the Banana, the Ginger, the Turmeric, the inebriating *Kava* (*Piper methysticum*), a kind of Arrow root, resembling the potato (*Tacca*), and the Saccharine Tee root (*Dracaena terminalis*) at the same time the best of portable fodder. The common timber for constructing houses, boats, various implements, and the best of fuel, is here the produce of a Mimosa (*Acacia heterophylla*). For lights and oil, the *too tooe* kernels (*Aleurites triloba*) produce an excellent and inexhaustible supply; the cocoa-nut and the fragrant *Pandanus* afford delicious food, cordage and mats, and the very reeds, reduced in size, which border the rivulets, are no other than the precious sugar-cane of commerce.

Leaving this favoured region of perpetual mildness, I now arrived on the shores of California, at Monterey. The early spring (March) had already spread out its varied carpet of flowers; all of them had to me the charm of novelty, and many were adorned with the most brilliant and varied hues. The forest trees were new to my view. A magpie, almost like that of Europe (but with a yellow bill), chattered from the branches of an Oak, with leaves like those of the Holly (*Quercus agrifolia*). A thorny Gooseberry, forming a small tree, appeared clad with pendulous flowers as brilliant as those of a Fuchsia. A new Plane tree spread its wide arms over the dried-up rivulets. A Ceanothus, attaining the magnitude of a small tree, loaded with sky-blue withered flowers, lay on the rude wood-pile, consigned to the menial office of affording fuel. Already the cheerful mocking-bird sent forth his varied melody, with rapture imitating the novel notes of his neighbouring songsters. The scenery was mountainous and varied, one vast wilderness, neglected and uncultivated; the very cattle appeared as wild as the bison of the prairies, and the prowling wolves (*Coyotes*) well fed, were as tame as dogs, and every night yelled familiarly through the village. In this region the Olive and the Vine throve with luxuriance and teemed with fruit; the Prickly Pears (*Cactus*) became small trees, and the rare blooming Aloe (*Agave americana*) appeared consigned without care to the hedge row of the garden.

After a perilous passage around Cape Horn, the dreary extremity of South America, amidst mountains of ice which opposed our progress in unusual array, we arrived again at the shores of the Atlantic. Once more I hailed those delightful scenes of nature with which I had been so long associated. I rambled again through the shade of the Atlantic forests, or culled some rare productions of Flora in their native wilds. But the "oft told tale" approaches to its close, and I must now bid a long adieu to the "new world," its sylvan scenes, its mountains, wilds and plains, and henceforth, in the evening of my career, I return, almost an exile to the land of my nativity!

THOMAS NUTTALL
AND F. ANDREW MICHAUX
[*The North American Sylva* (1849)]

A Country Boy Discovers Flowers

[*In England the farmer-boy essayist Richard Jefferies holds somewhat the same position among "nature writers" as Thoreau does in America. Jefferies was much less philosophical but the two actually were kin in their passionate love of the spectacle of living things.*]

BEFORE I had any conscious thought it was a delight to me to find wild flowers, just to see them. It was a pleasure to gather them and to take them home; a pleasure to show them to others—to keep them as long as they would live, to decorate the room with them, to arrange them carelessly with grasses, green sprays, tree-bloom—large branches of chestnut snapped off, and set by a picture perhaps. Without conscious thought of seasons and the advancing hours to light on the white wild violet, the meadow orchis, the blue veronica, the blue meadow cranes-bill; feeling the warmth and delight of the increasing sun-rays, but not recognizing whence or why it was joy. All the world is young to a boy, and thought has not entered into it; even the old men with gray hair do not seem old; different but not aged, the idea of age has not been mastered. A boy has to frown and study, and then does not grasp what long

years mean. The various hues of the petals pleased without any knowledge of colour-contrasts, no note even of colour except that it was
bright, and the mind was made happy without consideration of those
ideals and hopes afterwards associated with the azure sky above the fir-
tree. A fresh footpath, a fresh flower, a fresh delight. The reeds, the
grasses, the rushes—unknown and new things at every step—something
always to find; no barren spot anywhere, or sameness. Every day the
grass painted anew, and its green seen for the first time; not the old
green, but a novel hue and spectacle, like the first view of the sea.

If we had never before looked upon the earth, but suddenly
came to it man or woman grown, set down in the midst of a summer
mead, would it not seem to us a radiant vision? The hues, the shapes, the
song and life of birds, above all the sunlight, the breath of heaven, resting
on it; the mind would be filled with its glory, unable to grasp it, hardly
believing that such things could be mere matter and no more. Like a
dream of some spirit-land it would appear, scarce fit to be touched lest
it should fall to pieces, too beautiful to be long watched lest it should
fade away. So it seemed to me as a boy, sweet and new like this each
morning; and even now, after the years that have passed, and the lines
they have worn in the forehead, the summer mead shines as bright and
fresh as when my foot first touched the grass. It has another meaning
now; the sunshine and the flowers speak differently, for a heart that has
once known sorrow reads behind the page, and sees sadness in joy. But
the freshness is still there, the dew washes the colours before dawn. Unconscious happiness in finding wild flowers—unconscious and unques-
tioning, and therefore unbounded.

I used to stand by the mower and follow the scythe sweeping
down thousands of the broad-flowered daisies, the knotted knapweeds,
the blue scabious, the yellow rattles, sweeping so close and true that
nothing escaped; and yet, although I had seen so many hundreds of
each, although I had lifted armfuls day after day, still they were fresh.
They never lost their newness, and even now each time I gather a wild
flower it feels a new thing. The greenfinches came to the falling swathe
so near to us they seemed to have no fear; but I remember the yellow-
hammers most, whose colour, like that of the wild flowers and the sky,
has never faded from my memory. The greenfinches sank into the fallen
swathe, the loose grass gave under their weight and let them bathe in
flowers.

One yellowhammer sat on a branch of ash the live-long morning, still singing in the sun; his bright head, his clean bright yellow
gaudy as Spain, was drawn like a brush charged heavily with colour

across the retina, painting it deeply, for there on the eye's memory it endures, though that was boyhood and this is manhood, still unchanged. The field—Stewart's Marsh—the very tree, young ash timber, the branch projecting over the sward, I could make a map of them. Sometimes I think sun-painted colours are brighter to me than to many, and more strongly affect the nerves of the eye. Straw going by the road on a dusky winter's day seems so pleasantly golden, the sheaves lying aslant at the top, and these bundles of yellow tubes thrown up against the dark ivy on the opposite wall. Tiles, red burned, or orange coated, the sea sometimes cleanly definite, the shadows of trees in a thin wood where there is room for shadows to form and fall; some such shadows are sharper than light, and have a faint blue tint. Not only in summer but in cold winter, and not only romantic things but plain matter-of-fact things, as a waggon freshly painted red beside the wright's shop, stand out as if wet with colour and delicately pencilled at the edges. It must be out of doors; nothing indoors looks like this.

Pictures are very dull and gloomy to it, and very contrasted colours like those the French use are necessary to fix the attention. Their dashes of pink and scarlet bring the faint shadow of the sun into the room. As for our painters, their works are hung behind a curtain, and we have to peer patiently through the dusk of evening to see what they mean. Out-of-door colours do not need to be gaudy—a mere dull stake of wood thrust in the ground often stands out sharper than the pink flashes of the French studio; a faggot; the outline of a leaf; low tints without reflecting power strike the eye as a bell the ear. To me they are intensely clear, and the clearer the greater the pleasure. It is often too great, for it takes me away from solid pursuits merely to receive the impression, as water is still to reflect the trees. To me it is very painful when illness blots the definition of outdoor things, so wearisome not to see them rightly, and more oppressive than actual pain. I feel as if I was struggling to wake up with dim, half-opened lids and heavy mind. This one yellowhammer still sits on the ash branch in Stewart's Marsh over the sward, singing in the sun, his feathers freshly wet with colour, the same sun-song, and will sing to me so long as the heart shall beat.

The first conscious thought about wild flowers was to find out their names—the first conscious pleasure—and then I began to see so many that I had not previously noticed. Once you wish to identify them there is nothing escapes, down to the little white chickweed of the path and the moss of the wall. I put my hand on the bridge across the brook to lean over and look down into the water. Are there any fish? The bricks of the pier are covered with green, like a wall-painting to the surface of the stream, mosses along the lines of the mortar, and among the moss little plants—what are these? In the dry sunlit lane I look up to the top of the great wall about some domain, where the green figs look over upright on their stalks; there are dry plants on the coping— what are these? Some growing thus, high in the air, on stone, and in the chinks of the tower, suspended in dry air and sunshine; some low down under the arch of the bridge over the brook, out of sight utterly, unless you stoop by the brink of the water and project yourself forward to examine under. The kingfisher sees them as he shoots through the barrel of the culvert. There the sun direct never shines upon them, but the sunlight thrown up by the ripples runs all day in bright bars along the vault of the arch, playing on them. The stream arranges the sand in the shallow in bars, minute fixed undulations; the stream arranges the sunshine in successive flashes, undulating as if the sun, drowsy in the heat, were idly closing and unclosing his eyelids for sleep. Plants everywhere, hiding behind every tree, under the leaves, in the shady places, beside the dry furrows of the field; they are only just behind something, hidden openly. The instant you look for them they multiply a hundredfold; if you sit on the beach and begin to count the pebbles by you, their number instantly increases to infinity by virtue of that conscious act.

The bird's-foot lotus was the first. The boy must have seen it, must have trodden on it in the bare woodland pastures, certainly run about on it, with wet naked feet from the bathing; but the boy was not conscious of it. This was the first, when the desire came to identify and to know, fixing upon it by means of a pale and feeble picture. In the largest pasture there were different soils and climates; it was so large it seemed a little country of itself then—the more so because the ground rose and fell, making a ridge to divide the view and enlarge by uncertainty. The high sandy soil on the ridge where the rabbits had their warren; the rocky soil of the quarry; the long grass by the elms where the rooks built, under whose nests there were vast unpalatable mushrooms—the true mushrooms with salmon gills grew nearer the warren; the slope towards the nut-tree hedge and spring. Several climates in one field: the wintry ridge over which leaves were always driving in all four seasons of the year; the level sunny plain and fallen cromlech still tall enough for a gnomon and to cast its shadow in the treeless drought; the moist, warm, grassy depression; the lotus-grown slope, warm and dry.

If you have been living in one house in the country for some time, and then go on a visit to another, though hardly half a mile distant, you will find a change in the air, the feeling, and tone of the place. It is close by, but it is not the same. To discover these minute differences,

which make one locality healthy and home happy, and the next adjoining unhealthy, the Chinese have invented the science of Feng-shui,
spying about with cabalistic mystery, casting the horoscope of an acre.
There is something in all superstitions; they are often the foundation of
science. Superstition having made the discovery, science composes a
lecture on the reason why, and claims the credit. Bird's-foot lotus means
a fortunate spot, dry, warm—so far as soil is concerned. If you were
going to live out of doors, you might safely build your kibitka where
you found it. Wandering with the pictured flower-book, just purchased,
over the windy ridge where last year's skeleton leaves, blown out from
the alder copse below, came on with grasshopper motion—lifted and
laid down by the wind, lifted and laid down—I sat on the sward of the
sheltered slope, and instantly recognized the orange-red claws of the
flower beside me. That was the first; and this very morning, I dread to
consider how many years afterwards, I found a plant on a wall which
I do not know. I shall have to trace out its genealogy and emblazon its
shield. So many years and still only at the beginning—the beginning, too,
of the beginning—for as yet I have not thought of the garden or conservatory flowers (which are wild flowers somewhere), or of the tropics,
or the prairies. . . .

    I came every day to walk slowly up and down the plain road,
by the starry flowers under the ash-green boughs; ash is the coolest,
softest green. The bees went drifting over by my head; as they cleared
the hedges they passed by my ears, the wind singing in their shrill wings.
White tent-walls of cloud—a warm white, being full to overflowing of
sunshine—stretched across from ash-top to ash-top, a cloud-canvas roof,
a tent-palace of the delicious air. For of all things there is none so sweet
as sweet air—one great flower it is, drawn round about, over, and enclosing, like Aphrodite's arms; as if the dome of the sky were a bell-flower
drooping down over us, and the magical essence of it filling all the room
of the earth. Sweetest of all things is wild-flower air. Full of their ideal
the starry flowers strained upwards on the bank, striving to keep above
the rude grasses that pushed by them; genius has ever had such a struggle. The plain road was made beautiful by the many thoughts it gave.
I came every morning to stay by the star-lit bank.

    A friend said, "Why do you go the same road every day?
Why not have a change and walk somewhere else sometimes? Why
keep on up and down the same place?" I could not answer; till then it
had not occurred to me that I did always go one way; as for the reason
of it I could not tell; I continued in my old mind while the summers
went away. Not till years afterwards was I able to see why I went the

same round and did not care for change. I do not want change: I want the same old and loved things, the same wild-flowers, the same trees and soft ash-green; the turtle-doves, the blackbirds, the coloured yellow-hammer sing, sing, singing so long as there is light to cast a shadow on the dial, for such is the measure of his song, and I want them in the same place. Let me find them morning after morning, the starry-white petals radiating, striving upwards to their ideal. Let me see the idle shadows resting on the white dust; let me hear the humble-bees, and stay to look down on the rich dandelion disk. Let me see the very thistles opening their great crowns—I should miss the thistles; the reed-grasses hiding the moorhen; the bryony bine, at first crudely ambitious and lifted by force of youthful sap straight above the hedgerow to sink of its own weight presently and progress with crafty tendrils; swifts shot through the air with outstretched wings like crescent-headed shaftless arrows darted from the clouds; the chaffinch with a feather in her bill; all the living staircase of the spring, step by step, upwards to the great gallery of the summer—let me watch the same succession year by year.

RICHARD JEFFERIES
[*The Open Air* (1885)]

Wild Gardens of the Yosemite

[*If Richard Jefferies was a tamer Thoreau, John Muir was a wilder one. He wandered as freely over the vast stretches of the western mountains as Thoreau did over his small parish.*]

W H E N California was wild, it was the floweriest part of the continent. And perhaps it is so still, notwithstanding the lowland flora has in great part vanished before the farmers' flocks and ploughs. So exuberant was the bloom of the main valley of the state, it would still have been extravagantly rich had ninety-nine out of every hundred of its crowded flowers been taken away—far flowerier than the beautiful prairies of Illinois and Wisconsin, or the savannas of the Southern states. In the early spring it was a smooth, evenly planted sheet of purple and gold, one mass of bloom more than four hundred miles long, with scarce a green leaf in sight.

Still more interesting is the rich and wonderfully varied flora of the mountains. Going up the Sierra across the Yosemite Park to the Summit peaks, thirteen thousand feet high, you find as much variety in the vegetation as in the scenery. Change succeeds change with bewildering rapidity, for in a few days you pass through as many climates and floras, ranged one above another, as you would in walking along the lowlands to the Arctic Ocean.

And to the variety due to climate there is added that caused by the topographical features of the different regions. Again, the vegetation is profoundly varied by the peculiar distribution of the soil and moisture. Broad and deep moraines, ancient and well weathered, are spread over the lower regions, rough and comparatively recent and unweathered moraines over the middle and upper regions, alternating with bare ridges and domes and glacier-polished pavements, the highest in the icy recesses of the peaks, raw and shifting, some of them being still in process of formation, and of course scarcely planted as yet.

Besides these main soil-beds there are many others comparatively small, reformations of both glacial and weather soils, sifted, sorted out, and deposited by running water and the wind on gentle slopes and in all sorts of hollows, pot-holes, valleys, lake basins, etc.—some in dry and breezy situations, others sheltered and kept moist by lakes, streams, and waftings of waterfall spray, making comfortable homes for plants widely varied. In general, glaciers give soil to high and low places almost alike, while water currents are dispensers of special blessings, constantly tending to make the ridges poorer and the valleys richer. Glaciers mingle all kinds of material together, mud particles and boulders fifty feet in diameter: water, whether in oozing currents or passionate torrents, discriminates both in the size and shape of the material it carries. Glacier mud is the finest meal ground for any use in the Park, and its transportation into lakes and as foundations for flowery garden meadows was the first work that the young rivers were called on to do. Bogs occur only in shallow alpine basins where the climate is cool enough for sphagnum, and where the surrounding topographical conditions are such that they are safe, even in the most copious rains and thaws, from the action of flood currents capable of carrying rough gravel and sand, but where the water supply is nevertheless constant. The mosses dying from year to year gradually give rise to those rich spongy peat-beds in which so many of our best alpine plants delight to dwell. The strong winds that occasionally sweep the high Sierra play a more important part in the distribution of special soil-beds than is at first sight recognized, carrying forward considerable quantities of sand and gravel, flakes of mica, etc., and depositing them in fields and beds beautifully ruffled and embroidered and adapted to the wants of some of the hardiest and handsomest of the alpine shrubs and flowers. The more resisting of the smooth, solid, glacier-polished domes and ridges can hardly be said to have any soil at all, while others beginning to give way to the weather are thinly sprinkled with coarse angular gravel. Some of them are full of crystals, which as the surface of the rock is decomposed are set free, covering the summits and rolling down the sides in minute avalanches, giving rise to zones and beds of crystalline soil. In some instances the various crystals occur only here and there, sprinkled in the gray gravel like daisies in a sod; but in others half or more is made up of crystals, and the glow of the imbedded or loosely strewn gems and their colored gleams and glintings at different times of the day when the sun is shining might well exhilarate the flowers that grow among them, and console them for being so completely outshone.

These radiant sheets and belts and dome-encircling rings of crystals are the most beautiful of all the Sierra soil-beds, while the huge taluses ranged along the walls of the great cañons are the deepest and roughest. Instead of being slowly weathered and accumulated from the cliffs overhead like common taluses, they were all formed suddenly and simultaneously by an earthquake that occurred at least three centuries ago. Though thus hurled into existence at a single effort, they are the least changeable and destructible of all the soil formations in the range. Excepting those which were launched directly into the channels of rivers, scarcely one of their wedged and interlocked boulders has been moved since the day of their creation, and though mostly made up of huge angular blocks of granite, many of them from ten to fifty feet cube, trees and shrubs make out to live and thrive on them, and even delicate herbaceous plants—draperia, collomia, zauschneria, etc.—soothing their rugged features with gardens and groves. In general views of the Park scarce a hint is given of its floral wealth. Only by patiently, lovingly sauntering about in it will you discover that it is all more or less flowery, the forests as well as the open spaces, and the mountain tops and rugged slopes around the glaciers as well as the sunny meadows.

Even the majestic cañon cliffs, seemingly absolutely flawless for thousands of feet and necessarily doomed to eternal sterility, are cheered with happy flowers on invisible niches and ledges wherever the slightest grip for a root can be found; as if Nature, like an enthusiastic gardener, could not resist the temptation to plant flowers everywhere. On high, dry rocky summits and plateaus, most of the plants are so small they make but little show even when in bloom. But in the opener parts of the main forests, the meadows, stream banks, and the level floors of Yosemite valleys the vegetation is exceedingly rich in flowers, some of the lilies and larkspurs being from eight to ten feet high. And on the upper meadows there are miles of blue gentians and daisies, white and blue violets; and great breadths of rosy purple heathworts covering rocky moraines with a marvelous abundance of bloom, enlivened by humming-birds, butterflies and a host of other insects as beautiful as flowers. In the lower and middle regions, also, many of the most extensive beds of bloom are in great part made by shrubs—adenostoma, manzanita, ceanothus, chamaebatia, cherry, rose, rubus, spiraea, shad, laurel, azalea, honeysuckle, calycanthus, ribes, philadelphus, and many others, the sunny spaces about them bright and fragrant with mints, lupines, geraniums, lilies, daisies, goldenrods, castilleias, gilias, pentstemons, etc.

Adenostoma fasciculatum is a handsome, hardy, heathlike shrub belonging to the rose family, flourishing on dry ground below the pine belt, and often covering areas of twenty or thirty square miles of rolling sun-beaten hills and dales with a dense, dark green, almost impenetrable chaparral, which in the distance looks like Scotch heather. It is about six to eight feet high, has slender elastic branches, red shreddy bark, needle-shaped leaves, and small white flowers in panicles about a foot long, making glorious sheets of fragrant bloom in the spring. To running fires it offers no resistance, vanishing with the few other flowery shrubs and vines and liliaceous plants that grow with it about as fast as dry grass, leaving nothing but ashes. But with wonderful vigor it rises again and again in fresh beauty from the root, and calls back to its hospitable mansions the multitude of wild animals that had to flee for their lives.

As soon as you enter the pine woods you meet the charming little Chamaebatia foliolosa, one of the handsomest of the Park shrubs, next in fineness and beauty to the heathworts of the alpine regions. Like adenostoma it belongs to the rose family, is from twelve to eighteen inches high, has brown bark, slender branches, white flowers like those of the strawberry, and thrice-pinnate glandular, yellow-green leaves, finely cut and fernlike, as if unusual pains had been taken in fashioning them. Where there is plenty of sunshine at an elevation of three thousand to six thousand feet, it makes a close, continuous growth, leaf touching leaf over hundreds of acres, spreading a handsome mantle beneath the yellow and sugar pines. Here and there a lily rises above it, an arching bunch of tall bromus, and at wide intervals a rosebush or clump of ceanothus or manzanita, but there are no rough weeds mixed with it—no roughness of any sort.

Perhaps the most widely distributed of all the Park shrubs and of the Sierra in general, certainly the most strikingly characteristic, are the many species of manzanita (*Arctostaphylos*). Though one species, the Uva-ursi, or bearberry—the kinikinic of the Western Indians—extends around the world, the greater part of them are Californian. They are mostly from four to ten feet high, round-headed, with innumerable branches, brown or red bark, pale green leaves set on edge, and a rich profusion of small, pink, narrow-throated, urn-shaped flowers like those of arbutus. The branches are knotty, zigzaggy, and about as rigid as bones, and the bark is so thin and smooth, both trunk and branches seem to be naked, looking as if they had been peeled, polished, and painted red. The wood also is red, hard, and heavy.

These grand bushes seldom fail to engage the attention of the traveler and hold it, especially if he has to pass through closely planted fields of them such as grow on moraine slopes at an elevation of about seven thousand feet, and in cañons choked with earthquake boulders; for they make the most uncompromisingly stubborn of all chaparral. Even bears take pains to go around the stoutest patches if possible, and when compelled to force a passage leave tufts of hair and broken branches to mark their way, while less skillful mountaineers under like circumstances sometimes lose most of their clothing and all their temper.

The manzanitas like sunny ground. On warm ridges and sandy flats at the foot of sun-beaten cañon cliffs, some of the tallest specimens have well-defined trunks six inches to a foot or more thick, and stand apart in orchard-like growths which in bloomtime are among the finest garden sights in the Park. The largest I ever saw had a round, slightly fluted trunk nearly four feet in diameter, which at a height of only eighteen inches from the ground dissolved into a wilderness of branches, rising and spreading to a height and width of about twelve feet. In spring every bush over all the mountains is covered with rosy flowers, in autumn with fruit. The red pleasantly acid berries, about the size of peas, are like little apples, and the hungry mountaineer is glad to eat them, though half their bulk is made up of hard seeds. Indians, bears, coyotes, foxes, birds, and other mountain people live on them for months.

Associated with manzanita there are six or seven species of ceanothus, flowery, fragrant, and altogether delightful shrubs, growing in glorious abundance in the forests on sunny or half-shaded ground, up to an elevation of about nine thousand feet above the sea. In the sugar-pine woods the most beautiful species is C. integerrimus, often called California lilac, or deer brush. It is five or six feet high, smooth, slender, willowy, with bright foliage and abundance of blue flowers in close, showy panicles. Two species, prostratus and procumbens, spread handsome blue-flowered mats and rugs on warm ridges beneath the pines, and offer delightful beds to the tired mountaineers. The commonest species, C. cordulatus, is mostly restricted to the silver fir belt. It is white-flowered and thorny, and makes extensive thickets of tangled chaparral, far too dense to wade through, and too deep and loose to walk on, though it is pressed flat every winter by ten or fifteen feet of snow.

Above these thorny beds, sometimes mixed with them, a very wild, red-fruited cherry grows in magnificent tangles, fragrant and white as snow when in bloom. The fruit is small and rather bitter, not so good as the black, puckery chokecherry that grows in the cañons, but thrushes, robins, chipmunks like it. Below the cherry tangles, chinquapin and goldcup oak spread generous mantles of chaparral, and with hazel and ribes thickets in adjacent glens help to clothe and adorn the rocky wilderness, and produce food for the many mouths Nature has to fill. Azalea occidentalis is the glory of cool streams and meadows. It is from two to five feet high, has bright green leaves and a rich profusion of large, fragrant white and yellow flowers, which are in prime beauty in June, July, and August, according to the elevation (from three thousand to six thousand feet). Only the purple-flowered rhododendron of the redwood forests rivals or surpasses it in superb abounding bloom.

Back a little way from the azalea-bordered streams, a small wild rose makes thickets, often several acres in extent, deliciously fragrant on dewy mornings and after showers, the fragrance mingled with the music of birds nesting in them. And not far from these rose gardens Rubus Nutkanus covers the ground with broad velvety leaves and pure white flowers as large as those of its neighbor the rose, and finer in texture; followed at the end of summer by soft red berries good for bird and beast and man also. This is the commonest and the most beautiful of the whole blessed flowery fruity genus.

The glory of the alpine region in bloomtime are the heathworts, cassiope, bryanthus, kalmia, and vaccinium, enriched here and there by the alpine honeysuckle, Lonicera conjugialis, and by the purple-flowered Primula suffruticosa, the only primrose discovered in California, and the only shrubby species in the genus. The lowly, hardy, adventurous cassiope has exceedingly slender creeping branches, scalelike leaves, and pale pink or white waxen bell flowers. Few plants, large or small, so well endure hard weather and rough ground over so great a range. In July it spreads a wavering, interrupted belt of the loveliest bloom around glacier lakes and meadows and across wild moory expanses, between roaring streams, all along the Sierra, and northward beneath cold skies by way of the mountain chains of Oregon, Washington, British Columbia, and Alaska, to the Arctic regions; gradually descending, until at the north end of the continent it reaches the level of the sea; blooming as profusely and at about the same time on mossy frozen tundras as on the high Sierra moraines.

Bryanthus, the companion of cassiope, accompanies it as far north as southeastern Alaska, where together they weave thick plushy beds on rounded mountain tops above the glaciers. It grows mostly at slightly lower elevations; the upper margin of what may be called the bryanthus belt in the Sierra, uniting with and overlapping the lower margin of the cassiope. The wide bell-shaped flowers are bright purple, about three fourths of an inch in diameter, hundreds to the square yard, the young branches, mostly erect, being covered with them. No Highlander in heather enjoys more luxurious rest than the Sierra mountaineer in a bed of blooming bryanthus. And imagine the show on calm dewy mornings, when there is a radiant globe in the throat of every flower, and smaller gems on the needle-shaped leaves, the sunbeams pouring through them.

In the same wild, cold region the tiny Vaccinium myrtillus, mixed with kalmia and dwarf willows, spread thinner carpets, the down-pressed matted leaves profusely sprinkled with pink bells; and on higher sandy slopes you will find several alpine species of eriogonum with gorgeous bossy masses of yellow bloom, and the lovely Arctic daisy with many blessed companions; charming plants, gentle mountaineers, Nature's darlings, which seem always the finer the higher and stormier their homes. . . .

Considering the lilies as you go up the mountains, the first you come to is L. Pardalinum, with large orange-yellow, purple-spotted flowers big enough for babies' bonnets. It is seldom found higher than thirty-five hundred feet above the sea, grows in magnificent groups of fifty to a hundred or more, in romantic waterfall dells in the pine woods shaded by overarching maple and willow, alder and dogwood, with bushes in front of the embowering trees for a border, and ferns and sedges in front of the bushes; while the bed of black humus in which the bulbs are set is carpeted with mosses and liverworts. These richly furnished lily gardens are the pride of the falls on the lower tributaries of the Tuolumne and Merced rivers, falls not like those of Yosemite valleys—coming from the sky with rock-shaking thunder tones—but small, with low, kind voices cheerily singing in calm leafy bowers, self-contained, keeping their snowy skirts well about them, yet furnishing plenty of spray for the lilies.

The Washington lily (*L. Washingtonianum*) is white, deliciously fragrant, moderate in size, with three to ten flowered racemes. The largest I ever measured was eight feet high, the raceme two feet long, with fifty-two flowers, fifteen of them open; the others had faded or were still in the bud. This famous lily is distributed over the sunny portions of the sugar-pine woods, never in large garden companies like pardalinum, but widely scattered, standing up to the waist in dense ceanothus and manzanita chaparral, waving its lovely flowers above the blooming wilderness of brush, and giving their fragrance to the breeze. These stony, thorny jungles are about the last places in the mountains in which one would look for lilies. But though they toil not nor spin, like other people under adverse circumstances, they have to do the best they can. Because their large bulbs are good to eat they are dug up by Indians and bears; therefore, like hunted animals, they seek refuge in the chaparral, where among the boulders and tough tangled roots they are comparatively safe. This is the favorite Sierra lily, and it is now growing in all the best parks and gardens of the world.

The showiest gardens in the Park lie imbedded in the silver fir forests on the top of the main dividing ridges or hang like gayly colored scarfs down their sides. Their wet places are in great part taken up by veratrum, a robust broad-leaved plant determined to be seen, and habenaria and spiranthes; the drier parts by tall columbines, larkspurs, castilleias, lupines, hosackias, erigerons, valerian, etc., standing deep in grass, with violets here and there around the borders. But the finest feature of these forest gardens is Lilium parvum. It varies greatly in size, the tallest being from six to nine feet high, with splendid racemes of ten to fifty small orange-colored flowers, which rock and wave with great dignity above the other flowers in the infrequent winds that fall over the protecting wall of trees. Though rather frail-looking it is strong, reaching prime vigor and beauty eight thousand feet above the sea, and in some places venturing as high as eleven thousand.

Calochortus, or Mariposa tulip, is a unique genus of many species confined to the California side of the continent; charming plants, somewhat resembling the tulips of Europe, but far finer. The richest calochortus region lies below the western boundary of the Park; still five or six species are included. C. Nuttallii is common on moraines in the forests of the two-leaved pine; and C. caeruleus and nudus, very slender, lowly species, may be found in moist garden spots near Yose-

mite. C. albus, with pure white flowers, growing in shady places among
the foothill shrubs, is, I think, the very loveliest of all the lily family—
a spotless soul, plant saint, that every one must love and so be made
better. It puts the wildest mountaineer on his good behavior. With this
plant the whole world would seem rich though none other existed. Next
after Calochortus, Brodiaea is the most interesting genus. Nearly all the
many species have beautiful showy heads of blue, lilac, and yellow
flowers, enriching the gardens of the lower pine region. Other liliaceous
plants likely to attract attention are the blue-flowered camassia, the bulbs
of which are prized as food by Indians; fritillaria, smilacina, chloragalum,
and the twining climbing stropholirion. . . .

Thousands of the most interesting gardens in the Park are never
seen, for they are small and lie far up on ledges and terraces of the sheer
cañon walls, wherever a strip of soil, however narrow and shallow, can
rest. The birds, winds, and down-washing rains have planted them with
all sorts of hardy mountain flowers, and where there is sufficient moisture
they flourish in profusion. Many of them are watered by little streams
that seem lost on the tremendous precipices, clinging to the face of the
rock in lacelike strips, and dripping from ledge to ledge, too silent to be
called falls, pathless wanderers from the upper meadows, which for
centuries have been seeking a way down to the rivers they belong to,
without having worn as yet any appreciable channel, mostly evaporated
or given to the plants they meet before reaching the foot of the cliffs.
To these unnoticed streams the finest of the cliff gardens owe their
luxuriance and freshness of beauty. In the larger ones ferns and showy
flowers flourish in wonderful profusion—woodwardia, columbine, collomia, castilleia, draperia, geranium, erythraea, pink and scarlet mimulus,
hosackia, saxifrage, sunflowers and daisies, and azalea, spiraea, and calycanthus, a few specimens of each that seem to have been culled from the
large gardens above and beneath them. Even lilies are occasionally found
in these irrigated cliff gardens, swinging their bells over the giddy
precipices, seemingly as happy as their relatives down in the waterfall
dells. Most of the cliff gardens, however, are dependent on summer
showers, and though from the shallowness of the soil-beds they are often
dry, they still display a surprising number of bright flowers—scarlet
zauschneria, purple bush penstemon, mints, gilias, and bosses of glowing
golden bahia. Nor is there any lack of commoner plants; the homely
yarrow is often found in them, and sweet clover and honeysuckle for
the bees.

In the upper cañons, where the walls are inclined at so low an
angle that they are loaded with moraine material, through which peren-

nial streams percolate in broad diffused currents, there are long wavering garden beds, that seem to be descending through the forest like cascades, their fluent lines suggesting motion, swaying from side to side of the forested banks, surging up here and there over island-like boulder piles, or dividing and flowing around them. In some of these floral cascades the vegetation is chiefly sedges and grasses ruffled with willows; in others showy flowers like those of the lily gardens on the main divides. Another curious and picturesque series of wall gardens are made by thin streams that ooze slowly from moraines and slip gently over smooth glaciated slopes. From particles of sand and mud they carry, a pair of lobe-shaped sheets of soil an inch or two thick are gradually formed, one of them hanging down from the brow of the slope, the other leaning up from the foot of it, like stalactite and stalagmite, the soil being held together by the flowery, moisture-loving plants growing in it.

JOHN MUIR
[*Our National Parks* (1901)]

John Burroughs Takes a Walk

[*John Burroughs may have been a lesser man than either Thoreau or Muir, but he was far more widely read—partly at least because Theodore Roosevelt helped make him in the popular mind the representative defender of the simple life in a more and more complex civilization.*]

NEARLY every season I make the acquaintance of one or more new flowers. It takes years to exhaust the botanical treasures of any one considerable neighborhood, unless one makes a dead set at it, like an herbalist. One likes to have his floral acquaintances come to him easily and naturally, like his other friends. Some pleasant occasion should bring you together.

Several of our harmless little wild flowers have been absurdly named out of the old mythologies: thus, Indian cucumber root, one of Thoreau's favorite flowers, is named after the sorceress Medea and is called "medeola," because it was at one time thought to possess rare medicinal properties; and medicine and sorcery have always been more or less confounded in the opinion of mankind. It is a pretty and decorative sort of plant with, when perfect, two stages or platforms of leaves, one above the other. You see a whorl of five or six leaves, a foot or more from the ground, which seems to bear a standard with another whorl of three leaves at the top of it. The small, yellowish, recurved flowers shoot out from above this top whorl. The whole expression of the plant is singularly slender and graceful. Sometimes, probably the first year, it only attains to the first circle of leaves. This is the platform from which it will rear its flower column the next year. Its white, tuberous root is crisp and tender and leaves in the mouth distinctly the taste of cucumber. Whether or not the Indians used it as a relish as we do the cucumber, I do not know.

Still another pretty flower that perpetuates the name of a Grecian nymph, a flower that was a new find to me a few summers ago, is the arethusa. Arethusa was one of the nymphs who attended Diana and was by that goddess turned into a fountain, that she might escape the god of the river, Alpheus, who became desperately in love with her on seeing her at her bath. Our arethusa is one of the prettiest of the orchids and has been pursued through many a marsh and quaking bog by her lovers. She is a bright pink-purple flower an inch or more long, with the odor of sweet violets. The sepals and petals rise up and arch over the column, which we may call the heart of the flower, as if shielding it. In Plymouth County, Massachusetts, where the arethusa seems common, I have heard it called Indian pink.

My second new acquaintance the same season was the showy lady's-slipper. Most of the floral ladies leave their slippers in swampy places in the woods; only the stemless one (*Cypripedium acaule*) leaves hers on dry ground before she reaches the swamp, commonly under evergreen trees, where the carpet of pine needles will not hurt her feet. But one may penetrate many wet, mucky places in the woods before he finds the prettiest of them all, the showy lady's-slipper—the prettiest slipper, but the stoutest and coarsest plant; the flower large and very showy, white, tinged with purple in front; the stem two feet high, very leafy, and coarser than bearweed. Report had come to me, through my botanizing neighbor, that in a certain quaking sphagnum bog in the woods the showy lady's-slipper could be found. The locality proved to be the marrowy grave of an extinct lake or black tarn. On the borders of it the white azalea was in bloom, fast fading. In the midst of it were spruces and black ash and giant ferns and, low in the spongy, mossy bottom, the pitcher plant. The lady's-slipper grew in little groups and companies all about. Never have I beheld a prettier sight—so gay, so festive, so holiday looking. Were they so many gay bonnets rising above the foliage? or were they flocks of white doves with purple-stained breasts just lifting up their wings to take flight? or were they little fleets of fairy boats, with sail set, tossing on a mimic sea of wild, weedy growths? Such images throng the mind on recalling the scene and only faintly hint its beauty and animation. The long, erect, white sepals do much to give the alert, tossing look which the flower wears. The dim light, too, of its secluded haunts, and its snowy purity and freshness, contribute to the impression it makes. The purple tinge is like a stain of wine which has slightly overflowed the brim of the inflated lip or sac and run part way down its snowy sides.

This lady's-slipper is one of the rarest and choicest of our wild flowers, and its haunts and its beauty are known only to the few.

A few summers ago I struck a new and beautiful plant in the shape of a weed that had only recently appeared in that part of the country. I was walking through an August meadow when I saw, on a little knoll, a bit of most vivid orange, verging on a crimson. I knew of no flower of such a complexion frequenting such a place as that. On investigation, it proved to be a stranger. It had a rough, hairy, leafless stem about a foot high, surmounted by a corymbose cluster of flowers or flower heads of dark vivid orange color. The leaves were deeply notched and toothed, very bristly, and were pressed flat to the ground. The whole plant was a veritable Esau for hairs, and it seemed to lay hold upon the ground as if it was not going to let go easily. And what a fiery plume it had!

The next day, in another field a mile away, I chanced upon more of the flowers. On making inquiry, I found that a small patch or colony of the plants had appeared that season or had first been noticed then, in a meadow well known to me from boyhood. They had been cut down with the grass in early July, and the first week in August had shot up and bloomed again. I found the spot aflame with them. Their leaves covered every inch of the surface where they stood, and not a spear of grass grew there. They were taking slow but complete possession; they were devouring the meadow by inches. The plant seemed to be a species of hieracium, or hawkweed, or some closely allied species of the composite family, but I could not find it mentioned in our botanies.

A few days later, on the edge of an adjoining county ten miles distant, I found, probably, its headquarters. It had appeared there a few years before and was thought to have escaped from some farmer's door-yard. Patches of it were appearing here and there in the fields, and the farmers were thoroughly alive to the danger and were fighting it like fire. Its seeds are winged like those of the dandelion, and it sows itself far and near. It would be a beautiful acquisition to our midsummer fields, supplying a tint as brilliant as that given by the scarlet poppies to English grain fields. But it would be an expensive one, as it usurps the land completely.*

Our seacoast flowers are probably more brilliant in color than the same flowers in the interior. I thought the wild rose on the Massachusetts coast deeper tinted and more fragrant than those I was used to. The steeplebush, or hardhack, had more color, as had the rose gerardia and several other plants.

But when vivid color is wanted, what can surpass or equal our cardinal flower? There is a glow about this flower as if color emanated from it as from a live coal. The eye is baffled and does not seem to reach the surface of the petal; it does not see the texture or material part as it does in other flowers, but rests in a steady, still radiance. It is not so much something colored as it is color itself. And then the moist, cool, shady places it affects, usually where it has no floral rivals and where the large, dark shadows need just such a dab of fire! Often, too, we see it double, its reflected image in some dark pool heightening its effect. I never have found it with its only rival in color, the monarda or bee balm, a species of mint. Farther north, the cardinal flower seems to fail, and the monarda takes its place, growing in similar localities. It stands up two feet high or more, and the flowers show like a broad scarlet cap.

The only thing I have seen in this country that calls to mind the green grain fields of Britain splashed with scarlet poppies may be witnessed in August in the marshes of the lower Hudson, when the broad sedgy and flaggy spaces are sprinkled with the great marsh mallow. It is a most pleasing spectacle—level stretches of dark green flag or waving marsh grass kindled on every square yard by the bright pink blossoms, like great burning coals fanned in the breeze. The mallow is not so deeply colored as the poppy, but it is much larger and has the tint of youth and happiness. It is an immigrant from Europe, but it is making itself at home in our great river meadows.

The same day your eye is attracted by the mallows, as your train skirts or cuts through the broad marshes, it will revel with delight in the masses of fresh bright color afforded by the purple loosestrife,

* This observation was made ten years ago. I have since learned that the plant is *Hieracium aurantiacum*, from Europe, a kind of hawkweed. It is fast becoming a common weed in New York and New England.

which grows in similar localities and shows here and there like purple bonfires. It is a tall plant, grows in dense masses, and affords a most striking border to the broad spaces dotted with the mallow. It, too, came to us from overseas and first appeared along the Wallkill many years ago.

One sometimes seems to discover a familiar wild flower anew by coming upon it in some peculiar and striking situation. Our columbine is at all times and in all places one of the most exquisitely beautiful of flowers; yet one spring day, when I saw it growing out of a small seam on the face of a great lichen-covered wall of rock, where no soil or mold was visible—a jet of foliage and color shooting out of a black line on the face of a perpendicular mountain wall and rising up like a tiny fountain, its drops turning to flame-colored jewels that hung and danced in the air against the gray rocky surface—its beauty became something magical and audacious. On little narrow shelves in the rocky wall the corydalis was blooming, and among the loose boulders at its base the bloodroot shone conspicuous, suggesting snow rather than anything more sanguine.

ARBUTUS

Sequestered flower of April days,
Thy covert bloom in forest ways
    A spell about me weaves;
Thy frosted petals faint pink glow,
Crystals pure like urns of snow
That all with incense overflow,
Half hid beneath the leaves.

Certain flowers one makes special expeditions for every season. They are limited in their ranges and must generally be sought for in particular haunts. How many excursions to the woods does the delicious trailing arbutus give rise to! There are arbutus days in one's calendar, days when the trailing flower fairly calls him to the woods. With me, they come the latter part of April. The grass is greening here and there on the moist slopes and by the spring runs; the first furrow has been struck by the farmer; the liverleaf is in the height of its beauty, and the bright constellations of the bloodroot shine out here and there.

The arriving swallows twitter above the woods; the first che-wink rustles the dry leaves; the northward-bound thrushes, the hermit and the gray-cheeked, flit here and there before you. The robin, the sparrow, and the bluebird are building their first nests, and the first shad are making their way slowly up the Hudson. Indeed, the season is fairly under way when the trailing arbutus comes. Now look out for troops of boys and girls going to the woods to gather it! and let them look out that in their greed they do not exterminate it. Within reach of our large towns, the choicer spring wild flowers are hunted mercilessly. Every fresh party from town raids them as if bent upon their destruction. One day, about ten miles from one of our Hudson River cities, there got into the train six young women loaded down with vast sheaves and bundles of trailing arbutus. Each one of them had enough for forty. They had apparently made a clean sweep of the woods. It was a pretty sight—the pink and white of the girls and the pink and white of the flowers! And the car, too, was suddenly filled with perfume—the breath of spring loaded the air; but I thought it a pity to ravish the woods in that way. The next party was probably equally greedy and, because a handful was desirable, thought an armful proportionately so; till, by and by, the flower will be driven from those woods.

Another flower that one makes special excursions for is the pond lily. The pond lily is a star and easily takes the first place among lilies; and the expeditions to her haunts and the gathering her where she rocks upon the dark secluded waters of some pool or lakelet are the crown and summit of the floral expeditions of summer. It is the expedition about which more things gather than almost any other: you want your boat, you want your lunch, you want your friend or friends with you. You are going to put in the greater part of the day; you are going to picnic in the woods and indulge in a "green thought in a green shade." When my friend and I go for pond lilies, we have to traverse a distance of three miles with our boat in a wagon. The road is what is called a "back road," and leads through woods most of the way. Black Pond, where the lilies grow, lies about one hundred feet higher than the Hudson, from which it is separated by a range of rather bold wooded heights, one of which might well be called Mount Hymettus, for I have found a great deal of wild honey in the forest that covers it.

Our road leads us along this stream, across its rude bridges, through dark hemlock and pine woods under gray, rocky walls, now past a black pool, then within sight or hearing of a foaming rapid or fall, till we strike the outlet of the long level that leads to the lake. In this we launch our boat and paddle slowly upward over its dark surface, now pushing our way through half-submerged treetops, then ducking under the trunk of an overturned tree which bridges the stream and makes a convenient way for the squirrels and wood mice, or else forcing the boat over it when it is sunk a few inches below the surface.

As we come in sight of the lilies, where they cover the water at the outlet of the lake, a brisk gust of wind, as if it had been waiting to surprise us, sweeps down and causes every leaf to leap from the water and show its pink underside. Was it a fluttering of hundreds of wings, or the clapping of a multitude of hands? But there rocked the lilies with their golden hearts open to the sun and their tender white petals as fresh as crystals of snow. What a queenly flower, indeed, the type of un-sullied purity and sweetness! Its root, like a black, corrugated, ugly reptile, clinging to the slime, but its flower in purity and whiteness like a star. There is something very pretty in the closed bud making its way up through the water to meet the sun; and there is something touching in the flower closing itself up again after its brief career and slowly burying itself beneath the dark wave. One almost fancies a sad, regretful look in it as the stem draws it downward to mature its seed on the sunless bottom. The pond lily is a flower of the morning; it closes a little after noon.

In our walks we note the most showy and beautiful flowers but not always the most interesting. Who, for instance, pauses to con-sider that early species of everlasting, commonly called mouse-ear, that grows nearly everywhere by the roadside or about poor fields? It begins to be noticeable in May, its whitish downy appearance, its groups of slender stalks crowned with a corymb of paperlike buds, contrasting it with the fresh green of surrounding grass or weeds. It is a member of a very large family, the *Compositae*, and does not attract one by its beauty; but it is interesting because of its many curious traits and habits. For instance, it is dioecious, that is, the two sexes are represented by separate plants; and what is more curious, these plants are usually found sepa-rated from each other in well-defined groups, like the men and women in an old-fashioned country church—always in groups; here a group of females, there, a few yards away, a group of males. The females may be known by their more slender and graceful appearance and, as the season advances, by their outstripping the males in growth. Indeed, they be-come real amazons in comparison with their brothers. The staminate or male plants grow but a few inches high; the heads are round and have a more dusky or freckled appearance than do the pistillate; and as soon as they have shed their pollen their work is done, they are of no further use, and by the middle of May or before, their heads droop, their stalks wither, and their general collapse sets in. Then the other sex, or pistillate plants, seem to have taken a new lease of life; they wax strong, they shoot up with the growing grass and keep their heads above it; they are alert and active; they bend in the breeze; their long, tapering flower heads take on a tinge of color, and life seems full of purpose and enjoyment with them. I have discovered, too, that they are real sun worshipers; that they turn their faces to the east in the morning and follow the sun in his course across the sky till they all bend to the west at his going down. On the other hand, their brothers have stood stiff and stupid and unresponsive to any influence of sky and air, so far as I could see, till they drooped and died.

Another curious thing is that the females seem vastly more numerous—I should say almost ten times as abundant. You have to hunt for the males; the others you see far off. One season I used every day to pass several groups or circles of females in the grass by the roadside. I noted how they grew and turned their faces sunward. I observed how alert and vigorous they were, and what a purplish tinge came over their mammae-shaped flower heads as June approached. I looked for the males; to the east, south, west, none could be found for hundreds of yards. On the north, about two hundred feet away, I found a small colony of meek and lowly males. I wondered by what agency fertilization would take place—by insects, or by the wind? I suspected it would not take place. No insects seemed to visit the flowers, and the wind surely could not be relied upon to hit the mark so far off and from such an unlikely corner, too. But by some means the vitalizing dust seemed to have been conveyed. Early in June, the plants began to shed their down, or seed-bearing pappus, still carrying their heads at the top of the grass, so that the breezes could have free access to them and sow the seeds far and wide.

As the seeds are sown broadcast by the wind, I was at first puzzled to know how the two sexes were kept separate and always in little communities, till I perceived, what I might have read in the botany, that the plant is perennial and spreads by offsets and runners, like the strawberry. This would of course keep the two kinds in groups by themselves.

Another plant which has interesting ways and is beautiful besides is the adder's-tongue, or yellow erythronium, the earliest of the lilies and one of the most pleasing. The April sunshine is fairly reflected in its revolute flowers. The lilies have bulbs that sit on or near the top of the ground. The onion is a fair type of the lily in this respect. But here is a lily with the bulb deep in the ground. How it gets there is well worth investigating. The botany says the bulb is deep in the ground, but offers no explanation. Now, it is only the bulbs of the older or flowering plants that are deep in the ground. The bulbs of the young plants are near the top of the ground. The young plants have but one leaf, the older or flowering ones have two. If you happen to be in the woods at the right time in early April, you may see these leaves compactly rolled together, piercing the matted coating of sere leaves that covers the ground like some sharp-pointed instrument. They do not burst their covering or lift it up but pierce through it like an awl.

But how does the old bulb get so deep into the ground? In digging some of them up one spring in an old meadow bottom, I had to cleave the tough fibrous sod to a depth of eight inches. The smaller ones were barely two inches below the surface. Of course they all started from the seed at the surface of the soil. The young botanist or nature lover will find here a field for original research. If, in late May or early June, after the leaves of the plant have disappeared, he finds the ground where they stood showing curious, looping, twisting growths or roots of a greenish white color, let him examine them. They are as smooth and as large as an angleworm, and very brittle. Both ends will be found in the ground, one attached to the old bulb, the other boring or drilling downward and enlarged till it suggests the new bulb. I do not know that this mother root in all cases comes to the surface. Why it should come at all is a mystery, unless it be in some way to get more power for the downward thrust. My own observations upon the subject are not complete, but I think in the foregoing I have given the clew as to how the bulb each year sinks deeper and deeper into the ground.

It is a pity that this graceful and abundant flower has no good and appropriate common name. It is the earliest of the true lilies, and it has all the grace and charm that belong to this order of flowers. *Erythronium*, its botanical name, is not good, as it is derived from a Greek word that means red, while one species of our flower is yellow and the other is white. How it came to be called "adder's-tongue" I do not know; probably from the spotted character of the leaf, which might suggest a snake, though it in no wise resembles a snake's tongue. A fawn is spotted, too, and "fawn lily" would be better than "adder's-tongue." Still better is the name "trout lily," which has recently been proposed for this plant. It blooms along the trout streams, and its leaf is as mottled as a trout's back. The name "dog's-tooth" may have been suggested by the shape and color of the bud, but how the "violet" came to be added is a puzzle, as it has not one feature of the violet. It is only another illustration of the haphazard way in which our wild flowers, as well as our birds, have been named.

In my spring rambles I have sometimes come upon a solitary specimen of this yellow lily growing beside a mossy stone where the sunshine fell full upon it, and have thought it one of the most beautiful of our wild flowers. Its two leaves stand up like a fawn's ears, and this feature, with its recurved petals, gives it an alert, wide-awake look.

Another of our common wild flowers, which I always look at with an interrogation point in my mind, is the wild ginger. Why should this plant always hide its flower? Its two fuzzy, heart-shaped green leaves stand up very conspicuously amid the rocks or mossy stones; but its one curious, brown, bell-shaped flower is always hidden beneath the moss or dry leaves, as if too modest to face the light of the open woods. As a rule, the one thing which a plant is anxious to show and to make much of, and to flaunt before all the world, is its flower. But the wild ginger reverses the rule and blooms in secret. Instead of turning upward toward the light and air, it turns downward toward the darkness and the silence. It has no corolla, but what the botanists call a lurid or brown-purple calyx, which is conspicuous like a corolla. Its root leaves in the mouth a taste precisely like that of ginger.

This plant and the closed gentian are apparent exceptions, in their manner of blooming, to the general habit of the rest of our flowers. The closed gentian does not hide its flower, but the corolla never opens; it always remains a closed bud. I used to think that this gentian could never experience the benefits of insect visits, which Darwin showed us were of such importance in the vegetable world. I once plucked one of the flowers into which a bumblebee had forced his way, but he had never come out; the flower was his tomb. I am assured, however, by recent observers, that the bumblebee does successfully enter the closed corolla, and thus distributes its pollen.

There is yet another curious exception which I will mention, namely, the witch hazel. All our trees and plants bloom in the spring except this one species; this blooms in the fall. Just as its leaves are fading and falling, its flowers appear, giving out an odor along the bushy lanes and margins of the woods that is to the nose like cool water to the hand. Why it should bloom in the fall instead of in the spring is a mystery. And it is probably because of this very curious trait that its branches are used as divining rods by certain credulous persons to point out where springs of water and precious metals are hidden.

JOHN BURROUGHS
[*Riverby* (1894) and *Signs and Seasons* (1886)]

In Defense of Weeds

[*Stretching a point, most gardeners will agree that wild flowers and even weeds have their place—but that it is not in a garden. At least one Victorian thought a little differently.*]

I N new gardens it is possible, and not very difficult, to keep the weeds under; but in old gardens it is almost impossible. It is an old and very true gardening proverb, that one year's seed is many years' weed; or as Hamlet laments, "An unweeded garden grows to seed," and so "things rank and gross in nature possess it merely." In the history of an old garden there must have often been a one year's seed; and there must be in it from time to time many an unweeded corner. But I have almost an affection for weeds, a decided affection for some of them, and I have not much sympathy with those who say that a garden is not worth looking at unless it is as clean as a newly-swept floor; it is a counsel of perfection, which I have no great wish to reach. A weed is but a good plant in the wrong place; I say a *good* plant advisedly, having a full faith that where nature plants it, it fills a right place. Daisies are not perhaps in their right place in lawns, but I should be sorry to see my lawn quite free from them, and so I am sure would the children. Buttercups have a shining beauty of petal that is not surpassed by any flower, and I do not think that Jean Ingelow's comparison of a field of buttercups to the Field of the Cloth of Gold, to the great advantage of the buttercups, is much exaggerated; but they must be kept out of the garden. The weeds that chiefly trouble me in April are the two veronicas, *V. agrestis* and *V. Buxbaumi*; either of them might lay claim to the title of "the little speedwell's darling blue," and they are so short-lived that they do little real harm; still, they give a good deal of trouble. But some weeds are so beautiful that I should certainly grow them in the garden, if only they could be kept in place, and if they were not already too abundant. I should be sorry to banish from my walls the creeping toad flax and the

yellow fumitory, and as long as they keep to the walls they do no harm. But there are two plants that are sad weeds, but which, if lost, would be sorely missed. The dandelion is one—

> The flower
> That blows a globe of after arrowlets.

Surely no other flower can surpass it for beauty of foliage, beauty of shape, and rich beauty of colouring. The second weed that I often wish to transplant into my garden, but dare not, is the goosegrass, or silver weed, *Potentilla anserina*. Its beautiful leaves have a silver sheen that make it very attractive; but it is better kept outside the garden, and it grows everywhere. It is found in the Arctic regions and it is found in New Zealand, and so has as wide a range as almost any known plant, except, perhaps, the little fern *Cystopteris fragilis*, which not only grows as far north as lat. 76 deg., and as far south as New Zealand, but was also found by Whymper in the Equatorial Andes.

But it is not only for their beauty that I have an affection for some of the weeds, but, speaking as a gardener, I am sure that they are often very useful. We may see how in a hedgerow the most delicate plants nestle themselves close to and under those of the coarsest growth, and seem all the better for it; and I have seen many instances in which delicate seeds and young cuttings have been saved when protected by weeds, when those not so protected have perished. One of the most interesting gardens and the most untidy I ever saw was Professor Syme's in Fifeshire. It was a mass of weeds, and rampant weeds; but among the weeds, and apparently rejoicing in them, was a collection of some of the rarest plants, growing in greater luxuriance than I had ever seen else-where. The weeds keep the earth moist, and prevent the radiation of heat, and how much they do so most of us can see by observing the plantains on our lawns. I am not fond of plantains on lawns, and get rid of them; but some will remain, and on them I have often noticed that in a slight hoar-frost no hoar-frost is formed on the plantains; the broad leaves lying flat on the ground keep in the earth-heat. I am tempted to say more about weeds and their uses, but instead of doing so I will refer—and those who do not know the book will thank me for doing so —to one of Burroughs' charming little books, *Pepacton*, where there is a long chapter on the use and beauty of weeds. I will, however, quote another American writer, Hawthorne, who is quite enthusiastic in his praise of weeds. "There is," he says, "a sort of sacredness about them. Perhaps if we could penetrate Nature's secrets we should find that what we call weeds are more essential to the well-being of the world than the most precious fruit or grain." This is perhaps somewhat exaggerated, but there is a good truth in it.

HENRY N. ELLACOMBE
[*In a Gloucestershire Garden* (1895)]

Blitz Flowers

[*When man disturbs the balance of nature, even ever so slightly and over no matter how small an area, he is sure to change the spontaneous flora of that area. Open a field, cut through a road, or even disturb slightly the soil and new plants take over while old ones disappear. During the "blitz" on London there was a very grand disturbance indeed with some curious results which greatly interested London botanists.*]

LONDON, July 25.—London, paradoxically, is the gayest where she has been most blitzed. The wounds made this summer by flying bombs are, of course, still raw and bare, but cellars and courts shattered into rubble by the German raids of 1940–'41 have been taken over by an army of weeds which have turned them into wild gardens, sometimes as gay as any tilled by human hands.

There is the brilliant rose-purple plant that Londoners call rose-bay willow herb. Americans call it fireweed because it blazes wherever a forest fire has raged. It will not grow in the shade, but there is little shade as yet in the London ruins. It likes potash, and the ruins are full of wood ash. It sweeps across this pockmarked city and turns what might have been scars into flaming beauty. You see it everywhere—great meadows of it in Lambeth, where solid tracts were blitzed; waves of it about St. Paul's. Behind Westminster Abbey bits of it are high up where second-story fireplaces still cling to the hanging walls.

The fireweed plant gives the characteristic rose-purple and green color tone to what look like vacant lots all over London—the blitz sites.

London has done a neat job of ordering and inclosing these

ruined patches. Dangerous walls have been tumbled down, rubble and bricks heaped and piled, and neat four-foot brick walls today guard the passer-by on the pavement from the cellar holes. Some of these holes have been sealed in and filled as temporary reservoirs, and the image of clumps of fireweed reflected in the water gives added beauty to the picture.

Few of the old ruins are bare. Plant life creeps in almost at once. Only two years after the big blitz of 1940–'41, the present director of the Royal Botanical Garden at Kew, Professor E. J. Salisbury, has identified ninety-five species of plants, not counting mosses and fungi growing in the bomb sites. He also eliminated from his count the species found in areas which had formerly been gardens. He counted only plant immigrants into London since the blitz.

Contrasting with the rose-purple of the fireweed are everywhere fiery yellow patches of groundsel, or ragwort, a bushy plant with chrysanthemum-like leaves and golden daisy-like blossoms. Three species are abundant in the ruins. The least conspicuous common groundsel is an old resident of England, but the most striking of the three, curiously, is a native of Sicily, at home among the volcanic ashes of Mount Etna. This gay flower was introduced into the botanical gardens at Oxford in 1794 and in England is called the Oxford Ragwort. Its present wild abundance dates from the blitz.

Most of the weeds and wild flowers of the blitz sites are familiar to Americans: red and white clover, musk mallow, evening primrose, chamomile, white and purple-flowering nightshade, wild lettuce, sow thistle, Canada thistle, yellow rocket, hedge mustard, dandelion, knotweed, the various docks, lambs quarters (better known as pigweed), the coarse plant that Americans call horseweed, but in London is known as the Canadian fleabane; the daisy-like pest which Litchfield County, Conn., calls Germanweed, but which erudite Londoners, generally mispronouncing its Latin name, call "gallant soldiers." And the rank, rounded leaves of the common coltsfoot, which in early spring puts up dandelion-like flowers, are part of the picture of almost every blitz site.

The tree of heaven, the Ailanthus, which some of us call the Manhattan back-yard tree and which Betty Smith made famous in "A Tree Grows in Brooklyn," is already beginning to overshadow the wild flowers in some blitz cellars. But the most common tree to start growing in the ruins is the Goat Willow. There are also incipient poplars and sycamores, presumably seeded from the green squares that dot old London.

A few flowers known to Americans as garden plants are fre-

quently part of the wild gardens in the cellars of London, notably poppies, calendula, larkspur, candytuft and hollyhock, all of which are
common sights about Holborn and in the great devastated tracts behind
St. Paul's.

Here and there among brick piles in this moist climate of
London, ferns have sprung up—sometimes the handsome male fern,
which looks at a distance like the spinulose ferns our florists pack with
roses, but more often the common bracken. Both grow in the churchyard
of St. James's, in Piccadilly, behind Charing Cross station and at Amen
Corner. In some cellars behind St. Paul's, bracken is beginning to form
miniature bracken heaths.

The botanists say that the most abundant plants on the bomb
sites are those with parachute attachments for their seeds. The weed-
like yarrow, common beside the well traveled paths on the embank-
ments, is seldom seen in the ruins. Its seeds are usually carried in mud
attached to boots or tires, and neither boots nor tires climb down into
London's cellar ruins. The most abundant blitz plants—fireweed, ground-
sels and horseweed—are all air-distributed. Birds carry some seeds, but
birds have little interest in cellar sites until vegetation has established
itself there, providing food for them.

Today the blitz sites are untended gardens. In another few
years the shade provided by these plant pioneers will doubtless permit
new types of plant life to appear, and the reigning wild beauties of
today will disappear. But London's ruins are not likely to pass through
what the botanists call a normal cycle, for London is full of plans and
dreams of new types of houses and gardens to spring up where the
Germans have so expensively destroyed the old.

LEWIS GANNETT
[In the New York *Herald Tribune* (1944)]

Early Settlers

[*An astonishing number of our most familiar "native wild flowers" are
not native at all. Or perhaps it would be more hospitable to say that, like
most Americans, they have not been native for very long. Most of them*

came as unobserved immigrants in imported grain or in the ballast of ships.]

D R I V E along any New England road today, and note the "wild" flowers that give it character: most of them are immigrants from Europe, strangers who arrived and made themselves at home with the white man. We recognize the pale pink bouncing Bet and the abundant banks of tawny day lilies as "escapes" from vanished gardens—partly because they tend to linger in the neighborhood of betraying lilac bushes and apple trees. But even deep into the woods along the old cart roads, other plant immigrants have wandered.

The yellow rocket and wild mustard that gleam in May; most of the clovers—the red, the pink alsike, the yellow hop, and the tall sweet white and sweet yellow clover—are immigrants. So are the feathery white wild carrot ("Queen Anne's lace") and the familiar yellow wild parsnip, the daisies and the starry yarrow, the sky-blue chicory and the coarse blueweed that looks so lovely at a distance (I brought some of it into my garden once and had a time getting rid of it). So too are a golden army: the roadside buttercups, dandelions, butter-and-eggs, St.-John's wort, the delicate celandine poppy, tansy, the velvety-leaved mulleins, and the great coarse elecampane that some call "wild sunflower."

Ezra probably never saw a black-eyed Susan; it came from our own West, years later, with clover seed. Our commoner thistles are from Europe, even that which we miscall Canada thistle. So is teasel. The handsome orange hawkweed, often called "devil's paintbrush," and the brilliant spiked loosestrife that paints the marshes purple in August, both invaded this countryside within the memory of living man; the pestiferous shrubby cinquefoil (which our farmers call "hardhack," the name I give to steeplebush) is another European invader. Our "wild" roadsides are not native American at all.

Weeding in our gardens today, we are mostly rescuing European flowers and vegetables from European weeds. Not merely the useful timothy and redtop but the pernicious crab, quack, bent, foxtail, and wire grasses are importations; so is that pesky tiny daisy-like weed that my neighbors dub "Germanweed" and the more poetic call "gallant soldiers." So are the wiry-rooted sheep sorrel and the tough-rooted big docks, including the clinging burdock, most of our stinging nettles, the woolly catnip and the smoother peppermint, the ugly common plantain and the pretty little thyme-leaved speedwell that nestles in the lawn, shepherd's purse, purple self-heal and the creeping gill-over-the-ground, the nightshade that is not really so deadly as its name indicates, and the little cheese mallow whose fruits the children munch, almost all the various pigweeds, both the common chickweed that blooms, in a year of thaws, during every month of the calendar, and the coarser mouse-ear chickweed.

A historical botanist could prolong that list almost infinitely. It is long enough to make this clear: the Cream Hill roadsides do not look today at all as they did in anyone's great-great-grandfather's time—not, at least, until mid-August, when the goldenrods flame. Our goldenrods and asters are native American. Ezra too must have admired them, when he rode his horse up from New Haven to inspect his tenant farms, his saddlebags prudently packed with sermons. Possibly he dismounted now and then to pick a native bottle gentian in the August woods, or, in September, to look closer at the reflection of the sky in a swampy patch of fringed gentian. His diary does not say. It details the salaries of Connecticut parsons; it comments on local industries and even reflects on the deplorable sexual customs of Indians, but it never mentions a wild flower.

LEWIS GANNETT
[*Cream Hill* (1949)]

Plant Invaders

[*Most of the introduced plants Mr. Gannett lists are well-behaved and we are glad to have them. Every now and then, however, some new-comer likes his new home too well. The plant rivals, insect enemies and diseases of his native habitat are not present to check his growth. He becomes a pest or even, in the two terrifying examples which follow, a positive disaster.*]

MILE after mile the lowland road leading back to New Orleans was bordered by wide ditches choked from bank to bank with water hyacinths. That morning a newspaper headline had announced that a

Louisiana congressman had introduced a bill in Washington, D.C., to appropriate $25,000,000 for clearing southern streams and canals of water hyacinths. This runaway plant was introduced from South America into Louisiana at the time of the 1884 New Orleans Cotton Exposition. Its rapid reproduction has made it a multimillion-dollar pest.

A clump of water hyacinths will sometimes double in size in 20 days. A single square foot of these waterweeds may become 1,000 square feet in six months' time. Ten years after a woman in Florida tossed a few hyacinths from her fish pool into the St. Johns River the descendants of those plants spread in great rafts over 50,000,000 square yards of inland waters. The only natural checks upon the plant seem to be salt water and a temperature below 28 degrees F. It has no serious insect foes. Attempts to poison the hyacinths injured livestock and killed fish. A letter to a Florida newspaper once suggested that the hippopotamus ought to be introduced into the state to eat up the water hyacinths. So far the most successful method of dealing with the swift reproduction of the plant is the circular saws of government launches that chop up the rafts into small pieces which float out to sea or are hauled up on the banks to dry out and die. But as soon as the saws stop the plants gain ground. We passed one government boat moored in a roadside canal. It was completely surrounded by water hyacinths.

At one time, I was told, the army engineers, in their work of maintaining navigable streams, had virtually wiped out the plant in Louisiana. Then a new colonel arrived to take charge. Running down the list of funds appropriated for the year, he came to the item:

"Water Hyacinth Control . . . $10,000."

"What are water hyacinths?"

An assistant explained.

"Let's see some!"

So well had the work been done and so nearly were the plants eradicated that a long drive revealed only a few plants. Declaring that this was the silliest waste of taxpayers' money he had ever encountered, the colonel blue-penciled the whole appropriation. The fight against the water hyacinth stopped. Before it was resumed, the swiftly multiplying plant had got its second wind.

As we drove along we saw how its rapid multiplication—stimulated now by the spring—was playing a role in an endless battle that rages over this lowland region. This is the struggle between land and water. Curiously enough, the hyacinth, a plant that lives in water and depends upon water for its existence, fights on the side of the land. We saw a sequence of events taking place along the old canals. First the hyacinth got control. The canal became more and more choked. Cattails sprang up along the banks. They edged farther and farther out. And finally willows took root. Unless man interfered, the canal was doomed. Eventually its water would be replaced by silt and swampy land.

EDWIN WAY TEALE
[*North with the Spring* (1951)]

THERE is at least one case of very successfully setting a Bug to catch a Vegetable. The vicious vegetable was the prickly pear, a cactus that grows as a succession of thick, oval, slab-shaped leaves, and is harmless enough in California, though in Australia it grew until it covered the entire country over huge areas. It threatened to drive men out from whole districts; and a cactus is a particularly unpleasant plant to be driven out by.

The introduction of the prickly pear into Australia has been blamed upon Captain Arthur Phillip, in 1787. On his way out with the first colonists he stopped at Rio de Janeiro in Brazil and took in prickly pear plants and cochineal insects (which feed on them) "to dye his soldiers' coats red." But the only prickly pear found near Rio de Janeiro was a different species, not the one that became a pest, so Captain Phillip can be exonerated. The species that got completely out of hand is believed to have been introduced in 1839, as one plant sent in a flowerpot to Scone, New South Wales. Cuttings were sent from place to place, and people used the plant as hedges around their homesteads. Though it finally became overwhelming, its progress was very slow and deliberate. About 1870 it began to get beyond control. By 1900 it had claimed an area of about ten million acres, and no means was known of stopping it. By 1920 it covered sixty million acres and still no effective means of control was known. Mechanically grubbing it up was out of the question, and the best thing known was poisoning it with arsenic, though this was quite uneconomical. Its rate of spread was estimated at one million acres per year, which is nearly two acres a minute, so there was no time to be lost.

Bugs proved to be the answer to the prickly pear. There were previous examples, in Hawaii, of controlling undesirable vegetables by means of insects that eat them, carefully introduced without any of their normal insect enemies. It was necessary to make quite certain that the insects could not, by any chance, turn their attention to any valuable plants. Very careful tests are always carried out, first in the insect's own country, and when the insect is sent over it is always carefully guarded in an insectary and experimented with further before being released. The most useful insect brought in was a South American moth which has been given the very appropriate Latin name of *Cactoblastis cactorum*. The first and only consignment was 2750 eggs of this moth in 1925. Bred in the insectary, the moths from these eggs laid eggs to the number of about 100,000. The second generation yielded 2,540,000 eggs, an increase of nearly a thousandfold, all within a year. The moths had passed the final, exacting tests to make certain that they could do no harm, and they were then released in various localities. What followed exceeded the entomologists' most hopeful expectations: the caterpillars, burrowing inside the fleshy pads of the rank, abundant vegetation, utterly blasted the cactus. Around all the centers where the insect had been released were stretches where nothing could be seen but chewed up and decaying bits of prickly pear.

The new moth was spectacular, but not entirely perfect. There were some areas where it was not completely successful, and in some places there were varieties of prickly pear which it found less attractive than the variety that caused the main infestation. Also it did not spread well; around each center where it had been released it would expand its area of operation only slowly. The adult moths are able to fly for some distance, but apparently they seldom do so, and they lay their eggs very close to where they themselves have lived. In addition the very completeness of its work on the leaves caused a slight disadvantage, in this way: soon after the introduction of Cactoblastis, the pear would be ruined as far as the eye could see; the roots, however, would not be destroyed, and at the next summer (December in Australia) new growth would be put out. But the caterpillars in that locality would have practically died out, having eaten up all their food supply; only after some time could their number be built up again, and thus a year or two more would be required before the prickly pear was finally under control.

The answer to these objections was provided by other insects, for a whole battery was introduced. There was a sucking bug which would wander over the leaves and introduce its long beak to suck the sap; this worked particularly well on the succulent new growth put out from the roots after attack by Cactoblastis: it would not quite kill the plant, but would weaken it up for the attack of yet a third worker, a white fluffy little mealybug which is actually the cochineal of Captain Phillip's original intention. These insects preferred plants already weakened, but there was also a little eight-legged mite which like Cactoblastis would go straight to healthy pear. This mite is as good a "spreader" as Cactoblastis is a poor one, and it does this without even being able to fly: the minute young mites are very easily caught by the wind and carried for long distances, and if they happen to light on a cactus they may start a new infestation. So easily are the tiny creatures blown about that when the mite was brought to Australia, it escaped from the quarantine insectary where it was undergoing the final tests to make quite sure that it would not prove harmful.

By the early nineteen thirties, Australia had broken the back of the prickly pear problem. In just under a hundred years, the harm that originally came in a flowerpot to Scone, New South Wales, had been undone. The prickly pear was no longer advancing, it was in rapid retreat, and huge areas could again be lived in by man, untroubled by a horrible spiny vegetable. The various insects that won this battle now have a struggle for existence among themselves, competing for the available food supply; this struggle has been won by Cactoblastis, and the other insects are now scarce and rather difficult to find.

Live creatures are curious things. They are never quite predictable, and in their comings and goings from one continent to another the strangest consequences are sometimes produced, as byproducts, as it were. In Australia a battery of insects serves to keep down, though not eliminate, the prickly pear. In Madagascar the prickly pear was present, but was by no means a serious menace. One of the cactus-eating insects that were taken to Australia became introduced in Madagascar by mistake, and—though it was not Cactoblastis, which was the most successful in Australia, but one of the lesser fry—it completely eliminated the prickly pear from Madagascar, rather to the annoyance of the inhabitants, who used to employ the plant in a mild way as cattle feed.

ANTHONY STANDEN
[*Insect Invaders* (1943)]

Wild Flowers as Gifts

[*To Emerson nature was rather more a philosophical abstraction than something known in intimate detail. But about its more general aspects he could be characteristically eloquent.*]

IF, at any time, it comes into my head that a present is due from me to somebody, I am puzzled what to give, until the opportunity is gone. Flowers and fruits are always fit presents—flowers, because they are a proud assertion that a ray of beauty outvalues all the utilities of the world. These gay natures contrast with the somewhat stern countenance of ordinary nature; they are like music heard out of a workhouse. Nature does not cocker us; we are children, not pets; she is not fond; everything is dealt to us without fear or favor, after severe universal laws. Yet these delicate flowers look like the frolic and interference of love and beauty. Men used to tell us that we love flattery, even though we are not deceived by it, because it shows that we are of importance enough to be courted. Something like that pleasure, the flowers give us: what am I to whom these sweet hints are addressed? Fruits are acceptable gifts, because they are the flower of commodities, and admit of fantastic values being attached to them. If a man should send to me to come a hundred miles to visit him, and should set before me a basket of fine summer fruit, I should think there was some proportion between the labor and the reward.

RALPH WALDO EMERSON
["Gifts," in *Essays, Second Series* (1844)]

Having Your Cake Without Eating It

[*Henry Thoreau was always on the lookout for good ways of doing without. Here he tells us how to have the best part of a farm without having any of it.*]

AT a certain season of our life we are accustomed to consider every spot as the possible site of a house. I have thus surveyed the country on every side within a dozen miles of where I live. In imagination I have bought all the farms in succession, for all were to be bought, and I knew their price. I walked over each farmer's premises, tasted his wild apples, discoursed on husbandry with him, took his farm at his price, at any price, mortgaging it to him in my mind; even put a higher price on it—took everything but a deed of it—took his word for his deed, for I dearly love to talk—cultivated it, and him too to some extent, I trust, and withdrew when I had enjoyed it long enough, leaving him to carry it on. This experience entitled me to be regarded as a sort of real-estate broker by my friends. Wherever I sat, there I might live, and the landscape radiated from me accordingly. What is a house but a *sedes*, a seat? —better if a country seat. I discovered many a site for a house not likely to be soon improved, which some might have thought too far from the village, but to my eyes the village was too far from it. Well, there I might live, I said; and there I did live, for an hour, a summer and a winter life; saw how I could let the years run off, buffet the winter through, and see the spring come in. The future inhabitants of this region, wherever they may place their houses, may be sure that they have been anticipated. An afternoon sufficed to lay out the land into orchard, woodlot, and pasture, and to decide what fine oaks or pines should be left to stand before the door, and whence each blasted tree could be seen to the best advantage; and then I let it lie, fallow perchance, for a man is rich in proportion to the number of things which he can afford to let alone.

My imagination carried me so far that I even had the refusal of several farms—the refusal was all I wanted—but I never got my fingers burned by actual possession. The nearest that I came to actual possession was when I bought the Hollowell place, and had begun to sort my seeds, and collected materials with which to make a wheelbarrow to carry it on or off with; but before the owner gave me a deed of it, his wife— every man has such a wife—changed her mind and wished to keep it, and he offered me ten dollars to release him. Now, to speak the truth, I had but ten cents in the world, and it surpassed my arithmetic to tell, if I was that man who had ten cents, or who had a farm, or ten dollars, or all together. However, I let him keep the ten dollars and the farm too, for I had carried it far enough; or rather, to be generous, I sold him the farm for just what I gave for it, and, as he was not a rich man, made him a present of ten dollars, and still had my ten cents, and seeds, and materials for a wheelbarrow left. I found thus that I had been a rich man without any damage to my poverty. But I retained the landscape, and I have since annually carried off what it yielded without a wheelbarrow. With respect to landscapes—

I am monarch of all I *survey*,
My right there is none to dispute.

I have frequently seen a poet withdraw, having enjoyed the most valuable part of a farm, while the crusty farmer supposed that he had got a few wild apples only. Why, the owner does not know it for many years when a poet has put his farm in rhyme, the most admirable kind of invisible fence, has fairly impounded it, milked it, skimmed it, and got all the cream, and left the farmer only the skimmed milk.

HENRY DAVID THOREAU
[*Walden* (1854)]

Section Nine

THE JUNGLE,
THE DESERT, AND
THE TUNDRA

Never to have seen anything but the temperate zone is to have lived on the fringe of the World. Between the tropic of Capricorn and the tropic of Cancer live the majority of all the plant species. . . . Not to struggle and economize and somehow see the tropics puts you, in my opinion, in the class with the boys who could never scrape together enough pennies to see the circus. They never wanted to badly enough, that's all.

DAVID FAIRCHILD

What Samuel Butler called "the rights of the vegetables" are little respected in New England. The casual walker plucks a flower here, breaks a branch there, and treads down the struggling shrub in his path. In the desert, one walks circumspectly and one thinks twice before seizing even a branch which does not at first sight look spiny. One knows that the rights of the vegetables are being looked after by the only parties likely, in the long run, to look out for anyone's rights— the parties most directly concerned.

JOSEPH WOOD KRUTCH

Melville in Eden

[*When Herman Melville was young he sought innocence in the tropics before pursuing the embodiment of evil in a whale. Inevitably he celebrated the breadfruit which does not have to be earned by the sweat of the brow.*]

THE celebrity of the bread-fruit tree, and the conspicuous place it occupies in a Typee bill of fare, induces me to give at some length a general description of the tree, and the various modes in which the fruit is prepared.

The bread-fruit tree, in its glorious prime, is a grand and towering object, forming the same feature in a Marquesan landscape that the patriarchal elm does in New England scenery. The latter tree it not a little resembles in height, in the wide spread of its stalwart branches, and in its venerable and imposing aspect.

The leaves of the bread-fruit are of great size, and their edges are cut and scolloped as fantastically as those of a lady's lace collar. As they annually tend toward decay, they almost rival, in the brilliant variety of their gradually changing hues, the fleeting shades of the expiring dolphin. The autumnal tints of our American forests, glorious as they are, sink into nothing in comparison with this tree.

The leaf, in one particular stage, when nearly all the prismatic colours are blended on its surface, is often converted by the natives into a superb and striking head-dress. The principal fibre traversing its length being split open a convenient distance, and the elastic sides of the aperture pressed apart, the head is inserted between them, the leaf drooping on one side, with its forward half turned jauntily up on the brows, and the remaining part spreading laterally behind the ears.

The fruit somewhat resembles in magnitude and general appearance one of our citron melons of ordinary size; but, unlike the citron, it has no sectional lines drawn along the outside. Its surface is dotted all over with little conical prominences, looking not unlike the knobs on an antiquated church door. The rind is perhaps an eighth of an inch in thickness; and denuded of this, at the time when it is in the greatest perfection, the fruit presents a beautiful globe of white pulp, the whole of which may be eaten, with the exception of a slender core, which is easily removed.

The bread-fruit, however, is never used, and is indeed altogether unfit to be eaten, until submitted in one form or other to the action of fire.

The most simple manner in which this operation is performed, and, I think, the best, consists in placing any number of the freshly-plucked fruit, when in a particular state of greenness, among the embers of a fire, in the same way that you would roast a potato. After the lapse of ten or fifteen minutes, the green rind embrowns and cracks, showing through the fissures in its sides the milk-white interior. As soon as it cools, the rind drops off, and you then have the soft round pulp in its purest and most delicious state. Thus eaten, it has a mild and pleasing flavour.

Sometimes after having been roasted in the fire, the natives snatch it briskly from the embers, and permitting it to slip out of the yielding rind into a vessel of cold water, stir up the mixture, which they call "bo-a-sho." I never could endure this compound, and indeed the preparation is not greatly in vogue among the more polite Typees.

There is one form, however, in which the fruit is occasionally served, that renders it a dish fit for a king. As soon as it is taken from the fire the exterior is removed, the core extracted, and the remaining part is placed in a sort of shallow stone mortar, and briskly worked with a pestle of the same substance. While one person is performing this operation, another takes a ripe cocoa-nut, and breaking it in half, which they also do very cleverly, proceeds to grate the juicy meat into fine particles. This is done by means of a piece of mother-of-pearl shell, lashed firmly to the extreme end of a heavy stick, with its straight side accurately notched like a saw. The stick is sometimes a grotesquely formed limb of a tree, with three or four branches twisting from its body like so many shapeless legs, and sustaining it two or three feet from the ground.

The native, first placing a calabash beneath the nose, as it were, of his curious-looking log-steed, for the purpose of receiving the grated fragments as they fall, mounts astride of it as if it were a hobby-horse, and twirling the inside of one of his hemispheres of cocoa-nut around the sharp teeth of the mother-of-pearl shell, the pure white meat falls in snowy showers into the receptacle provided. Having obtained a quantity sufficient for his purpose, he places it in a bag made of the net-like fibrous substance attached to all cocoa-nut trees, and compressing it over the bread-fruit, which being now sufficiently pounded, is put into a wooden bowl—extracts a thick creamy milk. The delicious liquid soon bubbles round the fruit, and leaves it at last just peeping above its surface.

This preparation is called "kokoo," and a most luscious preparation it is. The hobby-horse and the pestle and mortar were in great requisition during the time I remained in the house of Marheyo, and Kory-Kory had frequent occasion to show his skill in their use.

But the great staple articles of food into which the bread-fruit is converted by these natives are known respectively by the names of "amar" and "poee-poee."

At certain seasons of the year, when the fruit of the hundred groves of the valley has reached its maturity, and hangs in golden spheres from every branch, the islanders assemble in harvest groups, and garner in the abundance which surrounds them. The trees are stripped of their nodding burdens, which, easily freed from the rind and core, are gathered together in capacious wooden vessels, where the pulpy fruit is soon worked by a stone pestle, vigorously applied, into a blended mass of a doughy consistency, called by the natives "tutao." This is then divided into separate parcels, which, after being made up into stout packages, enveloped in successive folds of leaves, and bound round with thongs of bark, are stored away in large receptacles hollowed in the earth from whence they are drawn as occasion may require.

In this condition the tutao sometimes remains for years, and even is thought to improve by age. Before it is fit to be eaten, however, it has to undergo an additional process. A primitive oven is scooped in the ground, and its bottom being loosely covered with stones, a large fire is kindled within it. As soon as the requisite degree of heat is attained, the embers are removed, and the surface of the stones being covered with thick layers of leaves, one of the larger packages of tutao is deposited upon them, and overspread with another layer of leaves. The whole is then quickly heaped up with earth, and forms a sloping mound.

The tutao thus baked is called "amar"; the action of the oven having converted it into an amber-coloured cakey substance, a little tart, but not at all disagreeable to the taste. By another and final process the "amar" is changed into "poee-poee." This transition is rapidly effected. The amar is placed in a vessel, and mixed with water until it gains a proper pudding-like consistency, when, without further preparation, it is in readiness for use. This is the form in which the tutao is generally consumed. The singular mode of eating it I have already described.

Were it not that the bread-fruit is thus capable of being preserved for a length of time, the natives might be reduced to a state of starvation; for, owing to some unknown cause, the trees sometimes fail to bear fruit; and on such occasions the islanders chiefly depend upon the supplies they have been enabled to store away.

This stately tree, which is rarely met with upon the Sandwich Islands, and then only of a very inferior quality, and at Tahiti does not abound to a degree that renders its fruit the principal article of food, attains its greatest excellence in the genial climate of the Marquesan Group, where it grows to an enormous magnitude, and flourishes in the utmost abundance.

HERMAN MELVILLE
[*Typee* (1846)]

Darwin in South America

[*The Charles Darwin who, as naturalist, sailed around the world in H.M.S. Beagle had no premonition that some of the observations he made would start him on a line of thought destined to set the whole world by the ears. But he looked closely at everything; and like so many from the temperate climes he was half stunned by the profusion of the tropics.*]

ON leaving Ascension, we sailed for Bahia, on the coast of Brazil, in order to complete the chronometrical measurement of the world. We arrived there on August 1st, and stayed four days, during which I took several long walks. I was glad to find my enjoyment in tropical scenery had not decreased from the want of novelty, even in the slightest degree. The elements of the scenery are so simple, that they are worth mentioning, as a proof on what trifling circumstances exquisite natural beauty depends.

The country may be described as a level plain of about three hundred feet in elevation, which in all parts has been worn into flat-bottomed valleys. This structure is remarkable in a granitic land, but is nearly universal in all those softer formations of which plains are usually composed. The whole surface is covered by various kinds of stately trees, interspersed with patches of cultivated ground, out of which houses, convents, and chapels arise. It must be remembered that within the tropics, the wild luxuriance of nature is not lost even in the vicinity of large cities: for the natural vegetation of the hedges and hill-sides overpowers in picturesque effect the artificial labour of man. Hence, there are only a few spots where the bright red soil affords a strong contrast with the universal clothing of green. From the edges of the plain there are distant views either of the ocean, or of the great Bay with its low-wooded shores, and on which numerous boats and canoes show their white sails. Excepting from these points, the scene is extremely limited; following the level pathways, on each hand, only glimpses into the wooded valleys below can be obtained. The houses I may add, and especially the sacred edifices, are built in a peculiar and rather fantastic style of architecture. They are all whitewashed; so that when illumined by the brilliant sun of midday, and as seen against the pale blue sky of the horizon, they stand out more like shadows than real buildings.

Such are the elements of the scenery, but it is a hopeless attempt to paint the general effect. Learned naturalists describe these scenes of the tropics by naming a multitude of objects, and mentioning some characteristic feature of each. To a learned traveller this possibly may communicate some definite ideas: but who else from seeing a plant in an herbarium can imagine its appearance when growing in its native soil? Who from seeing choice plants in a hothouse, can magnify some into the dimensions of forest trees, and crowd others into an entangled jungle? Who when examining in the cabinet of the entomologist the gay exotic butterflies, and singular cicadas, will associate with these lifeless objects, the ceaseless harsh music of the latter, and the lazy flight of the former—the sure accompaniments of the still, glowing noonday of the tropics? It is when the sun has attained its greatest height, that such scenes should be viewed: then the dense splendid foliage of the mango hides the ground with its darkest shade, whilst the upper branches are rendered from the profusion of light of the most brilliant green. In the temperate zones the case is different—the vegetation there is not so dark or so rich, and hence the rays of the declining sun, tinged of a red, purple, or bright yellow color, add most to the beauties of those climes.

When quietly walking along the shady pathways, and admiring each successive view, I wished to find language to express my ideas. Epithet after epithet was found too weak to convey to those who have not visited the intertropical regions, the sensation of delight which the mind experiences. I have said that the plants in a hothouse fail to communicate a just idea of the vegetation, yet I must recur to it. The land is one great wild, untidy, luxuriant hothouse, made by Nature for herself, but taken possession of by man, who has studded it with gay houses and formal gardens. How great would be the desire in every admirer of nature to behold, if such were possible, the scenery of another planet! yet to every person in Europe, it may be truly said, that at the distance of only a few degrees from his native soil, the glories of another world are opened to him. In my last walk I stopped again and again to gaze on these beauties, and endeavoured to fix in my mind for ever, an impression which at the time I knew sooner or later must fail. The form of the orange-tree, the cocoa-nut, the palm, the mango, the tree-fern, the banana, will remain clear and separate; but the thousand beauties which unite these into one perfect scene must fade away; yet they will leave, like a tale heard in childhood, a picture full of indistinct, but most beautiful figures.

CHARLES DARWIN
[*The Voyage of the Beagle* (1839)]

Wallace Describes the Tropics

[*After his one great voyage the ailing Darwin stayed quietly at home with his books, his simple experiments, and his thoughts. Meanwhile Alfred Russel Wallace was spending most of the early half of his long life in remote jungles. He was, of course, to arrive independently at many of the same conclusions Darwin had reached concerning evolution and the role of natural selection. Here he describes certain aspects of the tropical vegetation few have ever known so well.*]

W I T H but few and unimportant exceptions a great forest band from a thousand to fifteen hundred miles in width girdles the earth at the equator, clothing hill, plain, and mountain with an evergreen mantle. Lofty peaks and precipitous ridges are sometimes bare, but often the woody covering continues to a height of eight or ten thousand feet, as in some of the volcanic mountains of Java and on portions of the Eastern Andes. . . .

It is not easy to fix upon the most distinctive features of these virgin forests, which nevertheless impress themselves upon the beholder as something quite unlike those of temperate lands, and as possessing a grandeur and sublimity altogether their own. Amid the countless modifications in detail which these forests present, we shall endeavour to point out the chief peculiarities as well as the more interesting phenomena which generally characterise them.

The observer new to the scene would perhaps be first struck by the varied yet symmetrical trunks, which rise up with perfect straightness to a great height without a branch, and which, being placed at a considerable average distance apart, give an impression similar to that produced by the columns of some enormous building. Overhead, at a height, perhaps of a hundred and fifty feet, is an almost unbroken canopy of foliage formed by the meeting together of these great trees and their interlacing branches; and this canopy is usually so dense that but an indistinct glimmer of the sky is to be seen, and even the intense tropical sunlight only penetrates to the ground subdued and broken up into scattered fragments. There is a weird gloom and a solemn silence, which combine to produce a sense of the vast—the primeval—almost of the infinite. It is a world in which man seems an intruder, and where he feels overwhelmed by the contemplation of the ever-acting forces which, from the simple elements of the atmosphere, build up the great mass of vegetation which overshadows and almost seems to oppress the earth.

Passing from the general impression to the elements of which the scene is composed, the observer is struck by the great diversity of the details amid the general uniformity. Instead of endless repetitions of the same forms of trunk such as are to be seen in our pine, or oak, or beechwoods, the eye wanders from one tree to another and rarely detects two together of the same species. All are tall and upright columns, but they differ from each other more than do the columns of Gothic, Greek, and Egyptian temples. Some are almost cylindrical, rising up out of the ground as if their bases were concealed by accumulations of the soil; others get much thicker near the ground like our spreading oaks; others again, and these are very characteristic, send out towards the base flat and wing-like projections. These projections are thin slabs radiating from the main trunk, from which they stand out like the buttresses of a Gothic cathedral. They rise to various heights on the tree, from five or six to twenty or thirty feet; they often divide as they approach the ground, and sometimes twist and curve along the surface for a considerable distance, forming elevated and greatly compressed roots. These buttresses are sometimes so large that the spaces between them if roofed over would form huts capable of containing several persons. Their use is evidently to give the tree an extended base, and so assist the subterranean roots in maintaining in an erect position so lofty a column crowned by a broad and massive head of branches and foliage. The buttressed trees belong to a variety of distinct groups. Thus, many of the Bombaceae or silk-cotton trees, several of the Leguminosae, and perhaps many trees belonging to other natural orders, possess these appendages.

There is another form of tree, hardly less curious, in which the trunk, though generally straight and cylindrical, is deeply furrowed and indented, appearing as if made up of a number of small trees grown together at the centre. Sometimes the junction of what seem to be the component parts is so imperfect that gaps or holes are left by which you can see through the trunk in various places. At first one is disposed to think this is caused by accident or decay, but repeated examination shows it to be due to the natural growth of the tree. The accompanying outline sections of one of these trees that was cut down exhibits its character. It was a noble forest tree, more than two hundred feet high, but rather slender in proportion, and it was by no means an extreme example of its class. This peculiar form is probably produced by the downward growth of aerial roots, like some New Zealand trees whose growth has been traced, and of whose different stages drawings may be seen at the Library of the Linnaean Society. These commence their existence as parasitical climbers, which take root in the fork of some forest tree and send down aerial roots which clasp round the stem that upholds them. As these roots increase in size and grow together laterally they cause the death of their foster-parent. The climber then grows rapidly, sending out large branches above and spreading roots below, and as the supporting tree decays away the aerial roots grow together and form a new trunk, more or less furrowed and buttressed, but exhibiting no other marks of its exceptional origin. Aerial-rooted forest trees —like that figured in my *Malay Archipelago*—and the equally remarkable fig-trees of various species, whose trunks are formed by a miniature forest of aerial roots, sometimes separate, sometimes matted together, are characteristic of the Eastern tropics, but appear to be rare or altogether unknown in America, and can therefore hardly be included among the general characteristics of the equatorial zone.

Besides the varieties of form, however, the tree-trunks of these forests present many peculiarities of colour and texture. The majority are rather smooth-barked, and many are of peculiar whitish, green, yellowish, or brown colours, or occasionally nearly black. Some are perfectly smooth, others deeply cracked and furrowed, while in a considerable number the bark splits off in flakes or hangs down in long fibrous ribands. Spined or prickly trunks (except of palms) are rare in the damp equatorial forests. Turning our gaze upwards from the stems to the foliage, we find two types of leaf not common in the temperate zone, although the great mass of the trees offer nothing very remarkable in this respect. First, we have many trees with large, thick, and glossy leaves, like those of the cherry-laurel or the magnolia, but even larger, smoother, and more symmetrical. The leaves of the Asiatic caoutchouc tree (Ficus elastica), so often cultivated in houses, is a type of this class, which has a very fine effect among the more ordinary-looking foliage. Contrasted with this is the fine pinnate foliage of some of the largest forest trees, which, seen far aloft against the sky, looks as delicate as that of the sensitive mimosa. . . .

Among the minor but not unimportant peculiarities that characterise these lofty forests is the curious way in which many of the smaller trees have their flowers situated on the main trunk or larger branches instead of on the upper part of the tree. The cacao-tree is a well-known example of this peculiarity, which is not uncommon in tropical forests; and some of the smaller trunks are occasionally almost hidden by the quantity of fruit produced on them. One of the most beautiful examples of this mode of flowering is a small tree of the genus Polyalthea, belonging to the family of the custard-apples, not uncommon in the forests of north-western Borneo. Its slender trunk, about fifteen or twenty feet high, was completely covered with star-shaped flowers, three inches across and of a rich orange-red colour, making the trees look as if they had been artificially decorated with brilliant garlands. The recent discoveries as to the important part played by insects in the fertilisation of flowers offers a very probable explanation of this peculiarity. Bees and butterflies are the greatest flower-haunters. The former love the sun and frequent open grounds or the flowery tops of the lofty forest trees fully exposed to the sun and air. The forest shades are frequented by thousands of butterflies, but these mostly keep near the ground, where they have a free passage among the tree-trunks and visit the flowering shrubs and herbaceous plants. To attract these it is necessary that flowers should be low down and conspicuous. If they grew in the usual way on the tops of these smaller trees overshadowed by the dense canopy above them they would be out of sight of both groups of insects; but being placed openly on the stems, and in the greatest profusion, they cannot fail to attract the attention of the wandering butterflies. . . .

Next to the trees themselves the most conspicuous and remarkable feature of the tropical forests is the profusion of woody creepers and climbers that everywhere meet the eye. They twist around the slenderer stems, they drop down pendent from the branches, they stretch tightly from tree to tree, they hang looped in huge festoons from bough to bough, they twist in great serpentine coils or lie in entangled masses on the ground. Some are slender, smooth, and root-like; others are rugged or knotted; often they are twined together into veritable cables; some are flat like ribands, others are curiously waved and indented. Where they spring from or how they grow is at first a complete puzzle. They pass overhead from tree to tree, they stretch in tight cordage like the rigging of a ship from the top of one tree to the base of another, and the upper regions of the forest often seem full of them without our being able to detect any earth-growing stem from which they arise. The conclusion is at length forced upon us that these woody climbers must possess the two qualities of very long life and almost indefinite longitudinal growth, for by these suppositions alone can we explain their characteristic features. The growth of climbers, even more than all other plants, is upward towards the light. In the shade of the forest they rarely or never flower, and seldom even produce foliage, but when they have reached the summit of the tree that supports them, they expand under the genial influence of light and air, and often cover their foster-parent with blossoms not its own. Here, as a rule, the climber's growth would cease; but the time comes when the supporting tree rots and falls, and the creeper comes with it in torn and tangled masses to the ground. But though its foster-parent is dead it has itself received no permanent injury, but shoots out again till it finds a fresh support, mounts another tree, and again puts forth its leaves and flowers. In time the old tree rots entirely away and the creeper remains tangled on the ground. Sometimes branches only fall and carry a portion of the creeper tightly stretched to an adjoining tree; at other times the whole tree is arrested by a neighbour, to which the creeper soon transfers itself in order to reach the upper light. When by the fall of a branch the creepers are left hanging in the air, they may be blown about by the wind and catch hold of trees growing up beneath them, and thus become festooned from one tree to another. When these accidents and changes have been again and again repeated the climber may have travelled very far from its parent stem, and may have mounted to the tree tops and descended again to the earth several times over. Only in this way does it seem possible to explain the wonderfully complex manner in which these climbing plants wander up and down the forest as if guided by the strangest caprices, or how they become so crossed and tangled together in the wildest confusion.

The variety in the length, thickness, strength, and toughness of these climbers enables the natives of tropical countries to put them to various uses. Almost every kind of cordage is supplied by them. Some will stand in water without rotting, and are used for cables, for lines to which are attached fish-traps, and to bind and strengthen the wooden anchors used generally in the East. Boats and even large sailing vessels are built, whose planks are entirely fastened together by this kind of cordage skilfully applied to internal ribs. For the better kinds of houses, smooth and uniform varieties are chosen, so that the beams and rafters can be bound together with neatness, strength, and uniformity, as is especially observable among the indigenes of the Amazonian forests. When baskets of great strength are required special kinds of creepers are used; and to serve almost every purpose for which we should need a rope or a chain, the tropical savage adopts some one of the numerous forest-ropes which long experience has shown to have qualities best adapted for it. Some are smooth and supple; some are tough and will bear twisting or tying; some will last longest in salt water, others in fresh; one is uninjured by the heat and smoke of fires, while another is bitter or otherwise prejudicial to insect enemies.

Besides these various kinds of trees and climbers, which form the great mass of the equatorial forests and determine their general aspect, there are a number of forms of plants which are always more or less present, though in some parts scarce and in others in great profusion, and which largely aid in giving a special character to tropical as distinguished from temperate vegetation. Such are the various groups of palms, ferns, ginger-worts, and wild plantains, arums, orchids, and bamboos. . . .

It is a very general opinion among inhabitants of our temperate climes that amid the luxuriant vegetation of the tropics there must be a grand display of floral beauty, and this idea is supported by the number of large and showy flowers cultivated in our hothouses. The fact is, however, that in proportion as the general vegetation becomes more luxuriant, flowers form a less and less prominent feature; and this rule applies not only to the tropics but to the temperate and frigid zones. It is amid the scanty vegetation of the higher mountains and towards the limits of perpetual snow that the alpine flowers are most brilliant and conspicuous. Our own meadows and pastures and hillsides produce more gay flowers than our woods and forests; and, in the tropics, it is in the parts where vegetation is less dense and luxuriant that flowers most abound. In the damp and uniform climate of the equatorial zone the mass of vegetation is greater and more varied than in any other part of the globe, but in the great virgin forests themselves flowers are rarely seen. After describing the forests of the Lower Amazon, Mr. Bates asks: "But where were the flowers? To our great disappointment we saw none, or only such as were insignificant in appearance. Orchids are rare in the dense forests of the lowlands, and I believe it is now tolerably well ascertained that the majority of the forest trees in equatorial Brazil have small and inconspicuous flowers." My friend Dr. Richard Spruce assured me that by far the greater part of the plants gathered by him in equatorial America had inconspicuous green or white flowers. My own observations in the Aru Islands for six months, and in Borneo for more than a year, while living almost wholly in the forests, are quite in accordance with this view. Conspicuous masses of showy flowers are so rare that weeks and months may be passed without observing a single flowering plant worthy of special admiration. Occasionally some tree or shrub will be seen covered with magnificent yellow or crimson or purple flowers, but it is usually an oasis of colour in a desert of verdure, and therefore hardly affects the general aspect of the vegetation. The equatorial forest is too gloomy for flowers or generally even for much foliage, except of ferns and other shade-loving plants; and were it not that the forests are broken up by rivers and streams, by mountain ranges, by precipitous rocks and by deep ravines, there would be far fewer flowers visible than there are. Some of the great forest trees have showy blossoms, and when these are seen from an elevated point looking over an expanse of treetops the effect is very grand; but nothing is more erroneous than the statement sometimes made that tropical forest trees *generally* have showy flowers, for it is doubtful whether the proportion is at all greater in tropical than in temperate zones. On such natural exposures as steep mountain sides, the banks of rivers, or ledges of precipices, and on the margins of such artificial openings as roads and forest clearings, whatever floral beauty is to be found in the more luxuriant parts of the tropics is exhibited. But even in such favourable situations it is not the abundance and beauty of the flowers but the luxuriance and the freshness of the foliage, and the grace and infinite variety of the forms of vegetation, that will most attract the attention and extort the admiration of the traveller. Occasionally indeed you will come upon shrubs gay with blossoms or trees festooned with flowering creepers; but, on the other hand, you may travel for a hundred miles and see nothing but the varied greens of the forest foliage and the deep gloom of its tangled recesses. In Mr. Belt's *Naturalist in Nicaragua*, he thus describes the great virgin forests of that country which, being in a mountainous region and on the margin of the equatorial zone, are among the most favourable examples. "On each side of the road great trees towered up, carrying their crowns out of sight amongst a canopy of foliage, and with lianas hanging from nearly every bough, and passing from tree to tree, entangling the giants in a great network of coiling cables. Sometimes a tree appears covered with beautiful flowers which do not belong to it but to one of the lianas that twines through its branches and sends down great rope-like stems to the ground. Climbing ferns and vanilla cling to the trunks, and a thousand epiphytes perch themselves on the branches. Amongst these are large arums that send down long aerial roots, tough and strong, and are universally used instead of cordage by the natives. Amongst the undergrowth several small species of palms, varying in height from two to fifteen feet, are common; and now and then magnificent tree ferns sending off their feathery crowns twenty feet from the ground delight the sight by their graceful elegance. Great broad-leaved heliconias, leathery melastomae, and suc-culent-stemmed, lop-sided, leaved, and flesh-coloured begonias are abundant, and typical of tropical American forests; but not less so are the cecropia trees, with their white stems and large palmated leaves standing up like great candelabra. Sometimes the ground is carpeted with large flowers, yellow, pink, or white, that have fallen from some invisible tree-top above; or the air is filled with a delicious perfume, the source of which one seeks around in vain, for the flowers that cause it are far overhead out of sight, lost in the great overshadowing crown of verdure."

Although . . . it may be doubted whether light directly pro-duces floral colour, there can be no doubt that it is essential to the growth of vegetation and to the full development of foliage and of flowers. In the forests all trees, and shrubs, and creepers struggle upwards to the light, there to expand their blossoms and ripen their fruit. Hence, perhaps, the abundance of climbers which make use of their more sturdy companions to reach this necessary of vegetable life. Yet even on the upper surface of the forest, fully exposed to the light and heat of the tropical sun, there is no special development of coloured flowers. When from some elevated point you can gaze down upon an unbroken expanse of woody vegetation, it often happens that not a single patch of bright colour can be discerned. At other times, and especially at the beginning of the dry season, you may behold scattered at wide intervals over the mottled-green surface a few masses of yellow, white, pink, or more rarely of blue colour, indicating the position of handsome flowering trees.

The well-established relation between coloured flowers and the need of insects to fertilise them may perhaps be connected with the comparative scarcity of the former in the equatorial forests. The various forms of life are linked together in such mutual dependence that no one can inordinately increase without bringing about a corresponding increase or diminution of other forms. The insects which are best adapted to fertilise flowers cannot probably increase much beyond definite limits, because in doing so they would lead to a corresponding increase of insectivorous birds and other animals which would keep them down. The chief fertilisers—bees and butterflies—have enemies at every stage of their growth, from the egg to the perfect insect, and their numbers are, therefore, limited by causes quite independent of the supply of vegetable food. It may, therefore, be the case that the numbers of suitable insects are totally inadequate to the fertilisation of the countless millions of forest trees over such vast areas as the equatorial zone presents, and that, in consequence, a large proportion of the species have become adapted either for self-fertilisation, or for cross-fertilisation by the agency of the wind. Were there not some such limitation as this, we should expect that the continued struggle for existence among the plants of the tropical forests would have led to the acquisition, by a much larger proportion of them, of so valuable a character as bright-coloured flowers, this being almost a necessary preliminary to a participation in the benefits which have been proved to arise from cross-fertilisation by insect agency.

ALFRED RUSSEL WALLACE
[*Natural Selection and Tropical Nature* (1891)]

A Tropical Day

[*Henry Walter Bates belongs with the most remarkable of the mid-nineteenth-century explorer-naturalists. In 1848 at the age of twenty-three and without official or financial support he sailed for South America with the even more remarkable Alfred Russel Wallace. He spent eleven years on the upper Amazon, supporting himself largely by the specimens he sent back. Primarily an entomologist, he is said to have collected more than eight thousand species new to science. His account of his adventures contains many vivid glimpses of the jungle like the following description of a tropical day.*]

W E used to rise soon after dawn, when Isidoro would go down to the city, after supplying us with a cup of coffee, to purchase the fresh provisions for the day. The two hours before breakfast were devoted to ornithology. At that early period of the day the sky was invariably cloudless (the thermometer marking 72° or 73° Fahr.); the heavy dew or the previous night's rain, which lay on the moist foliage, becoming quickly dissipated by the glowing sun, which, rising straight out of the east, mounted rapidly towards the zenith. All nature was fresh, new leaf and flower-buds expanding rapidly. Some mornings a single tree would appear in flower amidst what was the preceding evening a uniform green mass of forest—a dome of blossom suddenly created as if by magic. . . .

In Europe, a woodland scene has its spring, its summer, its autumnal, and its winter aspects. In the equatorial forests the aspect is the same or nearly so every day in the year: budding, flowering, fruiting, and leaf-shedding are always going on in one species or other. The activity of birds and insects proceeds without interruption, each species having its own separate times; the colonies of wasps, for instance, do not die off annually, leaving only the queens, as in cold climates; but the succession of generations and colonies goes on incessantly. It is never either spring, summer, or autumn, but each day is a combination of all three. With the day and night always of equal length, the atmospheric disturbances of each day neutralising themselves before each succeeding morn; with the sun in its course proceeding mid-way across the sky, and the daily temperature the same within two or three degrees throughout the year—how grand in its perfect equilibrium and simplicity is the march of Nature under the equator!

HENRY WALTER BATES
[*The Naturalist on the River Amazons* (1863)]

To Blush Unseen

[*No part of the Arizona desert is hotter, drier or emptier than its south-western corner, which the army chose as the site for the training program known as "Operation Furnace." There an Iowa schoolteacher spent a year with her prospector husband looking for the gold they never found. They camped beside a rock until they exchanged it for the luxury of a shack to which even the irreducible minimum of water had to be hauled for miles across the sands. Bitterly loathing the desert at first, she gradually began to feel its fascination, and here describes perhaps its most striking miracle—the sudden flowering of a night-blooming cereus. This desert relative of a jungle species is for most of the year a dry stick which looks as unlikely to flower as Tannhäuser's staff. Then one night —and for one night only—it opens a huge, white and overpoweringly fragrant blossom obviously remembered from its jungle past.*]

SPRING was brief. In no time color that had appeared along the sandwashes vanished, and plants resumed their waiting—dry, apparently lifeless. Only the flaming tassels of the ocotillo brightened the ashen landscape.

Then, almost overnight, the cactus pageant began, and The Garden at the foot of the Copper Mountains was splashed with color like a painter's palette.

I had never dreamed that the viciously armored plants held

promise of such beauty. As the golden centers of the saguaro unfolded, as the creamy spikes of the yucca swayed in the hot dry wind, as the gorgeous jewels of all the other cacti flashed across the landscape, I lived in a world of enchantment. . . .

One warm May night we were all awakened by an overpowering fragrance floating up from the wash, the fragrance of tuberoses, regal lilies, jasmine, all the sweetest odors in the world, mixed together in an intoxicating perfume.

"Night-blooming cereus," Dad said from his cot over by the cookshade.

We lay discussing the miracle plant that could produce such a powerful perfume with nothing seemingly to draw life from but dry sand and rock. Dad promised to show me one of the plants in the morning.

The world was still cool and fresh and sweet, the birds were singing their dawn medleys when Dad tore strips from a white rag, stuffed them in his hip pocket, and announced that he was ready. Soon we were walking down the wash to The Garden, Dad stopping now and then to examine tangles of brush and cacti. I was surprised when he finally pointed out a single fluted stick, no more than a half inch across. It did not seem possible that such a dried stick of a plant could put forth a bud, to say nothing of a fragrant blossom.

We walked on, Dad's keen eyes scanning every patch of brush, even the smallest clumps in the center of bare spots. He pointed out several more of the budless plants, before he found one with a bud—a fleshy affair, somewhat like a lily bud. This time he tied one of the rags to a branch of brush directly over the plant so that I could find it again. To my amazement he soon found another budded plant and marked it, then another.

"The best way to find the plant is to track down the fragrance," he said. "But that would be quite a trick out here. The perfume travels a mighty long way these hot nights, and we don't want to be stumbling around and not know where we're goin'. So you watch these buds, and when you find one with white streaks showin' let me know. That will be The Night. We'll bring our flashlights and the lantern and sit up with it so you can see it bloom."

Every morning and evening when the shade lay in the canyon I made the rounds among my night-blooming plants, a number of which I discovered myself. The buds developed slowly or perhaps I was impatient. But at last came the evening when one was lifting its heavy head and when the white streaks Dad had mentioned showed

Inga Siliquis longissimis, vulgo Pacai. pag. 27

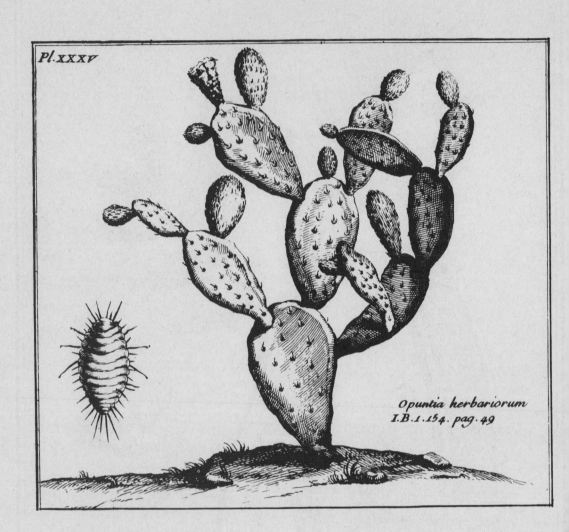

Pl. XXXV

Opuntia herbariorum
I.B.1.154. pag. 49

La Segadura

Original del Escultor Español Manuel Martínez Pintao
1925

between the folds of the sheath. A dilated bud gave its first hint of petals.

"She'll bloom tonight," Dad said, when I reported the progress of the bud. "Get your blankets and canteens ready and I'll fill the Coleman lantern and we'll all go and watch. No use to start till dark. Better get some sleep and I'll call you when it's midnight."

By midnight the moon was sailing high, the canyon almost as bright as day, and we didn't need the lantern, as the three of us accompanied by Foxie Dog followed the gleaming white pathway of the sandwash down into The Garden.

The bud had swollen considerably and was almost erect on its stem. It was loosening up, the white petals plainly visible in the moonlight. We spread our blankets on the sand and settled down to watch, Dad and Cap dozing at intervals for they were tired from work at the mine, but I was wide awake and sensitive to every sound and movement of the desert night.

Now and then I played my flashlight on the unfolding bud, though it was scarcely necessary with the moon pouring its light directly down on us as if it too were interested in this event.

A fox barked over among the rocks. Foxie Dog, curled beside Dad, whimpered. The men roused from their doze.

The bud was expanding in spasmodic jerks and beginning to send off sweet elusive perfume. We could almost see those creamy petals unfold. The perfume became heady, intoxicating. Breathlessly we watched. The night was so still it seemed to be watching too. At last a full-blown blossom, fully six inches across, gleamed in the white moonlight, its immaculate center filled with hundreds of waxy white stamens, yellow tipped, like so many lighted altar candles.

The Queen of the Night was in bloom!

Silently we worshipped. A moth fluttered up, quivered about the glistening petals, melted away in a moonbeam. Another moth floated up, sipped, was gone.

Cap's voice was reverent as he quoted,

Full many a flower is born to blush unseen,
And waste its sweetness on the desert air.

Not wasted, I thought, as we trod the path of moonbeams back to camp. Not wasted, but planted and tended by The Gardener, so that a human soul can for one brief hour forget its fear and satisfy its hunger.

OLGA WRIGHT SMITH
[*Gold on the Desert* (1956)]

Arctic Spring

[*A desert is not necessarily hot. As a matter of fact, the arctic tundra satisfies as well as our own Sonoran or Mohave deserts do the geographer's definition: "A desert is a region where the ground cover is not continuous." In all three cases the most obvious cause of desert conditions is scarcity of water. In the arctic, precipitation is scanty and such moisture as exists is locked up for a considerable portion of the year in the form of ice. Yet the tundra, like the warm deserts, blooms with brightly colored exuberance during its brief spring.*

No one knew the arctic better than Peter Freuchen or better described the fascination which it had for him. His last book, The Arctic Year, *was written in collaboration with a distinguished Danish naturalist and constitutes an almost encyclopedic compendium of information which manages to be at the same time almost a hymn to the awe and beauty of the north.*]

J U N E is the month of the year when the Arctic, more than any other part of the world, evidences huge differences between north and south. In Greenland, for example, the south is in full bloom—butterflies bring life to the landscape, bumblebees and snow buntings furnish music, and flowers show their colors in many places.

No less than 485 species of wild flowers have been identified and recorded in Greenland, and still botanists continue to discover new species for a hundred years ago only 311 were known. Of those now found in Greenland, 277 are arctic flowers, of which 20 are found nowhere else. This gives some little idea of the abundance of vegetation even in parts of the world usually regarded as barren and inhospitable. Even in the farthest north, in desertlike Peary Land, no less than 90 species of flowering plants have been found.

June is the month for flowering in the High Arctic, and in this respect it can be said to be the real spring month of the far north. Yet by far the majority of plants do not open their flowers until after the middle of the month, and this must certainly be considered a very late spring. The progress of flowering appears to be very similar all across the high-arctic zone, starting in the last week of May with the first blooms of the Purple Saxifrage, with Whitlow Grass and Cinquefoil following before the end of May. In June the Purple Saxifrage flowers everywhere, and gradually during the month a steadily increasing number of plant species burst into bloom. Careful counts have been made in many places over many years. As an example, a census carried out in northeast Greenland is enlightening. The first Purple Saxifrages flowered here on May 24, and before the end of the month 9 species were in flower. This number had increased to 38 by the middle of June. Then came the great floral period, between June 15 and June 24, when no less than 48 new species came into flower. In the last week of June, 6 more flowering plants were added. This does not mean that all species are in flower in June; in the present example, 35 species did not start flowering until some time in July. As a general rule, it can be said that in the High Arctic between a third and a half of the plant species do not open their flowers until July.

However, the end of June is the culminating period of vegetation. All the typical plants of the Arctic, all those that give the landscape its character by their great abundance, are then flowering or are in leaf. The late flowers appearing in July are much less conspicuous in the landscape than those of June, which make so great an impression because of the mass effect of the flowers of all the dominant plant species.

At this time of the year, when vegetation unfolds with startling suddenness and floral display reaches its maximum, the presence of moisture is of the greatest importance. The entire development of the vegetation depends on that, and all plant life adjusts itself to the fact that it now has easier access to moisture than at any time. Everywhere the ground is thawing, and the snow melts rapidly. The greater part of the melt-water, to be sure, rushes down from the heights in torrents, causing rivers to flood and channels to shift from year to year and spreading thick layers of debris over the plains, which results in great destruction to plant life. Still a fair amount seeps down through the frost-free upper one or two feet of the soil and is prevented from escaping by the permafrost. This percolating water forms the main supply for the plants. But it must be utilized in June when snow-melting takes place, for when this is over in July the ground becomes dry again.

Only a small part of the water utilized by the plants is furnished by the downfall, and this too can usually be used only in June. Earlier in spring the snowfall disappeared mainly by evaporation and left behind dry, still frozen ground through which water could not penetrate. The snow that falls in June melts on the ground where it lies. The fields and the slopes may be white in the morning and until noon, but before long the soil, warmed by the sun and already thawed, absorbs the melting snow, which easily penetrates to the roots of the plants. And for these, being in a period of rapid development and growth, water is of the most vital importance.

In the last week of June it no longer snows, except in rare instances, and the transition to summer is best indicated by the first rain. But apart from the rain and the melt-water in the ground, the plants have yet another source of moisture, which may be less obvious but both directly and indirectly is of great importance. Because the sun heats the land, cold winds often blow in from the sea in the latter part of June, and cause dense fogs to creep over the land and soak everything. Such fogs may occur day after day. The whole of the vegetation profits from them by direct absorption, but undoubtedly mosses and lichens derive the greatest advantage. Indirectly, the fog is also of significance for plant life because, when lying densely over the ground, it lessens evaporation considerably and therefore greatly aids the plants in their water economy.

The growth of flowers in June is not the only visible expression of activity in the plant world. June is characterized also by the leafing of the summer-green dwarf bushes, primarily the Dwarf Birch, the Bilberry and different willows. The first two do not appear in the most northern and barren regions but occur farther south in the high-arctic zone, not to mention the entire low-arctic region, where they cover extensive areas, and their leafing adds a fresh green touch to the landscape. Farther north, the White Heather is the only true heath-forming dwarf bush, and the areas covered with this plant become free of snow in the middle of June. Since the White Heather is winter-green the heaths become green all at once when the snow has disappeared.

However, not all the snow on the ground disappears in June, and the differences in the time at which it melts are of the greatest importance for the distribution of the plants. Everybody who has been up in the Arctic knows that the depth of snow varies greatly. The winter gales sweep the snow away from ridges, crests and peaks and deposit it in depressions and valleys, and the differences in snow cover thus created become especially noticeable in spring when the snow melts. Now it is significant for the plants that this uneven distribution of the snow is repeated every year. In areas that are free of snow in winter or that are clear of it early in spring, plant life naturally consists of extremely hardy species that are able to endure very low temperatures in winter, as well as strong wind erosion and further must face a severe exsiccation during the summer. Among such robust plants the most important are a number of heath plants, such as the Mountain Aven and the Crowberry. The Firemoss Cassiope also can be reckoned among them, since it requires only a thin and loose snow cover that melts in June. And the Purple Saxifrage, that heroic and inspiring plant of the early spring which, blossoming first, brings life to solitude, must not be forgotten; it often grows in places that are completely snow-free in winter.

Of course these robust plants, which expose themselves to such great dangers in winter, derive some advantage from their way of life. Since the arctic summer is so short, it is important that the plants profit by the light and the heat of the sun as early as possible in spring, as soon as the temperature at the surface of the soil is above the freezing point. The greater part of these early-blossoming plants require a rather long time for their development, including growth, flowering and the production of ripe seeds, and cannot afford to waste any of the brief growing season. Lack of time is a real danger for the high-arctic plants. Like the early-arriving birds in May which run a serious risk during harsh weather, a number of plants are bound to spend the winter without snow cover or with only a slight one in order to be able to start development so early in spring that they can complete the whole cycle before the fall sets in.

Time, then, is precious; the risk of being too late is obvious. Farther south, in our latitudes, an unfavorable spring causes a retardation of development, it is true, but a delay of a fortnight or even a month can easily be overcome during the long summer. But in the Arctic an inclement spring means not only a retardation of the advent of summer but a great reduction of the growing period. Although the plants are adapted to a very short summer, in unfavorable years such adaptation is insufficient. The plants that are on the northern limit of their distribution are overtaken by winter while still in flower. Under such conditions you may see the plants with frozen, vigorous leaves, with swelling buds, half-open or expanded flowers or half-ripe fruits. Thus, while still alive the plants have been paralyzed by the cold in fall.

The plants growing beneath the dense, late-melting snowdrifts, the so-called snow-bed plants, have troubles that are exactly opposite those of the early plants wintering in snowless ground. The snow-bed plants must reckon with a shortening of the growth season, and accordingly include only species that can exist with a greatly reduced vegetative period. On the other hand, the snow-bed plants derive great benefit from the protection against the cold offered by the snow cover. They can therefore afford to be frailer than those species that are exposed to the full force of the winter. In this respect, the snow-bed plants may be compared with the small mammals or the insects that winter beneath the snow protected from the icy cold.

The efficiency of the protection afforded by the high insulating power of the snow is shown by the fact that while the air temperature may sink as low as −25° F., the temperature two feet inside snowdrifts is as high as + 22°F. However, the main danger to the arctic plants is not the extreme cold but the desiccating winds of the polar winter. These give rise to some evaporation from the surface of the plants, slight though it may be. And since absorption of water from the frozen ground is impossible, the plants are doomed to death.

Snow-bed plants must accelerate their development even more than plants of the open field for they must pay for the protection of the snow by an inevitable shortening of the growth period. The last plants to appear from beneath the snow cover have scarcely six full weeks for the entire cycle, and no flowering plant can complete it faster than that. But all snow-bed plants are not so late as this; each species is adapted to its particular snow cover and its rate of growth bears a direct relation to the time it has at its disposal. The earliest snow-bed plants are exposed to the light in the latter part of June, about one month later than the earliest plants of snow-free ground. The last snow-bed plants do not appear until after the middle of July. Beneath snowdrifts that melt still later than that, there will not be any flowering plants at all, although sometimes some mosses may be found growing there.

Thus, immediately upon appearing, the snow-bed vegetation are subjected to the most intense heat of the summer. The plants are capable, therefore, of growing at an amazing rate, the rapidity of their development being unsurpassed anywhere among flowering plants throughout the world. The prefloral period, the time interval from when the plant is thawed out of the snow until its incipient flowering, covers only one or two weeks, the average being ten days and the briefest six days. The plants wintering on almost snow-free soil and exposed to light early in spring also develop very rapidly, although not as fast as the snow-bed plants. The period from thawing until they start flowering generally lasts for 15 to 22 days and only occasionally longer.

The astonishing rapidity of development accounts for the sudden, almost instantaneous appearance of the arctic flowers, which from early times has impressed travelers in the polar world. The unfolding of this concentrated display of life is considerably aided by the sudden rise of temperature in the arctic spring and by the continuous sunlight, which permits uninterrupted plant activity during the twenty-four hours of the day. But this is not enough to explain the remarkable rapidity of development. The thawing, awakening, growth, differentiation of organs, and formation of flowers could not possibly take place within one or two weeks even under the most favorable conditions. The inherent passiveness of living tissue would slow down growth and would prevent the completion of the reproductive cycle before fall, with the result that the plant soon would be exterminated. This does not happen, because all the organs in the plant have been prepared long beforehand. It is just like the metamorphosis of a caterpillar. After the long resting period in winter the pupa bursts and the full grown, mature butterfly crawls out, completely developed.

In practically all high-arctic plants, the life cycle cannot be completed within one year; they are what botanists call perennial plants. Most species require many years from germination to the first flowering. In their youth, they gradually build up leaves and stems before they start the development of flowers, and this immature stage may last for ten years or more. Even when the flower buds start their growth they do not unfold the flowers the same summer, but spend the winter in varying stages of development, ranging from the first incipient differentiation of the flowering organs to the completely developed flower buds with full-grown pollen. These buds are, of course, not injured by frost.

The stage in which the buds spend the winter rest is constant for each species, although the buds of about 10 per cent of all arctic plants show no periodicity and may winter in any stage. A few species, and they must be regarded as exceptions, may winter with ripening fruits, unfolded flowers or just buds, and in these it appears to be mere chance how far the plant has progressed in its development before it is arrested by the frost. When spring comes, it resumes its development quite uninjured.

In most cases, the flower buds begin their development in the spring a full year before the flowering takes place, but in particularly slow-growing species the flower buds may begin their development two years before the flowering. Owing to the early formation of the flowers, they are fully developed when they start activity in the spring, and consequently they are able to unfold within a few weeks.

Annual plants—that is, species able to complete their life cycle within the same summer—are extremely scarce in the high-arctic region, and constitute only 1 per cent of the species. These plants are very small, often less than a half inch high, and this minuteness is probably the reason why they are able to complete their entire development within 5 to 6 weeks.

PETER FREUCHEN
AND FINN SALOMONSEN
[*The Arctic Year* (1958)]

Night on the Desert

[*Lorus and Margery Milne (who always work together as naturalists and writers) had the happy idea of taking the World of Night as a subject. One of their vivid passages describes the blooming of the yucca during a night on the southwestern desert. Most night-blooming plants are fertilized by moths and are usually white because whiteness is most visible in darkness.*]

SINCE almost three-fourths of the earth's surface is open water—oceans, lakes, and rivers—it seems scarcely reasonable that any land should be so dry. Yet of the total area of the continents, more than a twelfth is desert, where the annual rainfall rarely reaches as much as ten inches. Sometimes a whole year goes by with no rain at all. Little or no subsurface water can be reached, and plants must either hoard moisture from one shower to another, or remain dormant for many months, even years.

The critical problem is always water. In the intense light of day, a small area of green plant can capture all the sun energy needed since the rate of growth is so limited by drought. Any excess of surface above ground invites extra loss of moisture. In consequence, the plants of the desert are largely hidden. Enormous root systems, specialized for storing water and for capturing any that may sink in after a rain, spread out in all directions and meet their neighbors. Exposed to air may be only low woody shrubs, each separated widely from the next by areas of naked soil.

To wander on foot through a desert, particularly after dark, is to sense the uniqueness of living conditions there. In the cactus forests of Arizona, on a night-time stroll with naturalist-philosopher Joseph Wood Krutch and William Woodin III of the Desert Museum in Tucson, we threaded our way between prickly pear and barrel cactus, past waist-high chollas and clumps of eight-foot catclaw wands. At intervals a giant saguaro was silhouetted against the sky. Some of them rose as much as thirty feet from the desert floor, their spine-set accordion pleats imprisoning six to seven tons of water. Their blunt, curved branches suggest grotesque arms, somehow frozen by the heat in the middle of a gesture. Even these monster green reservoirs do not dispel the feeling that all vegetation in the desert grows low, grows spines, grows slowly.

In the side of many a saguaro, a circular hole can be seen— the doorway to the cactus woodpecker's flask-shaped nest. These birds hollow out a cavity from the soft wet heart of the plant, and wait until scar tissue seals the surface with a firm liner. Year after year the flicker-sized woodpecker may nest in the same place. Eventually the hole goes vacant. A diminutive squatter, the elf owl, moves in and takes advantage of the cavity.

It was this new tenant that we sought in the saguaro forest, for elf owls live nowhere else in the world. From time to time one darted through the night beside us, carrying home to the hungry young a grasshopper or other insect. Some owls held more than one victim, and the assorted legs stuck out around the bird's bill like stiff whiskers. These and the disproportionately large yellow eyes seemed the only landmarks on the smooth little flying ball of feathers.

William Woodin had been our companion previously on a night field trip in a Panamanian jungle, and it was natural that we should compare the tropics with the desert. In the rain forest the bulk of vegetation had been almost invisibly high overhead, so that around us bare poles climbed at intervals from the naked, slippery mud. In the cactus forest the plants were almost entirely subterranean; our feet skidded in the coarse soil, and only the glaring stars told us that the saguaro trunks supported no canopy of leaves. Both regions had their pit-vipers, and lest we step on one, we kept our flashlamps burning. The tropics held fer-de-lance and bushmaster, the desert its own rattlesnakes and those specialists of sandy slopes, the sidewinders. . . .

Through May the saguaros flower. In June their fruit split

open, revealing a red jacket and pulp, set with hundreds of black seeds. They tumble to the ground and there are set upon by rodents, coyotes, birds, and men. The pulp is vaguely sweet. The seeds have thin skins, and concentrated nourishment. It is doubtful whether one seed in ten thousand has a chance to germinate.

Other desert plants are correspondingly profligate: the yuccas, shaking seeds noisily from split brown pods; creosote bushes broadcasting their furry white fruit balls; cottonwoods along the dry washes liberating myriads of fluffy seeds into the wind. . . .

The rate of growth of a yucca flower stalk is so fast as to be almost visible. A foot per day is common, far outdistancing the familiar but smaller asparagus which it resembles.

A similar flower stalk is produced by century plants (aloes of the genus *Agave*) as their final fling in life. They raise the stalk fifteen to twenty feet in less than three weeks. For years each *Agave* has stored water and sun energy in the heavy bases of its long, bayonet-shaped leaves. One leaf may weigh well over two pounds, its green pulp reinforced by stiff white flat fibers similar to those taken from commercial sisal for use in ropes and nets. Yet when the mature leaves reach full development, the aloe squanders all its resources on a gamble for the future. Swiftly it flowers and tempts pollinating birds and insects with nectar and perfume.

Much sugar-rich sap flows into the upthrusting flower stalk, giving energy for the rapid growth. Men have learned to rob the plant. They amputate the bud, scoop out a cavity holding half a gallon or more, and collect the juice as the sweet base for the beer-like *pulque* and the distilled liquor *tequila*. The raw liquid is so attractive to wild animals that the collecting cavity must be covered each evening with the saw-edged leaves, or coyotes will drink it dry.

Other plant denizens of the desert wait for night before unfurling their buds. The various kinds of night-blooming cereus clamber over other vegetation or lie prostrate on the dry soil. Mexican peasants believe that these plants time their flowering to match San Juan's Day— June 24, the supposed birthdate of John the Baptist. Actually they open a few blossoms each night for a protracted period in late spring. Each flower begins to spread its water-lily-like petals about sundown, and in an hour or so is fully open. Around the many yellow-tipped stamens the glistening white petals may spread as widely as fifteen inches across. The blossom liberates a powerful fragrance into the darkness. Hawkmoths whirr to this perfume across the desert, feast on the freely proferred sugar water, and accomplish pollination for the plant. The Indians name this cactus the "Desert Queen," and mention it in many of their legends.

LORUS J. AND MARGERY MILNE
[*The World of Night* (1956)]

A Tropical Garden

[*For many years David Fairchild searched around the world for new or improved varieties of useful plants. Through the Division of Plant Introduction of the United States Department of Agriculture he contributed to American agriculture innumerable now-important crops. But his interest in plant life was aesthetic as well as utilitarian, and he had an especial love of the tropics. His garden in Florida is still one of Miami's great show places.*]

I THINK if some one were to ask me, "What did you like best in Morocco?", I should answer unhesitatingly "The Garden of the Oudaias in Rabat." I have seen beautiful gardens in England and Scotland and surrounding the Châteaux along the Loire, I know Versailles, and Pierrefonds and many others in France, Dutch and Belgian and Swedish gardens, the palace gardens of Bavaria and Austria, as well as lovely Miramar which Maximilian built on the Adriatic, and that other garden of royalty, the Kaiser's retreat on a mountain top in Corfu, and also his Potsdam gardens. I have wandered in many a charming villa garden of Italy and Sicily and seen the famous gardens of the Alhambra, Cintra and the lovely Monserrat near Lisbon; I know the remarkable gardens of Cape Town and those of Melbourne and Sydney and of Rio de Janeiro, and also the notable gardens of the New England States, the pretentious but altogether charming ones of Southern California, the incomparable Magnolia Garden near Charleston, and all of the large botanic gardens of the tropics including those of Peradeniya in Ceylon, and Buitenzorg Java, and the superb creations of Japanese and Chinese landscape art. I admit that no gardens are comparable, that each is in a sense the loveliest thing of its kind, but to me this garden in Rabat is the most remarkable of them all from the standpoint of its impression of complete simplicity and beauty of proportion. It is not a collection of plants and I am aware that many of my gardening friends would sniff at the meager show of species, for they could count off on their fingers many more growing in their own gardens. But I maintain that a garden is more than a collection of flowering plants, it is a work of art demanding the highest form of artistic skill. There must not be a single jarring note of color or grotesqueness of form, or error of proportion in the whole creation. The garden of the Oudaias, I found to be such a creation.

When I try to describe it I seem paralyzed, I simply cannot do it. I can see in my imagination its red-brown castellated walls on which the storks were nesting. I can hear their raucous calls. I see the blue morning-glories covering great spaces below the turrets where we used to walk. I hear the faint sound of the blindfolded donkey as it turned the water wheel near the Meder-sea and the trickling water falling into the lily tank near by. I see the long pergolas made of irregular poles and reeds on which the grapevines were casting flickering shadows on the paths beneath. I remember beds of blue and white verbenas below the level of the walks with here and there, regardless of any order, a pomegranate or apricot or orange tree, and the low-clipped hedge of lavender enclosing them. Beside the softly modeled broad steps that led from one level of the garden to another the broad-leaved Acanthus was in flower and yuccas were starting to send up their spikes of blooms. The large-flowered Datura arborea and some broad-leaved banana plants filled one corner of the great walled-in space. Through a superbly proportioned Moorish archway groups of white-robed Arabs were strolling, fans in hand, to the little café which overlooks the river Bou-reg-reg and the white-walled town of Sale on the other side, from which, in the years gone by, the Barbary Pirates sailed forth to capture and bring back the white slaves for their Seraglios.

We sat one afternoon in this little café and tried in vain to discover in what lay the incredible fascination of all around us. We were conscious that many a man of great wealth would give a fortune to have his own garden one-half so charming. How would it be possible to bring into anything he might build the element of the fortuitous which was everywhere about us? The terrace alone, built perhaps by slaves, was fitted against the cliff as securely as a swallow would tie its little nest to the rocks. The different levels and the winding paths from one to the other were built to fit the irregularities of the rocks. Every bench on which the Arabs sat and smoked showed the hand marks of the workmen. Not a straight line was anywhere to be found, not a corner that had been made sharp by the use of a trowel and straightedge. The arbor over our heads was made of canes with about as much idea of regularity as though some darky fresh from the cotton fields of the South had made it from the canes and poles growing by the stream. Everything which an American mason would do to make his work perfect had here not been done, but the one thing which in the great majority of cases an American cement worker would not pay attention to—the proportions of every detail, had been as scrupulously adhered to as are the proportions of a swallow's nest adhered to by the birds that build it. I sometimes think as I shudder before some frightful residence or some perfectly terrible bedding on a lawn, that we Americans are too self-conscious to do things simply.

DAVID FAIRCHILD
[*Exploring for Plants* (1930)]

Section Ten

SOME USEFUL PLANTS

The profit of the earth is for all.

ECCLESIASTES

For a high-minded man agriculture is the best of all occupations.

XENOPHON

When Adam delved and Eve span,
Who was then the gentleman?

ANONYMOUS
14th century

There is no ancient gentlemen but gardeners.

SHAKESPEARE
Hamlet

The First Farmers

[*Millions of years before primitive man invented agriculture certain insects—ants as well as at least one species of beetle and one species of termite—were planting, fertilizing and cultivating underground fungus gardens. Thomas Belt, a Victorian geologist with a passionate side interest in natural history, was the first to observe that the so-called "leaf-cutter ants" did not eat the leaves they cut but used them to mulch their "mushroom gardens." His account (since abundantly confirmed) first appeared in* The Naturalist in Nicaragua.]

IN June 1869, very soon after the formation of my garden, the leaf-cutting ants came down upon it, and at once commenced denuding the young bananas, orange, and mango trees of their leaves. I followed up the paths of the invading hosts to their nest, which was about one hundred yards distant, close to the edge of the forest. The nest was not a very large one, the low mound of earth covering it being about four yards in diameter. At first I tried to stop the holes up, but fresh ones were immediately opened out; I then dug down below the mound, and laid bare the chambers beneath, filled with ant-food and young ants in every stage of growth; but I soon found that the underground ramifications extended so far, and to so great a depth, while the ants were continually at work making fresh excavations, that it would be an immense task to eradicate them by such means; and notwithstanding all the digging I had done the first day, I found them the next as busily at work as ever at my garden, which they were rapidly defoliating. . . .

It was fully twelve months before my garden was again invaded. I had then a number of rose-trees and also cabbages growing, which the ants seemed to prefer to everything else. The rose-trees were soon defoliated, and great havoc was made amongst the cabbages. I followed them to their nest, and found it about two hundred yards from the one of the year before. I poured down the burrows, as before, several buckets of water with carbolic acid. The water is required to carry the acid down to the lowest chambers. The ants, as before, were at once withdrawn from my garden; and two days afterwards, on visiting the place, I found all the survivors at work on one track that led directly to the old nest of the year before, where they were busily employed making fresh excavations. Many were bringing along pieces of the ant-food from the old to the new nests; others carried the undeveloped white pupae and larvae. It was a wholesale and entire migration; and the next day the formicarium down which I had last poured the carbolic acid was entirely deserted. I afterwards found that when much disturbed, and many of the ants destroyed, the survivors migrate to a new locality. I do not doubt that some of the leading minds in this formicarium recollected the nest of the year before, and directed the migration to it. . . .

Notwithstanding that these ants are so common throughout tropical America, and have excited the attention of nearly every traveller, there still remains much doubt as to the use to which the leaves are put. Some naturalists have supposed that they use them directly as food; others, that they roof their underground nests with them. I believe the real use they make of them is as a manure, on which grows a minute species of fungus, on which they feed; that they are, in reality, mushroom growers and eaters. This explanation is so extraordinary and unexpected, that I may be permitted to enter somewhat at length on the facts that led me to adopt it. When I first began my warfare against the ants that attacked my garden, I dug down deeply into some of their nests. In our mining operations we also, on two occasions, carried our excavations from below up through very large formicariums, so that all their underground workings were exposed to observation. I found their nests below to consist of numerous rounded chambers, about as large as a man's head, connected together by tunnelled passages leading from one chamber to another. Notwithstanding that many columns of the ants were continually carrying in the cut leaves, I could never find any quantity of these in the burrows, and it was evident that they were used up in some way immediately they were brought in. The chambers were always about three parts filled with a speckled, brown, flocculent, spongy-looking mass of a light and loosely connected substance.

Throughout these masses were numerous ants belonging to the smallest division of the workers, which do not engage in leaf-carrying. Along with them were pupae and larvae, not gathered together, but dispersed, apparently irregularly, throughout the flocculent mass. This mass, which I have called the ant-food, proved, on examination, to be composed of minutely subdivided pieces of leaves, withered to a brown colour, and overgrown and lightly connected together by a minute white fungus that ramified in every direction throughout it. I not only found this fungus in every chamber I opened, but also in the chambers of the nest of a distinct species that generally comes out only in the night-time, often entering houses and carrying off various farinaceous substances, and which does not make mounds above its nests, but long, winding passages, terminating in chambers similar to the common species, and always, like them, three parts filled with flocculent masses of fungus-covered vegetable matter, amongst which are the ant-nurses and imma-ture ants. When a nest is disturbed, and the masses of ant-food spread about, the ants are in great concern to carry every morsel of it under shelter again; and sometimes, when I had dug into a nest, I found the next day all the earth thrown out filled with little pits that the ants had dug into it to get out the covered up food. When they migrate from one part to another, they also carry with them all the ant-food from their old habitations. That they do not eat the leaves themselves I convinced myself; for I found near the tenanted chambers, deserted ones filled with the refuse particles of leaves that had been exhausted as manure for the fungus, and were now left, and served as food for larvae of *Staphylinidae* and other beetles.

These ants do not confine themselves to leaves, but also carry off any vegetable substance that they find suitable for growing the fungus on. They are very partial to the inside white rind of oranges, and I have also seen them cutting up and carrying off the flowers of certain shrubs, the leaves of which they neglected. They are particular about the ventilation of their underground chambers, and have numerous holes leading up to the surface from them. These they open out or close up, apparently to keep up a regular degree of temperature below. The great care they take that the pieces of leaves they carry into the nest should be neither too dry nor too damp, is also consistent with the idea that the object is the growth of a fungus that requires particular conditions of temperature and moisture to ensure its vigorous growth. If a sudden shower should come on, the ants do not carry the wet pieces into the burrows, but throw them down near the entrances. Should the weather clear up again, these pieces are picked up when nearly dried, and taken inside; should the rain, however, continue, they get sodden down into the ground, and are left there. On the contrary, in dry and hot weather, when the leaves would get dried up before they could be conveyed to the nest, the ants, when in exposed situations, do not go out at all during the hot hours, but bring in their leafy burdens in the cool of the day and during the night. As soon as the pieces of leaves are carried in they must be cut up by the small class of workers into little pieces. I have never seen the smallest class of ants carrying in leaves; their duties appear to be inside, cutting them up into smaller fragments, and nursing the immature ants. I have, however, seen them running out along the paths with the others; but instead of helping to carry in the burdens, they climb on the top of the pieces which are being carried along by the middle-sized workers, and so get a ride home again. It is very probable that they take a run out merely for air and exercise. The largest class of what are called workers are, I believe, the directors and protectors of the others. They are never seen out of the nest, excepting on particular occasions, such as the migrations of the ants, and when one of the working columns or nests is attacked; and then come stalking up, and attacking the enemy with their strong jaws. Sometimes, when digging into the burrows, one of these giants has unperceived climbed up my dress, and the first intimation of his presence has been the burying of his jaws in my neck, from which he would not fail to draw the blood. The stately observant way in which they stalk about, and their great size, compared with the others, always impressed me with the idea that in their bulky heads lay the brains that directed the community in its various duties. Many of their actions, such as that I have mentioned of two relays of workmen carrying out the ant-food, can scarcely be blind instinct. Some of the ants make mistakes, and carry in unsuitable leaves. Thus grass is nearly always rejected by them, yet I have seen some ants, perhaps young ones, carrying in leaves of grass. After a while these pieces were invariably brought out again and thrown away. I can imagine a young ant getting a severe earwigging from one of the major-domos for its stupidity.

THOMAS BELT
[*The Naturalist in Nicaragua* (1874)]

How Corn Came to the Indian

[*If agriculture was invented first by the insects, they kept their secret from primitive man. How it first developed no one knows but many primitive people have legends to account for the introduction of their most important food crop. This is the tale the Seneca Indians tell of the great gift of corn.*]

IN ancient times there was a village situated on the banks of a river. The chief source of subsistence of the people was the natural products of forest and stream—that is to say, game and fish, berries and various edible roots and tubers.

There came a day when the people dwelling in this village were told by an old woman that she heard the voice of a woman singing on the river; and she told them further that the words used by this strange singer were: "Luxuriant and fine are the planted fields which we have planted. My grandmother and my ancestors have planted them."

After hearing this singing for 10 nights the old woman said to her family and neighbors: "Let us go out to see what this singing means; perhaps some woman has fallen into the water, and it may be she who is singing in the middle of the river." They did go to the river bank, but saw nothing, and they returned much chagrined at their failure to discover the singer.

On the tenth night following, the woman again began to sing, seemingly from the middle of the river not very far from the village. Again she sang: "Luxuriant and fine are the planted fields [of corn] where I swell, going to and fro. Luxuriant and fine are the planted fields [of corn] which we have planted. My grandmother and my ancestors have planted them." Then the women of the village, going to the river bank for three nights, sang songs of welcome and recognition, and on the third night these women perceived that the singer on the river had drawn nearer to them. On the fourth night the women watching with their children on the river bank, and singing in response to the singing on the river, were surprised to see coming toward them a large number of women. Thereupon one of the girls exclaimed: "Oh, grandmother, do not let these women seize us," and the children fled from the place. But the spokeswoman, who was the eldest person present, said: "I alone shall remain here to await whatever may befall me, and I do so because my granddaughter, who is coming, is in need of pity and aid."

At this the woman, the midstream singer, exclaimed: "Oh, my grandmother! take me hence. I am not able to go there [where you now are]." Then the grandmother (so called by the courtesy of clan kinship) placed her canoe of birch bark in the stream and soon by rapid paddling reached the side of the young woman who had been singing in midstream. She found her granddaughter lying on the back of a beaver, which mysteriously held her above the water. The granddaughter was the first to speak, saying: "Oh, my grandmother! take me hence." The grandmother, replying: "Oh, my grandchild! your wish shall be fulfilled," at once proceeded to place her granddaughter in the canoe, after which she headed for the shore of the stream, paddling to the landing place in a short time. When they had landed, the young woman said: "Oh, grandmother! now leave me here. I will remain here, and you must come after me in the morning. Nothing shall happen to me in the meantime." The grandmother at once returned to her own lodge, where, of course, she related in detail what had taken place.

Early the next morning she returned to the landing place where she had left her granddaughter (by courtesy). There she saw only the growing stalk of a plant. Drawing near to this she found growing on the stalk an ear of corn, and breaking it off she carried it back to her lodge, where she hung it up on a roof-supporting pole hard by the fireplace.

It came to pass during the following night that the grandmother, so called, had a dream or vision, in which the young woman who had been singing in midstream said to her, "Oh, my grandmother, you should unhang me from this place, for it is indeed too hot here. You should place me in the ground—plant me—and then leave me there; for I will provide for you and your people, you human beings. So kindly place me under the ground." This dream came to the old woman three nights in succession. So she took down the ear of corn, and after shelling it she planted the grains of corn in the ground just as she had been instructed to do by the dream.

But on the following night the grandmother again dreamed, and the young woman in the dream said to her, "You and your people must

care for me. You must not permit weeds to kill me. You shall see me
sprout and grow to maturity; and it is a truth that in the future all the
people who shall be born will see that I will provide for their welfare.
So you must take care of me. You will see, you and your people, a great
multitude of people who are about to arrive here. You will see, I say,
that I will provide for all during the time the earth shall be in existence.
You shall now learn what is a well-known truth—that is, that I am corn;
I am native corn; I am sweet corn. I am the first corn that came or was
delivered to this earth." For three successive nights the grandmother, so
called, had this same dream or vision, hence she came to regard it as a
direct intimation to her regarding the disposition to be made of the corn
on the ear which she had found on the bank of the river. So forcibly did
the injunctions impress her that she planted the corn in the ground as
directed; and she carefully followed the directions of the Corn Maiden
as to the care required by the growing corn to enable it to mature and to
prevent it being choked to death by weeds.

In the autumn the old woman harvested her corn, and taking
it into her lodge she divided it into as many portions as there were families in the village of her people. Then she gave a portion to the chief
matron in each lodge, telling each that the corn should be used in the
spring for seed and also how it should be planted and cultivated. Afterward she returned to her own lodge. She was greatly rejoiced at the
prospect of her people having something which would supply them
with a staple food, if they would only properly care for it.

In a short time after reaching her own lodge she lay down on
her couch to rest for the night; but she had hardly fallen asleep before
she had another dream, or vision, of the Corn Maiden. In this dream the
Corn Maiden said to her: "You must tell my children [the human
beings] that they must not waste in any manner the corn which shall
grow to maturity in the future. It is well known that those who do not
honor and properly care for me invariably come to want and destitution;
for unless they act so toward me when I leave I shall take all the corn
and other seed away. And, grandmother, you must tell all these things
to your people and kindred."

[*Seneca Fiction, Legends, and Myths* (1910–11)
32d Annual Report of the Bureau of American Ethnology]

Incense from the East

[*The elder Pliny's vast and uncritical compilation called* Natural History *is the most complete existing summary of all the ancient world knew, thought it knew, or guessed on its subject. It includes travelers' tales, practical descriptions of horticultural methods, and gross superstitions. In a typical passage the author summarizes what he has heard about the valued but mysterious frankincense which the Romans valued no less than the ancient Hebrews.*]

N O R is it by any means agreed what is the appearance of the incense-tree. We have sent several expeditions against Arabia, and the Roman arms have penetrated into the greater part of that country; indeed, Caius Caesar, the son of Augustus, even earned considerable renown there; and yet this tree has been described by no Latin writer, at least that I know of. The descriptions given of it by the Greek writers vary very considerably: some of them say that it has exactly the leaf of the pear-tree, only somewhat smaller, and of a grass-green colour. Others, again, say, that it has a rather reddish leaf, like that of the mastich, and others, that it is a kind of terebinth, and that King Antigonus, to whom a branch of it was brought, was of that opinion. King Juba, in the work which he wrote and dedicated to Caius Caesar, the son of Augustus, who was inflamed by the wide-spread renown of Arabia, states, that the tree has a spiral stem, and that the branches bear a considerable resemblance to those of the Pontic maple, while it secretes a sort of juice very similar to that of the almond-tree. Such, he says, is the appearance of the tree as seen in Carmania and Egypt, where it was introduced and planted under the auspices of the Ptolemies when reigning there. It is well known that it has a bark not unlike that of the laurel, and, indeed, some persons have asserted that their leaves are similar. At all events, such was the case with the tree as it grew at Sardes: for the kings of Asia also took con-

siderable care to have it planted there. The ambassadors who in my time
have come to Rome from Arabia, have made all these matters more
uncertain, even, than they were before; a thing at which we may justly
be surprised, seeing that some sprigs even of the incense-tree have been
brought among us, from which we have some reason to conclude that
the parent tree is round and tapering, and that it puts forth its shoots
from a trunk that is entirely free from knots.

In former times, when they had fewer opportunities of selling
it, they used to gather the frankincense only once a year; but at the
present day, as there is a much greater demand for it, there is a second
crop as well. The first, and what we may call the natural, vintage, takes
place about the rising of the Dog-star, a period when the heat is most
intense; on which occasion they cut the tree where the bark appears to
be the fullest of juice, and extremely thin, from being distended to the
greatest extent. The incision thus made is gradually extended, but nothing is removed; the consequence of which is, that an unctuous foam
oozes forth, which gradually coagulates and thickens. When the nature
of the locality requires it, this juice is received upon mats of palm-leaves,
though in some places the space around the tree is made hard by being
well rammed down for the purpose. The frankincense that is gathered
after the former method, is in the purest state, though that which falls
on the ground is the heaviest in weight: that which adheres to the tree
is pared off with an iron instrument, which accounts for its being found
mingled with pieces of bark.

The forest is allotted in certain portions, and such is the mutual
probity of the owners, that it is quite safe from all depredation; indeed,
there is no one left to watch the trees after the incisions are made, and
yet no one is ever known to plunder his neighbour. But, by Hercules! at
Alexandria, where the incense is dressed for sale, the workshops can
never be guarded with sufficient care; a seal is even placed upon the
workmen's aprons, and a mask put upon the head, or else a net with
very close meshes, while the people are stripped naked before they are
allowed to leave work. So true it is that punishments afford less security
among us than is to be found by these Arabians amid their woods and
forests! The incense which has accumulated during the summer is
gathered in the autumn: it is the purest of all, and is of a white colour.
The second gathering takes place in spring, incisions being made in the
bark for that purpose during the winter: this, however, is of a red
colour, and not to be compared with the other incense. The first, or
superior kind of incense, is known as carfiathum, the latter is called
dathiathum. It is thought, also, that the incense which is gathered from

the tree while young is the whitest, though the produce of the old trees has the most powerful smell; some persons, too, have an impression that the best incense is found in the islands, but Juba asserts that no incense at all is grown there.

PLINY THE ELDER
[*Natural History* (1st century A.D.)]

Virgil's Advice to Farmers

[*No present-day poet would be likely to write a treatise on agriculture and no present-day agriculturist likely to set forth his conclusions in verse. Perhaps this is because we are likely to think that the poetry and the prose of farming (and of pretty much everything else) are two very different things. We may have lost as well as gained something by this dissociation, and in any event it did not always exist. Virgil's* Georgics *were intended to be sound both practically and poetically. His ideal farmer would have been a man much like the neighbor described by Thoreau in the paragraphs which immediately follow this excerpt from* The Georgics.]

I N the dawn of spring, when icy streams trickle melting from the hoar mountains, and the crumbling clod breaks its chain at the west wind's touch, even then I would fain see the plough driven deep till the bull groans again, and the share rubbed in the furrow till it shines. That is the corn-field to give an answer, full though late, to the grasping farmer's prayer, which has twice been laid bare to summer heat, and twice to winter cold—that is the corn-field to burst the barns with its unmeasured crop. Before, however, our share breaks the crust of an unknown soil, our care should be to understand the winds and the divers humours of the sky, and the traditional culture and habitude of the land, what each clime produces and what each disowns. Here you see corn crops, there grapes have kindlier growth: other spots are green with the young of trees and grass that comes unbidden. Only see how it is Tmolus that sends us its saffron fragrance, India its ivory, the soft Arab his frankincense, the naked Chalybs, again, his iron, Pontus its potent castor, Epirus the prizes of the mares of Elis! Such is the chain of law, such the eternal covenant with which Nature has bound certain climes, from the day when Deucalion first hurled his stones on the unpeopled earth—stones, whence sprang man's race, hard as they. Come, then, and let your rich soil, soon as ever the year begins, be turned up by the bullock's strength —let the clods be exposed for Summer to bake them to dust with its full mellow suns; but if the land be not fertile, be content to wait till Arcturus, and then just raise the surface with a shallow furrow—in the one case, that a luxuriant crop may not be choked with weeds; in the other, that the barren seed may not lose the little moisture it has.

Moreover, in alternate years, you will let your fields lie fallow after reaping, and suffer the scurf to harden on the inactive plain; or you will sow your golden spelt when another star arises; where you lately took off the rattling pods of a luxuriant bean crop, or the yield of the slender vetch and the bitter lupine's brittle stems and echoing jungle. For a plain is parched by a crop of flax; parched by the oat, parched by the poppy steeped in slumberous Lethe. Yet rotation will lighten the strain; only think of the dried-up soil and be not afraid to give it its fill of rich manure—think of the exhausted field, and fling about the grimy ashes broadcast. Then, under the change of produce, the land gets equal rest, and you escape the thanklessness of an unploughed soil. Oft, too, has it been found of use to set a barren field on fire, and let the crackling flames burn up the light stubble: whether it be that the land derives hidden strength and fattening nourishment from the process, or that the fire bakes out any distemper it may have, and sweats out its superfluous moisture, or that the heat opens fresh passages and secret apertures through which life-juice may come to the tender blades, or that it makes the land harder, and binds up its gaping pores, that so the subtle shower and the fierce sun's unusual tyranny, and the north wind's searching cold may have no power to parch it to the quick. Great, aye, great are his services to the land who breaks up its sluggish clods with the harrow, and drags over them his wicker hurdles: the golden corn-goddess eyes him from her Olympian height with no idle regard; great, too, his, who having once broken through the land's crust, and made it lift its ridgy back, turns his plough, and drives through it a second time crosswise, and piles earth again and again, and bows her fields to his will.

A wet summer and a fine winter should be the farmer's prayer. From winter's dust comes great joy to the corn, joy to the land. No tillage gives Mysia such cause for boasting, or Gargarus for wondering at his own harvest. Why talk of the man who having cast his seed, follows up the blow with his rake, and levels the bare sandy ridges, and then when the corn is springing up, brings on it streaming waters, that follow as he leads; and when the scorched land is in a glow, and the corn blades dying—O joy! from the brow of the channelled slope entices the floods? See! down it tumbles, waking hoarse murmurs among the smooth stones, and allaying the sun-struck ground as it bubbles on. Why talk of him, who in his care lest the weight of the ear should overbear the stems, grazes down the luxuriance of the crop while yet in the blade, when the springing corn has just reached the furrow's top; or of him, who drains off the whole watery contents of a marsh by absorbent sand —especially where, in the treacherous seasons, a river overflows, and covers whole acres with a coat of mud, making the hollow furrows steam again with the reeking moisture?

VIRGIL
[*The Georgics* (1st century B.C.)
TRANSLATED BY JOHN CONINGTON]

A Poetical Farmer

[*No New England farmer ever wrote a* Georgics *but if we may believe Thoreau there was one who might be called a "mute inglorious Virgil."*]

OCT. 4, 1851. . . . Minott is perhaps the most poetical farmer, the one who most realizes to me the poetry of the farmer's life, that I know. He does nothing with haste and drudgery, but everything as if he loved it. He makes the most of his labor, and takes infinite satisfaction in every part of it. He is not looking forward to the sale of his crops, but he is paid by the constant satisfaction which his labor yields him. He has not too much land to trouble him, too much work to do, no hired man nor boy, but simply to amuse himself and live. He cares not so much to raise a large crop as to do his work well. He knows every pin and nail in his barn. If any part of it is to be floored, he lets no hired man rob him of that amusement, but he goes slowly to the woods, and at his leisure selects a pitch-pine tree, cuts it, and hauls it or gets it hauled to the mill; and so he knows the history of his barn floor. Farming is an amusement which has lasted him longer than gunning or fishing. He is never in a hurry to get his garden planted, and yet it is always planted soon enough, and none in the town is kept so beautifully clean. He always prophesies a failure of the crops, and yet is satisfied with what he gets. His barn floor is fastened down with oak pins, and he prefers them to iron spikes, which he says will rust and give way. He handles and amuses himself with every ear of his corn crop as much as a child with his playthings, and so his small crop goes a great way. He might well cry if it were carried to market. The seed of weeds is no longer in his soil. He loves to walk in a swamp in windy weather, and hear the wind groan through the pines. He indulges in no luxury of food, or dress, or furniture, yet he is not penurious, but merely simple. If his sister dies before him, he may have to go to the almshouse in his old age, yet he is not poor, for he does not want riches. With never failing rheumatism and trembling hands, he seems yet to enjoy perennial health. Though he never reads a book since he finished the "Naval Monument," he speaks the best of English. . . .

Nov. 7, 1857.   Minott adorns whatever part of nature he touches. Whichever way he walks he transfigures the earth for me. If a common man speaks of Walden Pond to me, I see only a shallow, dull-colored body of water, without reflections, or peculiar color, but if Minott speaks of it, I see the green water and reflected hills at once, for he *has been* there. I hear the rustle of leaves from woods which he goes through. . . .

Dec. 11, 1856.   Minott tells me that his and his sister's wood-lot contains about ten acres, and has, with a very slight exception at one time, supplied all their fuel for thirty years, and he thinks would constantly continue to do so. They keep one fire all the time, and two some of the time, and burn about eight cords in a year. He knows his wood-lot, and what grows in it, as well as an ordinary farmer does his corn-field, for he has cut his own wood till within two or three years, knows the history of every stump on it, and the age of every sapling, knows how many beech-trees and black birches there are, as another knows his pear or cherry trees. It is more economical as well as more poetical to have a wood-lot, and cut and get your own wood from year to year than to buy it at your own door. Minott may say to his trees, "Submit to my axe; I cut your father on this very spot." How many sweet passages there must have been in his life there, chopping all alone in the short winter days! How many rabbits, partridges, foxes he saw! A rill runs through the lot where he quenched his thirst, and several times he has laid it bare. At last rheumatism has made him a prisoner, and he is compelled to let a stranger, a vandal it may be, go into his lot with an axe. It is fit that he should be buried there.

HENRY DAVID THOREAU

[*Journal*]

Thomas Jefferson, Gardener

[*The garden book of Thomas Jefferson reveals that among his innumerable interests gardening was not the least. The following letter written from France shows him ardently engaged upon what was once thought a chief obligation of the traveler—the search for foreign examples which might prove useful at home.*]

I WAS induced, in the course of my journey through the south of France, to pay very particular attention to the objects of their culture, because the resemblance of their climate to that of the southern parts of the United States, authorizes us to presume we may adopt any of their articles of culture, which we would wish for. We should not wish for their wines, though they are good and abundant. The culture of the vine is not desirable in lands capable of producing anything else. It is a species of gambling, and of desperate gambling too, wherein, whether you make much or nothing, you are equally ruined. The middling crop alone is the saving point, and that the seasons seldom hit. Accordingly, we see much wretchedness among this class of cultivators. Wine, too, is so cheap in these countries, that a laborer with us, employed in the culture of any other article, may exchange it for wine, more and better than he could raise himself. It is a resource for a country, the whole of whose good soil is otherwise employed, and which still has some barren spots, and surplus of population to employ on them. There the vine is good, because it is something in the place of nothing. It may become a resource to us at a still earlier period; when the increase of population shall increase our productions beyond the demand for them, both at home and abroad. Instead of going on to make an useless surplus of them, we may employ our supernumerary hands on the vine. But that period is not yet arrived.

The almond tree is also so precarious, that none can depend for subsistence on its produce, but persons of capital.

The caper, though a more tender plant, is more certain in its produce, because a mound of earth of the size of a cucumber hill, thrown over the plant in the fall, protects it effectually against the cold of winter. When the danger of frost is over in the spring, they uncover it, and begin its culture. There is a great deal of this in the neighborhood of Toulon. The plants are set about eight feet apart, and yield, one year with another, about two pounds of caper each, worth on the spot sixpence sterling per pound. They require little culture, and this may be performed either with the plough or hoe. The principal work is the gathering of the fruit as it forms. Every plant must be picked every other day, from the last of June till the middle of October. But this is the work of women and children. This plant does well in any kind of soil which is dry, or even in walls where there is no soil, and it lasts the life of man. Toulon would be the proper port to apply for them. I must observe, that the preceding details cannot be relied on with the fullest certainty, because, in the canton where this plant is cultivated, the inhabitants speak no written language, but a medley, which I could understand but very imperfectly.

The fig and mulberry are so well known in America, that nothing need be said of them. Their culture, too, is by women and children, and, therefore, earnestly to be desired in countries where there are slaves. In these, the women and children are often employed in labors disproportioned to their sex and age. By presenting to the master objects of culture, easier and equally beneficial, all temptation to misemploy them would be removed, and the lot of this tender part of our species be much softened. By varying, too, the articles of culture, we multiply the chances for making something, and disarm the seasons in a proportionable degree, of their calamitous effects.

The olive is a tree the least known in America, and yet the most worthy of being known. Of all the gifts of heaven to man, it is next to the most precious, if it be not the most precious. Perhaps it may claim a preference even to bread, because there is such an infinitude of vegetables, which it renders a proper and comfortable nourishment. In passing the Alps at the Col de Tende, where they are mere masses of rock, wherever there happens to be a little soil, there are a number of olive trees, and a village supported by them. Take away these trees, and the same ground in corn would not support a single family. A pound of oil, which can be bought for three or four pence sterling, is equivalent to many pounds of flesh, by the quantity of vegetables it will prepare, and render fit and comfortable food. Without this tree, the country of Provence and territory of Genoa would not support one-half, perhaps not one-third, their present inhabitants. The nature of the soil is of little consequence if it be dry. The trees are planted from fifteen to twenty feet apart, and when tolerably good, will yield fifteen or twenty pounds of oil yearly, one with another. There are trees which yield much more. They begin to render good crops at twenty years old, and last till killed by cold, which happens at some time or other, even in their best positions in France. But they put out again from their roots. In Italy, I am told, they have trees two hundred years old. They afford an easy but constant employment through the year, and require so little nourishment, that if the soil be fit for any other production, it may be cultivated among the olive trees without injuring them. The northern limits of this tree are the mountains of Cevennes, from about the meridian of Carcassonne to the Rhone, and from thence, the Alps and the Apennines as far as Genoa, I know, and how much farther I am not informed. The shelter of these mountains may be considered as equivalent to a degree and a half of latitude, at least, because westward of the commencement of the Cevennes, there are no olive trees in 43½° or even 43° of latitude, whereas, we find them *now* on the Rhone at Pierrelatte, in 44½°, and *formerly* they were at Tains, above the mouth of the Isere, in 45°, sheltered by the near approach of the Cevennes and Alps, which only leave there a passage for the Rhone. Whether such a shelter exists or not in the States of South Carolina and Georgia, I know not. But this we may say, either that it exists or that it is not necessary there, because we know that they produce the orange in open air; and wherever the orange will stand at all, experience shows that the olive will stand well, being a hardier tree. Notwithstanding the great quantities of oil made in France, they have not enough for their own consumption, and, therefore import from other countries. This is an article, the consumption of which will always keep pace with its production. Raise it, and it begets its own demand. Little is carried to America, because Europe has it not to spare. We, therefore, have not learned the use of it. But cover the southern States with it, and every man will become a consumer of oil, within whose reach it can be brought in point of price. If the memory of those persons is held in great respect in South Carolina who introduced there the culture of rice, a plant which sows life and death with almost equal hand, what obligations would be due to him who should introduce the olive tree, and set the example of its culture! Were the owner of slaves to view it only as a means of bettering their condition, how much would he better that by planting one of those trees for every slave he possessed! Having been myself an eye witness to the blessings which this tree sheds on the poor, I never had my wishes so kindled for the introduction of any article of new culture into our own country. South Carolina and Georgia appear to me to be the States, wherein its success, in favorable positions at least, could not be doubted, and I flattered myself it would come within the views of the society for agriculture to begin the experiments which are to prove its practicability. Carcassonne is the place from which the plants may be most certainly and cheaply obtained. They can be sent from thence by water to Bordeaux, where they may be embarked on vessels bound for Charleston. There is too little intercourse between Charleston and Marseilles to propose this as the port of exportation. I offer my services to the society for the obtaining and forwarding any number of plants which may be desired.

Before I quit the subject of climates, and the plants adapted to them, I will add, as a matter of curiosity, and of some utility, too, that my journey through the southern parts of France, and the territory of Genoa, but still more the crossing of the Alps, enabled me to form a scale of the tenderer plants, and to arrange them according to their different powers of resisting cold. In passing the Alps at the Col de Tende, we cross three very high mountains successively. In ascending, we lose these plants, one after another, as we rise, and find them again in the contrary order as we descend on the other side; and this is repeated three times. Their order, proceeding from the tenderest to the hardiest, is as follows: caper, orange, palm, aloe, olive, pomegranate, walnut, fig, almond. But this must be understood of the plant only; for as to the fruit, the order is somewhat different. The caper, for example, is the tenderest plant, yet, being so easily protected, it is among the most certain in its fruit. The almond, the hardiest, loses its fruit the oftenest, on account of its forwardness. The palm, hardier than the caper and orange, never produces perfect fruit here.

I had the honor of sending you, the last year, some seeds of the sulla of Malta, or Spanish St. Foin. Lest they should have miscarried, I now pack with the rice a cannister of the same kind of seed, raised by myself. By Colonel Franks, in the month of February last, I sent a parcel

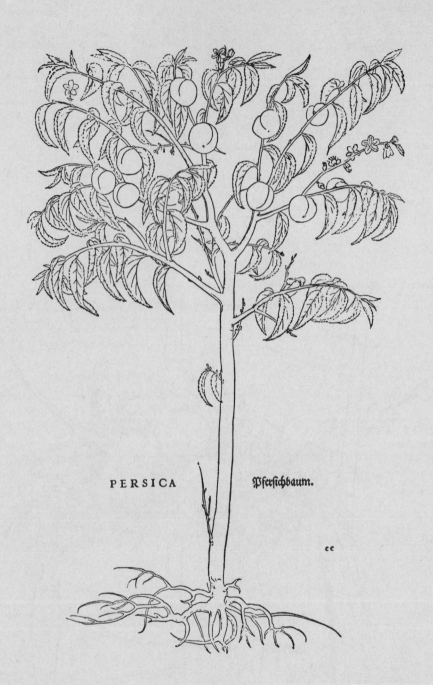

PERSICA   Pferſchbaum.

ee

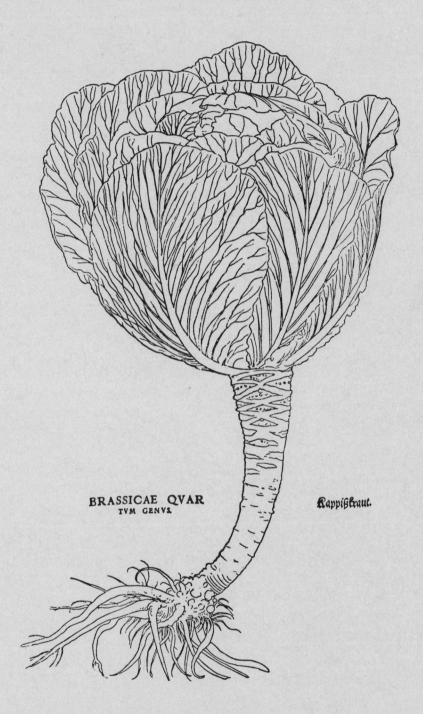

BRASSICAE QVAR
TVM GENVS.

Kappißkraut.

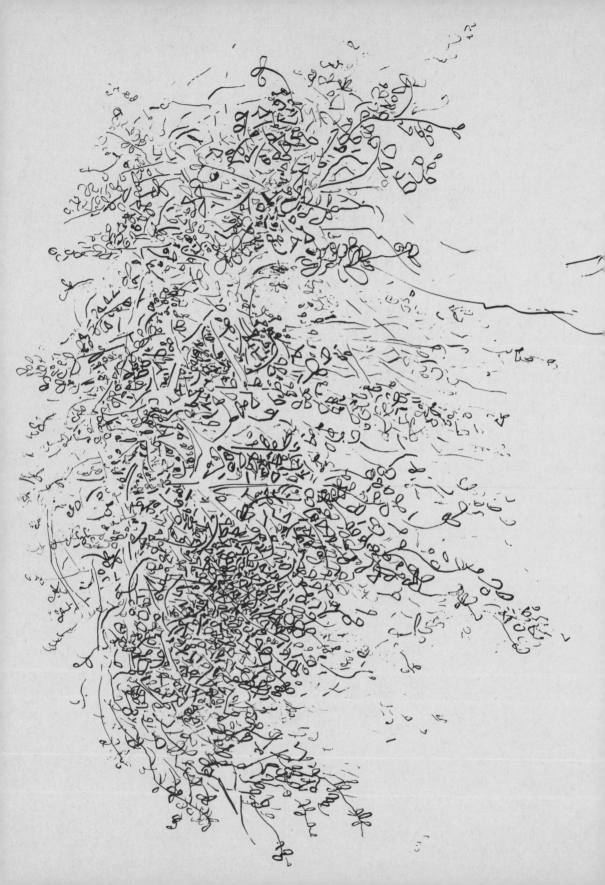

of acorns of the cork oak, which I desired him to ask the favor of the Delegates of South Carolina in Congress to forward to you.

THOMAS JEFFERSON
[Letter to William Drayton (Paris, July 30, 1787)]

Tobacco for Health

[*Whether or not tobacco is a "useful" plant has been a matter of opinion even since it was first brought to Europe. Certainly no other introduced from America conquered the world so quickly. In what is said to be the first account to be published in English the most marvelous virtues are ascribed to it. The author was a Spaniard named Nicholas Monardes and his translator one John Frampton, who published in 1580.*]

THIS Hearbe which commonly is called *Tabaco,* is an Hearbe of muche antiquitie, and knowen amongst the Indians, and in especially among them of the new Spayne, and after that those Countries were gotten by our Spaniardes, beying taught of the Indians, they did profite themselues with those things, in the wounds which they receiued in their Warres, healing themselues therewith to the great benefite.

Within these few yeeres [Monardes is writing in 1571] there hath beene brought into Spayne of it, more to adornate Gardens with the fairnesse thereof, and to geue a pleasant sight, than that it was thought to haue the maruelous medicinable vertues, which it hath, but nowe wee doe vse it more for his vertues, than for his fairenesse. For surely they are such which doe bring admiration. . . .

One of the meruelles of this hearbe, and that which bringeth most admiration, is, the maner howe the Priestes of the Indias did vse it, which was in this manner: when there was emongest the Indians any manner of businesse, of great importaunce, in the which the chiefe Gentlemen called *Casiques,* or any of the principall people of the countrie, had necessitie to consult with their Priestes, in any businesse of importance; they went and propounded their matter to their chiefe Priest, forthwith in their presence, he tooke certayne leues of the *Tabaco*, and cast them into the fire, and did receiue the smoke of them at his mouth, and at his nose with a Cane, and in taking of it, hee fell downe vppon the ground, as a Dead man, and remayning so, according to the quantitie of the smoke that he had taken, when the hearbe had done his worke, he did reuiue and awake, and gaue them their answeres, according to the visions, and illusions which hee sawe, whiles he was rapte in the same manner, and he did interprete to them, as to him seemed best, or as the Deuill had counselled him, geuing them continually doubtfull answeares, in such sorte, that howsoeuer it fell out, they might say that it was the same, which was declared, and the answeare that he made.

In like sort the rest of the Indians for their pastime, doe take the smoke of the *Tabaco*, too make themselues drunke withall, and to see the visions, and thinges that represent vnto them that wherein they doe delight: and other times thy take it to knowe their businesse, and successe, because conformable to that, whiche they haue seene beyng drunke therewith, euen so they judge of their businesse. And as the Deuil is a deceauer, and hath the knowledge of the vertue of hearbes, so he did shew the vertue of this Hearb, that by the meanes thereof, they might see their imaginations, and visions, that he hath represented to them, and by that meanes deceiue them.

JOHN FRAMPTON
[*Joyous News Out of Virginia*]

The Filthy Weed

[*An opinion very different from that of Monardes was expounded at length by no less a person than James I, a pedantic Scot who was also one of the last defenders in England of the belief in witches and who prided himself almost as much upon his learning and his poetical gifts as upon his mastery of kingcraft.*]

✗

T H A T the manifolde abuses of this vile custome of *Tobacco* taking, may the better be espied, it is fit, that first you enter into consideration both of the first originall thereof, and likewise of the reasons of the first entry thereof into this Countrey. For certainely as such customes, that haue their first institution either from a godly, necessary, or honorable ground, and are first brought in, by the meanes of some worthy, vertuous, and great Personage, are euer, and most iustly, holden in great and reuerent estimation and account, by all wise, vertuous, and temperate spirits: So should it by the contrary, iustly bring a great disgrace into that sort of customes, which hauing their originall from base corruption and barbarity, doe in like sort, make their first entry into a Countrey, by an inconsiderate and childish affectation of Noueltie, as is the true case of the first inuention of *Tobacco* taking, and of the first entry thereof among vs. For *Tobacco* being a common herbe, which (though vnder diuers names) growes almost euery where, was first found out by some of the barbarous *Indians*, to be a Preseruatiue, or Antidot against the Pockes, a filthy disease, whereunto these barbarous people are (as all men know) very much subiect, what through the vncleanly and adust constitution of their bodies, and what through the intemperate heate of their Climat: so that as from them was first brought into Christendome, that most detestable disease, so from them likewise was brought this vse of *Tobacco*, as a stinking and vnsauorie Antidot, for so corrupted and execrable a Maladie, the stinking Suffumigation whereof they yet vse against that disease, making so one canker or venime to eate out another.

    And now good Countrey men let vs (I pray you) consider, what honour or policie can mooue vs to imitate the barbarous and beastly maners of the wilde, godlesse, and slauish *Indians*, especially in so vile and stinking a custome? Shall wee that disdaine to imitate the maners of our neighbour *France* (hauing the stile of the first Christian King-dom) and that cannot endure the spirit of the Spaniards (their King being now comparable in largenes of Dominions, to the great Emperor of *Turkie*) Shall wee, I say, that haue bene so long ciuill and wealthy in Peace, famous and inuincible in Warre, fortunate in both, we that haue bene euer able to aide any of our neighbours (but neuer deafed any of their eares with any of our supplications for assistance) shall we, I say, without blushing, abase our selues so farre, as to imitate these beastly *Indians*, slaues to the *Spaniards*, refuse to the world, and as yet aliens from the Holy Couenant of God? Why doe we not as well imitate them in walking naked as they doe? in preferring glasses, feathers, and such toyes, to golde and precious stones, as they do? yea why do we not denie God and adore the Deuill, as they doe?

Now to the corrupted basenesse of the first vse of this *Tobacco*, doeth very well agree the foolish and groundlesse first entry thereof into this Kingdome. It is not so long since the first entry of this abuse amongst vs here, as this present age cannot yet very well remember, both the first Author, and the forme of the first introduction of it amongst vs. It was neither brought in by King, great Conquerour, nor learned Doctor of Phisicke.

With the report of a great discouery for a Conquest, some two or three Sauage men, were brought in, together with this Sauage custome. But the pitie is, the poore wilde barbarous men died, but that vile barbarous custome is yet aliue, yea in fresh vigor: so as it seemes a miracle to me, how a custome springing from so vile a ground, and brought in by a father so generally hated, should be welcomed vpon so slender a warrant. For if they that first put it in practise heere, had remembred for what respect it was vsed by them from whence it came, I am sure they would haue bene loath, to haue taken so farre the imputation of that disease vpon them as they did, by vsing the cure thereof. For *Sanis non est opus medico*, and counter-poisons are neuer vsed, but where poyson is thought to precede. . . .

Thus hauing, as I truste, sufficiently answered the most principall arguments that are vsed in defence of this vile custome, it rests onely to informe you what sinnes and vanities you commit in the filthie abuse thereof. First, are you not guiltie of sinnefull and shamefull lust? (for lust may bee as well in any of the senses as in feeling) that although you bee troubled with no disease, but in perfect health, yet can you neither be merry at an Ordinarie, nor lasciuious in the Stewes, if you lacke *Tobacco* to prouoke your appetite to any of those sorts of recreation, lusting after it as the children of Israel did in the wildernesse after Quales? Secondly it is, as you vse or rather abuse it, a branche of the sinne of drunkennesse, which is the roote of all sinnes: for as the onely delight that drunkards take in Wine is in the strength of the taste, and the force of the fume thereof that mounts vp to the braine: for no drunkards loue any weake, or sweete drinke: for are not those (I meane the strong heate and the fume) the onely qualities that make *Tobacco* so delectable to all the louers of it? And as no man likes strong headie drinke the first day (because *nemo repente fit turpissimus*) but by custome is piece and piece allured, while in the ende, a drunkard will haue as great a thirst to bee drunke, as a sober man to quench his thirst with a draught when hee hath need of it: So is not this the very case of all the great takers of *Tobacco*? which therefore they themselues do attribute to a bewitching qualitie in it. Thirdly, is it not the greatest sinne of all, that you the people of all sortes of this Kingdome, who are created and ordeined by God to bestowe both your persons and goods for the maintenance both of the honour and safetie of your King and Commonwealthy, should disable your selues in both? In your persons hauing by this continuall vile custome brought your selues to this shameful imbecilitie, that you are not able to ride or walke the iourney of a Iewes Sabboth, but you must haue a reekie cole brought you from the next poore house to kindle your *Tobacco* with? whereas he cannot be thought able for any seruice in the warres, that cannot endure oftentimes the want of meate, drinke and sleepe, much more then must hee endure the want of *Tobacco*. But now if it were time of warres, and that you were to make some sudden *Caualcado* vpon your enemies, if any of you should seeke leisure to stay behinde his fellowe for taking of *Tobacco*, for my part I should neuer bee sorie for any euill chance that might befall him. To take a custome in any thing that cannot bee left againe, is most harmefull to the people of any land. *Mollicies* and delicacie were the wracke and ouerthrow, first of the Persian, and next of the Romane Empire. And this very custome of taking *Tobacco* (whereof our present purpose is) is euen at this day accounted so effeminate among the Indians themselues, as in the market they will offer no price for a slaue to be sold, whome they finde to be a great *Tobacco* taker.

Now how you are by this custome disabled in your goods, let the Gentry of this land beare witnesse, some of them bestowing three, some foure hundred pounds a yeere vpon this precious stinke, which I am sure might be bestowed vpon many farre better vses. I read indeede of a knauish Courtier, who for abusing the fauour of the Emperour *Alexander Seuerus* his Master by taking bribes to intercede, for sundry persons in his masters eare, (for whom he neuer once opened his mouth) was iustly choked with smoke, with this doome, *Fumo pereat, qui fumum vendidit:* but of so many smoke-buyers, as are at this present in this kingdome, I neuer read nor heard. . . .

And is it not a great vanitie, that a man cannot heartily welcome his friend now, but straight they must bee in hand with *Tobacco*? No it is become in place of a cure, a point of good fellowship, and he that will refuse to take a pipe of *Tobacco* among his fellowes, (though by his own election he would rather feele the sauour of a Sinke) is accounted peeuish and no good company, euen as they doe with tippeling in the cold Easterne Countries. Yea the Mistresse cannot in a more manerly kinde, entertaine her seruant, then by giuing him out of her faire hand a pipe of *Tobacco*. But herein is not onely a great vanitie, but a great contempt of Gods good giftes, that the sweetenesse of mans breath, being a good gift of God, should be willfully corrupted by this stinking smoke. . . .

Haue you not reason then to bee ashamed, and to forbeare this filthie noueltie, so basely grounded, so foolishly receiued and so grossely mistaken in the right vse thereof? In your abuse thereof sinning against God, harming your selues both in persons and goods, and raking also thereby the markes and notes of vanitie vpon you: by the custome thereof making your selues to be wondered at by all forraine ciuil Nations, and by all strangers that come among you, to be scorned and contemned. A custome lothsome to the eye, hatefull to the nose, harmefull to the braine, dangerous to the Lungs, and in the blacke stinking fume thereof, neerest resembling the horrible Stigian smoke of the pit that is bottomelesse.

JAMES I
[*Counterblast Against Tobacco* (1604)]

The Secret of Curare

[*Botanists have often been intrepid as well as learned, and sometimes they have been eccentric as well. For instance there was William Turner, author of the best sixteenth-century English herbal, who was also Dean of Wells Cathedral and so opposed to anything which suggested popery that he trained his dog to snatch the square hats off the heads of any Anglican bishops who happened to visit him. But the palm for eccentricity certainly goes to the wealthy Yorkshire squire Charles Waterton who chose to spend eight of his young years making natural-history observations in British Guiana and his old age on his estate which had been transformed into a fantastic zoo where he could live intimately with his animals. His horses were kept in stables where they faced one another for conversation; a sloth slept in his bedroom; and his chimpanzee was kissed affectionately every night before he retired. In South*

America he once rode a crocodile; once slept with a fourteen-foot snake just to find out what it would be like; and repeatedly kept his big toe outside the tent flap in the hope that it would be bitten by a vampire bat. In England he kept a natural-history diary of which the following is a typical entry: "This day I took up a flower-pot which I had buried in the ground. In it I had incarcerated three toads amongst a little soil. I found all three alive. Two of them were bleached. The other was black. I gave them their liberty and told them to enjoy the spring."

Waterton's main purpose in visiting South America was to discover how the arrow poison curare was prepared. The following excerpt from his Wanderings *describes the success of this undertaking.*]

IT has been already remarked, that in the extensive wilds of Demerara and Essequibo, far away from any European settlement, there is a tribe of Indians who are known by the name of Macoushi.

Though the wourali-poison is used by all the South American savages betwixt the Amazons and the Oroonoque, still this tribe makes it stronger than any of the rest. The Indians in the vicinity of the Rio Negro are aware of this, and come to the Macoushi country to purchase it. . . .

Wishful to obtain the best information concerning this poison, and as repeated inquiries, in lieu of dissipating the surrounding shade, did but tend more and more to darken the little light that existed, I determined to penetrate into the country where the poisonous ingredients grow, where this pernicious composition is prepared, and where it is constantly used. Success attended the adventure; and the information acquired made amends for one hundred and twenty days passed in the solitudes of Guiana, and afforded a balm to the wounds and bruises which every traveller must expect to receive who wanders through a thorny and obstructed path. . . .

A day or two before the Macoushi Indian prepares his poison, he goes into the forest in quest of the ingredients. A vine grows in these wilds, which is called Wourali. It is from this that the poison takes its name, and it is the principal ingredient. When he has procured enough of this, he digs up a root of a very bitter taste, ties them together, and then looks about for two kinds of bulbous plants, which contain a green and glutinous juice. He fills a little quake, which he carries on his back, with the stalks of these; and lastly, ranges up and down till he finds two species of ants. One of them is very large and black, and so venomous, that its sting produces a fever; it is most commonly to be met with on the ground. The other is a little red ant, which stings like a nettle, and generally has its nest under the leaf of a shrub. After obtaining these, he has no more need to range the forest.

A quantity of the strongest Indian pepper is used; but this he has already planted round his hut. The pounded fangs of the Labarri snake, and those of the Couanacouchi, are likewise added. These he commonly has in store; for when he kills a snake, he generally extracts the fangs, and keeps them by him.

Having thus found the necessary ingredients, he scrapes the wourali vine and bitter root into thin shavings, and puts them into a kind of colander made of leaves: this he holds over an earthen pot, and pours water on the shavings: the liquor which comes through has the appearance of coffee. When a sufficient quantity has been procured, the shavings are thrown aside. He then bruises the bulbous stalks, and squeezes a proportionate quantity of their juice through his hands into the pot. Lastly, the snakes' fangs, ants, and pepper are bruised, and thrown into it. It is then placed on a slow fire, and as it boils, more of the juice of the wourali is added, according as it may be found necessary, and the scum is taken off with a leaf: it remains on the fire till reduced to a thick syrup of a deep brown colour. As soon as it has arrived at this state, a few arrows are poisoned with it, to try its strength. If it answer the expectations, it is poured out into a calabash, or little pot of Indian manufacture, which is carefully covered with a couple of leaves, and over them a piece of deer's skin, tied round with a cord. They keep it in the most dry part of the hut; and from time to time suspend it over the fire, to counteract the effects of dampness.

The act of preparing this poison is not considered as a common one: the savage may shape his bow, fasten the barb on the point of his arrow, and make his other implements of destruction, either lying in his hammock, or in the midst of his family; but, if he has to prepare the wourali-poison, many precautions are supposed to be necessary.

The women and young girls are not allowed to be present, lest the Yabahou, or evil spirit, should do them harm. The shed under which it has been boiled is pronounced polluted, and abandoned ever after. He who makes the poison must eat nothing that morning, and must continue fasting as long as the operation lasts. The pot in which it is boiled must be a new one, and must never have held anything before, otherwise the poison would be deficient in strength: add to this, that the operator must take particular care not to expose himself to the vapour which arises from it while on the fire.

Though this and other precautions are taken, such as frequently washing the face and hands, still the Indians think that it affects the health; and the operator either is, or, what is more probable, supposes himself to be, sick for some days after.

Thus it appears that the making the wourali-poison is considered as a gloomy and mysterious operation; and it would seem that they imagine it affects others as well as him who boils it; for an Indian agreed one evening to make some for me, but the next morning, he declined having anything to do with it, alleging that his wife was with child!

Here it might be asked, are all the ingredients just mentioned necessary, in order to produce the wourali-poison? Though our opinions and conjectures may militate against the absolute necessity of some of them, still it would be hardly fair to pronounce them added by the hand of superstition, till proof positive can be obtained.

We might argue on the subject, and, by bringing forward instances of Indian superstition, draw our conclusion by inference, and still remain in doubt on this head. You know superstition to be the off-spring of ignorance, and of course that it takes up its abode amongst the rudest tribes of uncivilized man. It even too often resides with man in his more enlightened state.

The Augustan age furnishes numerous examples. A bone snatched from the jaws of a fasting bitch, and a feather from the wing of a night owl—"osa ab ore rapta jejunae canis, plumamque nocturnae strigis"—were necessary for Canidia's incantations. And in aftertimes, parson Evans, the Welshman, was treated must ungenteelly by an enraged spirit, solely because he had forgotten a fumigation in his witch-work.

If, then, enlightened man lets his better sense give way, and believes, or allows himself to be persuaded, that certain substances and actions, in reality of no avail, possess a virtue which renders them useful in producing the wished-for effects; may not the wild, untaught, unenlightened savage of Guiana add an ingredient which, on account of the harm it does him, he fancies may be useful to the perfection of his poison, though in fact it be of no use at all? If a bone snatched from the jaws of a fasting bitch be thought necessary in incantation; or if witch-craft have recourse to the raiment of the owl, because it resorts to the tombs and mausoleums of the dead, and wails and hovers about at the time that the rest of animated nature sleeps; certainly the savage may imagine that the ants, whose sting causes a fever, and the teeth of the Labarri and Couanacouchi snakes, which convey death in a very short space of time, are essentially necessary in the composition of his poison; and being once impressed with this idea, he will add them every time he makes the poison, and transmit the absolute use of them to his posterity. The question to be answered seems not to be, if it is natural for the Indians to mix these ingredients, but, if they are essential to make the poison.

So much for the preparing of this vegetable essence; terrible importer of death, into whatever animal it enters. Let us now see how it is used; let us examine the weapons which bear it to its destination, and take a view of the poor victim, from the time he receives his wound till death comes to his relief.

When a native of Macoushia goes in quest of feathered game or other birds, he seldom carries his bow and arrows. It is the blow-pipe he then uses. This extraordinary tube of death is, perhaps one of the greatest natural curiosities of Guiana. It is not found in the country of the Macoushi. Those Indians tell you that it grows to the southwest of them, in the wilds which extend betwixt them and the Rio Negro. The reed must grow to an amazing length, as the part the Indians use is from ten to eleven feet long, and no tapering can be perceived in it, one end being as thick as the other. It is of a bright yellow colour, perfectly smooth both inside and out. It grows hollow; nor is there the least appearance of a knot or joint throughout the whole extent. The natives call it Ourah. This, of itself, is too slender to answer the end of a blow-pipe; but there is a species of palma, larger and stronger, and common in Guiana, and this the Indians make use of as a case, in which they put the ourah. It is brown, susceptible of a fine polish, and appears as if it has joints five or six inches from each other. It is called Samourah, and the pulp inside is easily extracted, by steeping it for a few days in water.

Thus the ourah and samourah, one within the other form the blow-pipe of Guiana. The end which is applied to the mouth is tied round with a small silk-grass cord, to prevent its splitting; and the other end, which is apt to strike against the ground, is secured by the seed of the Acuero fruit, cut horizontally through the middle, with a hole made in the end, through which is put the extremity of the blow-pipe. It is fastened on with string on the outside, and the inside is filled up with wild bees'-wax.

The arrow is from nine to ten inches long. It is made out of the leaf of a species of palm-tree, called Coucourite, hard and brittle, and pointed as sharp as a needle. About an inch of the pointed end is poisoned. The other end is burnt to make it still harder, and wild cotton is put round it for about an inch and a half. It requires considerable practice to put on this cotton well. It must just be large enough to fit the hollow of the tube, and taper off to nothing downwards. They tie it on with a thread of the silk-grass, to prevent its slipping off the arrow. . . .

The flesh of the game is not in the least injured by the poison, nor does it appear to corrupt sooner than that killed by the gun or knife. The body of this fowl was kept for sixteen hours, in a climate damp and rainy, and within seven degrees of the equator; at the end of which time it had contracted no bad smell whatever, and there were no symptoms of putrefaction, saving that, just round the wound, the flesh appeared somewhat discoloured.

The Indian, on his return home, carefully suspends his blow-pipe from the top of his spiral roof; seldom placing it in an oblique position, lest it should receive a cast.

Here let the blow-pipe remain suspended, while you take a view of the arms which are made to slay the larger beasts of the forest.

When the Indian intends to chase the peccari, or surprise the deer, or rouse the tapir from his marshy retreat, he carries his bow and arrows, which are very different from the weapons already described. . . .

Thus the savage of Guiana, independent of the common weapons of destruction, has it in his power to prepare a poison, by which he can generally ensure to himself a supply of animal food; and the food so destroyed imbibes no deleterious qualities. Nature has been bountiful to him. She has not only ordered poisonous herbs and roots to grow in the unbounded forests through which he strays, but has also furnished an excellent reed for his arrows, and another, still more singular, for his blow-pipe; and planted trees of an amazing hard, tough, and elastic texture, out of which he forms his bows. And in order that nothing might be wanting, she has superadded a tree which yields him a fine wax and disseminated up and down a plant not unlike that of the pine-apple, which affords him capital bow-strings.

CHARLES WATERTON
[*Wanderings in South America* (1828)]

Indians and Rubber

[*Ours is the Age of Rubber almost as much as it is the Age of Steel, and it is startling to realize that we call it "rubber" because for more than three hundred years after Europeans first met it in Mexico the only practical use they made of it was as a "rubber" or "eraser" for pencil marks. The Mexicans themselves made bouncing balls to play with, but it was not until the discovery in 1839 of the process called "vulcanizing" that men anywhere began to become dependent upon it. To Charles Waterton (whom we have just met watching Indians make curare) it was still little more than a curiosity.*]

HERE grows the tree from which the gum-elastic is got: it is large, and as tall as any in the forest. The wood has much the appearance of sycamore. The gum is contained in the bark: when that is cut through, it oozes out very freely: it is quite white, and looks as rich as cream: it hardens almost immediately as it issues from the tree; so that it is very easy to collect a ball, by forming the juice into a globular shape as fast as it comes out: it becomes nearly black by being exposed to the air, and is real India-rubber without undergoing any process. . . .

If ever there should be a great demand for large supplies of gum-elastic, commonly called India-rubber, it may be procured in abundance far away in the wilds of Demerara and Essequibo.

Some years ago, when I was in the Macoushi country there was a capital trick played upon me about India-rubber. It is almost too good to be left out of these Wanderings, and it shows that the wild and uneducated Indian is not without abilities. Weary and sick, and feeble through loss of blood, I arrived at some Indian huts, which were about two hours distant from the place where the gum-elastic trees grow. After a day and a night's rest I went to them, and with my own hands made a fine ball of pure India-rubber; it hardened immediately it became exposed to the air, and its elasticity was almost incredible.

While procuring it, exposure to the rain, which fell in torrents, brought on a return of inflammation in the stomach, and I was obliged to have recourse again to the lancet, and to use it with an unsparing hand. I wanted another ball, but was not in a state the next morning to proceed to the trees. A fine interesting young Indian observing my eagerness to have it, tendered his services, and asked me two handsful of fish-hooks for his trouble.

Off he went, and to my great surprise returned in a very short time. Bearing in mind the trouble and time it had cost me to make a ball, I could account for this Indian's expedition in no other way except that, being an inhabitant of the forest, he knew how to go about his work in a much shorter way than I did. His ball, to be sure, had very little elasticity in it. I tried it repeatedly, but it never rebounded a yard high. The young Indian watched me with great gravity, and when I made him understand that I expected the ball would dance better, he called another Indian, who knew a little English, to assure me that I might be quite easy on that score. The young rogue, in order to render me a complete dupe, brought the new moon to his aid. He gave me to understand that the ball was like the little moon, which he pointed to, and by the time it grew big and old, the ball would bounce beautifully. This satisfied me, and I gave him the fish-hooks, which he received without the least change of countenance.

I bounced the ball repeatedly for two months after, but I found that it still remained in its infancy. At last I suspected that the savage (to use a vulgar phrase) had come Yorkshire over me; and so I determined to find out how he had managed to take me in. I cut the ball in two, and then saw what a taught trick he had played me. It seems he had chewed some leaves into a lump, the size of a walnut, and then dipped them in the liquid gum-elastic. It immediately received a coat about as thick as a sixpence. He then rolled some more leaves round it, and gave it another coat. He seems to have continued this process till he made the ball considerably larger than the one I had procured; and in order to put his roguery out of all chance of detection, he made the last and outer coat thicker than a dollar. This Indian would, no doubt, have thriven well in some of our great towns.

CHARLES WATERTON
[*Wanderings in South America* (1828)]

Section Eleven

MECHANISMS
AND MYSTERIES

The learn'd is happy Nature to explore,
The fool is happy that he knows no more.

ALEXANDER POPE

To myself I seem to have been only like a boy playing on the sea-shore, and
diverting myself in now and then finding a smoother pebble or a prettier shell
than ordinary, whilst the great ocean of truth lay all undiscovered before me.

ISAAC NEWTON

The Wisdom of God

[*No Englishman did more to make natural history a genuine science than John Ray of Cambridge University. Besides many technical papers he published (1691)* The Wisdom of God Manifested in the Works of the Creation, *which remained for nearly a century the most read exposition and defense of the aims and justification of what was not yet called "biology."*]

Of the visible Works of God and their Division

I COME now to take a view of the Works of the Creation, and to observe something of the Wisdom of God discernible in the Formation of them, in their Order and Harmony, and in their Ends and Uses. And first I shall run them over slightly, remarking chiefly what is obvious and expos'd to the Eyes and Notice of the more careless and incurious Observer. Secondly, I shall select one or two particular Pieces, and take a more exact survey of them; tho' even in these more will escape our notice than can be discover'd by the most diligent Scrutiny; For our Eyes and Senses, however arm'd or assisted, are too gross to discern the Curiosity of the Workmanship of Nature, or those minute Parts by which it acts, and of which Bodies are compos'd; and our Understanding too dark and infirm to discover and comprehend all the Ends and Uses to which the infinitely wise Creator did design them.

But before I proceed, being put in mind thereof by the mention of the assistance of our Eyes, I cannot omit one general Observation concerning the curiosity of the Works of Nature in comparison of the Works of Art, which I shall propose in the late Bishop of *Chester's* Words, *Treat. of Nat. Religion*, Lib. 1, C.6. "The Observations which have been made in these latter times by the help of the *Microscope*, since we had the use and improvement of it, discover a vast difference between Natural and Artificial Things. What ever is natural, beheld through that appears exquisitely form'd, and adorn'd with all imaginable Elegancy and Beauty. There are such inimitable gildings in the smallest Seeds of Plants, but especially in the parts of Animals, in the Head or Eye of a small Fly; such Accuracy, Order and Symmetry in the frame of the most minute Creatures, a *Louse*, for example, or a *Mite*, as no Man were able to conceive without seeing of them. Whereas the most curious Works of Art, the sharpest and finest Needle doth appear as a blunt rough Bar of Iron, coming from the Furnace or the Forge: the most accurate Engravings or Embossments seem such rude, bungling, and deform'd Work, as if they had been done with a Mattock or Trowel; so vast a difference is there betwixt the skill of Nature, and the Rudeness and Imperfection of Art. I might add, that the Works of Nature, the better Lights and Glasses you use, the more clearer and exactly form'd they appear; whereas the effects of Human Art, the more curiously they are view'd and examin'd, the more of Deformity they discover.". . .

Of Vegetables or Plants

I have now done with Inanimate Bodies both simple and mix'd. The Animate are,

First, Such as are endued only with a Vegetative Soul, and therefore commonly called *Vegetables* or *Plants*; of which if we consider either their stature and shape, or their age and duration, we shall find it wonderful: For why should some Plants rise up to a great height, others creep upon the ground, which perhaps may have equal *Seeds*, nay, the lesser Plant many times the greater Seed? Why should each particular so observe its kind, as constantly to produce the same Leaf for consistency, figure, division, and edging; and bring forth the same kind of Flower, and Fruit, and Seed, and that tho' you translate it into a Soil which naturally puts forth no such kind of Plant, so that it is some Λόγ⊙· σπερμαΐικὸς, which doth effect this or rather some intelligent *plastick Nature*; as we have before intimated: For what account can be given of the determination of the growth and magnitude of Plants from Mechanical Principles, of *Matter mov'd* without the Presidency and Guidance of some superiour Agent? Why may not Trees grow up as high as the Clouds or Vapours ascend, or if you say the Cold of the superiour Air checks them, why may they not spread and extend their lateral Branches so far 'till their distance from the Center of Gravity depress them to the Earth, be the Tree never so high? How comes it to pass that tho' by Culture and Manure they may be highly improv'd, and augmented to a double, treble, nay some a much greater proportion in magnitude of all their Parts; yet is this advance restrain'd within certain limits? There is a *maximum quod sic* which they cannot exceed. You can by no Culture or Art extend a *Fennel Stalk* to the stature and bigness of an *Oak:* Then why should some be very long-lived, others only Annual or Biennial? How can we imagine that any Laws of Motion can determine the *Situation* of the *Leaves*, to come forth by pairs, or alternately, or circling the Stalk, the *Flowers* to grow singly, or in company and tufts, to come forth the bosoms of the Leaves and Branches, or on the tops of Branches and Stalks; the *Figure* of the Leaves, that they should be divided into so many Jags or Escallops, and curiously indented round the edges; as also of the Flower-leaves, their number and site, the figure and number of the *stamina* and their *apices*, the figure of the *Stile* and Seed-vessel, and the number of Cells into which it is divided. That all this be done, and all these parts duly propor-tion'd one to another, there seems to be necessary some intelligent *plastick Nature*, which may understand and regulate the whole Oecon-omy of the Plant: For this cannot be the Vegetative Soul, because that is material and divisible together with the Body: Which appears in that a Branch cut off of a Plant will take Root, and grow, and become a perfect Plant it self, as we have already observ'd. I had almost forgotten the complication of the Seed-leaves of some Plants in the Seed, which is so strange, that one cannot believe it to be done by Matter, however mov'd by any Laws or Rules imaginable. Some of them being so close plaited, and straitly folded up and thrust together within the Membranes of the Seed, that it would puzzle a Man to imitate it, and yet none of the Folds sticking or growing together; so that they may easily be taken out of their Cases, and spread and extended even with ones Fingers.

Secondly, If we consider each particular part of a Plant, we shall find it not without its End or Use: The *Roots* for its stability and drawing Nourishment from the Earth. The *Fibres* to contain and convey the Sap. Besides which there is a large sort of Vessels to contain the proper and specifick Juice of the Plant: and others to carry Air for such a kind of Respiration as it needeth; of which we have already spoken. The outer and inner Bark in Trees serve to defend the Trunk and

Boughs from the excesses of Heat and Cold and Drought, and to convey the Sap for the Annual augmentation of the Tree. For in truth every Tree may in some sense be said to be an Annual Plant, both Leaf, Flower and Fruit, proceeding from the Coat that was superinduc'd over the Wood the last Year, which Coat also never beareth any more, but together with the old Wood serves as a Form or Block to sustain the succeeding annual Coat. The *Leaves* before the *Gemma* or Bud be explicated to embrace and defend, the Flower and Fruit, which is even then perfectly form'd; afterwards to preserve the Branches, Flowers and Fruit from the Injuries of the Summer Sun, which would too much parch and dry them, if they lay open and expos'd to its Beams without any Shelter; the Leaves, I say, qualifie and contemper the Heat, and serve also to hinder the too hasty evaporation of the moisture about the Root: But the principle use of the Leaves (as we learn of Seignior *Malpighii*, Monsieur *Perault*, and Monsieur *Mariotte*) is to concoct and prepare the Sap for the nourishment of the Fruit, and the whole Plant, not only that which ascends from the Root, but what they take in from without, from the Dew, moist Air and Rain. This they prove because many Trees, if despoil'd of their Leaves, will die; as it happens sometimes in *Mulberry-Trees*, when they are pluck'd off to feed *Silk-worms*. And because if in Summer-time you denude a Vine-branch of its Leaves, the Grapes will never come to maturity: But tho' you expose the Grapes to the Sunbeams, if you pluck not off the Leaves, they will ripen notwithstanding. That there is a regress of the Sap in Plants from above downwards; and that this descendent Juice is that which principally nourisheth both Fruit and Plant, is clearly proved by the Experiments of Seignior *Malpighii*, and those rare ones of an Ingenious Country Man of our own *Thomas Brotherton* Esquire, of which I shall mention only one, that is, If you cut off a Ring of Bark from the Trunk of any Tree, that part of the Tree above the Barked Ring shall grow and encrease in bigness, but not that beneath.

But whether there be such a constant circulation of the Sap in Plants as there is of the Blood in Animals, as they would from hence infer, there is some reason to doubt. I might add hereto the pleasant and delectable, cooling and refreshing Shade they afford in the Summer-time; which was very much esteem'd by the Inhabitants of hot Countries, who always took great delight and pleasure to sit in the open Air, under shady Trees; Hence that Expression so often repeated in Scripture, of every Man's *sitting under his own Vine, and under his own Fig-tree*, where also they us'd to eat; as appears by *Abraham*'s entertaining the Angels under a Tree, and standing by them when they did eat,

Gen. 18.8. Moreover the Leaves of Plants are very beautiful and ornamental. That there is great pulchritude and comeliness of Proportion in
the Leaves, Flowers and Fruits of Plants, is attested by the general Ver-
dict of Mankind, as Dr. *More* and others well observe. The adorning
and beautifying of Temples and Buildings in all Ages, is an evident and
undeniable Testimony of this: For what is more ordinary with *Archi-
tects* than the taking in Leaves and Flowers and Fruitage for the garnish-
ing of their Work; as the *Roman* the Leaves of *Acanthus sat.* and the
Jewish of *Palm-Trees* and *Pomegranets:* And these more frequently
than any of the five regular Solids, as being more comely and pleasant
to behold. If any Man shall object, that comeliness of Proportion and
Beauty is but a meer Conceit, and that all things are alike handsome to
some Men who have as good Eyes as others; and that this appears by
the variation of Fashions, which doth so alter Mens Fancies, that what
e'er-while seem'd very handsome and comely, when it is once worn out
of fashion appears very absurd, uncouth and ridiculous. To this I answer,
that Custom and Use doth much in those Things where little of Proportion and Symmetry shew themselves, or which are alike comely and
beautiful, to disparage the one, and commend the other. But there are
degrees of Things; for (that I may use Dr. *More*'s Words) I dare appeal
to any Man that is not sunk into so forlorn a pitch of degeneracy, that
he is as stupid to these things as the basest Beasts, whether, for example,
a rightly-cut *Tetraedrum*, *Cube* or *Icosaedrum*, have no more Pulchritude in them than any rude broken Stone, lying in the Field or High-
ways; or to name other solid Figures, which tho' they be not regular
properly so call'd, yet have a setled *Idea* and Nature, as a *Cone*, *Sphere*
or *Cylender*, whether the sight of those do not more gratify the Minds
of Men, and pretend to more elegancy of shape than those rude cuttings
or chippings of Free-stone that fall from the Mason's hands, and serve
for nothing but to fill up the middle of the Wall, as fit to be hid from
the Eyes of Men for their ugliness. And therefore it is observable, that
if Nature shape any thing but near to this *Geometrical Accuracy*, that
we take notice of it with much content and pleasure, and greedily
gather and treasure it up. As if it be but exactly round, as those Spherical
Stones found in *Cuba*, and some also in our own Land, or have but its
sides parallel, as those rhomboideal *Selenites* found near St. *Ives* in
Huntingtonshire, and many other places in *England*. Whereas ordinary
Stones of rude and uncertain Figures we pass by, and take no notice of
at all. But tho' the Figures of these Bodies be pleasing and agreeable to
our Minds, yet (as we have already observ'd) those of the Leaves,
Flowers and Fruits of Trees, more. And it is remarkable, that in the

Circumscription and Complication of many Leaves, Flowers, Fruits, and Seeds, Nature affects a regular Figure. Of a pentagonal or quincunial Disposition Sir *Thomas Brown* of *Norwich* produces several Examples in his Discourse about the *Quincunx*. And doubless Instances might be given in other regular Figures, were Men but observant.

The *Flowers* serve to cherish and defend the first and tender Rudiments of the Fruit: I might also add the masculine or prolifick Seed contain'd in the Chives or *Apices* of the *Stamina*. These beside the Elegancy of their Figures, are many of them endued with splendid and lovely Colours, and likewise most grateful and fragrant Odours. Indeed such is the beauty and lustre of some Flowers, that our Saviour saith of the Lilles of the Field (which some, not without reason, suppose to have been *Tulips*) that *Solomon in all his Glory was not arrayed like one of these*. And it is observ'd by *Spigelius*, That the Art of the most skilful Painter cannot so mingle and temper his Colours, as exactly to imitate or counterfeit the native ones of the Flowers of *Vegetables*.

As for the *Seeds* of *Plant*, Dr. *More* esteems it an evident sign of Divine Providence, that every Kind hath its Seed: For it being no necessary result of the Motion of the Matter, (as the whole contrivance of the Plant indeed is not) and it being of so great consequence, that they have Seed for the continuance and propagation of their own Species, and also for the gratifying Man's Art, Industry and Necessities, (for much of Husbandry and Gardening lies in this) it cannot but be an Act of Counsel to furnish the several Kinds of Plants with their Seeds.

Now the *Seed* being so necessary for the maintenance and encrease of the several *Species*, it is worthy the Observation, what Care is taken to secure and preserve it, being in some doubly and trebly defended. As for instance, in the *Walnut*, *Almond*, and *Plumbs* of all sorts, we have first a thick pulpy Covering, then a hard Shell, within which is the Seed enclos'd in a double Membrane. In the *Nutmeg* another Tegument is added besides all these, *viz.* the *Mace* between the green *Pericarpium* and the hard Shell, immediately enclosing the Kernel. Neither yet doth the exteriour Pulp of the Fruit or *Pericarpium* serve only for the defence and security of the Seed, whilst it hangs upon the Plant: But after it is mature and fallen upon the Earth, for the stercoration of the Soil, and promotion of the growth, tho' not the first germination of the Seminal Plant. Hence (as *Petrus de Crescentiis* tells us) Husbandmen to make their Vines bear, manure them with Vine-leaves, or the Husks of exprest Grapes, and that they observe those to be the most fruitful, which are so manured with their own: Which Observation holds true also in all other Trees and Herbs. But besides this use of the Pulp or *Pericarpium*, for the guard and benefit of the Seed, it serves also by a secondary intention of Nature in many Fruits for the Food and Sustenance of Man and other Animals.

Another thing worthy the noting in *Seeds*, and argumentative of Providence and Design, is that pappose Plumage growing upon the tops of some of them, whereby they are capable of being wafted with the Wind, and by that means scatter'd and disseminated far and wide.

Furthermore, most *Seeds* having in them a Seminal Plant perfectly form'd, as the Young is in the Womb of Animals, the elegant Complication thereof in some *Species* is a very pleasant and admirable Spectacle; so that no Man that hath a Soul in him can imagine or believe it was so form'd and folded up without Wisdom and Providence. But of this I have spoken already.

Lastly, The immense smalness of some Seeds, not to be seen by the naked Eye, so that the number of Seeds produced at once in some one Plant; as for example, *Reed-mace* [*Tipha Palustris*] *Harts-Tongue*, and many sorts of *Ferns*, may amount to a Million, is a convincing Argument of the infinite Understanding and Art of the former of them.

And it is remarkable that such *Mosses* as grow upon Walls, the Roofs of Houses and other high places, have Seeds so excessively small, that when shaken out of their Vessels they appear like Vapor or Smoke, so that they may either ascend of themselves, or by an easie impulse of the Wind be rais'd up to the tops of Houses, Walls or Rocks: And we need not wonder how the Mosses got thither, or imagine they sprung up spontaneously there.

I might also take notice of many other particulars concerning Vegetables, as First That because they are design'd for the Food of Animals, therefore Nature hath taken more extraordinary Care, and made more abundant Provision for their propagation and encrease; so that they are multiplied and propagated not only by the Seed, but many also by the Root, producing Off-sets or creeping under Ground, many by Strings or Wires running above Ground, as *Strawberry* and the like, some by Slips or Cuttings, and some by several of these Ways. And for the security of such *Species* as are produc'd only by Seed, it hath endued all Seed with a lasting Vitality, that so if by reason of excessive cold, or drought, or any other accident, it happen not to germinate the first Year, it will continue its fœcundity, I do not say two or three, nor six or seven, but even twenty or thirty Years; and when the Impediment is remov'd, the Earth in fit case, and the Season proper, spring up, bear Fruit, and continue its Species. Hence it is that Plants are sometimes lost for a while in places where they formerly abounded; and again, after some Years, appear new: lost either because the Springs were not proper for their germination, or because the Land was fallow'd, or because plenty of Weeds or other Herbs prevented their coming up, and the like: and *appearing* again when these Impediments are remov'd. Secondly, That some sorts of Plants, as *Vines*, all sorts of *Pulse*, *Hops*, *Briony*, all Pomiferous Herbs, *Pumpions, Melons, Gourds, Cucumbers*, and divers other *Species*, that are weak and unable to raise or support themselves, are either endued with a faculty of twining about others that are near, or else furnish'd with Claspers and Tendrils, whereby, as it were with Hands, they catch hold of them, and so ramping upon Trees, Shrubs, Hedges or Poles, they mount up to a great height, and secure themselves and their Fruit. Thirdly, That others are arm'd with Prickles and Thorns, to secure them from the browsing of Beasts, as also to shelter others that grow under them. Moreover they are hereby render'd very useful to Man, as if design'd by Nature to make both Quick and Dead Hedges and Fences. The great Naturalist *Pliny* hath given an ingenious Account of the Providence and Design of Nature in thus arming and fencing them in these Words. *Inde* (speaking of Nature) *excogitavit aliquas aspectu hispidas, tactu truces, ut tantùm non vocem ipsius Naturæ fingentis illas, rationemque reddentis exaudire videamur, ne se depascat avida quadrupes, ne procaces manus rapiant, ne neglecta vestigia obterant, ne insidens ales infringat; his muniendo aculeis telisque armando, remediis ut salva ac tuta sint. Ità hoc quoque quod in iis odimus hominum causâ excogitatum est.*

It is worthy the noting, That *Wheat* which is the best sort of Grain, of which the purest, most savory and wholesome Bread is made, is patient of both Extreams, heat and cold, growing and bringing its Seed to maturity, not only in temperate Countries, but also on one hand in the Cold and Northern, *viz. Scotland, Denmark*, &c. on the other, in the hottest and most Southerly, as *Egypt, Barbary, Mauritania*, the *East Indies, Guinea, Madagascar*, &c. scarce refusing any Climate.

Nor is it less observable, and not to be commemorated without Acknowledgment of the Divine Benignity to us, that (as *Pliny* rightly notes) nothing is more fruitful than *Wheat, Quod ei natura* (saith he) [*rectiùs naturæ Parens*] *tribuit, quòd eo maximè hominem alit, utpote cùm è modio, si & aptum solum, quale in Byzacio Africæ campo centeni quinquaginta modii reddentur. Misit ex eo loco Divo Augusto procurator ejus ex uno grano (vix credibile dictu)* 400 *paucis minus germina: Misit & Neroni similiter* 360 *stipulas ex uno grano.* "Which fertility Nature (he should have said, the Author of Nature) hath confer'd upon it, because it feeds Man chiefly with it. One Bushel, if sown in a fit and proper

Soil, such as is *Byzacium*, a Field of *Africa*, yielding 150 of annual encrease; *Augustus*'s *Procurator* sent him from that place 400 within a few Blades springing from the same Grain: And to *Nero* were sent thence 360." If *Pliny* a Heathen could make this fertility of Wheat argumentative of the Bounty of God to Man, making such plentiful Provision for him of that which is of most pleasant taste and wholesom nourishment, surely it ought not to be passed over by us *Christians* without notice taking and thanksgiving.

JOHN RAY

[The Wisdom of God Manifested in the Works of the Creation (1691)]

A Vegetable Flytrap

[The term "botanist" once meant a man who knew flowers and their names; who, in many cases, also grew them, or searched for them in the fields. Today when "botanist" is more likely than not to mean "plant scientist" and "plant scientist" is more likely than not to mean "physiologist," "pathologist," "cytologist" or "biochemist," many who are so described have little experience with plants in the field, little practical or aesthetic interest in growing them, and may not (as one professor of botany confessed to the compiler of this volume) know a dozen plants by sight. Their subtle and often important researches hardly come within the scope of a garden anthology, and would not even if (as is seldom the case) they were described in terms interesting or even comprehensible to the layman. In this aspect, botany—like so many of the other sciences—has simply moved away from the tangible and visible, and at the same time beyond what the experience of those not technically trained has prepared them to appreciate or understand.

One of the last giants of natural history whose researches and experiments were fundamentally a matter of common sense and of observations which could be made without either elaborate apparatus or recondite knowledge was Charles Darwin. Here is one of his characteristically simple papers.]

D U R I N G the summer of 1860, I was surprised by finding how large a number of insects were caught by the leaves of the common sun-dew (*Drosera rotundifolia*) on a heath in Sussex. I had heard that insects were thus caught, but knew nothing further on the subject. I gathered by chance a dozen plants, bearing fifty-six fully expanded leaves, and on thirty-one of these dead insects or remnants of them adhered; and, no doubt, many more would have been caught afterwards by these same leaves, and still more by those as yet not expanded. On one plant all six leaves had caught their prey; and on several plants very many leaves had caught more than a single insect. On one large leaf I found the remains of thirteen distinct insects. Flies (Diptera) are captured much oftener than other insects. The largest kind which I have seen caught was a small butterfly (*Caenonympha pamphilus*); but the Rev. H. M. Wilkinson informs me that he found a large living dragon-fly with its body firmly held by two leaves. As this plant is extremely common in some districts, the number of insects thus annually slaughtered must be prodigious. Many plants cause the death of insects, for instance the sticky buds of the horse-chestnut (*Aesculus hippocastanum*), without thereby receiving, as far as we can perceive, any advantage; but it was soon evident that Drosera was excellently adapted for the special purpose of catching insects, so that the subject seemed well worthy of investigation.

The results have proved highly remarkable; the more important ones being—firstly, the extraordinary sensitiveness of the glands to slight pressure and to minute doses of certain nitrogenous fluids, as shown by the movement of the so-called hairs or tentacles; secondly, the power possessed by the leaves of rendering soluble or digesting nitrogenous substances, and of afterwards absorbing them; thirdly, the changes which take place within the cells of the tentacles, when the glands are excited in various ways.

It is necessary, in the first place, to describe briefly the plant. It bears from two or three to five or six leaves, generally extended more or less horizontally, but sometimes standing vertically upwards. The shape and general appearance of a leaf is shown, as seen from above, . . . and as seen laterally. . . . The leaves are commonly a little broader than long, but this was not the case in the one here figured. The whole upper surface is covered with gland-bearing filaments, or tentacles, as I shall call them, from their manner of acting. The glands were counted on thirty-one leaves, but many of these were of unusually large size, and the average number was 192; the greatest number being 260, and the least 130. The glands are each surrounded by large drops of extremely viscid secretion, which, glittering in the sun, have given rise to the plant's poetical name of the sun-dew. . . .

If a small organic or inorganic object be placed on the glands in the centre of a leaf, these transmit a motor impulse to the marginal tentacles. The nearer ones are first affected and slowly bend towards the centre, and then those farther off, until at last all become closely inflected over the object. This takes place in from one hour to four or five or more hours. The difference in the time required depends on many circumstances; namely on the size of the object and on its nature, that is, whether it contains soluble matter of the proper kind; on the vigour and age of the leaf; whether it has lately been in action; and, according to Nitschke, on the temperature of the day, as likewise seemed to me to be the case. A living insect is a more efficient object than a dead one, as in struggling it presses against the glands of many tentacles. An insect, such as a fly, with thin integuments, through which animal matter in solution can readily pass into the surrounding dense secretion, is more efficient in causing prolonged inflection than an insect with a thick coat, such as a beetle. The inflection of the tentacles takes place indifferently in the light and darkness; and the plant is not subject to any nocturnal movement of so-called sleep. . . .

It is a still more important fact (as we shall see more fully when we treat of the digestive power of the secretion) that when the tentacles become inflected, owing to the central glands having been stimulated mechanically, or by contact with animal matter, the secretion not only increases in quantity, but changes its nature and becomes acid; and this occurs before the glands have touched the object on the centre of the leaf. This acid is of a different nature from that contained in the tissue of the leaves. As long as the tentacles remain closely inflected, the glands continue to secrete, and the secretion is acid; so that, if neutralised by carbonate of soda, it again becomes acid after a few hours. I have observed the same leaf with the tentacles closely inflected over rather indigestible substances, such as chemically prepared casein, pouring forth acid secretion for eight successive days, and over bits of bone for ten successive days.

The secretion seems to possess, like the gastric juice of the higher animals, some antiseptic power. During very warm weather I placed close together two equal-sized bits of raw meat, one on a leaf of the Drosera, and the other surrounded by wet moss. They were thus left for 48 hrs., and then examined. The bit on the moss swarmed with infusoria, and was so much decayed that the transverse striae on the muscular fibres could no longer be clearly distinguished; whilst the bit on the leaf, which was bathed by the secretion, was free from infusoria, and its striae were perfectly distinct in the central and undissolved portion. In like manner small cubes of albumen and cheese placed on wet moss became threaded with filaments of mould, and had their surfaces slightly discoloured and disintegrated; whilst those on the leaves of Drosera remained clean, the albumen being changed into transparent fluid.

As soon as tentacles, which have remained closely inflected during several days over an object, begin to re-expand, their glands secrete less freely, or cease to secrete, and are left dry. In this state they are covered with a film of whitish, semi-fibrous matter, which was held in solution by the secretion. The drying of the glands during the act of re-expansion is of some little service to the plant; for I have often observed that objects adhering to the leaves could then be blown away by a breath of air; the leaves being thus left unencumbered and free for future action. Nevertheless, it often happens that all the glands do not become completely dry; and in this case delicate objects, such as fragile insects, are sometimes torn by the re-expansion of the tentacles into fragments, which remain scattered all over the leaf. After the re-expansion is complete, the glands quickly begin to re-secrete, and as soon as full-sized drops are formed, the tentacles are ready to clasp a new object.

When an insect alights on the central disc, it is instantly entangled by the viscid secretion, and the surrounding tentacles after a time begin to bend, and ultimately clasp it on all sides. Insects are generally killed, according to Dr. Nitschke, in about a quarter of an hour, owing to their tracheae being closed by the secretion. If an insect adheres to only a few of the glands of the exterior tentacles, these soon become inflected and carry their prey to the tentacles next succeeding them inwards; these then bend inwards, and so onwards, until the insect is ultimately carried by a curious sort of rolling movement to the centre of the leaf. Then, after an interval, the tentacles on all sides become inflected and bathe their prey with their secretion, in the same manner as if the insect had first alighted on the central disc. It is surprising how minute an insect suffices to cause this action: for instance, I have seen one of the smallest species of gnats (Culex), which had just settled with its excessively delicate feet on the glands of the outermost tentacles, and these were already beginning to curve inwards, though not a single gland had as yet touched the body of the insect. Had I not interfered, this minute gnat would assuredly have been carried to the centre of the leaf and been securely clasped on all sides. We shall hereafter see what excessively small doses of certain organic fluids and saline solutions cause strongly marked inflection.

Whether insects alight on the leaves by mere chance, as a resting-place, or are attracted by the odour of the secretion, I know not. I suspect from the number of insects caught by the English species of Drosera, and from what I have observed with some exotic species kept in my greenhouse, that the odour is attractive. In this latter case the leaves may be compared with a baited trap; in the former case with a trap laid in a run frequented by game, but without any bait.

That the glands possess the power of absorption, is shown by their almost instantaneously becoming dark-coloured when given a minute quantity of carbonate of ammonia; the change of colour being chiefly or exclusively due to the rapid aggregation of their contents. When certain other fluids are added, they become pale-coloured. Their power of absorption is, however, best shown by the widely different results which follow, from placing drops of various nitrogenous and non-nitrogenous fluids of the same density on the glands of the disc, or on a single marginal gland; and likewise by the very different lengths of time during which the tentacles remain inflected over objects, which yield or do not yield soluble nitrogenous matter. This same conclusion might indeed have been inferred from the structure and movements of the leaves, which are so admirably adapted for capturing insects.

The absorption of animal matter from captured insects explains how Drosera can flourish in extremely poor peaty soil—in some cases where nothing but sphagnum moss grows, and mosses depend altogether on the atmosphere for their nourishment. Although the leaves at a hasty glance do not appear green, owing to the purple colour of the tentacles, yet the upper and lower surfaces of the blade, the pedicels of the central tentacles, and the petioles contain chlorophyll, so that, no doubt, the plant obtains and assimilates carbonic acid from the air. Nevertheless, considering the nature of the soil where it grows, the supply of nitrogen would be extremely limited, or quite deficient, unless the plant had the power of obtaining this important element from captured insects. We can thus understand how it is that the roots are so poorly developed. These usually consist of only two or three slightly divided branches, from half to one inch in length, furnished with absorbent hairs. It appears, therefore, that the roots serve only to imbibe water; though, no doubt, they would absorb nutritious matter if present in the soil; for as we shall hereafter see, they absorb a weak solution of carbonate of ammonia. A plant of Drosera, with the edges of its leaves curled inwards, so as to form a temporary stomach, with the glands of the closely inflected tentacles pouring forth their acid secretion, which dissolves animal matter, afterwards to be absorbed, may be said to feed like an animal. But, differently from an animal, it drinks by means of its roots; and it must drink largely, so as to retain many drops of viscid fluid round the glands, sometimes as many as 260, exposed during the whole day to a glaring sun.

CHARLES DARWIN
[*Insectivorous Plants* (1875)]

Darwin Marshals an Argument

[*Charles Darwin was by no means the first to suggest that all plants and animals had a common origin and represented only the branches of a single family tree. His great originality lay in the fact that he first offered to the world a theory to explain* how *the differentiation might have come about and that he supplied much detailed evidence to support his theory. In this passage from* The Origin of Species *he explains what he means by "natural selection" and gives some examples of how he believed it had worked.*]

I T may be worth while to give another and more complex illustration of the action of natural selection. Certain plants excrete sweet juice, apparently for the sake of eliminating something injurious from the sap: this is effected, for instance, by glands at the base of the stipules in some Leguminosae, and at the backs of the leaves of the common laurel. This juice, though small in quantity, is greedily sought by insects; but their visits do not in any way benefit the plant. Now, let us suppose that the juice or nectar was excreted from the inside of the flowers of a certain number of plants of any species. Insects in seeking the nectar would get dusted with pollen, and would often transport it from one flower to another. The flowers of two distinct individuals of the same species would thus get crossed; and the act of crossing, as can be fully proved, gives rise to vigorous seedlings, which consequently would have the best chance of flourishing and surviving. The plants which produced flowers with the largest glands or nectaries, excreting most nectar, would oftenest be visited by insects, and would oftenest be crossed; and so in the long-run would gain the upper hand and form a local variety. The flowers, also, which had their stamens and pistils placed, in relation to the size and habits of the particular insect which visited them, so as to favor in any degree the transportal of the pollen, would likewise be favored. We might have taken the case of insects visiting flowers for the sake of collecting pollen instead of nectar; and as pollen is formed for the sole purpose of fertilization, its destruction appears to be a simple loss to the plant; yet if a little pollen were carried, at first occasionally and then habitually, by the pollen-devouring insects from flower to flower, and a cross thus effected, although nine-tenths of the pollen were destroyed it might still be a great gain to the plant to be thus robbed; and the individuals which produced more and more pollen, and had larger anthers, would be selected.

When our plant, by the above process long continued, had been rendered highly attractive to insects, they would, unintentionally on their part, regularly carry pollen from flower to flower; and that they do this effectually I could easily show by many striking facts. I will give only one, as likewise illustrating one step in the separation of the sexes of plants. Some holly-trees bear only male flowers, which have four stamens producing a rather small quantity of pollen, and a rudimentary pistil; other holly-trees bear only female flowers; these have a full-sized pistil, and four stamens with shrivelled anthers, in which not a grain of pollen can be detected. Having found a female tree exactly sixty yards from a male tree, I put the stigmas of twenty flowers, taken from different branches, under the microscope, and on all, without exception, there were a few pollen-grains, and on some a profusion. As the wind had set for several days from the female to the male tree, the pollen could not thus have been carried. The weather had been cold and boisterous and therefore not favorable to bees, nevertheless every female flower which I examined had been effectually fertilized by the bees, which had flown from tree to tree in search of nectar. But to return to our imaginary case; as soon as the plant had been rendered so highly attractive to insects that pollen was regularly carried from flower to flower, another process might commence. No naturalist doubts the advantage of what has been called the "physiological division of labor"; hence we may believe that it would be advantageous to a plant to produce stamens alone in one flower or on one whole plant, and pistils alone in another flower or on another plant. In plants under culture and placed under new conditions of life, sometimes the male organs and sometimes the female organs become more or less impotent; now if we suppose this to occur in ever so slight a degree under nature, then, as pollen is already carried regularly from flower to flower, and as a more complete separation of the sexes of our plant would be advantageous on the principle of the division of labor, individuals with this tendency more and more increased, would be continually favored or selected, until at last a complete separation of the sexes might be effected. It would take up too much space to show the various steps, through dimorphism and other means, by which the separation of the sexes in plants of various kinds is apparently now in progress; but I may add that some of the species of holly in North America are, according to Asa Gray, in an exactly intermediate condition, or, as he expresses it, are more or less dioeciously polygamous.

Let us now turn to the nectar-feeding insects; we may suppose the plant, of which we have been slowly increasing the nectar by continued selection, to be a common plant; and that certain insects depended in main part on its nectar for food. I could give many facts showing how anxious bees are to save time: for instance, their habit of cutting holes and sucking the nectar at the bases of certain flowers, which with a very little more trouble they can enter by the mouth. Bearing such facts in mind, it may be believed that under certain circumstances individual differences in the curvature or length of the proboscis, etc., too slight to be appreciated by us, might profit a bee or other insect, so that certain individuals would be able to obtain their food more quickly than others; and thus the communities to which they belonged would flourish and throw off many swarms inheriting the same peculiarities. The tubes of the corolla of the common red or incarnate clovers (Trifolium pratense and incarnatum) do not on a hasty glance appear to differ in length; yet the hive-bee can easily suck the nectar out of the incarnate clover, but not out of the common red clover, which is visited by humble-bees alone, so that whole fields of the red clover offer in vain an abundant supply of precious nectar to the hive-bee. That this nectar is much liked by the hive-bee is certain; for I have repeatedly seen, but only in the autumn, many hive-bees sucking the flowers through holes bitten in the base of the tube by humble-bees. The difference in the length of the corolla in the two kinds of clover, which determines the visits of the hive-bee, must be very trifling; for I have been assured that when red clover has been mown, the flowers of the second crop are somewhat smaller, and that these are visited by many hive-bees. I do not know whether this statement is accurate; nor whether another published statement can be trusted, namely, that the Ligurian bee, which is generally considered a mere variety of the common hive-bee, and which freely crosses with it, is able to reach and suck the nectar of the red clover. Thus, in a country where this kind of clover abounded, it might be a great advantage to the hive-bee to have a slightly longer or differently constructed proboscis. On the other hand, as the fertility of this clover absolutely depends on bees visiting the flowers, if humble-bees were to become rare in any country, it might be a great advantage to the plant to have a shorter or more deeply divided corolla, so that the hive-bees should be enabled to suck its flowers. Thus I can understand how a flower and a bee might slowly become, either simultaneously or one after the other, modified and adapted to each other in the most perfect manner, by the continued preservation of all the individuals which presented slight deviations of structure mutually favorable to each other.

I am well aware that this doctrine of natural selection, exemplified in the above imaginary instances, is open to the same objections which were first urged against Sir Charles Lyell's noble views on "the modern changes of the earth, as illustrative of geology"; but we now seldom hear the agencies which we see still at work, spoken of as trifling or insignificant, when used in explaining the excavation of the deepest valleys or the formation of long lines of inland cliffs. Natural selection acts only by the preservation and accumulation of small inherited modifications, each profitable to the preserved being; and as modern geology has almost banished such views as the excavation of a great valley by a single diluvial wave, so will natural selection banish the belief of the continued creation of new organic beings, or of any great and sudden modification in their structure.

CHARLES DARWIN
[*The Origin of Species* (1859)]

The Moth and the Candle

[*Since Darwin's time naturalists have been delighted and puzzled by the intimate relation between insects and flowers. Like Darwin, most still insist that, wonderful as this relationship is, chance and "natural selec-*

tion" can explain it. *Perhaps no other example puts that theory to so severe a test as the partnership between the yucca and the yucca moth, neither of which could survive as a species without the other.*]

T H E moth who singes his wings has pointed many a moral but he does not "desire" the flame, not even in the dim way that the first scorpion to leave the water may have "desired" to succeed in his dangerous adventure. The moth accomplishes no purpose of his own and none appropriate to nature at large. He is merely the victim of a situation which can seldom have arisen before man put in his appearance long after moths and many other insects had developed a tropism which was usually harmless during millions of years.

A moth's wings beat faster when light falls upon his eyes, and when it falls more strongly on one eye than on the other. Irresistibly his flight curves toward the source and if he reaches it, he dies—a victim of one of the mistakes which nature sometimes makes because even she cannot foresee every eventuality.

But in the case of a certain moth which lives in the desert and of a certain candle which grows there the situation is different.

Almost anywhere in the Southwest you will find as a conspicuous feature of the landscape one or another of the yuccas with their large bundle of stiff, sword-sharp leaves and, in early summer, an incredibly tall spire of innumerable creamy white blossoms held high on a great spike which shot up suddenly from the middle of the sword cluster. Pass by again in the fall and the spire will be bearing handsome pods which split open as they dry and scatter innumerable shiny black seeds on the sand. Though a bit difficult to gather, the pods make a fine addition to a winter bouquet and those who gather them often notice that each is perforated by at least one hole from which some insect has obviously emerged.

Sometimes the collector will search for a "perfect" specimen but perfect ones are not to be found. The "infestation" was necessary. Either the ovary from which the pod developed was "infested" or it didn't mature. Thereby hangs a tale as strange as any the desert has to tell and in certain important respects the most difficult to explain of all the strange tales which are told of the interdependence of insects and flowers. The hole was made by the larva of a moth, and just to make the question we are about to ask as neat as possible, it happens that certain species of yucca are still commonly called by the name which the Spaniards gave them: Our Lord's Candle.

Does Pronuba yuccasella, the moth in question, "desire" this particular candle? Please wait until you have heard the whole story before you answer.

Everybody—or at least everybody old enough to have been a child before directer methods of sex instruction came into fashion—knows about the bees and the flowers. If he did not lose all interest in the subject as he began to realize its remoter personal implications, he probably now knows at least in a very general way that many plants depend upon many insects and some, even, upon certain birds, to help them in what the eighteenth century liked to call "their nuptial rites." Orchard growers tend bees principally to increase their yield of apples and plums and pears; Darwin wrote a classic on the pollination of orchids; the Smyrna fig would not fruit in California until the particular wasp which acts as marriage broker for it in the Near East was imported to perform his function here, etc., etc.

But in every known case except that of the moth and the candle it is a somewhat one-sided affair with all the "intention" being on the part of the flower. Though the insect may be lured by a scent which it likes—even by the stench of rotten meat in the case of certain tropical blossoms pollinated by flesh-eating flies—and though he may be rewarded with nectar or with edible pollen, he does not do anything directly calculated to fertilize the flower. Sometimes the flower is so constructed that, for instance, the insect cannot get at the nectar without brushing against the pollen-bearing anthers and then against a stigma which will ultimately conduct the gene-bearing protoplasm of the pollen down to the ovules below. But he does not deliberately fertilize the plant and it would not affect his chances of passing on the torch to his posterity if the flower were not fertilized. The plant uses the insect but there is no active cooperation on the insect's part.

Consider, on the other hand, what happens in the unique case of the yucca and its attendant moth. In the first place, though there are many species of yuccas, only a single one of them—and it does not grow in this region—appears to be capable of getting along without the moth upon which all the rest depend. Moreover the moths, in their turn, are no less completely dependent upon the yuccas because their larva cannot feed upon anything except its maturing seeds. But this situation, which is odd without being unique, is not all. What *is* unique is the fact that the moth goes through a series of purposeful actions which have no other function except to fertilize a flower which could not be fertilized in any other way. If we naïvely interpreted its actions, we should find ourselves compelled to say that it "knows what it is doing."

The classic observation was made seventy-five years ago by the remarkable Missouri entomologist, Charles V. Riley, though the subject has been much studied and written about since Riley himself fully described the crucial, incredible event as he observed it on a cultivated species grown in the neighborhood of St. Louis. Several different insects frequent the flowers to eat the nectar or the pollen but perform no service in return. Meanwhile the female of the indispensable moth rests quietly in the half-closed blossoms.

When evening comes she goes in turn to several of the flowers just opening for their one night of perfect bloom. While the male, who has already done his duty, flutters uselessly about, she collects from the anthers a ball of the pollen which is surrounded by a sticky gum to prevent its accidental dispersal. After she has collected under her chin a mass somewhat larger than her head, she climbs the pistil of a different flower and into it she inserts her egg tube about a third of the way down from the top and injects several eggs. However she "knows" that if she left it at that her larva would have nothing to feed on. Accordingly, she mounts the rest of the way up the pistil, deposits the pollen ball on the stigma, and moves her head back and forth to rub the pollen well in. She eats neither nectar nor pollen. She gets no immediate benefit from her action. It has no purpose other than to fertilize the flower.

The insect which does these remarkable things is nothing much to look at—a little inch-long moth, silvery white in color and, so far as anyone knows, quite conventional in behavior except during the one great moment when it is impelled to act as though it knew a great deal about the physiology of plants as well as about the life history of its own species.

Most of what happens after the fertilization of the flower follows a familiar pattern. The flowers wither and a few days later the wormlike larva can be found. In time it will bore its way out of the maturing pod, drop to the ground, spin a cocoon a few inches below the surface, and there transform itself into an adult completely equipped to repeat, next year, the whole complicated process. Since there are commonly not more than two larvae per pod, they eat only a few of the perhaps two hundred seeds which the pod produces. From the standpoint of the yucca it is a very good arrangement since the sacrifice of a few seeds is a small price to pay for a very efficient job of fertilization. The staggering question for anyone who has committed himself to "explaining" nature is simply this: How on earth was such a system of mutual cooperation for individual ends ever worked out?

Evidently the yucca and the yucca moth came to their mutual understanding a long time ago—certainly before the plant genus had evolved the many species now flourishing—because, with the one exception previously mentioned, they all seem to be signatories to the agreement; certainly, also, long enough ago for the Pronuba moth to have itself evolved into at least several distinguishable species, because those which visit certain yuccas are slightly different from those which visit others. On the other hand, moth and yucca have not always worked together, because the flower continues to secrete a nectar which now merely attracts useless insects of various sorts and presumably it learned to do that at a time before Pronuba got into the habit of paying a visit on business of her own for which no honeyed inducement is necessary.

Apparently, sometime during the millennia when the two were engaged in a late phase of their evolution and separating themselves into the different species of moth and yucca, they must themselves have kept together. "Wherever thou goest I go," said the moth, because, again with the one single exception, where a yucca is native, so is a Pronuba. Attempt to grow the former outside its range and it may flower very nicely. But "no moth, no seed" seems to be the absolute rule.

William Trelease, student and monographer of the yucca genus, calls attention to the fact that "the mutual dependence seems absolute" and he then permits himself a cautious, scientific understatement when he remarks that the fact is "no doubt of the greatest suggestiveness," though "its meaning has escaped both botanists and zoologists."

Now the relatively simple one-sided arrangement which is so prevalent in the plant world is difficult enough to understand. Geology seems to demonstrate that the earliest flowering plants depended, as the conifers do today, upon the chance that some of their abundant pollen would be carried by the wind to the waiting ovaries. Then, since all organic matter is potentially edible by something, it is assumed that certain insects got into the habit of eating pollen, accidentally got some of it entangled in the hair on their bodies as many still do, and accidentally rubbed some of it off on the stigmas of the other flowers they visited. Since, for the plant, this was more effective than wind pollination and involved less waste of vital material, those plants which were most attractive to insects got along best. And as the degree of attractiveness accidentally varied, "natural selection" favored those which were most attractive, until gradually all the devices by which plants lure insects or birds—bright colored petals, nectar which serves the plant in no direct way, and perfume which leads the insect to the blossom; even the "guide lines" which sometimes mark the route to the nectar glands— were mechanically and necessarily developed.

Gardeners usually hate "bugs," but if the evolutionists are right, there never would have been any flowers if it had not been for these same bugs. The flowers never waste their sweetness on the desert air or, for that matter, on the jungle air. In fact, they waste it only when nobody except a human being is there to smell it. It is for the bugs and for a few birds, not for men, that they dye their petals or waft their scents. And it is lucky for us that we either happen to like or have become "conditioned" to liking the colors and the odors which most insects and some birds like also. What a calamity for us if insects had been color blind, as all mammals below the primates are! Or if, worse yet, we had had our present taste in smells while all the insects preferred, as a few of them do, that odor of rotten meat which certain flowers dependent upon them abundantly provide. Would we ever have been able to discover thoughts too deep for tears in a gray flower which exhaled a terrific stench? Or would we have learned by now to consider it exquisite?

The whole story, as it is usually told, of how flowers developed is thus a rather tall tale, as indeed the whole story of evolution is. But it does fall just short of the completely incredible even though we are likely to feel an additional strain when we begin to bring in the more remarkable features and find ourselves compelled to believe in the gradual blind development of the more intricate devices by which a flower is often adapted to some particular insect or bird and the exact correspondence between, say, the length of a given flower's tube and the length of the moth's proboscis or the hummingbird's bill which is going to reach down into it. But when we come to Pronuba and the yucca we get something more staggering still. That two different organisms should have simultaneously adapted themselves one to another is, if I understood the laws of probability, at least four times as improbable as that one should have adapted itself to the other. I am not saying I don't believe it did. On the whole I think I do, at least with one reservation. But sometimes I can't help saying to myself, "A man who will believe that will believe anything." . . .

The Mr. Riley who first told the world about Pronuba was a distinguished entomologist. He had the confidence of his professional brethren and textbook after textbook has repeated his tale. But is it just possible that he was overenthusiastic? How many other people have watched the performance and can vouch for it from their own experience?

Well, I confess that the shadow of such doubts crossed my own mind. Of the various references to Pronuba with which I was familiar, only one after Riley's own seemed on internal evidence to be indubitably first hand. The most learned entomologist of this region where yucca flourishes confessed that he had never seen the performance and didn't know anybody who had. Not too willingly—since I knew the difficulties, which include, besides the dilatoriness of the insect, darkness, a limited blooming season, and flowers lifted high above one's head—I decided to try to see for myself. And not to sustain any suspense which any reader may feel, I did. Three times Pronuba demonstrated before my eyes how she performed the crucial act, mounting the pistil of the recently opened flower and with prolonged purposefulness rubbing the pistil vigorously to get the pollen well in.

Partly to avoid the possibility that some amateur alienist might telephone a mental hospital that for several evenings a maniac had been seen standing for two hours and more peering at yucca flowers with a flashlight, I decided to make my observations well out into the desert and some twenty miles from town. And for poetic if not for strictly scientific reasons it was a good idea. It is one thing to read about what Pronuba does. It would be quite another to see her at work in a neighbor's back yard. But the performance belongs properly among the mysteries which one can only appreciate fully when the context is remote from the human and as exclusively as possible in that of almost timeless nature.

The moonless night was brilliant with stars. In the distance a coyote pack obligingly set up its chorus which is as wild a sound as one is likely to hear anywhere. And then, presently, there was Pronuba, even more insignificant looking than I had expected her to be, performing her delicate operation precisely, no doubt, as her ancestors had performed it millions of times during millions of springs. On the horizon the lights of town were just visible. In all that town few knew about, perhaps none had ever seen, the strange actions of this silent moth without whom the tall spires of flowers would never conceive their seeds and without whom, therefore, the whole race of yuccas would gradually die out. It was for the almost invisible moth, not for you or me or any aesthetically appreciative human spectator, that the great masses of flowers were lifted high.

As little Pronuba moved her head back and forth I remembered the question once asked by the American essayist Charles D. Stewart after he had described what looked like a remarkably purposeful action on the part of a spider who suddenly cut the main cable of his web and thereby sent flying an intruder of another species with designs upon an insect caught in the owner's web. "Is it God who is doing these things," Stewart asked, "or is it a spider?"

Fabre would have answered without hesitation, "God." Most biologists would reply with equal assurance, "Neither." But few are willing to admit what seems to me not wholly improbable—namely that the spider himself had something to do with it.

JOSEPH WOOD KRUTCH
[*The Voice of the Desert* (1954)]

Animal or Vegetable?

[*Samuel Butler, the author of* The Way of All Flesh, *was, among so many other things, a highly unorthodox biologist. One of his notions was that plants were not as different from animals as is commonly supposed. Some of the consequences of that notion he develops in this essay.*]

W E seldom in everyday life come across anything as to which we are in doubt whether to call it animal or vegetable.

True, there are such living forms. There is one, for example, called *Volvox globator*, which begins life as a perfectly well-marked animal, swimming freely in whatever direction it thinks proper, and settling down eventually as a seaweed; and I believe there are other seaweeds within the scheme of whose existence a similar radical change of front is comprised; but these troublesome doubtful cases—these vermin, as it were, that infest the holes and corners and outlying districts of our classification—betray the same germs of incipient moral consciousness that certain other small creatures do when they hop away and keep themselves as far as possible out of sight.

When we come to think of it, it is our own fault if we find the classification of such a creature as the *Volvox globator* troublesome.

If people will use an organ which entered so little into the original scheme of animal or vegetable life as a microscope did, they must not complain at having to re-cast many of their old notions. If they extend their organization, it is inevitable that they should ere long have to extend their ideas. We cannot so much as touch the organization of any organism without to some extent remodelling its mind, and conversely we cannot produce any change, however slight, in the mind of any organism without to some extent remodelling its body at the same time. Body and mind (whatever these may be, for we know nothing of either of them by itself and apart from all admixture with the other) are so closely connected that to touch one is to touch both, and thus it happened that the tacking on of a microscope to our eyes has involved the tacking on of the idea of a *Volvox globator* to our minds. Such an addition to the family of our ideas must always remain a thorn in the sides of those who wish to tie up all animals with a piece of red tape neatly into one parcel and put them into a pigeon-hole docketed "Animal World, Royal Zoological Society," and to tie up all plants in another perfectly tidy parcel, and put them in another pigeon-hole docketed "Vegetable World, Royal Botanical Society." We have, however, ourselves only to thank if we are incommoded by a form which cannot properly be tied up and pigeon-holed as either animal or vegetable.

Left to itself the *Volvox globator* is not agressive. No quiet peaceable person going about the streets of London need be afraid of having a *Volvox globator* rush out upon him from round a corner, nor will he find himself rudely hustled by any other form of life about which he is in doubt whether it is animal or vegetable. If he will let the *Volvox globator* alone, the *Volvox globator* will let him alone; and if he will not let a sleeping *Volvox* lie, he must not cry out at finding it a much more difficult customer to tackle than he thought for. True, it is very small, but if Nature is in a mood for puzzling she can pack a large difficulty in a very little compass; she can ask a riddle in a very few words which it will take the best of us all his time to guess; nevertheless, if people will mind their own business, they will come across cats in plenty and cabbages in plenty, but unless they are under the influence of either drink or microscope they will not come across anything about which there shall be any doubt as to whether it is more cat than cabbage or cabbage than cat. Our initial assumption, therefore, that the organic world falls into two broadly marked, easily distinguishable groups—animal and vegetable—is not likely to be challenged.

This, indeed, is as notorious as it is true, but it is not so notorious how or why this subdivision has been effected.

I never remember to have seen the question, why there should be any subdivision in the organic world at all, even asked, much less answered. Why should there be more than one single form of life? Why not the amoeba, the whole amoeba, and nothing but the amoeba, as the only form of life upon the face of the globe? Why not if once an amoeba always an amoeba? or at any rate, why should there not have been one main class only, so that all forms of life should have been either animal or vegetable?

Again, if there was to be more than one main class, why should there be only two? Why not half a dozen at once?

The inorganic world falls into three main classes—solid, fluid, and gaseous.

The animal and vegetable kingdoms again are subdivided into an almost infinite number of subordinate groups. Why should not the main groups, if there were to be more than one, be more than two, and why should these two be so broadly distinguished from one another?

It has been said that plants were made so that animals might have something to eat. This sounds well.

A great many animals certainly do eat a great many vegetables, and the arrangement seems to suit them, but it is a long cry from this to saying that the sole object of plants in growing is a desire to gratify the animals who may be kind enough to come and eat them.

Most plants show unmistakable hostility to the animal world. They scratch, cut, prick, sting, make bad smells, secrete the most dreadful poisons, frighten insects with delicate nervous systems by exploding—as the balsam does when ripe on being touched—hide themselves, grow in inaccessible places, and tell lies so plausibly that they deceive even their subtlest foes.

Others, again, lay traps smeared with bird-lime to catch insects or persuade them to drown themselves in pitchers which they have made of their leaves; others make themselves into living rat-traps which close with a spring on any insect which comes within their reach. Others, again, notably a kind of orchis that grows in Borneo or South America, I forget which, make their flowers in the shape of a certain fly that is a great pillager of honey, and when the real fly approaches this orchis, it thinks it is already bespoken, and goes on to pillage some other flowers instead.

If, on the other hand, they think an animal can be of use to them, they will coax it by every artifice in their power. It is not doubted among botanists that the lovely colouring of many Alpine plants has been assumed for the express purpose of alluring insects to come and fertilize them, they well knowing that without special inducement the insects would not be at the trouble of flying such a long way up.

These facts, and a thousand others that speak volumes as to the morality or immorality of plants, will not be disputed by anyone who keeps an eye upon what is going on in the botanical world; but they do not point in the direction of thinking that plants grow out of pure disinterested regard and unselfish devotion to the interests of animals, nor even indeed that much love of any kind is lost between the two kingdoms.

We take the most succulent and defenceless grasses, and so dispose them that our cows and horses can get at them and devour them; and on this we say the grass grows that our cows may come and eat it. It is probable that the grass hates and despises our cows. Nothing can prosper without unbounded though perhaps tacit confidence in the superiority of its own judgment over that of everyone else. Growth is conceit in its extreme development: it is dogmatism incarnate. To have a form at all is to declare that form to be the best that organism can conceive, and the way in which any form will grow depends on the nature of the opinion or opinions which it may have adopted in its own person and in those of its ancestors.

An organism which thinks one set of opinions best will assume one shape; another, which takes a different view of life and of what it is that makes life worth living, will be in another shape; few naturalists will now dispute that the bodily form of any organism is the visible out-come and expression of its opinions.

We see small exemplifications of this principle in the play and expression of people's faces as their thoughts and feelings change. All action is based upon opinion—that is to say, upon conceit, conscious or unconscious, and growth, which is the most concentrated and essential form of organic action, must be founded upon conceit also.

To live at all is, as I have already said, to stick to it, offensively and defensively, that one is one's self right and everyone else wrong. Without this quiet, persistent self-esteem, no organism would be able to carry on the arduous task of living at all. No sooner does this confidence fail than an organism begins to decline in vigour. A dying animal or plant is one that has begun to lose confidence in itself.

Is it not probable that a good, healthy, substantial, well-to-do vegetable looks upon the animal world much as we do upon the vege-table? It may admire, and, perhaps, even patronizingly envy, some of the more picturesque among the animal forms with which it is familiar. "Consider the Solomons in all their glory," we may fancy one of them in a moment of self-abasement to exclaim; "they toil not, neither do they spin; but not a rose or a lily among you is arrayed as one of these poor despised monarchs."

Very likely they look upon the *Droserae*, for example, or fly-catching plants, as little better than mere animals, and speak of them as "animating," much as we say of dull, stupid people that they "vegetate." To them we must appear restless ne'er-do-weels, rolling-stones who will gather no moss, who cannot be conceived as ever feeling, much less understanding; for if we felt, they might argue with some speciousness, we should never be able to survive the ceaseless shocks to which our nervous systems are daily and hourly subjected. The wear and tear of animal life must, in their eyes, be insupportable by an organism that could really feel. They will, therefore, have probably settled it that plants alone can either feel or reason; all animal action being only reflex, and destitute of either consciousness or intelligence.

Assuredly, if they could know the way in which we commonly talk about them, they might be able to make a good case for thinking poorly of our intelligence; indeed, whenever I hear a man say that a thing which manages its affairs with so keen an eye to the main chance as a nettle or a blackberry, has no intelligence and does not understand its own business, on the ground that it shows no sign of understanding ours, I always feel that however little intelligence the plant may have the man has even less.

SAMUEL BUTLER
[*Collected Essays* (1887)]

An Ancient But Indispensable Art

[*Beverly Nichols is perhaps the best-known contemporary English writer about gardening as such. Since his interest is both practical and aesthetic, he often puts a discussion of methods into the form of a literary essay—as here in an account of propagation by cuttings.*]

THE birth of plants would form a theme for many sermons. My last miracle is concerned with the birth of a rose-geranium. To a professional gardener it will not be a miracle at all, but to many men it may seem as strange as it did, in those days, to me. For the average man's ignorance about the processes of reproduction in plants is far deeper than the average child's ignorance of similar processes in human beings. He seems to imagine that trees are brought in a black bag, and that crocuses fall from the mouths of storks. The only plant with whose genesis he is really familiar is the mistletoe, owing to the somewhat embarrassing ordeal which all mistletoes have to endure before they can establish themselves in life.

Of the mysteries of cuttings and layerings and divisions he knows nothing. It is a great pity. I do not mind sexual ignorance in the adolescent—in fact, I prefer it to the hideous precocity which certain shrill educationists wish to thrust upon the modern young. I think that the actions of sexual intercourse are, by the ordinations of anatomy, essentially grotesque, ugly and indecent. No amount of purple romantic veils can conceal this elementary biological fact. I grow hot and restive when I read novels about heroines who lie down on banks of heather, submit to a long embrace, and then discover to their great surprise, in the following October, that they are about to have a baby. Certain very definite and very ludicrous things have to be done before one has babies. One cannot have them with one eye on the sunset and the other eye on the *Oxford Book of English Verse.*

Plants do things much more delicately. I did not realize how delicately they did it till the episode of the rose-geranium.

The air was full of bronze whirling leaves, the rooks cawed distractedly, and underneath the great chestnut tree there echoed the perpetual plomp, plomp of nuts falling, splitting open when they hit the road, and sending the polished nuts spinning into the wet grass. I went out into the garden, and stood facing the wind. I was excited. I remember that I was humming the prelude of Cesar Franck's Prelude, Aria and Fugue. It is a grand thing to hum when there is a tang in the air and the sense of a dark cloak soon to be drawn over the world. Then I saw the rose-geranium.

It was shivering. One blossom endured bravely on the end of a stalk. It looked like a little hat . . . the summer hat that some wretched woman might hold on her head if she were caught in a thunderstorm at a garden party. The flower seemed to be appealing to me . . .

"Take me in, take me in . . . the frost is on its way . . . soon it will be here to kill me . . . take me in!"

I bent down. What was one to do? I did not dare to root up the whole plant and put it in a pot. That seemed too drastic a business altogether. Yet something had to be done. The rose-geranium was a lady in distress. One could not pass on and leave her bewailing in the storm, clinging on to her little pink hat with tired green fingers.

Then dimly through my mind floated the word "cutting." Why should I not take a cutting of the rose-geranium and put it in the greenhouse for the winter? Well . . . if you are a professional gardener you will be quite justified in asking impatiently "Why not, indeed? What is all the fuss about . . . a simple geranium cutting? Ridiculous!"

But you must remember that this was my first autumn in the garden. I had never "taken a cutting" before. And though I had heard that it could be done, was indeed done on a very large scale, the idea, when one came to put it into practice, seemed so fantastic that it made me tremble with apprehension.

Do you not realize that the whole thing is miraculous? It is exactly as though you were to cut off your wife's leg, stick it in the lawn, and be greeted on the following day by an entirely new woman, sprung from the leg, advancing across the lawn to meet you. Surely you would be surprised if, having snipped off your little finger, and pushed it into a flower pot, you were to find a miniature edition of yourself in the flower pot a day later? Even if you were prepared for it, your wife would think the whole thing highly suspicious, and might institute proceedings for divorce.

Yet this phenomenon, which sounds like the wildest fairy-tale when you apply it to human beings, does not arouse the least interest in many gardeners, who yawn as they take off their cuttings and push them into the appointed loam.

I am quite sure that I did not yawn as I cut off the little branch of the rose-geranium. For one thing, I was afraid that the gardener would see me and tell me that I was doing it all wrong. I did not care whether it was wrong or not. I wanted to do it all myself. So I went furtively to the greenhouse, found a pot, filled it with the richest earth I could find, and put it in.

The stem sank into the earth. I pressed it down to make it firm. I gave it a little water. Then I stood and watched it. It did nothing. It merely stood quite still, sweetly green. A faint echo of its scent drifted upwards . . . a scent that made one think of sun-kissed lemons, and roses after rain.

Then I pulled myself together, beetled my brows, squared my shoulders, and like a strong silent man, seized the pot and hid it. And rushed out into the night.

On the next day I went down to the greenhouse very early. The rose-geranium was drooping. My heart sank. I said to myself, "It is ridiculous to imagine that it could be as simple as all that. It *must* be more difficult. One probably has to take the cutting off at a special place on the stem, and put it in a peculiar sort of earth and say *ena mena mina mo* over it till it goes to sleep." However I gave it some water. It should have every chance.

The day after, the rose-geranium had picked up. My spirits soared. But only for a brief space. For was it not quite possible that its life was only being prolonged artificially by water? Would the leaves not have been just as fresh if the stem had merely been placed in a vase? How could one tell if the plant was really forming root? Only, apparently, by pulling it up to see. This, by superhuman effort, I refrained from doing.

And so for another ten days I remained in an agony of doubt. The watering was continued, and after each drink the little pot was put back in its hiding place behind a box of seedlings. But gradually, as the second week drew to an end, I began to feel more assured. When a whole fortnight had elapsed it seemed almost certain that something really was happening. The plant grew perkier every day and even if it had been in a vase of water its leaves could not have been a fresher green.

It was at the beginning of the third week that I knew. For as I was watering it I suddenly saw a tiny new speck of green protruding from the stem. Awed, I bent down and scrutinized it. I knew every detail of the rose-geranium, and this was something that had not been there before. A moment's examination proved that it was, beyond doubt, a new shoot. In other words, the plant had taken root!

Well . . . there we are. Today, I have a dozen flourishing bushy geraniums that have all sprung from the little cutting which was taken years ago. You will tell me that it is all very commonplace. Perhaps. However, for me it is so miraculous that I am going to draw a line, very quickly, at the end of this chapter, before I am tempted to break into blank verse.

BEVERLY NICHOLS
[*Down the Garden Path* (1936)]

Origin of the Petunia

[*Few, if any, of the garden flowers as we know them are entirely un-modified wildings or, except as escapes, known anywhere outside of cultivation. In the case of many, their lineage is so obscure that cultivated plants are the despair of plant taxonomists, though recent researches into the chromosomes have given a new clue to the ancestry of some.*

A relatively simple case is that of the Petunia which—in its old-fashioned form—is generally regarded as a cross between two South American species. During recent years it has been appearing in a be-wildering variety of new and extravagant forms, many of them "F₁ hybrids"—which is to say a first generation produced by hand pollination and not coming true from second-generation seeds. Their history would require a book to itself, but here is an interesting account by the great horticulturist of Cornell University, Liberty Hyde Bailey, of the early history of the old-time favorite.]

THE modern petunia is a strange compound of the two original species which were introduced to cultivation less than three-quarters of a century ago. The first petunia to be discovered was found by Commerson on the shores of the La Plata in South America, and from the dried specimens which he sent home the French botanist, Jussieu, constructed the genus Petunia, and named the plant *Petunia nyctaginiflora*, in allusion to the four-o'clock-like or nyctaginia-like flowers. The plant appears to have been introduced into cultivation in 1823. It was a plant of upright habit, thick, sticky leaves and stems, and very long-tubed white flowers, which exhale a strong perfume at nightfall. This plant, nearly or even wholly pure, is not infrequent in old gardens, and fair strains of it can be had in the market. I remember that it self-sowed year after year in the old garden in my younger days, and even now an occasional plant may be found in some undisturbed corner. . . . The stem leaves of this species are said to be sessile—or without stalks—but the lower leaves in strong specimens . . . are often conspicuously narrowed into long petioles. Possibly this is a mark of hybridity, but I am rather inclined to think that the pure species has the lower leaves prominently stalked. This old-fashioned petunia is a coarse plant, and is now little known. It was not a difficult matter for the second species to dislodge it.

This second species of petunia first flowered in the Glasgow Botanical Garden in July, 1831, from seeds sent the fall before from Buenos Ayres by Mr. Tweedie; and in 1831 an excellent colored plate was made of it, under the name of *Salpiglossis integrifolia*. This is a neater plant than the other, with a decumbent base, narrower leaves and small violet-purple flowers, which have a very broad or ventricose tube scarcely twice longer than the slender calyx-lobes. This neat little plant has been known under a variety of names, having been referred to Nierembergia by two or three botanists. Lindley was the first to refer it to the genus petunia, and called it *Petunia violacea*, the name which it still bears. It was also early known as *Petunia phoenicea*, but this name is forgotten by the present generation of gardeners. It became popular immediately upon its introduction. In August, 1833, Joseph Harrison wrote that it was "one of the most valuable acquisitions that has been made to our collections of late years."

Petunia violacea early hybridized with the older white petunia, *P. nyctaginiflora*, and as early as 1837 a number of these hybrids—indistinguishable from the common garden forms of the present day—were illustrated in colors in the Botanical Magazine. Sir W. J. Hooker, who described these hybrids, declared that "it must be confessed that here, as in many other vegetable productions, the art and skill of the horticulturist has improved nature." "Cultivation alone," he wrote, "has, indeed, very much increased the size of the flowers and foliage of this plant (*P. violacea*), so that it can scarcely be recognized as belonging to the same species as the native specimens sent by Mr. Tweedie." This was about the time that *Phlox Drummondii* was becoming popular in England, having been sent there from Texas, in 1835, by Drummond. These two plants were novelties. "These varieties of petunia and the *Phlox Drummondii*," Hooker continues, "were decidedly among the greatest ornaments of the greenhouse in the Glasgow Botanic Garden during the month of May (1836), a season too early for them to come to perfection in the open border." These hybrid petunias were even described as a distinct species, *Nierembergia Atkinsiana;* and this fact is still remembered in some books in *Petunia violacea* var. *Atkinsiana*. Harrison gave a colored plate of these hybrid petunias in 1837 in his

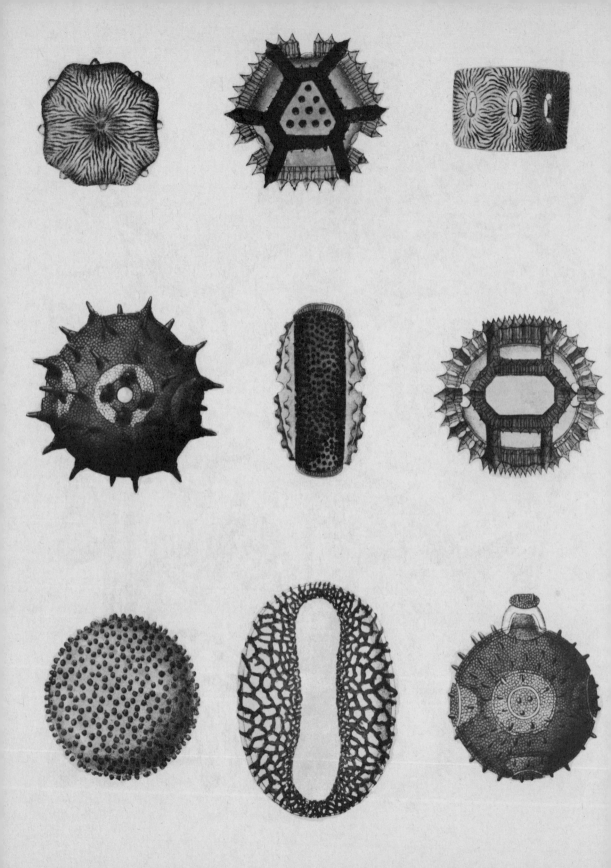

Floricultural Cabinet, but without description. He says, in an earlier issue of the magazine for that year, that the "impregnation of *P. violacea* and *P. nyctaginiflora* has produced several very charming varieties, such as pale pink with a dark center, sulphur with dark center, white with dark center, and others streaked and veined with dark. The size of the flowers of some of these hybrids has been much increased, some being three inches across." It would be interesting to know if *Petunia intermedia*, which was introduced about the same time as *P. violacea*, and which appears to be lost to cultivation, entered into any of these early hybrids. Here, then, our garden petunias started, as hybrids; but the most singular part of the history is that the true old *Petunia violacea* is lost to cultivation!

The pen drawing shows the closest approach to the true *P. violacea* which I have observed in several years' study of the petunia. Two or three plants came from a packet of mixed seed. But even this shows a flower-tube too long and a limb or border too wide; and perhaps the leaves are too broad. The nearest approach to the true species among the named varieties which I have seen, is the neat little white-tubed, purple-limbed Countess of Ellesmere. Vilmorin makes this variety a subdivision of *Petunia violacea*, and calls it Gloire de Segrez, or *Petunia violacea* var. *oculata*. I imagine that even Lindley did not have the pure species when he described *P. violacea* in 1833, for he says that it differs from *P. nyctaginiflora* "in nothing whatever except the inflated tube of its corolla and the size of its embryo." The common form of mixed garden petunia is a diffuse plant, low and slender, like the old *P. violacea*, but the tube is greatly lengthened and reduced in diameter by the influence of *P. nyctaginiflora*, and the colors sport into every combination of the purple and white of the original parents. These little petunias assume a fairly permanent light purple shade when left to themselves for a time, and they then reproduce themselves with tolerable accuracy; and they afford an admirable example of a hybrid which is abundantly fertile and which holds its own year after year.

Various curiously marked types of petunias have appeared and are lost. One of the early forms had a red body color, with grass-green borders. This was figured by Harrison in 1838 under the name of *Petunia marginata prasina*. These green-bordered strains appear now and then, and Mr. Carman, in using them in crossing experiments, obtained "rosettes of green leaves without the rudiments of calyx, corolla, stamens or pistils." A faintly striped variety, called *Petunia vittata*, was also figured by Harrison at the same time. The stripes originated in the throat of the flower and ran outwards, as they do in most of the striped sorts of the present day; but in 1844 he announced a variety, *Petunia Nixenii,* in which the stripes originate at the border of the flower and proceed inwards.

The most singular development in these hybrid petunias is the appearing of the very broad-mouthed fringed flowers, with short, sessile and more or less trough-like leaves. These highly developed forms may not come true from seed, but among any batch of seedlings flowers of the most remarkable beauty of shape and intensity of color may be found, and in some of them the texture of the flower is almost as firm as that of a rose petal.

L. H. BAILEY
[*The Survival of the Unlike* (1896)]

The Sleep of the Seed

[*No contemporary American "nature writer" has combined more successfully than Donald Culross Peattie sound knowledge and great enthusiasm with a gift for vivid presentation.*]

THE meaning of flowering is one and simple and to this purpose: that the speck of protoplasm inside the pollen grain—which is in the anther, which is borne on the stamen, which is enclosed by the petals—shall find its way to the bit of protoplasm which is within the ovule, which is in the ovary, which is inside the pistil at the heart of the flower.

Four hundred miles the pollen grain may travel to its goal, as when a high wind blows through a pine forest where the trees are loosing the dust of their fecundity. Or the consummating act may be immediate within the flower, as in those self-fertilizing blossoms where the anther rests right on the stigma. But whether it travels or breeds at home, the pollen grain, from the moment it quits the anther, is an independent plant.

It is a plant like no other, a plant reduced to a microscopic charge of one half of the life of its species. It is so tiny that it ranges from the giant grain of a pumpkin's pollen, all of a hundred-and-twenty-fifth of an inch through, to that of forget-me-not, which is one six-thousandth of an inch. It is so simplified that it comprises merely a sphere wrapped in one or two coats, within which is sheltered a male pro-embryo. This mere fraction of life, this dot of protoplasm, is crowded with the nuclei which carry the chromosomes, messengers of heredity.

Bearing the illimitable future of its kind, the pollen grain has an individual life span of a few hours, a few days, most exceptionally a year. For it is a plant without chlorophyll, and thus cannot work for a living; it has no reserve of food supply packed away with it, as a seed has. It is not yet even part of a seed; it is a spore, very special, highly evolved, a sex spore encapsuling the male generation of its race.

The ferns and the fungi and the brown seaweeds also confide their futures to the spore, but in these tribes it has the true sperm's power of driving toward its objective. The male pro-embryo of a flowering plant has lost the power of self-motility; it taxies within the golden pollen grain, borne by wind or wing.

At the mercy of such chance, tiny, frail and quick to die, the pollen grain is a spark of life that breathes, thirsts, is capable of growth, and can impregnate. It lives to no other purpose than to reach the female pro-embryo, which is charged with the other half of the race life. This female spore is locked up within the ovule, or unfertilized seed-to-be. One end of it is nutritive, and will form the future food supply of the seed; the other is strictly sexual and conjunctive. It is altogether just a little less nothing at all than the male pro-embryo, but it too carries in its nuclei the inscrutable pattern of chromosomes that spell destiny for its breed. . . .

Dry and avid of water, without a reserve of nourishment, on the verge of death, a lucky pollen grain arrives at the stigma. This has stickiness to catch the pollen, or a knobbed surface to hold it, or, as in the silk of a maize ear, feathery tendrils to seine the wind for it. And the glistening stigmatic fluid is food and drink to the pollen grain which swells with the moisture absorbed and swiftly thrusts out a tube that carries at its tip, as it grows, the male pro-embryo.

Down through the pistil grows the tube, down through the long style. Or right up it, in a nodding flower, gravity having no influence on the growth of the pollen tube, as it has on roots and stems. Or it prizes its way between the loose pistil cells, or it may secrete solvents that liquidate them as it grows. It lengthens out, and out—and not only from inner propulsions.

For it appears that the stigma and the ovules themselves lead it on, suck it in, by the eager secretion of exciting chemicals. This would seem a secret tightly hidden in the flower, but pollen placed on wet paper will grow straight to fragments of the stigma, to macerated ovules put near it in a film of water.

From the moment of pollination, when the grain arrives at the stigma, to fertilization, when the tube has reached the ovule, the growth of the pollen tube may be swift, as in our common stone fruits, when the act may take as little as nine hours. In pines and oaks, it is a matter of many months; in some of the cycads, of years.

Then when the tube has reached and penetrated the ovule, the male pro-embryo and the female pro-embryo meet. Their nuclei fuse, their chromosomes combine, mingling the dual heredity of all things born of sex. So the new life is conceived. The seed is set. The ovary grows great with it, the petals and stamens withering away from its crescent new estate.

So and so only is life created, by some spark from the burning brand of an old generation just touching and quickening the embryonic next. So and so only arises the wonderful, the fearful individuality of life's children, some forever destined to be less than the blood that made them, some to exceed it, all to struggle with the environment.

Once set, the seed begins its complex self-organization. The coats of the ovule become the coats of the seed, usually a hard outer one and a membranous inner. Within them, what was the structure of the ovule conditions the plan of the seed. At the ovule's nutritive end develops the seed's reserve food supply; the other end, where fusion with the male element took place, becomes the living embryo.

The scheme of storing nutriment is not known to the spores of the lowlier plants, and seeds by its possession have mastered the face of the earth. The food may lie quite outside the embryonic plantlet, visibly distinct, like the meat of a nut or the sweet kernel of a grain. Or it may lie in the seed-leaves, the fat cotyledons, nourishing them until they fill the whole cavity within the coats. Starch and protein, sometimes oil, or sugar or cellulose are packed away by an unthinking wisdom, provision for the days of growth.

For this the squirrels jump in the coloring trees of autumn; for this the chaff blows on the hot August air. But the seed's own vitality lies not in the meat but in its least conspicuous part—the embryo. In the seed of the common rush out on the marshes, it weighs but one sixty-eight thousandth of a grain. In a coconut it is a giant, weighing all of two grains, and still this is only one two-thousandths of the total weight of the coconut without its husk.

The embryo is the least part of a seed, and it is the life of the seed. In it lies the power of response unique to the living. From its beginning, the embryo answers opposite poles in its development. At its blunt end, it feels the pull of the root. At its acute tip, it pushes with the upward thrust of the shoot. Already, in its minutely integrated individuality, it perceives the difference between dark and day, down and up, earth and air. And it obeys the diametrically opposed commands of its nature to follow the cosmic stimuli. For the root obeys gravity, the shoot deliberately disobeys it. The shoot seeks light, the root shuns it. Their destinies are antipodal, and even the immature seed still upon the mother plant seems to know it.

It grows, in root and shoot, by swift repeated cellular division, the cleft passing right through the nucleus, each time shearing and sharing it fairly. At last, by crook, hook and bur, by wind or bird or wave, the seed is parted from the parent plant, and sets forth to seek its fortune.

Many and crafty are the devices by which these adventurers make their way in the world. Once Darwin grew a whole weed garden from seeds taken from the feet of migratory birds. Then there are the creeping fruits that hitch themselves along the ground by hygroscopic contortions of their spines. Dreadful are the travels of the porcupine grass, whose tails screw the grains forward, even into the flesh of prairie cattle and through the clothing of cowboys. Some fruits eject their seeds, as the pods dry and crack, to the distance of a foot, a yard, three yards. I used to hear, when I wrote in a Riviera garden, the whang of acanthus pods as they exploded in the arid summer afternoons. Even the modest violet pops its pods, and the touch-me-not is ever ready to do so. Fruits there are, and seeds, which remain buoyant in sea water for as much as four months, without becoming water-logged or losing their viability. So have the beaches of the Pacific isles been populated with a cosmopolitan strand flora. But the seeds and fruits with a fitness to travel by wind are beyond all numbering. They range from the minuteness of orchid seeds, fine as pollen, to the shining argosies of milkweed down blowing through our idle summer hours. By its winged seeds the cattail has encircled the earth, one species growing in the marshes of all continents. The seeds of the Spanish moss, which is a flowering plant and neither the moss nor the lichen it appears to be, are equipped with a parachute of sharp bristles that, when they lodge in the crevices of bark, serve to anchor the seed precisely where alone it can thrive.

Howsoever dispersed, whether it makes a happy landing or not, the seed cut off is another thing from the seed on the parent plant. There, in its immaturity, it was soft, watery, plump, vulnerable, and full of active life, its part dividing and differentiating to a nicety. But the seed on its own seems another plant. And now indeed is the plant reduced to first essentials.

Cramped into a tiny space where it cannot grow, it shrinks and shrinks. It loses water steadily, till it is desiccated to a Mojave dryness; every plant is a desert plant when it is a seed. The coats harden sometimes to stoniness; the tender cotyledons lose their green and become blanched as if in death, and the tiny true leaves of the embryo furl like conquered banners. Unresistant, the spark within allows itself to be immured alive; it is cut off as if in a coffin, from all the brightness of the world. The very breath drops lower, till at last, sometimes, no finest chemical test can prove that the seed does indeed still breathe. Vital chemistry stops like a run-down clock. There is a choked coagulation, and one cannot but remember the fabulous mystics of India who swallow their tongues and so by ceasing to live with any show of life, live on for years as men dead.

Among the longest lived and most impermeable of seeds, the more profound this look of death, the likelier it is that they still live. If they are really dead, they drink water like a dry log, swell up, even seem falsely to germinate by bursting with the slaking of their thirst. But the living seed seems to remain athirst voluntarily. By the depth of its sleep we know how stubbornly alive it is.

The secret of this life-in-death is the impermeability of the seed coat. In so far as the coat can shut out water and oxygen, and shut in the carbon dioxide evolved by the seed's own low but ever present metabolism, the sealed vitality can resist any summons, can sleep and, sleeping, endure. Without water there is no growth; with excess of carbon dioxide and deficiency of oxygen, there is anesthesia.

But even in the embryo's active youth, even as the petals began to shrivel about it, there was a beginning of this state of dormancy in the fruit. Withering spread like a contagion, like sleepiness when the Beauty pricked her finger on the spindle, over the whole life within the seed castle's walls. The deep sleep of the seed, provident as it appears, is due, then, not to the design of the future, but to the inevitabilities of the past. Forever, when we ask, Why? Nature gives no answer. Only when we ask, How? she permits us to discover. That inquiry is the field of science.

Antique organ, the seed was evolved by the seed-ferns in the Paleozoic; it is, historically, the oldest part of any plant that bears it. It is that generation, aspect, phase, in a plant's life that is least specialized, least adapted to the particular conditions of terrestrial life, and most ready for the cosmos.

For you can boil or freeze some seeds without necessarily killing them. Some resist continual boiling for forty-eight hours. Alfalfa, mustard and wheat seeds have been experimentally perforated to make them vulnerable, and then desiccated for six months, placed in a vacuum for a year, frozen for three weeks, next moved to a container where the temperature was like the cold of outer space. And still they germinated. Weed seeds were buried in glass bottles for forty years, and dug up and planted, twenty years after the first experimenter had died, and of them almost half were still alive. Seeds have been taken from herbarium sheets dated fifty years ago, and sown, and of these some still could grow. Lotus seeds four centuries old have been definitely known to retain viability; how much longer they might do so, no man can say. So naturally dormant are many seeds that they have a tendency to die in their sleep, smothered within their own obdurate walls. So that horticulturists, to obtain a satisfactory percentage of germination, have to file the coat, bore into it, break it off, leach it with acids.

If there is any living thing which might explain to us the mystery beyond this life, it should be seeds. We pour them curiously into the palm, dark as mystery, brown or gray as earth, bright sometimes with scarlet of those beads worked into Buddhist rosaries. We shake them there, gazing, but there is no answer to this knocking on the door. They will not tell where their life has gone, or if it is there, any more than the lips of the dead.

DONALD CULROSS PEATTIE
[*Flowering Earth* (1939)]

Flytraps and Pitcher Plants

[*Ever since they were first observed, the anomaly of flesh-eating plants has had for many observers a sort of horrid fascination. Darwin studied them extensively and wrote about them in his usual meticulous and detached fashion. In the little sketch which follows, a present-day naturalist permits himself to describe the reaction of one as much interested in his own human feelings as in the purely scientific facts. If one wonders why several different species of plants, not all members of the same family, should have developed several different devices for capturing insects and why they should all be characteristic of bog environments, the answer is quite simple. Bog soil is very deficient in the nitrogen which plant life needs but its want can be supplied by the protein found in the "flesh" of insects as well as in all animal tissues.]*

A S we stepped on the sphagnum carpet, a quick sensation of dizziness came over me. I stopped, wondering what was wrong. Dick and Tom walked on ahead. Watching them, I saw what was happening. With every step they took, the mat of sphagnum swayed and tilted. A hundred yards away, little ripples showed that the shore of the lake was moving up and down, and there was a faint buzzing sound as the swamp gas filtered up through the wet moss.

I walked on after Dick and Tom. They had stopped at a pitcher plant, its blossom richly purple, and Dick was examining one of the bulbous leaves. The pitcher was half-filled with water, in which three beetles lay drowned. Hours before, in search of pleasant food, they had crawled into the neck of the leaf, where slippery bristles slanted downward, and had not been able to crawl back. Now they, themselves, were succulent dinner to this insect-eating plant that had lured them to destruction with the sweet smell of nectar glands. I thought of the toad that feasts on mosquitoes, of mosquitoes that feast on the blood of man, of man that feasts on the flesh of other animals. The pitcher plant was in reasonably good company.

For half an hour we walked around on the tilting bog and examined the vegetation characteristic of such a place—the leather leaf shrub, its leaves shiny gray above and leather brown underneath, the cranberry bushes whose delicate blossoms seemed too fragile to produce so luscious a fruit, the yellow spatterdock that had made a military coalition with the sphagnum to destroy the lake with green.

But of all the bog flowers none, I think, is quite so lovely as the sundew, for all its amoral conduct. It lies half-hidden on the sphagnum, the copper-gold of its leaves tipped with translucent, sparkling drops. Though the small white blossom is pretty in the flowery way of most blossoms, it is the leaf that is spectacular—a small disc, no bigger than a dime, covered with short scarlet hairs, on the ends of which tiny globules, wonderfully bright, glisten like drops of early morning dew.

The glistening drops, however, are neither dew nor rain. They are formed from a sticky substance exuded from small glands at the ends of the scarlet hairs, and their purpose is sinister. If a small insect comes in contact with the drops, it will never be able to free itself. Slowly, inexorably, the hairs curl over the victim, the leaf partially closes, and the sundew digests its prey as thoroughly as if it had fallen into the bulbous leaf of the pitcher plant or upon the darting tongue of the toad.

While I was stooping down to admire the beauty of these miniature suns, the first of two strange things happened. A dragonfly with light blue body swooped down upon the clump of sundew as if to attack it. What prompted the attack I shall never know. Perhaps the dragonfly was merely clumsy; perhaps it saw an insect entangled in the sundew's scarlet hairs and meant to capture it. Whatever the reason, the dragonfly struck one of the golden discs with violence. He flew no farther. His flight ended as abruptly as if he had struck stone. Though his wings beat in a frenzy and though his slender body writhed and twisted, the moment he struck the diamond drops he became a helpless captive. I watched the struggle, fascinated and somewhat horrified, and then I remembered Tom. I stood up and started to call him, but did not do so. Death is a lonely event for man or dragonfly, and yet . . . Again I started to call, again stopped.

When I next looked down, the second strange thing had already happened, but because I had had my eyes on Tom I had not seen it occur. In some ways I am just as glad. Crossed against each other at right angles, two dragonflies now struggled to escape from the sparkling drops and closing tentacles. By this time, the wings of the first dragonfly were hardly moving, the body hardly twisting, but the second victim still clung piteously to hope. For awhile there was a frantic whir of wings, and then the whirring slowly subsided and the writhing of the body almost ceased. After a time both dragonflies were perfectly still, forming in death a sky-blue cross.

EDWIN L. PETERSON
[*Penn's Woods West* (1958)]

The Mating of Flowers

[*The author of the "Elegy Written in a Country Churchyard" was himself an enthusiastic botanist, so he must have known that he was being most poetically unscientific when he spoke of the flower that "wastes its sweetness on the desert air." If it pleased and attracted the pollinating insect it was intended to please, then it was not, from nature's standpoint, wasted even though no poet happened to be there to enjoy it.*

Prof. N. J. Berrill of McGill would not be likely to make that mistake. Though by specialty a geneticist with an especial interest in marine biology, he is the author of a number of popular books equally remarkable for their scientific accuracy and their sense of wonder. The following chapter from his Sex and the Nature of Things *emphasizes some facts about the pollination of flowers which gardeners do not usually think of—as, for example, that not only the perfume but also the color of a blossom often depends upon the insect or the bird it is intended to attract.*]

THIS is an interacting universe and it seems to me that few things show it so clearly as flowers and the animals which pollinate them. The making and mating of a flower has gone hand in hand with the evolutionary refinements of insects and of certain birds and mammals. Left alone to the sun and the wind, plants would never have evolved a flower as we know it, although our knowing and liking a flower has had nothing to do with it. Yet beauty, it is said, lies only in the eyes of the beholder— a half-truth if there ever was one—but it seems pretty certain that if insects had no eye for color, flowers would be without it. And if insects had no need of help in their unwitting services to the plant, flowers would not have the form they have. But it is not all insect. The beauty of symmetry is there, and no matter how far insects have called it forth, it is in itself the inborn rhythm of growth.

Flowers, apart from the seeds they bear, are accessory organs of reproduction as surely as the tail of a peacock, although their meaning was a mystery until two centuries ago. For where a cock has need to display to stimulate a hen, plants stand rooted where their roots sink down and their reproductive need is to exploit some go-between.

We need to go back to the age of conifers when all the forests were coniferous evergreens and beetles and reptiles dominated the animal world on land—a world of monotonous color and no song, a time when there were no birds, no butterflies, no mammals and no flowers to speak of. It seems somewhat dull and, when you think of beetles and dinosaurs as the best life could offer, rather horrible. Yet all that we have and are has come from that.

The plants of the age of conifers and reptiles were of separate sexes and depended upon the wind for pollination. Cross-fertilization was the rule, but the wind is never reliable and the pollen dust that must be shed to be effective is beyond imagination. In some, the pollen grains had wings to help them on their drifting flight. The eggs or seeds, in cones or on leaves, exuded drops of sap to trap what came their way.

The first flowers were beetle flowers and this seems to have been the beginning. Beetles feeding on the sap and resin of stems and leaves must have discovered that the liquid droplets from the male and female cones were odoriferous and nourishing—and some, returning regularly to feed on them, accidentally carried pollen to the eggs. And so it started. From this point on, as insects became more and more diversified, the flower came into being as a central stigma for the collection of pollen grains leading down to deep-seated eggs, surrounded by stamens for delivering pollen for the insect to take away to another flower. We can only speculate on how the changes came and I doubt that it is very profitable as yet for us to do so—beetle pollination may have brought the plant sexes together to become the hermaphrodite beetle flower, or this may have been the state of affairs from the beginning. It is hard to tell and we may never know. Yet the fact remains that beetle flowers are still the most primitive flowers we have.

The beetle flowers that still survive are most abundant in the tropics, and they attract their insect pollen-carriers by offering smells of the kind they like. The beetles are beetles and have not changed because of plants—they go their ancient way and feed on sap, fruit, leaves and the remains of any animals they find. They live in an aromatic world where sight is of less importance than odor. One group of beetle flowers has large, solitary blossoms and includes magnolias, pond lilies, California poppy and the wild rose; the other has clusters of smaller ones, like dogwood, elder and buckthorn. The beetles not only lap up nectar and other juices but feed upon the petals and stamens, and, to protect their eggs from the jaws of their pollinators, most beetle flowers keep them well below the floral crown. Most of them are primitive—they are large, bright and heavily scented, it seems, because the low-slung beetles have a sense of color and smell.

From here, we go on. In a changing world, cross-fertilization or cross-pollination has been necessary to produce progeny variable enough to cope with changing circumstances, and plants have had as much need of it as animals. And, without delving into history, we can see the wind again in trees of more modern kinds—in the catkins of the oak and birch, hazel and poplar, hanging so that the wind can blow their pollen far and wide. The female flower, if we can call the inconspicuous reproductive units by that colorful name, grows on the same tree as the male but not in the same place and opens at a slightly different time. The tree combines the sexes, but not in a single flower, which may be something old. Yet flowers by and large combine the sexes: a central pistil with pollen-receptive stigma at the top and eggs or ovules hidden in its base—the female unit; a ring or rings of stamens, bearing pollen-producing anthers, surrounding it—the male unit; and outer rings of leaflike protective structures, which may or may not be glorified as brightly colored petals, around the whole. Such is the flower in general, and its problems usually are two—how to become fertilized by pollen from another plant, and how to avoid becoming fertilized by its own.

Cross-fertilization produces a much wider range of variation among the offspring of either plants or animals, and it is this variety which is the raw material upon which natural selection works to bring about changes in the course of many generations. Where adaptability is all-important, this is essential. It may also be essential when the perfect type, so to speak, is hard to fix upon, and natural selection by external agencies may be relied on to weed out the progeny that are too different from their parents one way or another. Most animals depend upon it for either change or security, and inbreeding can be, but is not necessarily, dangerous. The point is that where there is any weakness in the stock, inbreeding intensifies it, while outbreeding may mask it.

But, in a very large number of flowering plants, strains have been evolved in the course of great periods of time that are more or less stabilized, and self-pollination has become substituted for cross-pollination. Grasses, for instance, are very well adapted to cross-pollination by the wind, yet many of them, including wheat, oats and barley, pollinate themselves. This is easily managed. The anthers simply burst before they are extruded from the flower and the trick is done—the wind is too late. A few flowers have gone even further and skip pollination altogether: the dandelion, for all its yellow invitation, sets seed without fertilization of any kind, whether from itself or from another plant. It is subsexual in the same sense as the summer broods of water fleas. The result is a plant that is wonderfully well suited to living in abundance in the places where you expect to see it. But it would have a harder time than most in adapting to a new set of circumstances.

Cross-pollination or cross-fertilization is still the rule, however, for the great majority, and many are the ways for ensuring it and avoiding the alternative. Some plants simply cannot self-pollinate—the dahlia is one of them. The pollen will not germinate on the stigma of a flower on the same plant.

In the end, as in the beginning, we need to turn to the animal kingdom, for unless we regard the flower as being no more than a circle of male stamens surrounding the female pistil, or groups of these clustered together, there is no sense to it. Its shape and color and size, all in fact that catches your eye and makes you catch your breath as well, is something added—and is there to attract and perhaps to force an insect or even a bird or a bat to bring to it pollen from another plant and take away some of its own. Darwin recognized this long ago and wrote a book about it. And so there are bee flowers and moth flowers, fly flowers and beetle flowers, and the bird flowers and bat flowers—all different from those of the wind.

How much of this is sex or reproduction, I am not sure, but this animal-vegetable relationship I think is fascinating, and demands attention.

Bee flowers include violets and verbena, some orchids, blue columbine, larkspur, monkshood, bleeding heart, many members of the snapdragon, mint and pea families and a host of others. You can add to the list as you will on any balmy summer day. They are all showy, with brightly colored petals, sweetly fragrant, and all offer nectar to the bees that come to them. The colors are mostly blue or yellow, or combinations of them, to conform to the color vision of the bee—for bees see a color range from yellow into the ultraviolet and are color blind to red. Bees like sweet or minty odors and fly only by day—and so the flowers are scented likewise and usually close at night. The bee settles on the flower and the long bee tongue dips deeply to the base of the tube of petals where the nectar lies, where most other insects cannot reach, picks up pollen on its body hairs unknowingly, and flies quickly to another flower of the same kind if possible. Pollen is brought and other pollen picked up, and each kind of bee is suited to its own group of flowers—or perhaps it is better put the other way, for while bumble-bees do not depend on monkshood for their living, monkshood cannot get along without the bumblebee and is limited to its range. Without bees of all sorts to pollinate their flowers, one hundred thousand species of plants or more would perish from the earth. It seems to me a heavy responsibility for one kind of insect to have to carry.

Moths and butterflies also have their flowers, each with its own characteristics. Moth flowers are morning glory, yellow columbine, tobacco, yucca, phlox, evening primrose and many orchids. Moths do not settle upon the flowers they suck but hover above them and lower their long tongues into the nectar—in tropical hawk moths they are sometimes ten inches long. Both sight and smell guide the moths, but since most of them fly during dusk or night the flowers run mainly to shades of white and to heavy fragrance; they are open in late afternoon or evening and stay closed during the day. Butterflies fly by day and it is then their flowers are open, and since, unlike the bees, a butterfly sees color well into the red, butterfly flowers tend to red and orange. And in both moth and butterfly flowers the nectar lies at the base of a long, slender, tubular spur, and there is a close matching of the length of the spur and the length of the tongue of the moth or butterfly that visits that particular flower. The fitting of tongue to spur holds insect and flower together, but whether the fitting is mutual or more or less one-sided is difficult to decide.

At the other extreme are the flowers of the short-tongued flies. And while the butterflies and moths have at least met the flowers part way, the flies act toward their flowers in an unskilled, stupid way that puts all of the burden upon the plant. They do not specialize in sucking nectar and feed on almost anything that stinks. It is the flower that exploits the fly and has taken on the quality of its disagreeable world —for flies smell their food and the odors they like the best we most abhor. Fly flowers are dull in color and rank in smell. A large-blossomed fly flower in Malaya smells like putrefying flesh, another smells like dung; there is a lily that smells of fish oil, and a Dutchman's-pipe like decaying vegetation. No food is offered to these low-caste pollinators— and the jack-in-the-pulpits even trap them for a day or two in order to douse them with pollen and take what they have. Bees are offered nectar, pollen, shelter and a landing platform, fragrance and bright colors; for flies there is only trouble, pitfalls, prisons and false allures!

Flowers have taken advantage, I was going to say, of birds and bats as well as bees; but, when reward is commensurate with the service, the advantage is mutual—you feel that nature broods upon the scene and pronounces magic words upon the visitor and visited.

Birds have powerful vision toward the red but not the blue, and have a poor sense of smell—you can almost guess the rest. Their flowers are red and yellow: red columbine, fuchsia, passion flower, hibiscus, and many cacti, orchids and others. Hummingbirds suck on the wing and favor the hanging types, the sunbirds of Africa and Asia do not and their flowers usually stand erect and provide a landing platform. Seeds are kept well out of harm's way from the beak, behind the floral parts, and petals are fused to form a tube which holds large amounts of thin nectar. The nectar tube often matches the length and curvature of the beak of the bird, while stamens are arranged so that they brush against its breast. The Mexican century plant lives only where hummingbirds can pollinate it. Its dependence is complete.

Bees, butterflies and birds seem to go naturally with flowers—but not a bat. Bats go out at night and see but poorly. Yet as birds and butterflies belong to daylight and color, bats and moths have the night and smell. Bat flowers are pollinated by certain tropical bats equipped with long slender snouts, protrudable tongues and shortened or missing front teeth, all of which fit them to feed on the flowers. In going from flower to flower, they carry the pollen. The flowers, which are tropical, are large and mostly white, open only at night and attract the bats by giving off a fermenting or fruitlike odor; the calabash, candle-tree and areca palm are among them.

Color dominates the scene around us and I think is what pleases us most. Yet we take it for granted. It is there to see—in flowers and butterflies and birds—but we didn't put it there and are only now beginning to realize how lucky we are that we can see it. For as far as we know, among the mammals, only the anthropoids have color vision. We and the apes and monkeys see color; moreover where else in the mammalian group can you find such colorful creatures as the blue-faced mandrill? The rest of the warm-blooded hairy folk apparently are color blind. They are drab enough to prove it.

Yet the colors we admire so much in the living world are there because the insects as a whole know one color from another. This we know—but the circumstantial evidence is there in any case. Flowers are colored primarily because insects exist that see color and make use of it. And the most colorful of insects—the butterflies—are colored in various ways for various reasons. One of these is sex and their own color vision; another is related to the fact that birds see color, too, and feed upon the insects. A butterfly needs to feed and mate; it also needs to avoid being eaten. And by playing both ends of the color scheme, the insect avoids a compromise.

The brightly colored upper surfaces of the wings of butterflies appear to be advertisements which bring notice of one insect to another, and the males locate their females by the colors and not by scent—although both vision and sense of smell may vary greatly among these insects, and what may be true of many may not be true of all. Yet butterflies have their enemies, especially among the birds, and color informs predators as well as prospective mates. So the under surface of the wings, which is all that shows when the insect is at rest, is camou-flaged in brownish break-up patterns which hide it from the bird; and in many forms the upper vivid surface may be over-bright as a warning that its owner has a bitter taste and is best left alone, or has decoy bands or eyespots that draw the fatal thrust away from vital centers. Sex flaunts its color when it can, but it is often unsafe to do so—and only plants appear to display it with impunity.

N . J . B E R R I L L
[*Sex and the Nature of Things* (1953)]